THE PSYCHOLOGY OF ART

THE PSYCHOLOGY OF ART

LEV SEMENOVICH VYGOTSKY

Introduction by A. N. Leontiev
Commentary by V. V. Ivanov

THE M.I.T. PRESS
Cambridge, Massachusetts, and London, England

Originally published in Russian under the title "Psikhologiia Iskusstva" Translated from the Russian by Scripta Technica, Inc.
English translation copyright © 1971 by The Massachusetts Institute of Technology
Set in Fototronic CRT Baskerville and printed and bound in the United States of America by The Colonial Press Inc.

ISBN 0 262 22013 X (hardcover)

Library of Congress catalog card number: 74-103904

INTRODUCTION

This book was penned by a great scholar, Lev Semenovich Vygotsky (1896–1934), the creator of an original branch of Soviet psychology, based on the sociohistorical nature of man's consciousness.

Vygotsky wrote *The Psychology of Art* some forty years ago, when Soviet psychology was coming into being. The battle was still raging against the openly idealistic psychology then in the ascendant at the major Soviet center of scientific psychology, the Psychological Institute of the University of Moscow, headed by G. I. Chelpanov. During the course of these disputes, which were waged with the goal of rebuilding the science of psychology on the foundations of Marxism, the progressive psychologists firmly established their new school of thoughts.

After the Second Conference on Psychoneurology in January 1924, the direction of the Psychological Institute passed into the hands of K. I. Kornilov. Many new people, some just beginning their careers, joined the Institute. Among these was Vygotsky, who at the time was only twenty-eight years old.

Appointed to the modest position of Junior Staff Scientist (or Staff Scientist, 2nd Class, as the rank was then known), Vygotsky from his very first days at the Institute showed astonishing energy. He presented a multitude of papers both at the Institute and at other scientific organizations in Moscow, and he lectured to students. He carried on his experimental research with a small group of young fellow psychologists, and at the same time he wrote a great deal. Early in 1925 he published a brilliant article, "Consciousness as a Problem in the Psychology of Behavior," [1] and in 1926 he completed his first important book, *The Psychology of Teaching*. The results of his experiments in the study of dominant reactions[2] came out almost at the same time. These works opened up a new phase in Vygotsky's career—his activities as a psychological scientist.

In the field of scientific psychology Vygotsky was both a new and exceptional arrival. As far as he was concerned, psychology had always been one of his closest interests, especially in relation to his preoccupation with art. Thus his crossing over into the field of psychology had its own internal logic. This logic was also reflected in the present work, a *transitional* book in every sense of the word.

In *The Psychology of Art* the author presents the results of his work in the years 1915 to 1922. The book also lays foundations for the new scientific ideas in psychology which constituted Vygotsky's main contribution to science and to which he devoted the remaining years—alas, all too few —of his life.

The Psychology of Art should be read on two levels: as the psychology of *art* and as the *psychology* of art. It is not difficult to recreate the historical context of this book for the reader. At the time of its first publication, Soviet art scholarship was in the process of taking its first few steps. It was a period in which old values were being re-examined, and the great "trial analysis" was beginning to pervade both art and literature. An atmosphere of divergent and contradictory trends prevailed among the Soviet intelligentsia. The phrase "socialist realism" had not yet been invented.

A comparison of Vygotsky's book with other writings on art of the early 1920's immediately shows it to be exceptional. In it the author turns to the classic forms of literature—the fable, the novel, and Shakespeare's tragedies. But his attention was not concentrated on the controversies raging then over formalism and symbolism, the futurists and the left front. The main problem to which he addressed himself was of broader and more general significance: just what does an artistic creation do, what transforms it into a work of art? This is actually the fundamental aesthetic problem; it cannot be disregarded if one is to estimate the real value of something new arising in the world of art.

Vygotsky approaches works of art from the point of view of a psychologist who has freed himself of the old subjective-empirical psychology. Thus, in his book he opposes the *psychologism* used traditionally in the interpretation of art. His method is objective and analytical. He believes that in analyzing the structure of a work of art one must recreate the response, the internal activity to which it gives rise. This concept gave Vygotsky the means of penetrating the secrets of the lasting value of great works of art, of discovering that force by which a Greek epic or a Shakespearean tragedy still continues, in Marx's words, "to provide us with artistic enjoyment and, in a certain respect, to serve us both as a norm and an unattainable model."

We must begin by clearing the way, by throwing out the many fallacious "solutions" that were proposed in the very extensive literature of the time. Thus, a good deal of Vygotsky's book is devoted to criticism of one-sided views of the specific qualities of art, its specific human and social functions. He is opposed to reducing the functions of art to a purely perceptive, gnostic function. If art does have a perceptive function, it becomes a function of *special* perception carried out by *particular* means. Art is not simply a matter of visual perception. Transformation into a figure or symbol does not of itself create a work of art. The "pictographic quality" of a production and its quality as a work of art are two very different things. The essence and function of art are not contained in form itself, for form does not exist alone and has no independence. Its true validity appears only when we consider it in relation to the material which it informs or "incarnates," as Vygotsky puts it, by giving it new life in the context of the work of art. From this standpoint, the author expresses his opposition to formalism in art, to the criticism of which he devotes a whole chapter of his book ("Art as Technique").

But is the specific quality of art perhaps embodied in the expression of emotional experience, the communication of feelings? Vygotsky rejects this solution as well. He opposes both the theory of the "contagion" of feelings and the purely hedonistic interpretation of the function of art.

Art, of course, "works" with human feelings, and a work of art incarnates this work. Sensations, emotions, and passions are part of the content of a work of art, but they are *transformed* in it. Just as artistic creation produces a transfiguration of the material of which the work of art is composed, it also causes a metamorphosis of feelings. The significance of this metamorphosis is, in Vygotsky's view, its transcendence of individual feelings and their generalization to the social plane. Thus, the significance and function of a poem about sorrow is not at all to transmit the author's sadness to the reader (that would be unhappy for art, remarks Vygotsky), but that it changes this sorrow in such a manner as to reveal something new and pertinent to man on a higher level of truth.

Only through the high quality of an artist's work can this metamorphosis, this elevation of feelings, be achieved. But the nature of the process itself is hidden from the investigator, just as it is concealed from the observations of the artist himself. What the student of art has before him is not the artist's work but its product—the artistic creation, the work of art in whose structure it is crystallized. This is a very precise thesis: human activity does not evaporate or disappear from its product; it merely changes within the work of art from a form of motion into a form of being, or state of existence as an object (*Gegenständlichkeit*).

An analysis of the structure of the artistic creation forms the principal content of Vygotsky's *The Psychology of Art*. Analysis of structure is usually associated in our minds with the idea of a purely formal analysis, divorced from the content of a work of art. But with Vygotsky, form is not separated from content; rather it *penetrates* into it. For the content of artistic production is not the material. Its *real* content is its effective content—that which determines the specific character of the aesthetic experience to which an artistic creation gives rise. Thus the content we have in mind is not simply injected into the work of art from the outside, but is *created* in it by the artist. The process of creation of this content is crystallized, embodied in the structure of the work of art, just as, say, a physiological function is embodied in the anatomy of an organ.

Study of the "anatomy" of an artistic product reveals the many levels of activity adequate to its full attainment. First of all, its real content requires mastering the properties of the material in which it is realized— the substantive form in which it finds its existence. To communicate the warmth, the quality of animation, the plasticity of the human body, the sculptor chooses cold marble, bronze, or grained wood; a colored wax figure does not belong in an art museum but in a waxworks.

We know that at times the mastery of the material properties of the substance from which the artist's creation is made attains extraordinary levels: it seems to the beholder that the stone out of which the *Winged Victory* of Samothrace was carved has neither mass nor weight. This feeling may be described as the result of "incarnation of matter by form." But this description is only tentative; for the truly determining factor is that which lies *beyond* the form and creates it. This is none other than the content incarnated in a work of art, its *meaning*. In the *Winged Victory* of Samothrace the meaning is flight, the triumph of victory.

The subject matter studied in *The Psychology of Art* is literature, a type of art especially hard to analyze, because its material is language; in other words the material has meaning, is *relevant* to the content embodied in it. In a work of literature, that which realizes its content may seem to be the same as the content itself. Here too, of course, there is an "incarnation" of the material, but an incarnation not just of its physical properties—not only of the "phasic" aspect of the words, as Vygotsky would have said—but of their intrinsic internal aspect, their semantic values. The meaning of the work of art becomes prejudiced and thereby rises above equality with the semantic value of the words.

One of the great merits of Vygotsky's book is its brilliant analysis of the overcoming of the "prosaism" of verbal material, of the elevation of its function in the structure of a work of literature. Yet this is only one level of analysis abstracted from the main level, which carries the structure within itself. The main factor is the movement which Vygotsky calls the "movement of opposite feelings." It is something like this which produces the effect of art and engenders its specific function.

The "opposition of feelings" suggests that the emotional, affective content of the work develops in two opposing directions which, however, strive to meet at a single crowning point. At this intersection, a brief joining or closure of the two decides the effect: a transformation and clarification of feelings.

To designate this important internal movement crystallized in the structure of a work of art, Vygotsky employs the classic term *catharsis.* The significance of this term, as Vygotsky uses it, is not the same as that assigned to it by Aristotle, nor as that acquired in Freudian psychology. To Vygotsky, catharsis is not simply the release of overwhelming affective attractions liberated, through art, from their "evil qualities." It is rather the resolution of a certain, merely personal conflict, the revelation of a higher, more general, human truth in the phenomena of life.

Vygotsky does not always use precise psychological concepts to express his thought. At the time this book was written, many of these concepts had not yet been worked out: there was as yet no doctrine of the sociohistorical nature of the human psyche, the elements of the "reactological" approach propagandized by K. N. Kornilov had not yet been surmounted; a concretely psychological theory of consciousness had merely been adumbrated in very general terms. In his book, therefore, Vygotsky expresses his own ideas quite often in words that are *not* his own. He quotes a great deal, even from authors whose general conceptions are basically alien to his own.

The Psychology of Art was not published during its author's lifetime. Was this a matter of accident, the result of an unfortunate chain of circumstances? It seems hardly likely. In the few years left him after he had written it, Vygotsky published about a hundred works, including a series of books beginning with his *Psychology of Teaching* (1926) and ending with his last, posthumously published *Thought and Language* (1934). The explanation probably lies in Vygotsky's internal motivations, as a result of which he virtually never again returned to the theme of art.[3]

The reasons for Vygotsky's failure to publish the present book were probably twofold. When he had finished his work on the manuscript, he had already become aware of the potentialities of a new direction in the science of psychology, to which he attributed a very great, even decisive, importance for understanding the mechanisms of artistic creativity and the specific functions of art. He was compelled to follow this direction in order to complete his work on the psychology of art and prove what still remained unproven.

Vygotsky clearly saw the incompleteness and imperfections of his work up to that point. At the beginning of the chapter in which he sets forth his own positive views—the theory of catharsis—he warns the reader: "The disclosure of the content of this formula of art as catharsis must remain outside the scope of this book. . . . Before this can be done," he writes, "further investigations in the areas of the various different arts would be needed." What he had in mind, of course, was not just the extension of what had already been learned to a wider sphere of phenomena. In a later article, on the psychology of the actor's creativity (written in 1932 and published after his death), Vygotsky not only entered a new field of art but also approached it from a new standpoint— the sociohistorical interpretation of the human mind, a view barely present in his earlier works.

Since it was much too brief and moreover devoted to the specialized problem of theatrical or dramatic feelings, this posthumous article was limited, in its treatment of the broader problems of the psychology of art, to only a few general theoretical statements. Yet these statements are extremely significant. They reveal retrospectively what was already present, in a germinal form, in *The Psychology of Art.*

"The laws of governing the interpretation of dramatic feelings must first be discovered," Vygotsky wrote, "within the framework of historical, not biological, psychology. The actor's expression of feelings achieves general significance and becomes meaningful only through inclusion in a broader system of *social psychology;* it is only then that the function of art can be understood."

"The psychology of the actor is of a historical and class-structured character" (author's italics).[4]—"The actor's life emerges not as a function of his own individual, spiritual existence but as a phenomenon that has an objective social value and serves as a transitional step from psychology to ideology." [5]

These words of Vygotsky's may be read as a sort of culminating point of all his efforts: the understanding of the function of art in the life of society and in the life of man as a sociohistorical being.

Vygotsky's *Psychology of Art* is a book that is far from having lost its value; it is a creative book and demands creative effort and attitude on the part of its reader. In the forty-odd years that have passed since it was written, Soviet psychologists have advanced a good deal, both during the remainder of Vygotsky's life and afterward. Thus, some of the psychological views expressed in this book must now be interpreted differently—from the standpoint of present psychological views of human activity and consciousness. This task, of course, will require further special investigation and cannot be fulfilled within the scope of a brief introduction.

Much of the content of Vygotsky's book has already been superseded. But from no work of science can one expect truth in the last instance or demand final, eternally valid solutions; these cannot be expected of Vygotsky's book. Its importance lies elsewhere: Vygotsky's writings retain their scientific urgency to this day; they continue to be printed and attract the attention of readers. Of how many of the studies to which Vygotsky referred can this be said? Very few. This fact alone reveals the lasting value of his ideas in scientific psychology.

We venture to think that his *Psychology of Art* will share the destiny of his other works—it will become part of the heritage of Soviet science.

A. N. Leontiev

NOTES

1. In *Psikhologiia i Marksizm* (*Psychology and Marxism*), edited by K. N. Kornilov, Leningrad-Moscow, 1925.

2. In *Problemy Sovremennoĭ Psikhologii* (*Problems of Contemporary Psychology*), edited by K. N. Kornilov, Leningrad, 1926.

3. His only other known writings on this subject are his earlier article, "Modern Psychology and Art," *Sovetskoe Iskusstvo* (*Soviet Art*), 1928, and an article published as an epilogue to R. M. Jakobson's book *Psikhologiia stenicheskikh chuvstv aktera* (*The Psychology of the Feelings of the Actor*), Moscow, 1936.

4. L. S. Vygotsky, "On the Problem of the Psychology of the Actor's Creativity," in R. M. Jakobson, *ibid.*, p. 204.

5. *Ibid.*, p. 211.

CONTENTS

Introduction by A. N. Leontiev   v

Preface   3

I. ON THE METHODOLOGY OF THE PROBLEM

1. *The Psychological Problem of Art*   9

   "Aesthetics from Above" and "Aesthetics from Below." Marxist Theory of Art and Psychology. Social and Individual Psychology of Art. Subjective and Objective Psychology of Art. The Objective-Analytical Method and Its Application.

II. CRITIQUE

2. *Art as Perception*   29

   Principles of Criticism. Art as Perception. Rationalization of This Formula. Criticism of the Theory of Forms. Practical Results of This Theory. Deficiencies of the Psychology of Forms. Dependence on Associative and Sensualistic Psychology.

3. *Art as Technique*   52

   Reaction to Intellectualism. Art as Technique. The Psychology of the Subject, the Hero. Literary Ideas and Feelings. Psychological Contradiction of Formalism. Shortcomings of the Psychology of Matter. Practice of Formalism. Elemental Hedonism.

4. *Art and Psychoanalysis*   71

   The Unconscious in the Psychology of Art. Psychoanalysis of Art. Deficiencies of the Social Psychology of Art. Critique of Pansexualism and Infantilism. The Role of Conscious Elements in Art. Practical Application of the Psychoanalytical Method.

III. ANALYSIS OF THE AESTHETIC REACTION

5. *Analysis of the Fable*   89

   Fable, Short Story, and Tragedy. Lessing's and Potebnia's Theories of the Fable. Fables in Prose and in Verse. Structural Elements of the Fable: Allegory, Use of Animals, the Moral, Anecdote, Lyrical Style, and Technique.

6. *The Subtle Poison, a Synthesis*   118

   The Source of Lyric, Epic, and Drama in the Fable. Krylov's Fables. Synthesis of the Fable. Affective Contradiction as the Psychological Basis of the Fable. Catastrophe of the Fable.

7. *Bunin's "Gentle Breath"*   145

   "Anatomy" and "Physiology" of the Narrative. Disposition and Composition. Characteristics of the Material. The Functional Significance of Composition. Auxiliary Methods. Affective Contradiction and Rejection of the Content of Form.

8. *The Tragedy of Hamlet, Prince of Denmark*   166
The Riddle of *Hamlet*. "Subjective" and "Objective" Solutions.
The Problem of Hamlet's Character. Structure of the Tragedy.
Fable and Subject. Identification of the Hero. Catastrophe.

IV. THE PSYCHOLOGY OF ART

9. *Art as a Catharsis*   199
Theory of Emotions and Fantasies. Principles of the Economy
of Force. Theory of Emotional Tone and Feeling. The Law of
the "Double Expression of Emotion" and the law of the "Reality
of Emotion." Central and Peripheral Discharge of Emotions.
Affective Contradiction and the Beginning of Antithesis. Catharsis. Rejection of the Content of Form.

10. *The Psychology of Art*   217
Verifying the Formula. Psychology of Verse. Lyric, and Epic.
Hero and Dramatis Personae. Drama. The Comic and the
Tragic. Theater. Painting, Drawing, Sculpture, Architecture.

11. *Art and Life*   240
Theory of Contamination. Significance of Art in Life. Social
Significance of Art. Art Criticism. Art and Teaching. The Art
of the future.

Commentary by V. V. Ivanov   263

Index   297

". . . *No one has hitherto laid down the limits to the powers of the body* . . . *But, it will be urged, it is impossible that solely from the laws of nature considered as extended substance, we should be able to deduce the causes of buildings, pictures, and things of that kind which are produced only by human art; nor would the human body, unless it were determined and led by the mind, be capable of building a single temple. However, I have just pointed out that the objectors cannot fix the limits of the body's power, or say what can be concluded from a consideration of its sole nature* . . ."

Benedict Spinoza, *Ethics,* Part III,
Postulate 2, Scholion
(translated from the Latin by
R. H. M. Elwes)

PREFACE

This book has come about as the result of a series of minor and some major studies in the areas of art and psychology. Three of my literary essays—on Krylov, on *Hamlet* [1]*, and on the composition of the short story—form the basis of my analyses here, as do a number of articles and notes published in various periodicals.[1] The different chapters of the present book will give only brief results, outlines, and summaries of these studies. It would be impossible, for example, to present an exhaustive analysis of *Hamlet* in a single chapter—this task alone calls for at least one other book. The search for a way out of the precarious confines of subjectivism has equally characterized Russian art scholarship and Russian psychology during the years of my studies. This tendency toward objectivism, toward a precise, materialistic, scientific approach to knowledge in both fields, gave rise to the present volume.

On the one hand, scholarly studies of art have increasingly felt the need for a psychological base. On the other hand, psychology, striving to understand and explain behavior as a whole, is inevitably drawn to the complicated problems of the aesthetic reaction. If we add to this the shift that is taking place in both areas of study, the present crisis of objectivism, we shall understand the full urgency of our subject. In fact, traditional art scholarship, whether consciously or unconsciously, has always been based on psychological assumptions. But the old popular psychology has ceased to be adequate for two reasons. In the first place, it was still capable of nourishing every kind of subjectivism in aesthetics,

* Numbers in square brackets refer to V. V. Ivanov's Commentary starting on p. 270.

but objective trends require objective presuppositions. Secondly, a new psychology which is rebuilding the time-honored foundations of all the so-called "sciences of the soul" is emerging. My purpose has been to reexamine the traditional psychology of art and to try to delineate a new field of investigation for objective psychology—to state the problem and merely suggest a method and some fundamental psychological principles of explanation, and no more.

In calling this book *The Psychology of Art*, I did not wish to imply that it would present a complete system or represent the whole gamut of problems and causes. My goal has been quite different: to offer not a system but a program; it was not the whole range of problems but the central problem that I kept constantly in mind and pursued as my goal.

I shall therefore leave to one side the controversies on psychologism in aesthetics and on the boundaries separating aesthetics from pure art scholarship. I agree with Lipps that aesthetics can be defined as a discipline of applied psychology, but I shall nowhere pose this problem as a whole. I propose to remain content with the methodological and theoretical laws of the psychological examination of art, along with every other attempt, pointing out the essential importance[2] of finding a place within the Marxist doctrine of art. Here my guideline has been the well-known Marxist position that the sociological view of art does not deny its aesthetic consideration; on the contrary, it opens wide the door to it and presupposes it, in Plekhanov's words, as its complement. Yet any aesthetic discussion of art, to the extent that it does not wish to depart from Marxist sociology, must constantly base itself on social psychology. It is easy to show that even those art scholars who quite properly separate their own field completely from aesthetics inevitably work into their treatment of the basic concepts and problems of art psychological axioms that are uncritical, arbitrary, and precarious. I share Utitz' view that art goes beyond the limits of aesthetics and even has features that are fundamentally different from aesthetic values, but that it begins with the aesthetic element and remains with it to the end. It is also clear to me that the psychology of art must be related to aesthetics as well, without losing sight of the line separating one area from the other.

It must be said that in the new art scholarship, as in objective psychology, the basic concepts and fundamental principles are in the process of being worked out, the first steps are still being taken. This is why a work that arises at the crossing of these two disciplines, and that desires to use the language of objective psychology in dealing with the objective facts of art, must necessarily be burdened by the circumstance that it remains ever at the threshold of the problem, not penetrating deeply or ranging widely within it. I have merely wished to develop the particular aspects of a psychological view of art and to note the central idea, the methods of working it out, and the content of the problem. If an objective psychology of art comes forth at the intersection of these three lines of thought, the present work may well be the small seed from which it will sprout.

The central idea of the psychology of art, I believe, is the recognition of the dominance of material over artistic form, or, what amounts to the same thing, the acknowledgement in art of the social techniques of emotions. The method of investigating this problem is the objective-analytical method which proceeds from an analysis of art in order to arrive at a psychological synthesis—the method of analysis of artistic systems of stimuli.[3] Along with Hennequin, I look upon a work of art as "a combination of aesthetic symbols aimed at arousing emotion in people," [4] and I attempt, by analyzing these symbols, to re-create the emotions corresponding to them. But the difference between my method and the aesthetic-psychological one is that I do not interpret these symbols as manifestations of the spiritual organization of the author or his readers [2]. I do not attempt to infer the psychology of an author or his readers from a work of art, since I know this cannot be done on the basis of an interpretation of symbols.

I shall attempt to study the pure and impersonal psychology of art [3] without reference to either the author or the reader, looking only at the form and material of the work of art. Let me explain. From Krylov's fables alone we should never be able to reconstruct his psychology, and the psychology of his readers will differ between people of the nineteenth and the twentieth centuries, and between groups, classes, ages, and individuals. But we can, by analyzing a fable, discover the psychological law on which it is based, the mechanism through which it acts; this we may call the psychology of the fable. Actually, of course, this law and this mechanism have nowhere acted in their pure form but have been complicated by a whole series of phenomena and processes upon which they have impinged. We were also quite right in eliminating from the psychology of the fable its concrete effect, just as the psychologist isolates a pure reaction, sensory or motor, selection or distinction, and studies it as an impersonal reaction.

Finally, the essence of the problem, I believe, is this: the theoretical and applied psychology of art should bring to light all the mechanisms that operate through art and should also provide the basis for all disciplines concerned with art.

The task of the present work is essentially one of synthesis. Müller-Freienfels has very rightly said that the psychologist of art resembles the biologist who can make a complete analysis of living matter and break it down into its component parts but is unable to recreate the living whole out of these parts or to discover the laws that govern this whole. A long series of publications has undertaken such a systematic analysis of the psychology of art, but I know of no work that has objectively posed and solved the problem of the psychological synthesis of art. In this sense, it seems to me, the present attempt does represent a new step and ventures to introduce certain new and hitherto unstated concepts into the field of scientific discussion. The new ideas which I consider my own in this book must of course be tested and criticized against other concepts and the facts. Yet at this time they seem reliable and mature enough to be presented in a book.

The general aim of this work has been the achievement of a degree of scientific soundness and sobriety in the psychology of art, the most speculative and mystically unclear area of psychology. My thought is expressed in those words of Spinoza [4] which appear in the epigraph at the beginning of the book. Like him, I have strived neither to be astonished, nor to laugh, nor to weep—but to understand.[5]

NOTES

1. Printed in M. Gorky's *Letopisi* (*Chronicles*), 1916–1917, on the new theater, on the novels of Bely, on Merezhkovskii, on V. Ivanov, and on other subjects; in *Zhizn Iskusstva* (*Life of Art*), 1922, on Shakespeare; in *Novaya Zhizn* (*New Life*), 1917, on Eichenwald; and in *Novyi Put* (*The New Path*), 1915–1917.

2. See A. Yevlakhov, *Vvedenie v filosofiu khudozhestvennovo tvorchestva* (*Introduction to the Philosophy of Artistic Creativity*), vol. III, Rostov-on-Don, 1917. Evlakhov ends his discussion of each system and terminates each of the six chapters of his volume with a section subheaded "The Need for Aesthetic-psychological Premises." This is his *ceterum censeo*.

3. By a similar method Sigmund Freud re-created the psychology of humor in his book, *Wit and Its Relation to the Unconscious*, New York: Moffat, Yard & Co., 1917. Such a method was also used in F. Zelinskii's investigation of the rhythm of artistic speech, from an analysis of form to the creation of an impersonal psychology of this form. See F. Zelinskii, "The Rhythm of Artistic Speech and Its Psychological Basis," in *Vestnik Psikhologii* (*Herald of Psychology*), Nos. 2, 4, 1906, which gives a psychological summary of the results.

4. E. Hennequin, "An Attempt to Create a Scientific Criticism: An Aesthetic Psychology," *Russkoe Bogatstvo* (*The Wealth of Russia*), 1892, p. 114.

5. See Spinoza's *Political Treatise*, chapter I, paragraph 4.

I ON THE METHODOLOGY
OF THE PROBLEM

1 THE PSYCHOLOGICAL PROBLEM OF ART

"AESTHETICS FROM ABOVE" AND "AESTHETICS FROM BELOW." MARXIST THEORY OF ART AND PSYCHOLOGY. SOCIAL AND INDIVIDUAL PSYCHOLOGY OF ART. SUBJECTIVE AND OBJECTIVE PSYCHOLOGY OF ART. THE OBJECTIVE-ANALYTICAL METHOD AND ITS APPLICATION.

If we were to draw a boundary dividing all the trends of contemporary aesthetics into two great directions, we would think of psychology. These two directions, the psychological and the nonpsychological, cover everything that is going on in aesthetics. Fechner aptly speaks of an "aesthetics from above" and an "aesthetics from below."

It might seem that we are dealing here not only with two different areas of one and the same science, but with two independent disciplines, each of which has its own subject and its own method of study. Some continue to regard aesthetics largely as a speculative science, while others, such as O. Külpe, are inclined to believe that "at the present time aesthetics is in a state of transition . . . the speculative method of post-Kantian idealism has almost completely been abandoned. Empirical investigation, however . . . is influenced by psychology. . . . To us aesthetics is the teaching of aesthetic behavior (*Verhalten*), that is to say, the general state produced in a person by an aesthetic impression. . . . We must regard aesthetics as the psychology of aesthetic enjoyment and artistic creativity." [1]

Volkelt holds the same view. "An aesthetic object" he says, ". . . acquires its specific aesthetic character only through the perception, feeling, and imagination of the person perceiving it." [2]

This idea of psychology has been recently espoused by such scholars as Veselovskii.[3] The general idea has been quite appropriately expressed by Volkelt: "Psychology must become the basis for aesthetics." [4]—"The first, most urgent task of aesthetics is, of course, to provide a detailed and subtle psychological analysis of art, rather than metaphysical speculations." [5]

A diametrically opposed view was held in the antipsychological trends of German philosophy, which became so powerful over the past decade, and a compendium of which can be found in H. Shpet's article.[6] The polemic between the adherents of the two viewpoints was carried on mainly with negative arguments and the demonstration of each other's weaknesses. The fundamental futility of this exercise made the debate tedious and delayed any practical solution of the problem.

Aesthetics from above drew its laws and evidence from the "nature of the soul," from metaphysical premises, or from speculative constructions. It took itself for a somewhat special existential category, and even such distinguished psychologists as Lipps did not escape this common fate. Aesthetics from below, on the other hand, concerned itself with extraordinarily primitive experiments in order to clarify the most basic aesthetic relationships; it was thus incapable of lifting itself even slightly above this combination of primordial and fundamentally meaningless facts. It became ever more obvious that both aesthetic trends were in the throes of a deep crisis. Many authors realized that the substance and nature of the crisis went far beyond what might have been regarded as the crisis of an individual trend. The original premises of both trends as well as their scientific bases of investigation and methods suddenly turned out to be false. This became obvious when the crisis spread to both the empirical psychology and the German idealistic philosophy of recent decades.

To break this deadlock, a radical change in the basic principles of investigation, the selection of totally new methods, and a new definition of the problem are necessary.

As concerns aesthetics from above, it is obvious that a theory can be developed only from sociological and historical bases. It is equally obvious that art will become the object of scientific study only if it is regarded as one of the vital functions of society [5], intimately connected with all the other spheres of social life in its material-historical state. Of all the sociological trends in art theory, the most consistent in its progress is the theory of historical materialism, which tries to base the scientific analysis of art on the principles applied to the study of all phenomena of social life [6]. From this point of view art is usually regarded as one of the forms of ideology arising, as do all other forms, as a structure superimposed on economic and productive relations. It is quite obvious that since aesthetics from below was always empirical and positive, the Marxist theory of art would make a clear-cut attempt to introduce such a psychology into aesthetics. Lunacharskii even goes so far as to view aesthetics as a branch of psychology. "Nonetheless, it would be quite superficial to assert that art has no evolutionary law of its own. The flow of water is determined by its bed and its banks. Sometimes water stretches out in a stagnant pond. Sometimes it flows in a calm majestic current. Then it may swirl and foam along a stony bed, or drop in waterfalls, turn right or left, or even turn back. But no matter how clear it is that the course of a brook is determined by the inflexible laws imposed by outside conditions, its essence is determined by the laws of hydrodynamics, laws which we cannot derive from the outward conditions of flow without having some knowledge about the nature of water." [7]

For this theory, the boundary that formerly divided aesthetics from above from aesthetics from below, follows a totally different course. Now it separates the sociology of art from the psychology of art and shows each of these fields its own characteristic point of view concerning one and the same object of investigation.

Plekhanov, in his studies on art, distinguishes very sharply between the two views. He points out that the psychological mechanisms which define the aesthetic behavior of man are determined by sociological causes. Therefore, psychology studies the effect of these mechanisms, while sociology studies their causality. "Man's nature is such that he can have aesthetic tastes and concepts. His environmental conditions make this possibility a reality; the environment accounts for the fact that a given social individual (or a given society, people, or class) has certain aesthetic tastes and concepts rather than others. . . ." [8] Thus, at various stages of his social evolution, man receives from nature different impressions, because he sees nature from different points of view.

Of course, the effect of the general laws governing man's psychological nature is not interrupted during any of these stages. But since at different periods "man's mind receives anything but homogeneous and identical material, it is not surprising that the results from processing that material are anything but identical." [9]—". . . to what extent can the psychological laws be regarded as a key to explanation of the history of ideology in general and the history of art in particular? In the psychology of seventeenth-century man, the principle of antithesis played exactly the same role as in that of our contemporaries. Why, then, are our aesthetic tastes diametrically opposed to those of seventeenth-century man? Because we find ourselves in a totally different condition. This means that we are about to reach a conclusion well known to us: the psychologic nature of man makes it possible for him to have aesthetic concepts, and Darwin's principle of antithesis (the Hegelian dialectic) plays an extremely important role, hitherto not sufficiently explained, in the mechanism of these concepts. Why, however, a given social individual has precisely these rather than other tastes; why he likes precisely these rather than other objects—this depends upon environmental conditions." [10]

Plekhanov, better than anyone else, was able to explain the theoretical and methodological need for the psychological investigation of the Marxist theory of art. In his words, "all ideologies have one common root: the psychology of a given era." [11]

Using the examples of Hugo, Berlioz, and Delacroix, he shows how the psychological romanticism of their era gave birth to three different forms of ideological romanticism in three completely different fields: poetry, music, and painting.[12] In the formula given by Plekhanov to express the relationship between the base and the superstructure, we have five sequential elements:

1. The state of productive forces
2. The economic conditions
3. The sociopolitical regime
4. The psyche of social man
5. Various ideologies reflecting the properties of this psyche.[13]

Thus, the psyche of social man is viewed as the general substratum common to all the ideologies of a given era, including art. And we also recognize that art is determined and conditioned by the psyche of social man.

Instead of the old antagonism, we now find some harmony between the psychological and antipsychological trends in aesthetics. There is also a more precise demarcation between them on the basis of Marxist sociology. This sociological system, the philosophy of historical materialism, is of course not likely to explain anything on the basis of human psyche as the ultimate cause. But it is also not likely to reject or ignore the psyche and the significance of its study as an auxiliary mechanism, which, together with economic relationships and the sociopolitical regime, generates ideologies. When investigating complex art forms, this theory insists on the need of studying the psyche, because the distance between economic relations and ideological form grows constantly greater; hence, art can no longer be explained as a direct consequence of economic conditions. Plekhanov had this in mind when he compared the dance of Australian aborigines with the eighteenth-century minuet. "To understand the dance of Australian native women, it suffices to know the role played in the tribal life of Australian aborigines by women gathering wild-growing plants. To understand the minuet, however, it does not suffice to know the economy of eighteenth-century France. We are dealing here with a dance that expresses the psychology of a nonproductive class. . . . Therefore, the economic 'factor' yields its place and position to the psychological factor. We must remember, however, that the emergence of nonproductive classes in human society is a product of economic evolution." [14]

Thus, the Marxist approach to art, especially in its more complex forms, necessarily involves the study of the psychophysical effect of artistic creation.

A subject of sociological investigation may be an ideology as such, or else it may be dependent upon certain forms of social evolution. But no sociological investigation per se (i.e., not complemented by psychological investigation) will ever be able to expose the prime cause of any ideology, the psyche of social man. To determine the methodological boundary between the different viewpoints, it is of paramount importance to understand what distinguishes psychology from ideology.

We can now understand the distinct role assigned to art as a special ideological form dealing with a totally distinct and peculiar aspect of the human psyche. And, if we are to understand this particular characteristic of art and to know what exactly distinguishes it and its action from all other ideological forms, we cannot but resort to psychological analysis. Art systematizes a very special sphere in the psyche of social man—his emotions. While it is true that all the realms of the psyche are generated by the same causes, it is also true that, by acting via various psychic modes of behavior (*Verhaltungsweisen*), these causes bring to life various ideological forms.

The old antagonism is therefore transformed into an alliance of two trends in aesthetics, each of which can become significant only within a general philosophical system. The reform of aesthetics from above is now under way, and is laid out in a number of works to such an extent that it is possible to study these problems in the spirit of historical materialism. On the other hand, as far as the psychology of art is concerned, things are totally different. There are difficulties and problems completely unknown to the conventional methodology of psychological aesthetics. One of these is the separation of social from individual psychology when studying art. The old viewpoint which did not admit a distinction between these two must be thoroughly revised. I feel that the conventional conception of the object and the subject of social psychology will turn out to be false at its very root if tested against the new approach. Indeed, the viewpoint of social psychology, or the psychology of peoples, as defined by Wundt, chose as the subject of its studies language, myths, customs, art, and religious systems, as well as juridical and ethical standards. There is no doubt that from the viewpoint of the new approach all this is no longer psychology but a conglomerate of ideology, or crystals of ideology. The task of psychology, however, is to study the solution per se, to study the social psyche and not the ideology. Language, customs, and myths are the results of the activity of the social psyche, not its process. Hence, when social psychology deals with the subject, it substitutes ideology for psychology. It is evident that the fundamental premise of conventional social psychology and of the upcoming collective reflexology, according to which the psychology of the individual is not fit to explain social psychology, will be shaken by the new methodological assumptions.

Bekhterev claims that ". . . obviously, the psychology of individuals is not suitable for explaining social movements. . . ." [15] The same view is held by other social psychologists (like McDougall, Le Bon, Freud, *et al.*), who regard the social psyche as secondary, originating from the psyche of the individual. They assume that there is a special individual psyche and that from the interaction of individual psyches or psychologies there arises a collective psyche or psychology common to all individuals. Thus, social psychology is regarded as the psychology of a collective individual, in the same way that a crowd is made up of single individuals, even though it has a supra-individual psychology. We see that non-Marxist social psychology has a primitive empirical approach to the social entity, regarding it as a crowd, a collective entity, a relation between individuals or persons. Society is taken to be an association of people, and it is regarded as an accessory activity of one individual. These psychologists do not admit that somewhere, in a remote and intimate corner of his thought, his feelings, etc., the psyche of an individual is social and socially conditioned. It is easy to show that the subject of social psychology is precisely the psyche of the single individual. Chelpanov's view, frequently quoted by others, according to which specifically Marxist psychology is a social psychology that studies the genesis of ideological forms according to a specifically Marxist method, involving the study of the origin of given forms based on the social economy, is incorrect. Equally incorrect is his view that empirical and experimental psychology cannot become Marxist, any more than mineralogy, physics, chemistry, etc., can. To corroborate his view, Chelpanov refers to Chapter VIII of Plekhanov's *Fundamental Problems of Marxism*, in which the author expounds the origin of ideologies. The exact opposite is more likely to be true, namely that only the individual (i.e., the empirical and experimental) psychology can become Marxist. Indeed, how can we distinguish social psychology from individual psychology if we deny the existence of a popular soul, a popular spirit, and so forth? Social psychology studies precisely the psyche of the single individual, and what he has in his mind. There is no other psyche to study. The rest is either metaphysics or ideology; hence, to assert that this psychology cannot become Marxist (i.e., social), just as mineralogy and chemistry cannot become Marxist, is tantamount to not understanding Marx's fundamental statement which says that "man in the most literal sense is a *zoon politicon*,* an animal to whom social intercourse is not only peculiar but necessary in order to stand out as a single individual." To assume the psyche of the single individual (the object of experimental and empirical psychology) to be as extrasocial as the object of mineralogy, means to assume a position diametrically opposed to Marxism. Of course, physics, chemistry, mineralogy, and so on, can be either Marxist or anti-Marxist if we take science to be not only a bare listing of facts, a catalogue of relationships and functions but a systematized knowledge of the world in its entirety.

There now remains only the question concerning the genesis of ideological forms. Is it really the task of social psychology to study the dependence of these forms on social economy? It seems to me that it is not. This is the general task of each particular discipline as a branch of general sociology. The history of religion and jurisprudence, the history of art, and the history of science accomplish this task for their own fields of endeavor.

The incorrectness of the previous point of view becomes evident not only from theoretical considerations but also from the practical experience of social psychology. Wundt, in establishing the origin of social creativity, was finally forced to resort to the creativity of the single individual.[16] He says that the creativity of one individual can be recognized by another individual as an adequate expression of his own ideas and emotions; hence, a number of different persons can be simultaneously the creators of one and the same concept. In criticizing Wundt, Bekhterev quite correctly shows that "in this case there can be obviously no social psychology since there are no new tasks other than those that are comprised in the psychology of single individuals." [17] As a matter of

* A social animal (Aristotle, *Politics* I. I.).

fact, the earlier viewpoint, according to which there is a fundamental distinction between the processes and the products of popular and individual creativity, appears now to have been unanimously discarded. Today no one would dare assert that an ancient *bylina* (a Russian popular epic) written from the words of an Arkhangel'sk fisherman, and a Pushkin poem carefully corrected and edited by the poet, are the products of different creative processes. The facts testify to exactly the opposite. Accurate investigation reveals that the difference here is purely quantitative. The narrator of the *bylina* does not recount it in exactly the same way in which he received it from his predecessor. He introduces changes, cuts, additions and he reshuffles words and parts. Thus, he becomes the author of that particular version using the ready-made standards and clichés of popular poetry. Hence, the notion that popular poetry is unsophisticated in the sense that it is created by an entire people and not by professionals (narrators, troubadours, storytellers) of artistic creativity applying a traditional, rich, and specialized technique to their craft and using it in exactly the same way as the writers of later periods, is completely wrong. On the other hand, an author who puts down in writing the product of his creativity is by no means the sole creator of his work. Pushkin, for example, is not the individual author of his poems. He did not invent the methods of writing verse and rhymes, or of construing a subject or theme in a specific way. Like the narrators of the *byliny,* he passes on the immense heritage of literary tradition which to a great extent depends on the evolution of language, verse-writing techniques, traditional subjects, themes, images, compositional subjects, and so on.

Were we to determine in a literary work what is created by the author himself and what he has taken ready-made from the literary tradition, we would find that the author's creativity amounts to selecting certain elements, combining them within given, generally accepted standards, transposing certain traditional elements into other systems [7], and so forth. In other words, in both the Arkhangel'sk narrators of *byliny* and in Pushkin we can always detect the existence of both elements: the individual authorship and the literary traditions. The difference, as stated before, consists only in the quantitative relationship between the two. In Pushkin the individual authorship prevails, while in the *bylina* narrative it is the literary tradition that prevails. To use Silverswan's well-chosen simile, both remind us of a swimmer crossing a river and being dragged away by the current. The swimmer's path, like the writer's creativity, is the resultant of two forces, the swimmer's own effort and the deviating force of the current.

We have enough reasons to assert that from a psychological point of

view there is no fundamental difference between the processes of popular and individual creativity. Thus, Freud is completely right when he
states that individual psychology from the incept is at the same time
also social psychology. Tarde's intermental psychology (interpsychol-
ogy) as well as the social psychology of other authors must therefore be
viewed in a completely different light.

In agreement with Siegel, de La Grasserie, Rossi, and others, I am inclined to believe that we must distinguish between social and collective
psychology, but I feel that the way to do this must be fundamentally
different. Because this distinction is based on the degree of organization
of the collective under study, this opinion is not generally accepted in
social psychology.

The difference becomes self-evident if we consider the psyche of the
single individual as the subject of social psychology. It is obvious that
the subject of individual psychology coincides with that of differential
psychology, the task of which is the study of individual differences in
single individuals. The concept of general reflexology, as opposed to
Bekhterev's collective reflexology, also completely coincides with this.
"In this respect there is a certain relation between the reflexology of the
single individual and collective reflexology; the former aims at clarifying the peculiarities of the single individual, tries to find differences in
the individual mentalities of persons, and show the reflexologic basis of
these differences, while collective reflexology, which studies mass or collective manifestations of correlative activity, is essentially aimed at
clarifying how social products of a correlative activity are obtained by
the correlation between single individuals in social groups and by
smoothing away their individual differences." [18]

It is obvious that we are dealing here with differential psychology in
the precise acceptance of that term. What, then, is the subject of collective psychology as such? There is a simple answer to this question: Everything within us is social, but this does not imply that all the properties of the psyche of an individual are inherent in all the other members
of this group as well. Only a certain part of the individual psychology
can be regarded as belonging to a given group, and this portion of individual psychology and its collective manifestations is studied by collective psychology when it looks into the psychology of the army, the
church, and so on.

Thus, instead of distinguishing between social and individual psychology, we must distinguish between social and collective psychology. The
difference between social and individual psychology in aesthetics appears to be the same as that between normative and descriptive aesthetics, because, as shown quite correctly by Münsterberg, historical aes-

thetics was connected with social psychology, and normative aesthetics with individual psychology.[19]

Far more important is the difference between subjective and objective psychology of art. The difference of the introspective method as applied to the study of aesthetic feelings becomes obvious from the individual properties of these feelings. By its very nature, an aesthetic feeling is incomprehensible and fundamentally obscure in its evolution to the person experiencing it. We do not really know or understand why we like or dislike an object. Anything we devise to explain its behavior is but an afterthought, an obvious rationalization of unconscious processes. The very substance of the experience, however, remains mysterious. The purpose of art is to disguise art, according to a French maxim. Psychology attempted to solve these problems experimentally, but all methods of experimental aesthetics, as applied by Fechner (the methods of selection, determination, and application) or approved by Külpe (method of selection, gradual change, and time variation),[20] are essentially not able to be anything but the simplest and most elementary aesthetic evaluations or appraisals.

In summarizing the results of this methodology, Frebes reaches very lamentable results.[21] Haman and Croce criticized it severely, and the latter bluntly called it aesthetic astrology.[22]

Not much better is the naive approach to studying art by exploring the artist's personality with such test questions as, "What would you do if your beloved betrayed you?"[23] Even if we were to take the artist's pulse or respiration or if the artist were asked to express himself on spring, summer, autumn, or winter during such a test—it still would be an ineffective, inefficient, and ridiculous way of studying the subject.

The fundamental error of experimental aesthetics consists in starting from the wrong end, that of aesthetic pleasure and aesthetic appraisal, all the while intentionally ignoring the fact that both pleasure and appraisal may be arbitrary, secondary, or even irrelevant features of aesthetic behavior. Another error is the inability to detect the specifics that distinguish an aesthetic experience from an ordinary one. Experimental aesthetics will never be able to achieve anything so long as it evaluates simple combinations of colors, sounds, lines, and so on, and fails to understand that these alone do not characterize aesthetic perception as such.

Finally, the third and most serious error of experimental aesthetics is the assumption that a complex aesthetic experience is the sum of individual minor aesthetic pleasures. The beauty of an architectural structure or of a musical composition can, according to this assumption, be comprehended as a summary expression of individual harmonies, chords, the golden section, and so on. It is obvious that for conventional aesthetics the terms "subjective" and "objective" were synonymous with psychological and nonpsychological aesthetics.[24] The concept of objective psychological aesthetics was a senseless and contradictory combination of concepts and words.

The great crisis in psychology today has split psychologists more or less into two camps: One of these has gone further and deeper into subjectivism than even Dilthey et al., obviously leaning toward pure Bergsonism. The other, ranging from America to Spain, is trying to create an objective psychology. American behaviorism, German Gestalt psychology, reflexology, and Marxist psychology are examples of such attempts. It is clear that this trend toward objectivism involves not only the methodology of conventional aesthetics but also that of psychological aesthetics. The major task of this psychology is therefore the creation of an objective method and system of art psychology; this is a matter of life and death for this entire field of knowledge. But in order to attempt the solution of this problem, one must first outline the psychological problem of art more precisely and only then begin studying its methods.

It can be shown quite readily that any investigation of art must necessarily operate with certain psychological premises and data. Lacking a finished psychological theory of art, these investigations use the vulgar day-to-day psychology along with domestic observations. It is easier to show by an example how unforgivable mistakes can make their way into serious books when they resort to commonplace psychology. One such error is the common psychological characterization of verse meter. In a recent book, Grigor'ev points out that the sincerity of the poet's emotions and feelings can be tested by a rhythmic curve devised by Andrei Bely for different poems. He describes the trochee psychologically as ". . . useful for expressing cheerful, dancing moods, as for example in 'Clouds are racing, clouds are whirling' " (a poem by Pushkin). But if a poet uses the trochee to express an elegiac mood, then it is evident that the mood is insincere or artificial, and the attempt to use the trochee for an elegy is as preposterous as, according to a witty remark by the poet Rukavishnikov, "an attempt to sculpture a Negro in white marble." [25]

It is enough to remind oneself of the Pushkin poem quoted by Grigor'ev or even of a single line from it ("plaintive squeals and howls are harrowing my soul"), to realize that here is no trace of the "cheerful, dancing mood" ascribed to the trochee. Instead, the poet uses the trochee in a lyrical poem to express a sombre, desperate mood. Grigor'ev calls this attempt as preposterous as sculpturing a Negro from white marble. Only a bad sculptor would paint a white marble statue of a Negro black, and only a bad psychologist would decree trochaic verses to be fit for expressing only cheerful, dancing moods. White marble statues may indeed represent Negroes, just as lyrical verses expressing sad or desperate moods may be trochaic. It is true, however, that both instances need a special explanation that can be given only by the psychology of art.

As an addendum to this we may bring up an analogous characterization of verse meters given by Yermakov: "In the poem 'A Wintery Road' (by Pushkin), the poet uses a sad, iambic meter for this highly sensitive work, and generates a feeling of intimate alienation and utter sadness. . . ." [26] This psychological construction cannot stand up against a simple fact—the poem "A Wintery Road" was written in pure trochaic tetrameters and not in "a sad, iambic meter." The psychologist who tries to understand Pushkin's melancholy from the iambic or his cheerfulness from the trochees has lost his way in broad daylight and has forgotten the scientifically established fact formulated by Gershenzon that "for Pushkin the meter is obviously immaterial. He uses the same meter to describe the parting from a beloved woman ("To the Shores of the Remote Fatherland"), the chasing of a mouse by a cat (in "Count Nulin"), the encounter of an angel with a demon, a captive siskin. . . ." [27]

We shall never be able to understand the laws governing the feelings and emotions in a work of art without proper psychological investigation. It is also remarkable that the sociological studies of art are unable to completely explain the mechanics of a work of art. A useful tool is the Darwinian "principle of antithesis" which Plekhanov employs to interpret many phenomena in art. [28] All this is evidence of the colossal complexity of the influences acting upon art, which cannot and must not be reduced to a primitive and single-valued form of expression. In the final analysis this is no more than the problem of the complex effect of a superstructure as broached by Marx when he says that certain periods of its (art's) blossoming do by no means correspond to the general progress of society, and that in the field of art, certain important art forms are possible only at a low stage in the evolution of art. However, the difficulty does not consist in the fact that Greek art and epics are associated with certain forms of social evolution. It consists rather in the fact that they continue to give us artistic pleasure and, to a certain extent, remain as standard and unattainable models.

We have here a precise formulation of the psychological problem of art. We must, in fact, determine the significance and action of the vitality and fascination of art which "are not in contradiction with the undeveloped social level from which they sprang," [Marx], rather than establish the origin of art as a factor of economy. Thus, the relationship between art and the economic conditions generating it turns out to be extremely complex.

This does not mean that social conditions do not completely determine the character and the effect of a work of art; it merely shows that they determine it indirectly. The feelings and emotions aroused by a work of art are socially conditioned. This is best shown by examples of Egyptian painting, where the form (stylization of the human figure) has most obviously the function of carrying a social message which is lacking in the object represented but is given it by art. If we expand this idea, we may juxtapose the effect of art and that of science and technology. Here, too, the problem of psychological aesthetics is solved by the same pattern as that for sociological aesthetics. We are ready to quote Gauzenshtein, substituting "psychology" for his "sociology": "A purely scientific sociology of art is a mathematical function." [29]—"Since art is form, sociology of art ultimately deserves this definition only when it is also a sociology of form. Sociology of content is possible and necessary, but it is not sociology of art in the proper sense, since sociology of art, in its precise meaning, can only be sociology of form. Sociology of content is nothing but general sociology, and it refers to the civil history of society rather than to its aesthetic history. Viewing a revolutionary painting by Delacroix from the standpoint of its sociological content is tantamount to examining the July revolution rather than studying the sociology of the formal element associated with Delacroix' great name." [30] Thus, the subject of this study is general psychology, not psychology of art. "The sociology of style can never be a sociology of an art form, for the sociology of style deals with the effect on form." [31]

Thus the question arises whether or not it is possible to determine some psychological laws of the effect of art on man. Extreme idealism tends to deny any regular pattern in art or psychological life. "Now as before and after, the soul is and will be for ever unfathomable. . . . There are no laws for the soul; hence, there are none for art." [32] But if we admit a pattern of regularity in one psychological life, we must necessarily refer to it to explain the workings of art, since these are always associated with our other forms of activity.

Hennequin's aesthetopsychological method involves, therefore, the correct idea that social psychology alone can give a proper base and direction to the art student. Unfortunately, this method became mired in what might be called a no man's land between sociology and psychology. It is therefore essential for any research in art psychology to determine clearly and unequivocally the substance of the psychological art problem as well as its boundaries. We agree with Külpe, according to whom aesthetics does not fundamentally shun psychology: "The fact that this relation with psychology is occasionally disputed is apparently due to an unessential inner discrepancy: some consider aesthetics' special tasks to be the application of a particular point of view to the study of psychic phenomena. Others regard them as the study of a peculiar region of facts which are usually investigated psychologically. In the former case we have an aesthetics of psychological facts, and in the latter, a psychology of aesthetic facts." [32]

The main task, however, is to distinguish art's psychological problem from its sociological one with utmost precision. On the basis of earlier arguments I feel that this is best achieved by using the psychology of a single individual. The generally accepted formula according to which the experiences, feelings, and emotions of an individual cannot be used as material for social psychology is obviously inapplicable here. It is not true that the psychology of an individual's experience in art is as little related to sociology as is a mineral or a chemical compound; but it is evident that studying the genesis of art and its dependence on sociological economy is the special subject of the history of art. Art per se, as a well-established trend, as the sum of available works, is an ideology like any other.

Thus, to be or not to be is a problem of method for objective psychology. The psychological study of art has hitherto followed but one of two trends: either the psychology of the creator (artist) was studied as it revealed itself in the work of art, or the psychology of the receptor (viewer, reader, etc.) was investigated. The imperfection and futility of both methods are sufficiently obvious. Considering the extraordinary complexity of creative processes and the total lack of knowledge about the laws governing the expression of the artist's psyche in his work makes it clear that we cannot work back from the work of art to the artist's psychology unless we resign ourselves to being lost forever in conjectures. Furthermore, Engels has shown that any ideology is always created with a false consciousness or, essentially, unconsciously. According to Marx, we cannot judge an individual on the basis of what he thinks of himself. Therefore we cannot judge a revolution on the basis of its consciousness. On the contrary, this consciousness must be explained by the contradictions of material life. In one of his letters Engels writes that ideology is a process performed by a so-called thinker in full consciousness, even though this consciousness is false. The real impelling forces that set him in motion remain unknown to him; otherwise this would not be an ideological process. Consequently, he can conceive of only the false or fictitious impelling forces.

Equally futile is the analysis of the emotions of the viewer, since he, too, is shrouded in the psyche's unconsciousness. It seems to me that another method for studying the psychology of art can be devised which, however, needs some methodological substantiation. One of the first, and easiest, objections against it is the one commonly raised against studying the unconscious by means of psychology. The unconscious, it is said, is by definition something we do not recognize; it is something unknown to us, and therefore it cannot become the subject of scientific investigation. This reasoning proceeds from the false assumption that we can study only what is directly recognizable. This is obviously a superficial approach, since we do study many things of which we have knowledge only from analogies, hypotheses, surmises, etc. Thus, we gather our ideas of the past from piecing together, in the most diverse fashion, data and material that frequently have no resemblance to these ideas or mental pictures, in the same way as "a zoologist, from the bone of an extinct animal, determines its size, appearance, life habits, feeding habits, and so forth. All this information is not immediately available to the zoologist, and is certainly not directly experienced by him; instead, it is the result of inferences and deductions from a few data directly recognizable from the bone." [33]

On the basis of these arguments we can now suggest a new method of art psychology, which in Müller-Freienfels' classification is termed the "objective-analytic method." [34] [8] Accordingly, the work of art, rather than its creator or its audience, should be taken as the basis for analysis. While it is true that a work of art as such is not an object of psychology (having no psyche of its own), we must remember that a historian, studying for instance the French revolution from materials that do not contain any of the objects of his study, finds himself faced with the necessity of actually creating the object of his study by means of indirect, that is, analytic methods. Indeed, this happens in a number of other disciplines and sciences. They search for the truth in a way similar to that of a court investigating a crime from leads, circumstantial or other evidence. Only a bad judge would pass a sentence on the basis of statements from either the defendant or the plaintiff, both of whom are prejudiced and bound to distort the truth. The psychologist operates in a similar fashion when he studies the statements of a reader or a viewer of a work of art. This does not mean, however, that a judge should not hear the interested parties—provided he takes their statements with a grain of salt. And the psychologist never refuses to use any material, even though he knows from the outset that it may not be correct. The judge establishes the truth by comparing various false statements, checking them against objective evidence, and so forth. The historian uses notoriously false or biased material most of the time; and like the historian or the geologist who first creates the object of his studies and only then subjects it to scrutiny, the psychologist is forced to resort to material evidence—the works of art—and create a corresponding psychology in order to be able to study the laws governing it. For the psychologist any work of art is a system of stimuli, consciously and intentionally organized in such a way as to excite an aesthetic reaction. By analyzing the structure of the stimuli we reconstruct the structure of the reaction. Here is a simple example: We study the rhythmic structure of a philological excerpt and deal with nonpsychological facts; but if we analyze it as being variously directed to cause a corresponding functional reaction, we create, proceeding from objective data, certain characteristics of the aesthetic reaction. It is obvious that the aesthetic reaction thus created is completely impersonal, that is, it does not belong to any single individual, nor does it reflect any concrete individual psychic process—which is its virtue. Thus we are able to determine the nature of aesthetic reaction in its pure form without confounding it with all the random processes accumulated with it in an individual's psyche.

This method guarantees a sufficient objectivity of results and of investigation, since it proceeds every time from the study of solid, objectively existing, accountable facts. Here is the formula of this method: from the form of the work of art, via the functional analysis of its elements and structure, recreate the aesthetic reaction and establish its general laws.

The task and the plan of the present book can be termed an attempt at applying this new method consistently and thoroughly to actual problems. This has obviously prevented us from pursuing any systematic tasks. We had to renounce the fundamental and consistent review of the entire material in the field of methodology, the critique of the study as such, the theoretical generalization of the results, and the establishment of their practical value. This, as a matter of fact, could become the subject of a host of further studies.

Many times I had to devise a way for solving the simplest problems and for testing the validity of the method. I have therefore chosen some fables, short stories, and tragedies to show with sufficient clearness how this method works.

I consider my task completed if this work will result in what may turn out to be a general outline of the psychology of art.

NOTES

1. O. Külpe, *Introduction to Philosophy,* translated by W. B. Pillsbury and E. B. Titchener, New York: The Macmillan Co., 1901, p. 98 *passim.*

2. J. I. Volkelt, *System der Ästhetik,* vol. I, Munich. Beck, 1900, p. 5.

3. B. M. Engelhardt, *A. N. Veselovskii,* Petrograd: Kolos, 1924, p. 212.

4. J. I. Volkelt, "Contemporary Problems in Aesthetics," *Obrazovanie (Education)* St. Petersburg, 1900, p. 192.

5. *Ibid.,* p. 208.

6. H. Shpet, "Problems of Contemporary Aesthetics," *Iskusstvo (Art),* 1923, no. 1.

7. A. V. Lunacharskii, *Osnovy pozitivnoi estetiki (Principles of Positive Aesthetics),* Moscow-Petrograd, 1923, pp. 123–124.

8. G. V. Plekhanov, *Iskusstvo (Art),* Moscow: Novaia Moskva, 1922, p. 46.

9. *Ibid.,* p. 56.

10. *Ibid.,* p. 54.

11. G. V. Plekhanov, *Osnovnye voprosy marksizma (Fundamental Problems of Marxism),* Moscow: Moskovskii rabochii, 1922, p. 76.

12. *Ibid.,* pp. 76–78.

13. *Ibid.,* p. 75.

14. *Ibid.,* p. 65.

15. V. M. Bekhterev, *Kollektivnaia refleksologiia (Collective Reflexology),* part I, Petrograd: Kolos, 1921, p. 14.

16. W. Wundt, *Völkerpsychologie,* part II, Leipzig: W. Engelmann, 1900–1909, p. 593.

17. V. M. Bekhterev, *Collective Reflexology,* part I, p. 15.

18. *Ibid.,* part II, p. 28.

19. See G. Münsterberg, *Grundzüge der Psychotechnik,* Leipzig, 1920.

20. O. Külpe, *Der gegenwärtige Stand der experimentalen Aesthetik,* 1906.

21. J. Frebes, *Lehrbuch der experimentalen Psychologie,* vol. II, 1922, p. 330.

22. R. Haman, "Aesthetics," *Problemy estetiki (Problems of Aesthetics),* Moscow, 1913; and B. Croce, *Aesthetics as the Science of Expression and General Linguistics,* translated by D. Ainslie, New York: Noonday Press, 1953.

23. V. M. Bekhterev, "The Artist's Personality in Reflexological Studies," in *Arena,* a theater anthology edited by E. Kuznetsov, St. Petersburg: Vremia, 1924, p. 35.

24. See E. Maiman, *Estetika (Aesthetics),* part I, chapter 3, Moscow, 1919; and *Sistema Estetiki (Aesthetic Systems),* part II, chapter 1, Moscow, 1920.

25. M. S. Grigor'ev, *Vvedenie v poetiku (Introduction to Poetics),* part I, Moscow, 1924, p. 38.

26. I. D. Yermakov, *Etiudi po psikhologii tvorchestva A. S. Pushkina (Essays on the Psychology of Pushkin's Art),* Moscow-Petrograd, 1923, p. 190. According to Vygotsky, this is a structural commentary on "The Hamlet of Kolomna," "The Prophet," and the minor tragedies.

27. M. Gershenzon, *Videnie poeta (A Poet's Vision),* Moscow, 1919, p. 17.

28. G. V. Plekhanov, *Art,* pp. 37–59.

29. V. Gauzenshtein, *Opyt sotsiologii Izobrazitelnovo (Experimentation in the Sociology of the Fine Arts),* Moscow: Novaia Moskva, 1924, p. 28.

30. *Ibid.,* p. 27.

31. V. Gauzenshtein, *Iskusstvo i obshchestvo* (*Art and Society*), Moscow: Novaia Moskva, 1923, p. 12.

32. I. Eichenwald, *Siluety russkikh pisatelei* (*Portraits of Russian Writers*), Moscow: Nauchnoe slovo, 1911, pp. 7–8.

33. B. Ivanovskii, *Metodologiia vvedeniia v nauku i filosofiiu* (*Methodology of the Introduction to Science and Philosophy*), 1923, p. 199.

34. R. Müller-Freienfels, *Psychologie der Kunst*, vol. I, Leipzig-Berlin, 1923, pp. 42–43.

II CRITIQUE

2 ART AS PERCEPTION

PRINCIPLES OF CRITICISM. ART AS PERCEPTION. RATIONALIZATION OF THIS FORMULA. CRITICISM OF THE THEORY OF FORMS. PRACTICAL RESULTS OF THIS THEORY. DEFICIENCIES OF THE PSYCHOLOGY OF FORMS. DEPENDENCE ON ASSOCIATIVE AND SENSUALISTIC PSYCHOLOGY.

There exist various psychological theories, each explaining in its own way the processes of artistic creativity or perception. Very few of them, however, have ever been pursued to an end. There is no completely and generally accepted system of art psychology. Some authors, such as Müller-Freienfels, who want to consolidate all that has been done in this field, give only an eclectic report or synopsis of disparate viewpoints. Most psychologists worked only on some particular problems of the general theory of art and proceeded in their research from different approaches, following divergent paths, and reaching different conclusions. Without a general idea or a valid methodological principle it is difficult to appraise systematically what psychology has achieved in this direction.

We can therefore investigate only those psychological theories of art which have been, or can be, developed into a systematic theory, and apply their premises to our study. In other words, we can approach critically only those psychological theories that operate with an objective-analytic method (an objective analysis of the work of art) and, proceeding from that analysis, develop a suitable psychology. Other methods of investigation are out of our reach. To check the results of our study with the aid of the facts and rules established earlier would require the final results of our study, since only the ultimate conclusions can be compared with the results of other investigations that have proceeded along a completely different path.

This procedure reduces the number of theories which can be subjected to critical investigation to three typical psychological systems, each of which is associated with a variety of partial studies, uncoordinated approaches, etc.

The critique which we intend to develop must, according to the interpretation and significance of the task set before us, proceed from the purely psychological strength and reliability of each theory. The merits of each theory in its own specialized field, such as linguistics or literature, will not be considered here.

The first and most widespread formula of art psychology goes back to W. von Humboldt; it defines art as perception. Potebnia adopted this as the basic principle in a number of his investigations. In a modified form, it approaches the widely held theory that comes to us from antiquity, according to which art is the perception of wisdom, and teaching and instruction are its main tasks. One of the fundamental views of this theory is the analogy between the activity and evolution of language and art. The psychological system of philology has shown that the word is divided into three basic elements: the sound, or external form; the image, or inner form; and the meaning, or significance. The inner form is understood to be the etymological form that expresses the content. Frequently this inner form is forgotten, or is displaced by the expanded meaning of the word. In other cases, however, this inner form can be readily determined. Etymological investigation reveals that where only the outward form and meaning were retained, the inner form existed once but was forgotten as the language evolved. For example, the Russian word for *mouse* once signified *thief* [9], and only by means of the inner form have the sounds acquired the meaning "mouse." In such words as *streetcar, newspaper, dogcart,* and so on, the inner form is still apparent, as is the fact that the image contained in these words is gradually being pushed out by their expanded content. This leads to a conflict between the original, stricter sense of these words and the subsequent broader application. When we say "old newspapers," or "horse-drawn dogcart," this conflict becomes obvious. To illustrate the significance of the inner form and its important role in an analogy with art, let us explore the phenomenon of synonyms. Two synonyms have the same content but a different sound form, because the inner form of each word is completely different. In Russian *moon* and *month* mean exactly the same thing. Etymologically, in Russian *moon* means something capricious [10], whimsical, changeable, and variable (alluding to the lunar phases), while *month* is a measure (alluding to measuring time by lunar phases). The difference between the two words is merely psychological. They lead to the same result, but with the aid of different thought processes. Similarly, two different clues may cause us to guess the same thing, but the mode of guessing will be different each time. Potebnia formulates this thought quite brilliantly: "The inner form of each word gives our thought a different direction. . . ." [1]

Psychologists have found the same three elements that make up a word are also found in a work of art. It is asserted that the psychological processes of the perception and creation of a work of art coincide with the identical processes of perception and creation of a word. "The same elemental forces," says Potebnia, "are also found in a work of art, and we can recognize them if we reason the following way: 'There is a marble statue (outer form) of a woman with sword and scales (inner form) representing justice (content).' We will find that in a work of art the image refers to the content, as in a word the concept refers to the sensory image or idea [11]. Instead of the 'content' of a work of art we may use a more common term, the 'idea.' " [2]

This analogy reveals the mechanism of the psychological processes that correspond to the creation of a work of art. It becomes obvious that the significance or descriptive power of a word equals its poetic value, so that the basis of an artistic experience is representation, and its general character traits are the common properties of the intellectual and perceiving processes. A child who has never before seen a glass sphere may call it a small watermelon, and explain the unusual and unknown experience by means of an old and familiar image. The familiar idea of a "small watermelon" helps the child to apperceive the new concept. "Shakespeare created Othello," says Ovsianiko-Kulikovskii, "to apperceive the idea of jealousy. The child has used 'small watermelon' to apperceive a glass sphere. . . . 'A glass sphere is nothing but a small watermelon,' says the child. 'Jealousy, that's Othello,' says Shakespeare. Successfully or not, the child has explained the glass sphere. Shakespeare has brilliantly explained jealousy, first to himself, and then to all of us." [3]

Thus, poetry or art is a special way of thinking [12] which, in the final analysis, leads to the same results as scientific knowledge (Shakespeare's explanation of jealousy), but in a different way. Art differs from science only in its method, in its way of experiencing and perceiving, in other words, psychologically. "Poetry and prose," says Potebnia, are first and foremost a 'certain way of thinking and perceiving.' " [4]—"Without an image there is no art, especially no poetry." [5]

According to this theory of artistic understanding, a work of art can be applied as a predicate to new, imperceptive phenomena or ideas, to apperceive them in the same way as the image in a word helps apperceive the new meaning. What we are unable to understand immediately and directly can be understood in a roundabout way, allegorically. The whole psychological effect of a work of art can then be entirely credited to this indirectness.

"In the Russian word *mouse,* according to Ovsianiko-Kulikovskii, the thought goes to the target, namely to the definition of the concept, following a direct path and making only one step. In the Sanskrit *mus* it takes an indirect path, first to the meaning *thief,* and from there to the meaning *mouse,* thus making two steps. Compared to the first rectilinear movement, the latter is more rhythmical . . . In the psychology of language, that is, in terms of realistic thinking (not always formally logical), what matters is *how* something is said, *how* it is thought, and *how* the content is presented, not *what* is said or thought." [6]

It is obvious therefore that we are dealing with an intellectual theory. Art requires brain work; all the rest is incidental in the psychology of art. "Art is a certain exercise for thought," says Ovsianiko-Kulikovskii.[7] The fact that art, whether created or perceived, is accompanied by strong emotions is said by these authors to be a marginal phenomenon and not a part of the process itself. It comes as a prize for the effort, because the image necessary to understand a certain idea, the predicate to this idea, "has been given me beforehand by the artist, and it came free." [8] The free feeling of relative lightness, of the parasitic enjoyment of exploiting somebody else's labor free of charge is the source of artistic enjoyment. In a manner of speaking, Shakespeare worked for us by finding for the idea of jealousy the fitting image of *Othello.* All the enjoyment we experience in reading *Othello* comes from the pleasant use of somebody else's work and from the exploitation without expense of somebody else's artistic creativity. It is interesting to note that this unilateral intellectualism of the system is openly admitted by all the most prominent representatives of this school. Hornfeld, for instance, says that the definition of art as perception "covers only one of the aspects of the artistic process." [9] He also points out that with such an interpretation of the psychology of art, the boundary between the process of scientific and artistic perception is effaced, that in this respect "the great scientific truths are similar to artistic images," and that, consequently, "this definition of poetry requires a subtler *differentia specifica* which is not easy to find." [10]

It is quite interesting that this theory is in conflict with the entire psychological tradition associated with the problem. The scholars have excluded all intellectual processes from aesthetic analysis. "Many theoreticians underscore so unilaterally that art is a matter of perception, fantasy, or feeling, contrasting art with science as the field of knowledge, that it may appear as irreconcilable with the theory of art if we assert that the process of thinking is also a part of artistic enjoyment." [11] This is one author's excuse for including the thinking process in the analysis of aesthetic enjoyment. Thought is used here as a cornerstone in the explanation of the art phenomenon.

This one-sided intellectualism revealed itself quite early, so that the second generation of researchers had to introduce substantial corrections to the theories of their teachers. Strictly speaking, from a psychological viewpoint, these corrections reduce to naught the teachers' assertions. None less than Ovsianiko-Kulikovskii had to come out with a teaching or theory, according to which lyrics are a special aspect of artistic creativity,[12] which reveals a "fundamental psychological difference" from the epic. The essence of lyrical art can be reduced to processes of perception, or to pure brainwork. The decisive role is played by emotion, an emotion so distinct that it can be separated from the secondary emotions that arise in the course of scientific and philosophical creativity. "Any human creativity involves emotions. In analyzing the psychology of mathematics, for example, we will discover a special kind of 'mathematical emotion.' However, no mathematician, philosopher, or experimental biologist will agree that his task consists of creating specific emotions associated with his field of endeavor. We cannot possibly speak of science or philosophy as emotional activities . . . Emotions play a dominant role in artistic creativity. They are generated by the content itself and can be of any sort or kind: grief, sorrow, pity, anger, sympathy, indignation, horror, and so on. These emotions per se are not lyrical, but they may incidentally include a lyrical 'streak' if the work of art has a lyrical form, as for instance a poem or a piece of rhythmic prose. Let us take the scene of Hector's farewell from *Andromache*. In reading it we may experience a strong emotion and may even be moved to tears. But this emotion has nothing lyrical in it since it is caused only by the emotional scene. However, accompanied by the rhythmic effect of the flowing hexameters, it causes lyrical emotion. The latter was more powerful in the days when Homer's poems were sung by blind rhapsodists accompanied by the sounds of the cithara. The rhythm of singing and music joins that of the verse. The lyrical element is strengthened and occasionally may even have replaced the emotion caused by the subject matter. To get this emotion in its pure form, without the admixture of its lyrical component, all we have to do is transpose the scene into prose devoid of any rhythmic cadence. Imagine, for instance, Hector's farewell from *Andromache* described by Pisemskii. 'You will experience true feelings of sympathy, compassion, and pity; you may even shed a tear; but there will be nothing lyrical about it.' " [13]

Thus, a huge area of art, namely, music, architecture, and poetry, is totally excluded from the theory that explains art as the result of an exercise of thought. We are forced not only to place these art forms into a subcategory within the art categories, but to view them as a special kind of creativity alien to the visual arts as well as to philosophy and to science, while standing in the same relation to both. However, we find it extremely difficult to draw a precise boundary between lyrical and non-lyrical art forms. In other words, if we admit that lyrical art forms require the work of something other than thought, we must also admit that any other art form has large areas where pure thought is by no means the only essential element. We will find, for instance, that such works as Goethe's *Faust,* or Pushkin's *Mozart and Salieri, The Stone Guest,* or *The Covetous Knight* belong to the syncretistic, or mixed, forms of art, semigraphic and semilyrical. We cannot perform the same operation on them which we have tried to perform on Hector's farewell scene. According to Ovsianiko-Kulikovskii's teachings there is no substantial difference between verse and prose, that is between measured and non-measured speech. Consequently there is no sign in the external form that would enable us to distinguish the visual arts from the lyrical arts. "The verse is nothing but pedantic prose in which metric uniformity has been maintained, whereas prose is a free verse in which iambi, trochees, etc, alternate freely and arbitrarily, and do not prevent certain prose (Turgenev's, for instance) from being more harmonious than some verse." [14]

We have also seen that in Hector's farewell scene our emotions are of two distinct kinds: those caused by the subject matter (namely, the emotions which would not disappear even if the scene were narrated by Pisemskii), and those generated by Homer's hexameters (namely, emotions which would have been lost or would not have even arisen had the scene been written by Pisemskii). But is there any work of art in which these additional emotions, caused by the form, are lacking? In other words, can we imagine a work of art which, if retold by Pisemskii, (so that only the content is retained, the external form vanishing completely), would not lose any of its intrinsic qualities? Analysis and everyday observation show, on the contrary, that in the visual arts the indissolubility of the form coincides with the indissolubility of the form of any lyrical poem. Ovsianiko-Kulikovskii attributes Tolstoy's *Anna Karenina* to the category of purely epic art. But here is what Tolstoy himself wrote about his novel, and, in particular, about its form: "If I wanted to put into other words what I intended to express by the novel, I would have to write exactly the same novel all over again. . . . And if the critics already have understood and are able to express and paraphrase what I wanted to say, then I must wholeheartedly congratulate them and boldly affirm *qu'ils en savent plus long que moi* . . . (that they know more about it than I . . .). If the nearsighted critics think I wanted to describe only what pleased me, how Oblonsky dines, and what beautiful shoulders Karenina has, they are wrong . . . In nearly everything I wrote I was guided by the need of gathering thoughts and connecting them to express myself, but each thought expressed separately loses its meaning and becomes insignificant if taken out of the context to which it belongs. The context itself is not made up of thoughts (I think) but of something else, and it is impossible to express in precise words the basis of this combination. But it can be done indirectly, using words to describe images, actions, and situations." [15]

Here Tolstoy refers quite explicitly to the subordination of thought in a work of art and shows why it is impossible to perform on *Anna Karenina* the operation suggested by Ovsianiko-Kulikovskii for Hector's farewell scene. It might seem that if *Anna Karenina* were re-narrated in our own words or in Pisemskii's, all of its intellectual features would be preserved. Since the novel is not written in hexameters, it is not entitled to additional lyrical emotions, and thus it would suffer no damage from such an operation. We discover, however, that to violate the combination of thoughts and words, that is, to destroy its form, is tantamount to destroying the novel, in the same way that transcribing a lyrical poem in Pisemskii's style is equivalent to destroying its lyricism. Other works mentioned by Ovsianiko-Kulikovskii, such as Pushkin's *The Captain's Daughter,* or Tolstoy's *War and Peace* are also unlikely to withstand this operation. It must be said that the basic operation of psychological analysis consists in this—real or imaginary—destruction of the form. The distinction between the effect of the most precise re-narration and that of the original work is the starting point for the analysis of the special emotion of form. The rationality of this system clearly reveals a complete lack of understanding of the psychology of form in a work of art. Neither Potebnia nor his pupils have ever been able to explain the special and quite specific effect generated by artistic form. This is what Potebnia has to say on the subject: "No matter what the particular solution of the problem of why poetic thinking (in its less complex forms), more than prosaic thinking, is closely related to the musicality of sounds, namely, tempo, rhythm, harmony, and association with melody, it cannot refute the position according to which poetic thinking can do without measures and meters, while prose can artificially (though with some harm to it) be given the form of verse." [16] It is obvious that meters or verses are not essential to a poetic work of art. It is equally obvious that a rule of mathematics or grammar expressed in verses is not a work of poetry. The belief that poetic thinking can be completely independent of any external form, as Potebnia asserts in the lines cited above, is a complete contradiction of the first axiom of the psychology of artistic form, which states that a work of art exerts its psychological effect only in its given form. Intellectual processes are only parts and components, or tools, in those combinations of words and thoughts which are the actual work of art. But this combination, the form of a work of art, is, as Tolstoy says, made up not of thoughts but of something else. In other words, the psychology of art does involve thought, but it is not, as a whole, the result of the labor of thought. The unusual psychological power of the artistic form was correctly understood by Tolstoy, who pointed out that any violation of that form, even if it is minimal, immediately wipes out the artistic effect: "I have already cited somewhere the profound statement on art of the Russian painter Briullov, but I cannot but repeat it once more because this statement, better than anything else, shows what can and what cannot be taught at school. As he was correcting the sketch of a pupil, Briullov gave it a few touches here and there, and the dull, drab sketch suddenly came to life. 'But you've *scarcely* touched it, and everything has changed!' said one of the pupils. 'Art begins where *scarcely* starts,' replied Briullov, expressing the most characteristic trait of art. This remark is true for all the arts, but its remarkable correctness can be best seen in the execution of music. . . . Let us take the three main conditions, the pitch, duration, and intensity of a sound. The execution or interpretation will only be artistic when the tone is no higher or lower than it should be, when the note is hit at its infinitely small center, when it is held exactly for the time required, and when the intensity of the sound is exactly the one required, neither weaker nor stronger. The slightest deviation in pitch of the note, the slightest increase or decrease in its duration, the slightest increase or decrease in intensity, and the interpretation is gone. The execution of the piece is no longer captivating. Thus, the 'intoxication' with the art of music which seems to be so easily induced, occurs only when the performer succeeds in finding those infinitely small instants necessary for a perfect interpretation. The same applies to all the arts: in painting, scarcely lighter or darker, scarcely higher or lower, slightly more to the left or right; in drama, the slightest increase or decrease of stress, or a minute acceleration or delay; in poetry, the slightest understatement, overstatement, or exaggeration—and there is no 'intoxication.' It occurs to the degree and extent in which the artist finds those infinitesimal elements which make up his work. There is no way to teach by external means how to discover and find these elements, since they can be found only when a person abandons himself entirely to feeling. No training or instruction can make a dancer keep in step with the music, a violinist or singer hit that minuscule but correct portion of a note, a painter draw the only proper line of all the possible ones, or the poet find the only correct combination of words. All this can be achieved only by feeling." [17]

The difference between a great conductor and an average one becomes obvious only in the performance of the same piece of music; the difference between a great painter and an imitator is to be sought in those infinitely small elements of the art that belong to the category of formal elements. "Art begins where *scarcely* starts" is tantamount to saying that art begins where form begins.

Thus, since form is characteristic of any work of art, whether lyrical or graphic, the particular emotion of a form becomes a necessary condition for artistic expression. This eliminates Ovsianiko-Kulikovskii's distinction, according to which in some arts the aesthetic enjoyment "comes more as the result of a process, as some sort of reward for the creativity of the artist, and for understanding and repeating someone else's creativity for anyone who perceives the work of art. It is different with architecture and lyrics, where these feelings appear primarily as a fundamental emotional feature in which the gravitational center of the work of art is concentrated, rather than as 'results' or 'rewards.' These arts may be called emotional, to distinguish them from the others which we might call intellectual or 'graphic'. . . . In the latter the emotional process is governed by the formula: from image to idea, and from idea to emotion. For the former, the formula is different: from the emotion generated by external form to another, stronger emotion, which arises because the external form has become the symbol of the idea of the subject." [18]

Both formulas are completely fallacious. As a matter of fact, it would be more correct to say that during the perception of graphic and lyrical art the emotional process evolves by the formula: from the emotion of form to something following it. In any event, the starting point, without which the understanding of art is impossible, is the emotion of form. This is best illustrated by the psychological operation performed by the author on Homer. This operation also disproves the assertion according to which art is brainwork. The emotion of art cannot be equated to the emotion accompanying "any act of predication, especially grammatical predication. The answer to the question has been given, the predicate has been found, and the subject experiences a form of mental satisfaction. An idea has been discovered, an image has been created, and the subject experiences a peculiar intellectual pleasure." [19]

This, as we have already shown, does away with any psychological difference between the intellectual pleasure derived from solving a mathematical problem and that derived from listening to a concert. Hornfeld is quite right when he states that "in this entirely perceptive theory the emotional elements of art are bypassed. This is the shortcoming of Potebnia's theory, a shortcoming of which he was aware and which he would have corrected had he continued his work." [20]

We do not know what Potebnia would have done, had he continued his work; but we do know what became of his theory, which was subsequently developed by his pupils. It excluded from his formula a great number of the arts, and contradicted the most evident facts when attempts were made to apply it to the remaining ones.

The intellectual operations and thinking processes in which works of art involve us do not belong to the psychology of art in the narrower sense of the word. They are the result, consequence, conclusion, or effect of a work of art, and they can occur only as a result of the fundamental effect generated by the work of art. The theory which starts out from this position behaves, as Shklovskii remarked quite wittily, like a horseman who wants to get on his horse but jumps over it. The theory misses the target and does not explain the psychology of art as such. The following simple examples illustrate our point. Valerii Briusov adopted this theory and claimed that any work of art, by some special method, leads to the same perception as does the course of a scientific proof. For instance, what we experience in reading Pushkin's poem *The Prophet* can also be described by scientific methods. "Pushkin proves the same idea using poetic means, namely by synthesizing concepts. But since the conclusion is wrong, there must be mistakes in the proofs. Indeed, we cannot accept the image of the seraphim, nor can we accept the substitution of the heart by coal, and so on. All the merits of Pushkin's poem notwithstanding . . . we can accept it only if we share the poet's viewpoint. Pushkin's *The Prophet* is a historic fact, as is, for instance, the teaching of the indivisibility of the atom." [21] The intellectual theory is pushed to absurd extremes here; hence, its psychological oddities and peculiarities are especially evident. It would appear that if a work of art contradicts scientific truths, it has the same value for us as the teaching of the indivisibility of the atom, that is, of an incorrect and therefore abandoned scientific theory. But then, about 99 percent of all the world's works of art should be discarded as material having only historical value. One of Pushkin's great poems begins with the words:

The earth is motionless: heaven's dome
Is held by Thee, Creator, so that
It will not fall on land and water
And crush us.

Every first-grader knows that the earth is not motionless but revolves. Thus these stanzas have no serious meaning for a civilized person. Why, then, do poets resort to obviously untrue and incorrect ideas? Marx points out that the most important problem in art is to explain why the Greek epics and the Shakespearean tragedies retain the significance of a standard and unattainable model to this day, despite the fact that the circumstances from which their ideas and concepts developed have long since disappeared. Greek art was able to evolve only from Greek mythology, but it continues to stir and excite us, even though Greek mythology has lost all real meaning for us, apart from a historical one. The best proof that in art this theory operates essentially with an extra-aesthetic moment is provided by the fate that befell Russian symbolism, the theoretical premises of which fully coincide with the theory under investigation.

Viacheslav Ivanov crystallized the conclusions reached by the Russian symbolists in the formula: "Symbolism lies beyond the aesthetic categories." [22] It is as though the processes of thinking and theory are all beyond the aesthetic categories and psychological experiences of art. Far from explaining to us the psychology of art, these processes require an explanation which can be given only on the basis of its scientific development.

A theory is best evaluated by means of those extreme conclusions, concerned with an entirely different field, which make it possible to verify its laws by using facts of a completely different category. It is interesting to follow the conclusions of the theory which we are studying and to apply them to the history of ideologies. At first sight the history of ideologies appears to be in perfect harmony with that of the constant change of social ideology caused by changes in production techniques. It apparently explains how and why changes in the psychological impression generated by the same work of art occur, despite the fact that the form of the work remains the same. Once we establish that the crux of the matter, so to speak, is not the content planned by the author but that attributed to it by the reader, it becomes obvious that the content of this work of art is a dependent and variable quantity, *a function of the psyche of social man*. "The artist's achievement is not found in the minimum content that he intended to give his work. Rather, it is mirrored in the flexibility of the image, in the capacity of the internal form to inspire different contents. A simple riddle (in which from a play on Russian words we have a window, a door, and a heap) can evoke the idea of the relationships between the different strata of a people to the flowering of political, moral, and scientific ideas. Such an interpretation of the riddle will be wrong only if we pretend that it is based on its objective meaning rather than on the personal feeling it brought about in us. There is a story about a poor fellow who wanted to get water from the river Sava to dilute some milk in a cup. As he was filling his cup, a wave from the river washed away the milk, whereupon he exclaimed, 'Sava, Sava, you haven't profited by this, but have only made me sad!' Someone may see in this tale the inexorable, cataclysmic, and destructive effect of world events, the bad luck and ill fate striking out at individuals, the cry that issues from the heart of a person stricken by an irreparable, and, from his subjective viewpoint, undeserved loss. Mistakes are easily made by imposing on a people one understanding or another, but it is obvious that stories like this live on for centuries, not because of their literal meaning but on account of the significance attached to them. This explains why the works of ignorant people and of dark ages can retain their artistic value even in advanced, sophisticated times. It also explains why, despite the alleged immortality of art, there comes a time when, with rising difficulties in understanding and with the inner form forgotten, works of art lose their value." [23]

This can account for the changeability of art in history. "Tolstoy compared the effect of a work of art with contagion; this comparison is particularly suitable in this case: I caught typhus from Ivan, but I'm suffering from my own typhus, not Ivan's. I have my own Hamlet, not Shakespeare's. Typhus is nothing but an abstraction necessary to theoretical thought and created by it. Each generation, each reader has his own Hamlet." [24]

This appears to explain the dependence of art on history quite well, but a comparison with Tolstoy's formula completely exposes the fallacy of this explanation. It is true that, for Tolstoy, art ceases to exist when one of its smallest components is violated. It is also true that for him a work of art is a complete formal tautonymy. In its form it is always equal to itself. "I have said what I have said"—this is an artist's only answer to the question of what he wanted to say with his work. The only way to reconfirm himself is to repeat the entire novel with the same words he used in the first place. Potebnia claims that a work of art is always allegorical. "I didn't say what I said, but something else," is his formula for a work of art. It is obvious that this theory does not explain the change in the psychology of art per se, but the change in the use of the work of art. Each generation, each era uses the work of art in its own way. To be used, a work of art has to be felt in the first place. But how it is felt by different generations and different eras the theory explains in a way that is not exactly historical. Ovsianiko-Kulikovskii points out that psychology of lyrics makes feeling a matter of work rather than of mind and establishes the following points: "The psychology of lyrics is characterized by certain special symptoms which distinguish it quite sharply from the psychology of other forms of creativity. . . . The distinctive features of lyrics must be recognized as eternal; they reveal themselves in the earliest stages of lyricism accessible to investigation and run through its entire history. All the changes to which they are subjected in the course of evolution not only do not violate their psychological nature, but contribute to making lyrical expression fuller and more complete." [25]

This shows quite clearly that since we talk about the psychology of art, in the proper acceptance of the word, it appears to be eternal. Despite all the changes, it expresses its nature more fully and seems to be not subject to the general law of historical evolution, at least in its substantial parts. If we remind ourselves of the fact that for our author lyrical emotion is general artistic emotion, i.e., emotion of form, we see that the psychology of art, in so far as it is the psychology of form, remains immutable and eternal. What changes and evolves from generation to generation is the way it is used and applied. The monstrous strain on our thought, which becomes evident, even conspicuous when we follow Potebnia and try to intoduce some meaning into a modest and unassuming riddle, is a direct consequence of the fact that the study is conducted in the area of the use and application of the riddle rather than in that of its actual meaning and nature. Virtually anything can be made meaningful. Hornfeld gives many examples of some nonsense or absurdity to which we give a meaning.[26] The inkspot tests conducted by Rohrschach show quite unmistakably that we give meaning, structure, and expression to the most absurd, random, and senseless accumulations of forms. In other words, a work of art by itself cannot be responsible for the thoughts and ideas it inspires. The thought or idea of political evolution, and of a varying approach to it from different quarters and viewpoints is certainly not contained in the modest riddle. If we replace its literal meaning (window, door, and heap) with an allegorical one, the riddle will stop functioning as a work of art. There would be, in fact, no difference between a riddle, a fable, and an extremely complex work if any and each of them could contain the greatest and most valuable thoughts and ideas. The difficulty does not consist in the fact that the use of a work of art in a specific era has its own, specific character, that the *Divina Commèdia* has a different social purpose in our time than in Dante's; rather, the difficulty consists in showing that the reader, who is under the influence of the same conventional emotions as any contemporary of Dante's, uses the same psychological mechanisms in a different way and experiences the *Commèdia* in a different way.

In other words, we have to show that not only do we interpret works of art differently, but we also experience and feel them differently. This is why Hornfeld entitled his paper on the subjectivity and changeability of understanding, "On Interpreting Works of Art." [27] It is important to show that the most objective and, it would seem, the purest visual art is —as Guyau showed for landscaping—in the final analysis the same lyrical emotion, that is, the specific emotion of the artistic form. "The world of *A Sportsman's Notebook*," says Gershenzon, "is a faithful representation of the peasantry of Orlov province in the 1840's; but if we take a closer look we discover that this world is a masquerade: the images of Turgenev's state of mind are disguised in the flesh, life, and psychology of Orlov peasants, and even in the landscape of Orlov province." [28]

And finally, the most important of all: The subjectivity of understanding, the meaning introduced by us, is definitely not a specific peculiarity of poetry. It is the sign of any understanding. As Humboldt quite rightly put it, any understanding is a non-understanding; that is to say, the thoughts instilled in us by someone's speech never coincide entirely with the thought in the mind of the speaker. Anyone listening to a speech and understanding it apperceives the words and their meaning in his own way, and the meaning of the speech will be a subjective one every time, no more and no less than the meaning of a work of art.

Briusov, following Potebnia, sees the peculiarity of poetry in that it uses synthetic views rather than analytic opinions as does science. "If the opinion, 'man is mortal,' is basically analytical—although we have arrived at it by induction, by observing that all people die—the poet's (Tyutchev) expression, 'the sound fell asleep,' is a synthetic statement. No matter how much one analyzes the term *sound,* the concept of *sleep* will not be found in it. Something from outside must be added, that is, synthesized into it, to obtain the concept of 'the sound fell asleep.' " [29] The trouble is, however, that our everyday language, our business and journalistic prose, is literally crammed with such synthetic statements. With the aid of such statements we shall never be able to find a specific indication of the psychology of art that distinguishes it from any other form of emotion. A newspaper statement to the effect that "the government fell" contains, in this context, as much synthesis as the expression "the sound fell asleep." Conversely, in poetry we find many such statements that cannot be recognized as being synthetic in the sense expounded. When Pushkin says "Love subjugates all ages," he makes a statement that is not at all synthetic, although it is quite poetic. We see that if we dwell on the intellectual processes initiated by a work of art, we are likely to lose the precise symptom or sign which distinguishes them from all other intellectual processes.

Another manifestation of poetic emotion adduced by this theory as a specific characteristic of poetry is the picturesqueness, or the emotional meaningfulness, of a concept. According to this theory, a work of art is all the more poetic, the more picturesque, graphic, obvious, and incisive the emotional image evoked in the mind of the reader. "If, for instance, in imagining a horse I take the time to think of a black horse galloping along, its mane waving, etc., my thought is bound to be artistic—it will perform a minor act of artistic creativity." [30]

Thus it would seem that any image-bearing concept is at the same time a poetic concept. Here we see a most obvious connection between Potebnia's theory and the associative and sensualistic trends in psychology on which all the teachings of this school are based. A tremendous upheaval has occurred in psychology since the merciless criticism of both these trends, as applied to the higher processes of thought and imagination, razed to the ground the old psychological system, and with it Potebnia's statements and the assertions based on it. The new psychology has shown quite correctly that the process of thinking, in its higher forms, occurs without the help of graphic concepts or images. The traditional doctrine, according to which thought is nothing but an association of images or concepts, appears to have been completely abandoned after the fundamental investigations of Bühler, Messer, Ach, Watt, and other psychologists of the Würzburg school. The absence of graphic concepts in other thinking processes may be regarded as quite an achievement of the new psychology; Külpe tries to reach extremely important conclusions for aesthetics as well. He points out that the traditional idea of the graphic character of a poetic image collapses under the new discoveries. "All we have to do is to take the observations of readers and listeners. Frequently we know what it is about; we understand the situation, the behavior, and the personality of the characters; but we think of the corresponding or graphic concept only accidentally." [31]

Schopenhauer says, "Were we to translate the speech we hear into images of fantasy rushing past us, images that grapple and intertwine as the words and their grammar flow by, what a confusion would seize our minds as we listen to someone, or read a book. In any event, this does not happen." Indeed, we would be appalled to think of the ugly distortion that could occur in a work of art if we were to translate into sensorial concepts the images used by the poet Lermontov:

In the aerial ocean
Without helms or sails,
Choruses and harmonies of stars
Silently float in the mist.

Were we to imagine graphically, as Ovsianiko-Kulikovskii suggests, the ocean, the helm, the upper regions of space, the mist, and the stars, the confusion would be such that nothing would be left of Lermontov's poem. Nearly all artistic descriptions are construed in such a way that their images cannot be translated into ordinary words or graphic concepts. How would one graphically imagine the following distich by Mandelstamm:

Burn on his lips, like black ice . . .
The knell of Stygian remembrances.

"Black ice burning" is utter nonsense if we picture it literally. The reader who attempts to visualize graphically the verses from *Solomon's Song,* "Thy hair is as a flock of goats that appear from Gilead; thy teeth are as a flock of sheep which go up from the washing . . ." will certainly get into trouble. The same thing would happen to him that happened to a fictitious sculptor in a poem by a Russian humorist: in trying to mold a statue of Shulamite to represent graphically the metaphors of the *Song of Songs* he produced a "bronze dunderhead, six ells long."

It is interesting to note that, when applied to riddles, such a remoteness of the image from its actual meaning vouches for the riddle's poetic effect. The proverb puts it correctly: between the riddle and its solution there are seven versts of truth (or untruth). Another variant expresses the same idea: between the riddle and its solution there are seven versts, whether of truth or untruth. If we eliminate the seven versts, we will kill the effect of the riddle. This is exactly what the teachers who wanted to replace the complicated and abstruse riddles of folklore with rational and educational ones did. They assigned to children such insipid riddles as: What is it that stands in the corner and sweeps the room? Answer: the broom. Riddles like that are completely devoid of any poetic significance and effect, because they lend themselves to total literal rationalization. Shklovskii points out quite correctly that the relationship of the image to the word signified by it does not justify Potebnia's rule according to which "the image is something much simpler and clearer than what is being explained;" that is, "since the purpose of representation is the close approximation of the image to our understanding, and since without this all graphicalness becomes meaningless, the image must be better known to us than that which it explains." [32] He adds, "This 'duty' is not fulfilled by Tyutchev's comparison of boundaries with deaf and dumb demons, or by Gogol's comparison of the sky with God's chasuble, or by Shakespeare's similes which astonish us because they are so strained." [33]

Let us state once more that any riddle always goes from the simpler to the more complicated image, and not vice versa. A riddle that asks "Iron boils in the meat pot—what is it?" and answers, "the horse's bit," gives an image that strikes us with its complexity as compared with the simplicity of the solution. This is always the case. When Gogol in his *Terrible Vengeance* gives his famous description of the Dnieper, he does not contribute to the objective representation of that river but creates a fantastic image of a marvellous stream that has nothing to do with the real Dnieper. He asserts that no river in the world equals the Dnieper, while in fact it is not among the world's largest rivers. He claims that only "an occasional bird reaches the middle of the Dnieper," while in fact any bird can fly from one bank to the other several times without effort. Thus, not only does he take us to the actual image of the river, but he takes us away from it in accordance with the purposes and intentions of his imaginative and romantic story. In the plot, the Dnieper is indeed an unusual and fantastic river.

This example from Gogol's work is frequently used in textbooks to show the difference between poetic and prosaic descriptions. The authors claim, in full agreement with Potebnia's theory, that Gogol's description differs from the one found in a geography book only in that he gives an imaginative and descriptive picture of the river, whereas the geography book gives a bare, matter-of-fact account of it. A simple analysis, however, reveals that the harmonic form of this rhythmic fragment and its hyperbolic, almost inconceivable, plasticity are meant to create a totally new meaning which is a requisite for the short story of which this fragment forms a part.

All this becomes quite evident when we consider that words, which are the basic material of any poetic work of art, are not necessarily graphic; so that the fundamental psychological error (usually made by sensualistic psychologists) consists in substituting words for graphic or descriptive images. "The material of poetry is made up of words, not of images or emotions," says Zhirmunskii.[34] The sensations and images evoked by words may not exist at all. At any rate they are only a subjective addition made by the reader to the meaning and significance of the words he reads. "To build an art with these images is impossible. Art requires completeness and precision; hence it cannot be left to the mercy of the reader's imagination. The work of art is created by the poet, not the reader." [35]

Words, by their very psychological nature, nearly always exclude graphic images. When a poet speaks of a horse, the word does not imply a flying mane, galloping, etc. Any such additional meaning is brought in (and usually quite arbitrarily) by the reader. By applying to these readers' additions Tolstoy's famous *scarcely*, we can see how unlikely such arbitrary, vague, and imprecise elements can be subjects of art. It is said that the reader or spectator completes with his imagination the picture or image created by the artist. Christiansen, however, has convincingly shown that this takes place only when the artist remains the master of the stirrings of our fancy, and when the formed elements predetermined quite precisely the work of our imagination. This happens with paintings representing depth or distance. But the artist must never allow our fancy or imagination to perform an arbitrary addition or completion. "An engraving shows all objects in black and white, but when we [actually] look at them, they seem different. We do not perceive them as black and white objects. We do not see the trees as being black, the meadows gray, and the sky white. Is this due to our imagination filling in the true colors of the landscape, putting forth a colorful image with green trees and meadows, gay flowers and blue skies instead of what the engraving actually shows? The artist, I suppose, might say 'Thanks so much for adding the work of ignoramuses and laymen to my creation.' A disharmony among the added colors may very well destroy his design. But stop to think for an instant. Do we really see the colors? Of course, we have the impression of a perfectly normal landscape with natural colors, but we do not actually see it. The impression remains outside the image." [36]

In a thorough investigation which immediately acquired great acclaim, Meyer has exhaustively shown that the very material used by poetry excludes a graphic and pictorial representation of the subject matter. He defined poetry as "the art of nonpictorial philological representation." [37] As he analyzes all the forms of philological representation and the origin of concepts, he concludes that imagery and sensorial obviousness are not the psychological property of poetic experience and emotion, and that the content of any poetic description is fundamentally extraimaginative. The same was shown by Christiansen by means of extremely astute observations and critique. He established that "the purpose of representing objects in art is to show the featureless impression of the object, not its sensorial image." [38] It is to Christiansen's merit to have proved this point also for the graphic arts, where obviously this

theory runs into heavy contradictions. "It is the established opinion that
the visual arts aim at the eyes, in order to enhance the visual property
of things. Is it possible that here art also strives toward something imageless, rather than toward the sensorial image of an object, considering
that it creates 'pictures' and is called visual?" [39] An analysis does show,
however, that "in the visual arts as well as in poetry the imageless impression is the final aim of representing an object. . . ." [40]

"Thus, at every point we were forced to contradict the dogma according to which art's end in itself is its emotional content. To entertain our
feelings is not the final purpose of an artistic design or plot. The most
important part in music is that which we cannot hear, in sculpture, that
which we cannot see or touch." [41] Wherever an image appears, intentional or not, it is never a sign of "poeticity." Speaking of Potebnia's
theory, Shklovskii remarks, "This construction is based on the equation: image equals poetry. In actual fact, however, there is no such
equality. For it to exist one would have to assume that any symbolic use
of a word is necessarily poetic, be it only for one brief instant when the
symbol is created. However, we can conceive of using a word in its indirect connotation without creating a poetic image. On the other hand,
words used in their direct meaning and put together in sentences that
do not evoke images may be works of poetry as, for instance, Pushkin's
poem 'I loved you once, perhaps this love. . . .' Imagery or symbolism
does not distinguish poetic language from prose." [42]

Finally, during the past ten years the most serious and shattering criticism has been leveled against the traditional theory of imagination as a
combination of images. Meinong's school (as well as the schools of other
researchers) showed with sufficient thoroughness that imagination and
fantasy must be regarded as functions servicing our emotional sphere,
and when they discover some exterior and superficial similarity with
mental processes, the reasoning is always based on emotion. Heinrich
Meyer discovered an extremely important property of this emotional
thinking. He found that the basic tendency of the facts of emotional
thinking is substantially different from that of discursive thinking. The
process of perception is pushed to the background and not recognized.
Consciousness performs *eine Vorstellungsgestaltung, nicht Auffassung* (representation of an image, not conception). The fundamental purpose of the
process is completely different, although the exterior forms may occasionally coincide. The activity of imagination consists of an order of
affects, like feelings which manifest themselves in expressive movements. There exist two opinions among psychologists as to whether
emotions increase or decrease under the effect of affective concepts:
Wundt maintained that emotions decrease, but Lehman held the oppo-

site view. If we apply to this question the principle of single-pole energy output as introduced by Kornilov in interpreting rational processes, we will see that in emotions as well as in thoughts an increase of the charge at the center leads to a weakening of the charge in the peripheral organs. Here and there the central and peripheral charges are in an inverse ratio to one another; consequently any increase from affective concepts represents basically an act of emotion, similar to acts complicating the reaction, by adding to it intellectual elements of choice, distinction, and so on. Since the intellect is nothing but inhibited will, we might possibly think of imagination as inhibited feeling. In any event, the obvious resemblance with rational processes cannot overshadow the fundamental differences which exist here. Even strictly perceptive opinions which refer to a work of art and are *Verständnis-Urteile* (judgments of comprehension) are not opinions but emotionally affective acts of thought. Thus when looking at Leonardo da Vinci's *Last Supper,* the thought arises that "this is Judas. He is obviously upset and has overturned the salt." Meyer explains this in the following way: "I recognize Judas only on the strength of the affective emotional way of representation." [43] This shows that the theory of graphic representation as well as the assertion concerning the rational character of aesthetic reaction runs into considerable opposition from psychologists. Where graphicalness is the result of the activity of the imagination, it obeys laws completely different from those of the usual creative imagination and the usual logical-discursive thinking. Art is the work of the intellect and of very special emotional thinking, but even after having introduced these corrections we have still to solve the problem confronting us. Not only do we have to establish with maximum precision how the laws of emotional thinking differ from other forms of this process; we also have to show how the psychology of art differs from other forms of that same emotional thinking.

Nothing reveals the impotence of the intellectual theory better and more fully than the practical results to which it has led. Any theory, in the final analysis, is by preference checked against the practical results issuing from it. The best evidence of whether a theory correctly recognizes and understands the phenomena with which it is concerned is given by the extent to which it controls these phenomena. Approaching the problem from a practical angle we see that this theory is totally incapable of mastering the facts of art. Neither in literature nor in the teaching of literature, in social critique, nor in the theory and psychology of creativity, has this theory given anything that could induce us to believe that it grasps one or the other law of the psychology of art. Instead of a history of literature, it has created a history of the Russian intelligentsia (Ovsianiko-Kulikovskii), a history of social thought (Ivanov-Razumnik), and a history of social movements (Pypin). In these superficial and methodologically inaccurate works the theory distorted the literature, which it used as material, and the social history which it tried to understand with the aid of literary phenomena and events. When an attempt was made to base an understanding of the intelligentsia of the 1820's upon *Eugene Onegin,* an equally distorted and incorrect view of the intelligentsia and of *Eugene Onegin* resulted. It is true that some traits of the intelligentsia of the 1820's can be found in *Eugene Onegin,* but these traits are so changed, transformed, compounded with others, and brought into a completely different connection with the plot, that on their basis it is as impossible to form a correct idea of this group in the 1820's as it is impossible to write a grammar of the Russian language on the basis of Pushkin's poetic language. No serious scholar or investigator could ever conclude, proceeding from the assumption that *Eugene Onegin* "reflects the Russian language," that the words in the Russian language distribute themselves in the form of iambic tetrameters, and rhyme in the way they rhyme in Pushkin's poem. Any attempt at perceiving anything through a work of art will fail as long as we have not learned to distinguish the auxiliary artistic techniques used by the poet to process the material he has taken from life.

There remains one last point to make. The general premise of this practical application of the theory, the typicalness of the work of art, must be taken with a good deal of circumspection and subjected to very accurate scrutiny. The artist does not give a collective photograph of life; hence, typicalness is by no means the feature he pursues. Thus, anyone endeavoring to investigate the history of the Russian intelligentsia on the basis of the Chatskiis and Pechorins risks remaining with completely fallacious ideas and understandings of the phenomena under study. With such a brand of scientific investigation we may hit the target no more than once in a thousand times. This, more than any theoretical considerations, testifies to the groundlessness and superficiality of the theory whose fine points we have just discussed.

NOTES

1. A. A. Potebnia, *Mysl' i yazyk* (*Thought and Language*), 3rd ed., Kharkov, 1913, p. 146.

2. *Ibid.*

3. D. N. Ovsianiko-Kulikovskii, *Yazyk i isskusstvo* (*Language and Art*), St. Petersburg, 1895, pp. 18–20.

4. A. A. Potebnia, "Poetry and Prose," "Tropes and Figures," and "Poetical and Mythical Thought," in *Iz zapisok po teorii slovesnosti* (*Notes on the Theory of Literature*), Kharkov, 1905, p. 97.

5. *Ibid.*, p. 83.

6. D. N. Ovsianiko-Kulikovskii, *Language and Art*, pp. 26, 28.

7. *Ibid.*, p. 63.

8. *Ibid.*, p. 36.

9. A. G. Hornfeld, *Puti tvorchestva* (*Paths of Creation*), a collection of articles on artistic writing, Petrograd: Kolos, 1922, p. 9.

10. *Ibid.*, p. 8.

11. R. Müller-Freienfels, *Psychologie der Kunst*, vol. I, p. 180.

12. See D. N. Ovsianiko-Kulikovskii, *Collected Works*, vol. VI, St. Petersburg, 1914. This volume includes "Psychology of Thought and Feeling," "Artistic Creation," "Lyrics as a Special Form of Creation," and "Crisis of Russian Ideologies."

13. *Ibid.*, pp. 173–175.

14. D. N. Ovsianiko-Kulikovskii, *Language and Art*, p. 55.

15. L. N. Tolstoy to N. N. Strakhov, April 23, 1876, in L. N. Tolstoy, *Collected Works*, vol. 62, Moscow, 1953, pp. 268–269.

16. A. A. Potebnia, *Notes on the Theory of Literature*, p. 97.

17. L. N. Tolstoy, *Collected Works*, vol. 30, Moscow, 1951, pp. 127–128.

18. D. N. Ovsianiko-Kulikovskii, *Language and Art*, pp. 70–71.

19. D. N. Ovsianiko-Kulikovskii, *Collected Works*, vol. VI, p. 199.

20. A. G. Hornfeld, *Boyeve otkliki na mirne temy* (*War Cries in Response to Peaceful Themes*), Leningrad: Kolos, 1924, p. 63.

21. V. I. Briusov, Ed., "Synthetics of Poetry," in *Problemy poetiki* (*Problems in Poetry*), Moscow-Leningrad: Zemlia i fabrika, 1925, pp. 19–20.

22. V. Ivanov, *Borozdy i meshi. Opyty esteticheskie i kriticheskie* (*Furrows and Boundaries: Aesthetic and Critical Essays*), Moscow: Musaget, 1916, p. 154.

23. A. A. Potebnia, *Thought and Language*, pp. 153–154.

24. A. G. Hornfeld, *Paths of Creation*, 114.

25. D. N. Ovsianiko-Kulikovskii, *Collected Works*, vol. VI, p. 165.

26. A. G. Hornfeld, *Paths of Creation*, p. 139.

27. *Ibid.*, pp. 95–153.

28. M. Gershenzon, *A Poet's Vision*, p. 11.

29. V. I. Briusov, "Synthetics of Poetry," p. 14.

30. D. N. Ovsianiko-Kulikovskii, *Language and Art*, p. 10.

31. O. Külpe, "The Contemporary Psychology of Thinking," *Novye idei v filosofii* (*New Ideas in Philosophy*) 16:73, 1914.

32. A. A. Potebnia, *Notes on the Theory of Literature*, pp. 29, 314.

33. V. Shklovskii, "Potebnia," *Poetika* (*Poetics*), a collection on the theory of poetic language (Petrograd) 3:5, 1919.

34. V. Zhirmunskii, "Tasks of Poetics," in a collection of articles entitled *Zadachi i metody izucheniia iskusstva* (*Problems and Methods in the Study of Art*), Petrograd: Academia, 1924, p. 131.

35. *Ibid.*, p. 130.

36. Christiansen, *Filosofiia iskusstva* (*Philosophy of Art*), 1911, p. 95.

37. A. Meyer, *Das Stilgesetz der Poesie,* Leipzig, 1901, p. IV.
38. Christiansen, *Philosophy of Art,* p. 90.
39. *Ibid.,* p. 92.
40. *Ibid.,* p. 97.
41. *Ibid.,* p. 109.
42. V. Shklovskii, "Potebnia," p. 4.
43. See H. Meyer, *Psychologie des emotionalen Denkens,* 1908.

3 ART AS TECHNIQUE

REACTION TO INTELLECTUALISM. ART AS TECHNIQUE. THE PSYCHOLOGY OF
THE SUBJECT, THE HERO. LITERARY IDEAS AND FEELINGS. PSYCHOLOGICAL
CONTRADICTION OF FORMALISM. SHORTCOMINGS OF THE PSYCHOLOGY OF
MATTER. PRACTICE OF FORMALISM. ELEMENTAL HEDONISM.

We have seen from the foregoing that the main shortcoming of the
prevalent psychological theory of art is its failure to understand the psychology of form. We have also seen that its fundamentally incorrect intellectualism and theory of representation have generated intricate and
confused ideas that have little connection with the actual problem. As a
reaction against this intellectualism a new formalistic trend arose,
formed, and developed solely as an opposition to the old system. This
trend focused upon a previously neglected concept: the concept of artistic form. It proceeded not only from earlier unsuccessful attempts to understand art by stripping it of its form but also from the fundamental
psychological fact which underlies all psychological theories of art. The
fact is that if we destroy the form of a work of art, it loses its aesthetic
effect. Hence, it was very tempting to conclude that the entire effect of a
work of art is due exclusively to its form. The new theoreticians proclaimed that art is pure form, completely independent of content. Art
was said to be a technique, an end in itself. Where the older scholars detected a complexity of thought, the new investigators saw only a play of

artistic form. Art was now being investigated from an angle completely different from the earlier scientific one. Shklovskii formulated the new approach as follows: "A literary work is pure form; it is neither a thing nor a material, but a relationship between materials. And like any relationship, it is one of zero dimension. Therefore the scale of the work is irrelevant. The arithmetic value of its numerator and denominator is unimportant. What is important is their ratio. Jocular, tragic, universal, or chamber works, juxtapositions of one world to another, or of a cat to a stone, are equal among themselves." [1]

Because of the change in their approach, the formalists had to give up the conventional concepts of form and content and replace them with the two new ideas of form and material. Whatever is readily available to the artist, such as words, sounds, plots, conventional images, and so on, is the material of a work of art and comprises the thoughts and ideas included in the work. The way in which this material is structured, placed, and distributed is called the form of this work, irrespective of whether we refer to the arrangement of sounds in a verse of poetry, to the arrangement of events in a story, or the sequence of thoughts in a monologue. Thus, the conventional concept of form was quite successfully expanded from a psychological viewpoint. Previously the scientific definition of form closely approached that in everyday use: science regarded form as something external, the sensorially recognizable aspect of a work—its outer shell, so to speak—so that elements like the pure sound elements of poetry or the combination of colors in paintings were considered form. The new approach broadened the significance of the term to include the universal principle of artistic creativity. Form is considered to be the artistic arrangement of the given material, made with the purpose of generating a specific aesthetic effect. This then is called an artistic technique. Any relationship of materials in a work of art will therefore either be *form* or *technique*. From this point of view a verse is not the ensemble of the sounds of which it consists but the sequence, or the alternating sequence, of their correlation. If we rearrange the words in a verse, the aggregate of the sounds composing it, namely its material, will remain unviolated, but its form, the verse or the meter, will disappear. In music, it is not the sum total of sounds which forms a melody, but the correlation of the ratio of the sounds. Similarly, any artistic technique is, in the final analysis, a construction of available material, a formation.

This is the viewpoint from which formalists approach the subject of a work of art, termed its content by earlier investigators. Most of the time the poet finds readily available the material, the events, actions, situations, and so forth, which constitute his story. His creativity amounts to his forming that material and giving it an artistic arrangement. This is analogous to the statement that a poet does not invent words but only arranges them to form a verse. "The methods and techniques of subject construction are similar and, in principle, equal to the techniques used for, say, sound instrumentation. Works of literature are a complex of sounds, articulate motions, and thoughts. The idea in a literary work is either the same material as the pronounced, or sound, portion of a morpheme, or an alien body." [2] Further, "a tale, a short story, or a novel are a combination of motives; a song is a combination of stylistic motives; hence, subject and *subjectness* are the same form as rhyme. The concept of *content* is completely unnecessary when we analyze a work of art from the viewpoint of its subject." [3]

The new school thus determines the relationship of the subject to the plot in the same way as it does that of the verse to the words composing it, or the melody to the notes composing it, or the form to its material. "The plot juxtaposes the subject: the events are the same, but they are narrated in the order in which they occur in the work, in the connection in which the work refers to them. . . ." In brief, the plot is "what actually happened," and the subject is "how the reader learned about it." [4]

". . . The plot is nothing but the material for the formulation of the subject," says Shklovskii. Thus, the subject of *Eugene Onegin* is not the story of his involvement with Tatiana but the treatment of that plot, brought about by introducing interruptions and deviations. [5]

The formalists approach the psychology of the characters and dramatis personae from precisely this point of view. We are to understand psychology only as a technique used by the artist, a technique in the sense that previously given psychological material is artificially and artistically transformed by the artist in connection with his aesthetic aims and purposes. Thus, we must seek the explanation of the psychology of characters and dramatis personae and their actions, not in the rules and laws of psychology, but in the aesthetic conditions set by the author's intentions. The reason for Hamlet's hesitating to kill the king must be sought not in the psychology of irresoluteness and lack of will but in the rules and laws of artistic construction. Hamlet's slowness and procrastination are nothing but an artistic device of the tragedy. He fails to kill the king immediately only because Shakespeare needed to protract the tragic action for strictly formal reasons, in the same way that a poet has to select words for his rhymes not because of the laws of phonetics, but because such are the tasks and purposes of his art. "The tragedy is protracted not because Schiller had to analyze the psychology of procrastination. On the contrary, Wallenstein procrastinates because the tragedy has to be held up, and the delay must be concealed. The same happens in *Hamlet*." [6]

Thus, the current idea that the psychology of avarice can be studied from *The Covetous Knight*, and the psychology of jealousy and envy from *Mozart and Salieri* is completely discredited, as are other equally popular ideas and theories according to which Pushkin's aim was to portray avarice or jealousy, while the reader's task is to recognize them. Both avarice and jealousy are, according to the new approach, the same raw material for an artistic construction as sounds are for a verse, or scales for a piano.

Why does King Lear not recognize Kent? Why do Kent and Lear not recognize Edgar? In the dance why do we see a plea after the consent? What separated and scattered Glan and Edvarda all over the world in Hamsun's *Pan*, even though they loved each other? [7] It is absurd to resort to psychology for an answer to these questions, because there is only one reason: artistic device or technique. Those who do not understand this also do not understand why words in a verse are arranged in an order different from that of common speech. Nor do they understand the totally new effect produced by this artificial distribution or arrangement of the material.

A similar change occurs in the conventional approach to a feeling that is said to be part of a work of art. Feelings, too, are only material or techniques. "Sentimentality cannot be the content of an art, if only for the simple reason that art has no content. To show things from 'a sentimental point of view' is a special mode of representation, as if it were; for instance, to show things from the viewpoint of a horse (Tolstoy's *Kholstomér, the Story of a Horse*) or of a giant (Swift).

"Art in its essence is unemotional . . . Art is pitiless or nonpitiful except in those cases when the feeling of compassion or pity is taken as material for constructing a work of art. But when we speak of material we must consider it from the viewpoint of composition, in the same way that we must see a driving belt as a part of an engine if we are to understand the engine, and not from the viewpoint of a vegetarian." [8]

Thus, emotions are only part of the artistic machine, the driving belt of artistic form.

It is obvious that with such an extreme change in the approach to art "we are talking not about the method of studying literature but about principles concerning the structure of literary science," according to Eichenbaum.[9] Indeed, we are not talking about changing the method of learning but about changing the most fundamental explanatory principle. The formalists proceed from the fact that they are through with the cheap and popular psychological doctrine of art and are therefore inclined to view their principle as the antipsychological principle par excellence. One of their methodological principles consists in renouncing any "psychologism" when setting up a theory of art. They try to study the artistic form as something completely objective, independent of thoughts, ideas, feelings, and other psychological material of which the forms consist. "Artistic creativity, says Eichenbaum, is suprapsychological in its essence; it does not belong to normal conventional emotional phenomena and is characterized by the fact that it rises above emotional empiricism. In this sense an emotional phenomenon, being a passive thing, must be distinguished from an intellectual phenomenon, and a personal phenomenon must be distinguished from an individual phenomenon." [10]

The formalists, however, suffer the same fate as all those art theoreticians who intend to construe their theories outside sociological and psychological foundations. Lanson puts it quite correctly: "We, the critics, do the same as Monsieur Jourdain. We 'talk in prose,' that is, we practice sociology without knowing it," and, like Molière's famous character, who found out only from his teacher that he had been talking in prose all his life, any scholar of art learns from the critic that he practiced sociology and psychology without knowing it, for Lanson's statement can also be applied to psychology.

It is quite easy to show that certain psychological premises underlie any formal principle, just as they underlie any form of art, and that the formalists are, in fact, forced to be psychologists and speak occasionally in an extremely complex, but quite psychological, prose. Tomashevskii's study, based upon this principle, begins with the words, "It is impossible to give an exact objective definition of the verse. It is impossible to lay down the basic characteristics that distinguish verse from prose. We recognize verses, or a poem, by perception. The feature of 'verse making' is born not only from the objective properties of poetic speech, but also from the conditions for its artistic perception and from the judgment of taste of the listener." [11]

This statement is equivalent to an admission that the formalistic theory has no objective data other than a psychological explanation with which to determine the nature of verse and prose, the two most obvious and clearcut formalistic devices or techniques. A superficial analysis of the formula proposed by the formalists leads to the same results. The formula "art as technique" immediately triggers the question, "technique for what?" Zhirmunskii quite correctly pointed out some time ago that technique for technique's sake, technique taken per se and not directed toward anything, is a trick, a gimmick. No matter how much the formalists try to leave this question unanswered, they, like Jourdain, answer it even though they are unaware of it. The answer is that an artistic device or technique has its own purpose which determines it completely and which cannot be defined in any terms other than psychological. The basis of this psychological theory is the teaching of the automatism of all habitual emotions. "If we begin to look into the general rules of perception and cognition, we find that once they are habitual, actions become automatic. All our habits belong to the unconscious-automatic domain. Everyone remembers the feeling he had when holding a pen in his hand for the first time, or speaking in a foreign language for the first time. Comparing this sensation with the one experienced when performing such an action for the tenthousandth time, one will agree with us. The automatization process accounts for certain rules of our prosaic speech, with its incomplete sentences and implied, half-uttered words . . . With such an algebraic method of thinking, things are grasped by numbers and size. We do not really see them but recognize them from their first indications, at first glance. A thing passes before our eyes wrapped in a bag, so to speak; we know that it exists and where it exists from the place it occupies, but we see only its surface . . . By restoring the feeling of life, by instilling feelings and sensations into things, so that a stone is really stony, we have what we call art. The purpose of art is to put feeling into objects by using sight rather than recognition. One technique of art is the device of the 'estrangement' of objects, a device which complicates the form that increases the difficulty and the duration of perception, since in art the perceptive process is an end in itself and must be prolonged. Art is a method of experiencing the making of a thing, but what is made is of no import in art." [12]

Thus we discover that the technique, or device, used to compose artistic form has its own purpose. In determining that purpose, the formalists run into a surprising contradiction when they affirm that neither things nor material nor content is essential in art, and then claim that the ultimate purpose of artistic form is to "make a thing felt," "make a stone stony," etc.; that is, to enhance and increase the sensorial experience of that very material, the significance of which was denied in the first place. Because of this contradiction, the formalists fail to discover the real, final significance of the rules of estrangement [13], since in the final analysis the purpose of this estrangement is to perceive an object. This fundamental shortcoming of formalism, the failure to understand the psychological significance of the material, leads to a sensualistic onesidedness similar to the intellectual onesidedness resulting from the failure of Potebnia's followers to understand form. The formalists assume that material is of no importance in art and that a poem on the destruction of the world and a poem about a cat or a stone are identical from the viewpoint of their poetic effect. Like Heine, they think that "in art, form is everything, and material is of no importance: Staub [a tailor] charges for a dress or a coat that he tailors from his own fabric exactly the same amount that he charges for tailoring the same garment from the customer's material. He asks to be paid only for the form, the material he gives away free." However, the investigators had to convince themselves that not all tailors are like Staub, and that in the case of a work of art we pay not only for the form but also for the material. Shklovskii himself affirms that the selection of the material is far from insignificant. He says, "Perceptible, significant quantities are chosen. Every epoch has its own index, its own list of subjects, forbidden because they are obsolete." [13] The fact is, however, that every epoch has not only a list of forbidden subjects but also one of subjects developed by it, which means that the subject itself, or the material used for its composition, is far from being insignificant in terms of the psychological effect of the entire work of art.

Zhirmunskii is quite correct in distinguishing two meanings in the formula "art as a device or technique": The first meaning regards a work of art as "an aesthetic system determined by the unity of the artistic task, that is, as a system of techniques and devices." [14]

It is obvious that in this case the technique or device is not an end in itself, but it acquires meaning and significance in relation to the overall task (assignment) to which it is subordinated. If we take the formula's second meaning, according to which not the method but the final aim of the investigation is important, and claim that "everything in art is only an artistic technique, there is nothing in art but a totality of devices and techniques," [15] then we are bound to run into a contradiction with the most obvious facts, which show that in the processes both of creation and of perception there are many tasks of a nonaesthetic nature; thus, what is known as "applied arts" is a device or a technique on the one hand, and a practical activity on the other. Instead of a formal theory we thus get "formalistic principles" and the completely false idea that subject, material, and content are of no importance in a work of art. Zhirmunskii quite correctly points out that the concept of poetic genre as a special compositional unity is associated with the definition of subjects. An ode, a poem, or a tragedy, each has its characteristic group of subjects.

The formalists could only come to these conclusions by proceeding from such a nonfigurative, subjectless art as music or pure ornament, and by interpreting any and all works of art as if they were ornaments. In an ornament the line has no purpose other than a formal one. This is why in all other art forms the formalists deny the existence of any informal or extraformal reality. "Hence," says Zhirmunskii, "the identification of the subject of *Eugene Onegin* with Rinaldo and Angelica's love story in Boiardo's *Orlando Innamorato*; the only difference is that Pushkin gives 'a complex psychological motivation for the timing of the lovers' attraction to one another,' while Boiardo 'explains the same situation as the work of magic or charms' . . . We could also include the well-known fable of the crane and the heron which uses the same compositional technique in a 'bare' form: 'A loves B, B does not love A; when B falls in love with A, A no longer loves B.' It would appear, however, that as far as the artistic effect of *Eugene Onegin* is concerned, its affinity with the fable is quite secondary; much more important is the deep qualitative difference that arises from the difference in the subject ('the arithmetical sense of the numerator and the denominator') of Onegin and Tatiana on the one hand, and the crane and the heron on the other." [16]

Christiansen's studies have shown that "the material of a work of art participates in the synthesis of the aesthetic object" [17] and that it does not obey the law of geometric relations, a law totally independent of the absolute magnitude of the terms participating in it. This can be readily proved if we maintain the form but change the absolute magnitude of the material. "A piece of music does not depend on the pitch of the tone, a work of sculpture does not depend on its absolute size; the deformation of an aesthetic object becomes universally noticeable only when the changes reach extremes." [18]

To determine the significance of the material, we have to perform an operation similar to the one by which we have determined the significance of form. By destroying the form, we see that we have destroyed the artistic effect; if we maintain the form and apply it to a completely different material we also distort the psychological effect of the work of art. Christiansen revealed the importance of this distortion by pointing out the difference between reproducing a print on silk, India paper, or heavy bond, or sculpturing a statue in marble or casting it in bronze, or translating a novel from one language into another. Furthermore, if we increase, or decrease somewhat, the absolute size of a painting, or change the tone of a melody, we again obtain a deformation. This is all the more obvious if we consider that Christiansen takes the material in its narrow acceptance, the substance or matter from which the work of art is made, and distinguishes separately the material content of the work of art with respect to which he reaches an identical conclusion. This does not mean, however, that the material or the subject content is of any significance or importance because of its nonaesthetic properties, such as the cost of bronze or marble, etc. "Although the effect of an object is independent of its nonaesthetic value, it can, nonetheless, become an important component of the synthesized object. . . . A well-painted bunch of radishes is better by far than a badly painted Madonna; hence the subject is completely irrelevant. . . . The artist who makes a good painting of a bunch of radishes may not be able to paint a good Madonna. . . . If the subject were completely irrelevant, nothing could prevent a painter from creating an equally beautiful painting on any subject. . . ." [19]

To understand the action and the effects of the material, we must consider the following two extremely important points. The first establishes the proposition that perception of a form in its simplest way is not, of itself, an aesthetic fact. We perceive forms at every step in our daily lives and, as recently shown by Köhler's brilliant experiments, form perception reaches very deep into the psyche of animals. Köhler trained a chicken to perceive relations, or forms. The bird was shown two pieces of paper: A was light gray and B was dark gray. Grains were glued to sheet A, but were loose on sheet B. After several tests the chicken was trained to go directly to the dark gray sheet B and pick up the grains there. At one point the chicken was faced with a new situation. The dark gray sheet B was kept, but the light gray sheet A was substituted by a new one, sheet C, which was even darker than sheet B. In the new combination, sheet B played the role of sheet A in the old combination. It would seem that the chicken, trained to pick the grains from sheet B, would now go directly to it, since the new sheet was unknown to it. This would have been the case if the training had been aimed at the absolute quality of color. Experiment showed, however, that the chicken turned to the new paper sheet C, and avoided the known sheet B, because it had been trained not to discern the absolute quality of color but its relative effect. The chicken did not react to sheet B, but to the darker of the two sheets presented. Since in the new combination sheet B does not play the same role as in the old one, it exerts a completely different effect. [20]

These historic psychological experiments show that the perception of forms and relations appears to be quite an elementary, and possibly even a primordial, act of the animal psyche, proving that not every perception of form need necessarily be artistic.

No less important is the second consideration, which also proceeds from the idea of form and shows that form in its full significance does not exist outside the material of which it consists. Relations and proportions depend upon the material to which they refer. We follow specific relations and proportions when we mold a figure in papier-mâché, but we follow different ones if we cast the same figure in bronze. A papier-mâché mask cannot produce exactly the same correlation as a bronze mask. Similarly, certain sound relations are possible only in Russian,

others only in German, and so on. We have one subject correlation of
ill-timed love affairs if we take Glan and Edvarda, another one if we
take Onegin and Tatiana, and a third, if we take the crane and the
heron. Thus any deformation of the material is at the same time a deformation of the form itself. We begin to understand now why a work of
art becomes irreparably distorted if we take its form and apply it to
some other material. With the other material that form turns out to be
something else entirely.

Thus the desire to avoid dualism when studying the psychology of art
distorts the only untouched factor and places it in a false light. "The
best and most obvious way to prove the significance of form or content
is to look at the consequences that arise when the form is removed, such
as for instance when describing a subject in plain words. Of course, the
artistic meaning of the content is lost, but does this mean that the effect
that issued from the form and content, fused into an artistic unit, depended entirely on the form? Such a conclusion would be as wrong as
the idea that all features and properties of water depend on the addition of hydrogen to oxygen, since without hydrogen there is nothing in
oxygen that could possibly recall water." [21]

Without touching on the material correctness of this comparison, and
leaving open the question whether form and content form a unit in the
same way that oxygen and hydrogen form water, we cannot but agree
with the logical correctness of the way the error in formalistic thinking
was detected. "The fact that form is extremely significant in a work of
art, that without a specific form there is no work of art, has been recognized long since and is not being debated here. But does this mean that
it is form alone that creates a work of art? Of course not. We could
prove this if we could take the form per se and show that certain indis-
putable works of art consist of it alone. But this, we claim, has not been
done and cannot be done." [22]

To continue this reasoning, we must mention that attempts have been
made to represent pure form, devoid of any content. These, however,
ended in the same psychological failure as the attempt to create artistic
content without form. The first group of such attempts consisted of taking a work of art, transposing it onto new material and observing the
deformation that occurred in it.

Other attempts consisted of the so-called material or substantial experiment, the clamorous failure of which illustrates, better than all theoretical speculations, the inconsistency of the one-sided teachings of the formalists.

Here, as always, we check the theory of art against its practice. Practical outcroppings of the ideas of formalism were the early ideology of

Russian futurism, the propagation of abstruse language, the absence of plots, etc. We see that practice has led the futurists to loudly repudiate all they had asserted in their manifestoes on the basis of theoretical assumptions: "We have destroyed all the punctuation marks, thereby for the first time emphasizing and recognizing the role of the word mass" —they claimed in paragraph 6 of their manifesto.[23]

In actual fact this means that the futurists have not only done away with punctuation marks in their verse-writing practices but have introduced a whole series of new punctuation marks, such as the famous dashed line of Maiakovskii's verse.

"We have shattered the rhythm," they announced in paragraph 8 of their manifesto, and in Pasternak's poetry they introduced a sample of choice and sophisticated rhythmic compositions that had been long absent in Russian poetry.

They preached abstruse language, proclaiming in paragraph 5 that abstruseness awakens creative fantasy and gives it freedom, does not offend it with anything concrete, since "sense or meaning make a word shrink, contort, and stay rigid as if it were petrified." [24] Actually however, they brought sense and meaning in art to hitherto unattained heights of sophistication [14], while Maiakovskii was busy composing advertisements in verse for Mossel'prom (Association of Moscow Enterprises Processing Agricultural Products).

They preached abstraction, but in fact composed exceptionally meaningful works, with both plots and subjects. They repudiated the old themes and plots, but Maiakovskii worked on the motif of tragic love, which can hardly be called novel. Thus, Russian futurism set up a natural experiment for formalistic principles, and that experiment showed beyond any doubt the incorrectness of the prevalent views [15].

The same happens if we apply to the formalistic principle those extreme conclusions to which it has led. We have pointed out that, as we determine the purpose of an artistic technique or device, it gets entangled in its own contradictions and ends by asserting what it denied or refuted in the first place. It is said that the principal task of a technique is to give life to things, but no word is said about the purpose of these live sensations and feelings; thus we automatically conclude that there is no other purpose, that such a process of perception is pleasant in itself and that art is an end in itself. All odd and complex compositions of art serve, in the final analysis, to give us the enjoyment of perceiving pleasant things. "The process of perception in art is an end in itself," asserts Shklovskii. This concept that the value in art is determined by the pleasure and delight it gives us suddenly reveals the psychological paucity of formalism. It takes us back to Kant, who said that "beautiful is what we like, irrespective of its meaning." According to the teaching of the formalists, the perception of an object is pleasant by itself, as the beautiful plumage of a bird is pleasant by itself, the color and shape of a flower, the coloring of a seashell (Kant's examples). This elementary hedonism—a return to the teaching of enjoyment and pleasure abandoned long ago—which we get from contemplating beautiful things, is possibly the weakest spot in the psychological theory of formalism [16]. To give an objective definition of a verse and distinguish it from prose without resorting to a psychological explanation is as impossible as solving the problem of the meaning and structure of the entire artistic form without having some specific idea about the psychology of art.

The fallibility of a theory which proclaims that the purpose of art is to create beautiful things and liven their perception is exposed by psychology with the reliability of a scientific or even mathematical truth. Of all of Volkelt's generalizations, none is so convincing as his laconic "art consists in dematerializing what is being represented." [25]

We can show not only by means of individual works of art but also by means of entire areas of artistic activity that in the end form transforms the material with which it operates, and the pleasure and enjoyment derived from the perception of this material can in no way be regarded as pleasure given by art. A far greater error, however, is the idea that pleasure or enjoyment of any sort be recognized as the basic and defining feature of the psychology of art. "People will understand the meaning of art," says Tolstoy, "when they stop thinking that the purpose of this activity is beauty, that is, enjoyment." He shows by means of a primitive example how things that are beautiful in themselves can be combined into a vulgar and trite work. A fairly stupid but very civilized lady once read Tolstoy a novel she had written. "The novel started like this: in a poetic forest, near the water, in a poetically white garment, with poetically flowing hair, the heroine was reading poetry. The action took place in Russia, and suddenly from behind the shrubs, there appeared the hero in a hat with a plume à la William Tell (thus it was written), with two poetically white dogs accompanying him. The authoress believed all this to be extremely poetical."

Was this novel with white dogs and other extremely beautiful things— the perception of which can only give pleasure and enjoyment—trite and vulgar only because the authoress was unable to raise the perception of these objects above the automatic level and "make a stone stony," that is, force the reader to sense a white dog and flowing hair and a hat with a plume? Is it not the other way round? The more acutely we sense and perceive these things, the worse it is for the novel.

Croce gives a brilliant criticism of aesthetic hedonism. He says that formal aesthetics, in particular Fechner's, has as its task the investigation of the objective conditions of beauty. "To what physical facts does beauty correspond? To what physical fact does ugliness correspond? It is as if we were to look at political economics for metabolic laws, using those processes which participate in metabolism." [26]

Croce has two other important considerations of the same subject. The first is a frank admission that the problem of the effect of material and form, as well as the problem of the poetic genre of the comical, the sweet and the tender, the humorous, the solemn, the ugly, and so forth in art can only be solved on the basis of psychology. Croce himself is not a partisan of psychology in aesthetics, but he realizes the complete inability of both aesthetics and philosophy to arrive at a solution to these problems. How much can we understand of the psychology of art if we are unable to understand at least the problem of the tragic and the comic and to distinguish between them? ". . . Since psychology (the purely empirical and descriptive character of which has come to be increasingly emphasized) is the naturalistic discipline which has as its aim the development of the types and patterns for man's spiritual life, none of these concepts belong to the domain of aesthetics or philosophy, and therefore must be assigned to psychology." [27]

This is also the case with formalism, which turned out to be incapable of correctly evaluating the effect of artistic form without resorting to psychological explanations. Croce's other consideration touches directly upon the psychological methods of solving this problem. He quite correctly opposes the formal trend taken by inductive aesthetics, because it started from the end, so to speak; it began by explaining the moment of enjoyment, which is precisely the point at which formalism stumbled. "It began quite consciously to collect beautiful objects, for example, stationery envelopes of different shapes and sizes. It tried to establish which of these generated the effect of beauty, and which generated that of ugliness . . . a coarse manila envelope, ugly in the eyes of a person who wishes to put into it a message of love, is better suited for a summons to appear in court. . . ." But this technique failed. They (the inductivists) resorted to a technique which discouraged the accuracy of the scientific method. They circulated their envelopes and conducted a poll. With a simple majority of votes they tried to establish what was beautiful and what was ugly. . . . Despite all efforts, inductive aesthetics has to this day failed to discover a single law.[28]

It is true that since Fechner formal experimental aesthetics has regarded a majority of votes as the decisive verdict concerning the truth and applicability of a psychological rule. This criterion has also been

applied by psychologists in many individual surveys, and many investigators still assume that if the overwhelming majority of test subjects
placed under identical conditions give similar or identical opinions,
they reflect the truth. One can hardly think of a more dangerous error
in psychology. All we have to do is to come up with a circumstance, applicable to all the test subjects, which would distort the results of their
statements and make them unreliable. Our search for the truth must
then fail. Psychologists know that there are many existing trends that
distort the truth—such as social prejudices, fashions, etc. These affect
every single test subject. It is as difficult to find the psychological truth
by this method as it is to get a correct self-estimate of a person. Since the
overwhelming majority of test subjects would maintain that they are
fairly intelligent persons, the psychologist following this method would
reach the strange conclusion that stupid people do not exist at all. Exactly the same happens when psychologists rely on statements from test
subjects queried about enjoyment or pleasure, if they do not establish
beforehand that the elements of such enjoyment, which are unexplained for the subject himself, are guided by forces incomprehensible
to the subject and require a deep and thorough analysis if the actual
facts are to be established. Wundt also exposed the error of the hedonistic approach to the psychology of art. He showed that we are dealing
here with an extremely complex activity in which the element of enjoyment plays an inconstant and frequently irrelevant role. He applied the
concepts of *Einfühlung* (empathy) developed by Lipps and Fischer, and
believed that the psychology of art "is best explained by the term 'Einfühlung,' which indicates that this psychological process is based on
feelings, but that these feelings are projected by the perceiving subject
onto the object." [29]

Wundt, however, does not say that all sensations and experiences are
feelings. He gives *Einfühlung* (the projecting of one's self into what is
seen) a very broad and fundamentally correct definition which we shall
adopt in our analysis of artistic activity. "The object acts as a will stim-
ulator," says Wundt, "but it does not perform an act of will. It generates
the urges or inhibitions of which action is composed, and these are projected onto the object so that it acts in different directions and runs into
the opposition and resistance of extraneous forces. By this projection
onto the object, the will stimuli make it come alive and relieve the spectator from performing the action." [30]

This is how Wundt views the process of an elementary aesthetic experience. He is therefore rather scornful about the work of Lange and
other psychologists who claim that "the artist and the spectator have no
other aim but enjoyment. . . . Was it Beethoven's aim to give pleasure

to himself and to others when in his Ninth Symphony he expressed all
the passions of the human soul from the deepest sorrow to the highest
joy?" [31] Wundt obviously wants to emphasize that although in everyday
conversation we carelessly state that the Ninth Symphony causes enjoyment, this is an unforgivable error on the part of the psychologist.

An individual example can best show how impotent the formal
method is—how it reveals the total inconsistency of elementary hedonism—if it is not supported by psychological explanations. I will show
this on the theoretical basis of the importance of sounds in verses, as developed by the formalists. They began by pointing out the importance
of the sound of a verse and claimed that "the perception of a poem usually amounts to perceiving its sound image. . . . Everybody knows how
difficult it is for us to understand the content of even the easiest, most
understandable poems." [32]

Proceeding from this correct observation, Yakubinskii reached the following conclusion. "In poetic thinking, sounds rise to the luminous surface of conscience. We establish an emotional relationship with them,
which in turn leads to bringing about a certain interdependence between the 'content' of the poem and its sound. The latter is enhanced
also by the expressive movements of the organs of speech." [33]

Thus, by means of objective form analysis, without resorting to psychology, we can only establish that sounds play an emotional role in the
perception of a poem. To explain this role, we must resort to psychology. Unimaginative attempts to determine the emotional properties of
sounds from their direct effect on us have no basis whatever. When Balmont determined the emotional content of the Russian alphabet, he
claimed that "a is the clearest and warmest sound, m is a sound of pain,
i is the "sound of astonishment or fear." [34] He supported these claims
with more or less convincing individual examples. However, we could
produce at least as many counterexamples. There are plenty of Russian
words containing an i that express neither astonishment nor fear. This
theory of phonetic symbolism, though longstanding, has been subject to
an infinite amount of criticism an infinite number of times [17].

Bely's calculations, which purport to show the deep significance of the
sounds r, d, and t in Blok's poetry,[35] and Balmont's considerations as
well remain scientifically unconvincing. Hornfeld refers to a clever remark by Mikhaĭlovskii concerning the theory that the sound a is imperative. "It is useful to note that according to the rules of the Russian language the a sound is used mostly by women: I, Anna, was beaten with a
stick; I, Barbara, was locked up in the women's quarters, etc.* Hence
the 'imperious character of the Russian woman.' " [36]

---

* In Russian, the third person singular, past tense, in the feminine gender always ends in a.

Wundt showed that phonetic symbolism [18] is very seldom encountered in a language and also that the number of words having some symbolic sound meaning is insignificant compared with the number of words having no sound meaning at all. Such investigators as Grammont [19] even discovered a psychological source for the phonetic expression of individual words. "All the sounds in a language, both consonants and vowels, can acquire significance and expression if supported by the meaning of the word in which they are encountered. If the meaning of the word does not support its sounds, then the sounds remain without expression. It is obvious that if a verse contains an accumulation of certain sound phenomena, the latter, depending on the idea they express, may be expressive. The same sound can be used to express ideas which are far removed from each other." [37]

The same view is put forth by Niepor, who cites a large number of expressive and inexpressive words constructed on the same sound. "There once was an idea that there is a mysterious link between the three 'o's of the word monotone and its meaning. Nothing of the sort exists in actual fact. The repetition of the same vowel occurs also in other words having a totally different meaning, such as, protocol, monopoly, chronology, zoology, and so on." As for expressive words, we quote Charles Balli. "If the sound of a word can be associated with its meaning, then certain sound combinations promote a certain emotional perception and bring about actual concepts and ideas; however, sounds by themselves are not capable of having similar effects." [38] Thus, all investigators agree that sounds in themselves have no emotional expression, and that by analyzing the properties of sounds per se we will never be able to establish correct rules concerning their effect on us. Sounds become meaningful only if the word is meaningful. Sounds can be meaningful if the verse is meaningful [20]. In other words, the perception of the value of the sounds in a verse is not an end in itself, as assumed by Shklovskii. It is rather the complex psychological effect of artistic composition and construction. Incidentally, the formalists themselves realized that they had to resort to the concepts of sound image instead of the emotional effects of individual sounds. D. Vygodsky in his study "The Fountain of Bakhchisáráy" asserts that the sound image and the selection of sounds based upon it are aimed not at producing a sensorial pleasure from the perception of the sounds, but at a prevailing meaning which "fills the poet's mind at a given instant" and is connected, as we may assume, with the extremely complex experiences and emotions of the poet. Thus Vygodsky surmises that the basis of the sound images in Pushkin's poem "The Fountain of Bakhchisáráy" is the name of Raevskaia.[39]

Eichenbaum criticizes Bely's position that "the poets' instrumentation subconsciously expresses the accompaniment of the intellectual content of poetry with external form." [40] He correctly points out that neither sound imitation nor elementary symbolism is characteristic of the sounds of a verse.[41] Hence, we can readily conclude that the purpose of the sound composition of a verse reaches far beyond the boundaries of the simple sensorial pleasure we may receive from sounds. What we intended to establish by means of the specific example of the study of sounds, can, strictly speaking, be applied to all problems that have been solved by formalistic methods. Everywhere we run into the fact that the psychology corresponding to the work of art under investigation is completely ignored, so that the work cannot be correctly interpreted by proceeding only from the analysis of its external and objective properties.

The fundamental principle of formalism is completely incapable of revealing and explaining the social-psychological content of art that changes historically and depends upon the selection of the subject, content, or material. Tolstoy criticized Goncharov, a quintessential urban man, who said that after Turgenev there was nothing left to write about in country life. "The life of rich people with their love affairs and discontent has an inexhaustible supply of plots and ideas. One character kisses his lady friend's palm of the hand, another kisses her elbow, the third kisses her somewhere else. One hero is miserable because he is bored and lazy, another, because he is not loved. And so Goncharov feels that variety is infinite in this field. . . . We think that the people of our time and society have very important and quite varied feelings, but in fact all the feelings of individuals of our society amount to three quite irrelevant and very uncomplicated emotions: pride, sex, and *Weltschmerz* (worldweariness). These three emotions and their ramifications make up the content of the art of the upper classes." [42]

Though we may not agree with Tolstoy, we cannot, however, deny that each period has its own psychological content and problems, and that historical research has sufficiently proved this to be true.

Formalism has come to the same conclusion, but from a different direction than that of Potebnia's followers. It proved powerless to change the psychological content of art and produced conclusions that not only explain nothing in psychology of art but themselves need to be explained by psychology of art. Russian formalism in its theoretical and practical failure, and despite its tremendous merits, reveals the weak spot of any theory of art which proceeds solely from the objective facts of the artistic form or content and avoids basing itself on the psychological theory of art.

NOTES

1. V. Shklovskii, "Rozanov," *Opoyaz* (Petrograd), 1921, p. 4. This is a collection (no. 4) on the theory of poetic language.

2. V. Shklovskii, "Association of Subject Composition with General Style Techniques," *Poetika* (*Poetics*), a collection of articles on the theory of poetic language (Petrograd) 3:143, 1919.

3. *Ibid.*, p. 144.

4. B. Tomashevskii, *Teoriia literatury* (*Poetika*) (*Theory of Literature: Poetics*), Leningrad: GIZ, 1925, p. 137.

5. V. Shklovskii, '*Tristram Shendi*' *Sterna i teoriia romana* (*Sterne's 'Tristram Shandy' and the Theory of the Novel*), *Opoyaz* (Petrograd), 1921, p. 39. This is part of a collection on the theory of poetic language (no. 4, part 2).

6. B. M. Eichenbaum, *Skvoz' literaturu* (*Through Literature*), *Academia* (Leningrad), 1924, p. 81.

7. V. Shklovskii, "Subject Composition with General Style Techniques," p. 115.

8. V. Shklovskii, " 'Tristram Shandy' and the Theory of the Novel," pp. 22–23.

9. B. M. Eichenbaum, "On the Problem of the 'Formalists,' " *Pechat i revolyutsiia* (*The Press and Revolution*) 5:2, 1924.

10. B. M. Eichenbaum, *Molodoi Tolstoi* (*The Young Tolstoy*), Petrograd-Berlin: Z. I. Grzhebin, 1922, p. 11.

11. B. Tomashevskii, "Russian Poetics: Metrics," *Academia* (Petrograd) 1923, p. 7.

12. V. Shklovskii, "Art as Technique," *Poetika* (*Poetics*) 3:104–105, 1919.

13. V. Shklovskii, "Rozanov," pp. 8–9.

14. V. Zhirmunskii, "Problems in the Theory of Literature, 1917–1926," *Academia* (Leningrad) 1928, p. 158.

15. *Ibid.*, p. 159.

16. *Ibid.*, pp. 171–172.

17. Christiansen, *Filosofiia iskusstva* (*Philosophy of Art*), 1911, p. 58.

18. *Ibid.*

19. *Ibid.*, p. 67.

20. K. Bühler, *Dukhovnoe razvitie rebenka* (*The Mental Development of the Child*) (in Russian translation), Moscow: Novaia Moskva, 1924, pp. 203–205.

21. S. Askol'dov, "Form and Content in the Art of the Word," in "Literary Thought," no. 3, a collection of articles published in *Mysl* (*Thought*) (Leningrad) 1925, pp. 312–313.

22. *Ibid.*, p. 327.

23. *Sadok sudei* (*A Hotbed of Judges*), vol. II, St. Petersburg: Zhuravl, 1914, p. 2.

24. A. Kruchenykh, *Deklaratsiia zaumnovo yazyka* (*Declaration of Abstruse Language*), Baku, 1921.

25. J. I. Volkelt, "Contemporary Problems in Aesthetics," *Obrazovanie* (*Education*) (St. Petersburg), 1900, p. 69.

26. B. Croce, *Aesthetics as the Science of Expression and General Linguistics,* translated by D. Ainslie, New York: Noonday Press, 1953, p. 123.

27. *Ibid.,* pp. 101–102.

28. *Ibid.,* p. 124.

29. W. Wundt, *Grundzüge der physiologischen Psychologie,* Leipzig: W. Engelmann, 1902–1903.

30. *Ibid.,* p. 223.

31. *Ibid.,* p. 245.

32. V. Shklovskii, "On Poetry and Abstruse Language," *Poetika (Poetics)* 3:22, 1919.

33. L. Yakubinskii, "The Sounds of Verse Language," *Poetika (Poetics)* 3:49, 1919.

34. K. Balmont, *Poeziia kak volshebstvo (Poetry as Magic),* Moscow: Skorpion, 1915, pp. 59–62 et seq.

35. A. Bely, "Blok's Poetry," *Vetv (Branch),* a collection of the Moscow Writers Club, Moscow: Severnye dni, 1917, pp. 282–283.

36. A. G. Hornfeld, *Boyeve otkliki (Fighting Spirit),* pp. 135–136.

37. M. Grammont, *Le Vers Français, ses moyens d'expression et son harmonie (The French Verse, Its Means of Expression and Harmony),* Paris, 1913, p. 206.

38. C. Balli, *Le Style Français* (in Russian translation), Moscow, 1961, p. 75.

39. See *The Poems, Prose and Plays of Alexander Pushkin,* edited by A. Yarmolinsky, New York: Random House, Inc., 1936.

40. A. Bely, "Blok's Poetry," p. 283.

41. B. M. Eichenbaum, "Through Literature," p. 204 ff.

42. L. N. Tolstoy, *Collected Works,* vol. 30, pp. 86–87.

4 ART AND PSYCHOANALYSIS

THE UNCONSCIOUS IN THE PSYCHOLOGY OF ART. PSYCHOANALYSIS OF ART. DEFICIENCIES OF THE SOCIAL PSYCHOLOGY OF ART. CRITIQUE OF PANSEXUALISM AND INFANTILISM. THE ROLE OF CONSCIOUS ELEMENTS IN ART. PRACTICAL APPLICATION OF THE PSYCHOANALYTICAL METHOD.

The two psychological theories of art just investigated have shown that we are not likely to find a solution to the fundamental problems of the psychology of art if we confine ourselves to analyzing processes that occur only at the conscious level. We will not discover the essence of the emotion that associates both the poet and the reader with art. One of the most characteristic aspects of art is that the processes involved in its creation and use appear to be obscure, unexplainable, and concealed from the conscious mind.

No one is able to put in precise and exact words why he likes a certain work of art. Words do not express the substantial and important aspects of an emotion, and, as already pointed out by Plato (in his *Ion* dialogue), the poets are the last to become aware of the methods they use for their creativity.

One does not need any particular psychological perspicacity to see that the most obvious reasons for an artistic effect are hidden in the subconscious [21], so that we can really tackle the problems of art only by penetrating into this area. The same thing happened with the analysis of the subconscious in art as with the introduction of this concept in psychology. The psychologists were inclined to believe that the subconscious, or unconscious, by definition is outside our consciousness, is concealed, and unknown to us. Consequently, by its very nature, it is something unrecognizable. As soon as we perceive the subconscious or unconscious, it ceases to be such; we are then dealing with facts belonging within the range of our normal psyche.

In the first chapter we showed that this approach is incorrect and that these considerations have been disproved in practice. We have also shown that science studies not only what is given and cognizable but the whole body of phenomena and facts that can be investigated indirectly, that is, by means of induction, reproduction, or analysis, and also with the aid of material that not only is totally different from the objects studied but is frequently and intentionally incorrect. Thus the unconscious does not become the subject of study for a psychologist by itself but indirectly through analysis of those traces which it leaves in our psyche. It is not separated from the conscious by some impregnable barrier. Processes generated in the subconscious frequently continue into our consciousness; conversely, many a conscious fact is pushed into the subconscious. In our minds there exists a continuous, lively, and dynamic connection between the two areas. The subconscious affects our actions and manifests itself in our behavior; thus we begin to understand it and learn about it and about the laws governing it.

With this approach the old method of interpreting the psyche of the author or the reader is no longer valid. Now, basically, we must take objective and reliable facts, from the analysis of which we can acquire some knowledge about subconscious processes. Obviously, these objective facts (in which the subconscious reveals itself most clearly) are the works of art themselves; they become the starting point for the analysis of the subconscious.

Any conscious and reasonable interpretation or comment given to a work of art by the artist or the reader must be regarded as a subsequent rationalization, as a self-deception, a justification before one's own intellect, or an explanation devised post factum.

The history of interpretation and critique, as well as that of the obvious meaning subsequently introduced by the reader into a work of art, is nothing but a history of rationalization which changes again and again according to the fashion of the time. The art systems that succeeded in explaining why the understanding of a work of art changed from one era to the next have essentially contributed very little to the psychology of art, because they succeeded only in explaining why the rationalization of artistic emotions changed and failed to explain how emotions changed.

Rank and Sachs correctly point out that the fundamental aesthetic problems remain unsolved "so long as our analysis is confined to processes that take place in the conscious domain . . . enjoyment of a work of art reaches its peak when we choke from emotion, when our hair stands on end because of fear, or when we can't control tears of sympathy or pity. We avoid these emotions in life but, oddly enough, seek them in art. Their effect on us is obviously quite different when they are the result of a work of art, and this aesthetic change from painful to enjoyable emotion is a problem, the solution to which can be found only by analyzing the subconscious." [1]

Psychoanalysis is a psychological system that studies subconscious life and its manifestations. Obviously, it was very tempting for psychoanalysts to try to apply their method to the interpretation of art problems. Psychoanalysis deals with two main facts of the manifestation of the subconscious: dreams and neuroses. Both facts, or forms, were understood and explained as a certain compromise or conflict between the conscious and the subconscious. The attempt was made to study art from the standpoint of these two basic elements. The psychoanalysts claim that art sits somewhere between a dream and a neurosis and that it is based upon a conflict which "is too mature for the dream, but not mature enough to be pathogenic." [2] In art, as in these two forms, the subconscious manifests itself in this conflict but in a slightly different way, although it (the subconscious) is of the same nature. "Psychologically speaking, the artist stands between the dreamer and the neurotic: the psychological process is essentially the same in all three. It differs only in the degree of intensity. . . ." [3] The easiest way to understand the psychoanalytical explanation of art is to follow the poet's explanation of his creativity and the reader's perception. Freud mentions two forms of subconscious manifestation which approach art more closely than either dream or neurosis: children's games and daydreaming fantasies. "It is wrong to assume," he says, "that the child does not approach seriously the world created by him; on the contrary, he takes his playing very seriously and does it with a great deal of animation. The opposite of play is not seriousness, but reality. Despite all the enthusiasm and distractions, the child distinguishes very well between the world created by him and reality and looks for support for imaginary objects and relations in the tangible and visible objects of real life. . . . The poet does the same things as the child at play: he creates a world, which he takes very seriously, with a lot of enthusiasm and animation, and at the same time very sharply sets it apart from reality." [4] When the child ceases to play, however, he is unable to give up the pleasures and enjoyment he derived from his play. Since he cannot find the source of this pleasure and enjoyment in the real world, he begins to replace play with daydreaming, as in the case of many adults, who indulge themselves in imagining the realization of their favorite erotic or other inclinations. ". . . So instead of playing, he is now daydreaming. He builds castles in Spain and creates what are known as 'dreams in a state of wakefulness.' " [5] Daydreaming has three elements that distinguish it from play and bring it closer to art. First, these fantasies may contain, as basic material, painful emotions which are enjoyable nonetheless; this characteristic recalls somewhat the change of affect in art. Rank claims that daydreams contain "situations which in reality could be quite painful; fantasy, nonetheless, depicts them with pleasure and enjoyment. The most common among these fantasies are death, pain, suffering, and accident. Poverty, illness, imprisonment, and dishonor occur quite frequently, no less so than the execution of an appalling crime followed by its discovery." [6]

In his analysis of children's play, however, Freud showed that a child frequently will go through painful experiences and emotions; for example, when playing doctor he repeats in his play all the procedures which in real life would have given him pain, tears, and sorrow.[7]

The same phenomena occur in our daydreams, but with an incomparably stronger and sharper intensity than in a child's play.

Freud's other basic distinction between daydreaming and children's play is the fact that the child is never ashamed of his game and does not conceal it from adults, whereas, "the adults are ashamed of their fantasies, conceal them from others, and hide them as their innermost secrets; they would rather confess a crime than reveal them. It is quite possible that each adult regards himself as the only person who has such fantasies and is completely unaware of the fact that they are probably quite widespread."

Finally, the third and most important element for understanding art is the source of these fantasies. It is those who are dissatisfied who most frequently have fantasies. Unsatisfied desires are the incentives and stimuli for reveries and fantasies. A fantasy is the realization of a desire, a compensation for a frustrated reality. Freud therefore assumes that the basis of poetic creativity, as well as the basis of dreams and fantasies, is unsatisfied desires, frequently such "of which we are ashamed, which we must conceal from ourselves, and which we therefore push into the subconscious." [8]

In this respect, the mechanism of the effect of art is quite similar to that of fantasy. Fantasy is usually provoked by a strong and real emotion which "awakens in the writer old memories and reminiscences, which usually refer to childhood emotions, to the starting point of a desire that finds its realization in the work of art. . . . Creativity, as the 'dream in a state of wakefulness,' is nothing but the continuation and substitution of an old child's game." [9] Thus a work of art is for the poet a means of satisfying unsatisfied and unrealized desires. How this is accomplished can be seen from the theory of affects developed in psychoanalysis. According to this theory, affects "may, and in some cases must, remain subconscious without losing their effect which invariably enters consciousness. Enjoyment, or the opposite emotion, which enters consciousness in this fashion, ties itself there to other affects, or to concepts referring to them. . . . A close associative link must exist between the two, and along the path broken by this association travel enjoyment and the energy tied to it. If this theory is correct, then it can be applied to our problem too. The solution would be approximately thus: a work of art generates conscious, subconscious, or unconscious affects, which are far more intense and frequently contrast with the conscious ones. The concepts that aid this solution must be chosen to have, along with conscious associations, a sufficient number of associations with typical subconscious complexes of affects. A work of art is capable of performing this complex task, because at its incept it played the same role in the psyche of the artist that it played for the listener; i.e., it afforded the possibility of challenge and a fantastic satisfaction of the subconscious desires they share." [10]

With this in mind, a number of investigators have developed a theory of poetic creativity in which they compare the artist to the neurotic, although they do agree with Steckel who rejects Lombroso's comparison of the genius with the lunatic. For them the poet is quite normal. He is a neurotic and "performs psychoanalysis on his poetic images. He treats strange images as the mirror of his soul. He lets his wild inclinations lead a life in the images composed from fantasy." Along with Heine they believe that poetry is a disease of man, and the question concerns only the types of mental disease that affect poets. Kovach sees the poet as a paranoiac who projects his ego outside himself, and the reader as a hysteric who subjectivizes the emotions and experiences of others. Rank is inclined to view the artist as hysterical rather than paranoid. At any rate, all agree that the poet in his creativity releases his subconscious inclinations and desires by means of the mechanism of transfer, or substitution, by associating earlier affects with new concepts. Therefore, as one of Shakespeare's heroes says, the poet bemoans his own sins in other people, and Hamlet's famous question, "What's Hecuba to him, or he to Hecuba, that he should weep for her?" is explained by Rank as the actor associating with Hecuba the affect generated by him, but in the tears apparently shed for Hecuba's ill fate he really bemoans his own misfortunes. We know of the famous admission of Gogol, who asserted that he had rid himself of his own shortcomings and vices by bestowing them upon his characters. Many other authors have made similar confessions; Rank notes, in part quite correctly, that "if Shakespeare could see through the soul of a wise man and a fool, a saint and a criminal, he not only subconsciously was all those (anyone of us could be), but he also had a gift which none of us has—namely the capacity of seeing and recognizing his own subconscious and creating in his fantasy what appear to be completely independent images." [11]

According to Müller-Freienfels, some psychoanalysts assert quite seriously that if Shakespeare and Dostoevsky did not become criminals, it is only because they described and represented murderers in their works and thus overcame their own criminal tendencies. Thus art becomes a sort of therapy [22] for both the artist and the spectator, a means of removing a conflict with the subconscious without lapsing into a neurosis. But since psychoanalysts are inclined to reduce all tendencies to one, and Rank takes, as the epigraph to his study, Hebbel's words, "It is astonishing to what extent all human inclinations can be reduced to one," they are bound therefore to reduce all poetry to sexual experiences and emotions and regard these as underlying any poetic activity, creativity, or perception. Sexual impulses, according to psychoanalysts, are the main reservoir of the subconscious, and the transfer of psychic energy performed in art is principally the sublimation of sexual energy, that is, a deviation from direct sexual aims and a transformation into creativity. Art is always based upon subconscious and repressed impulses and desires, which contradict our moral, cultural, and civilized requirements. This is why in art our forbidden desires achieve their satisfaction in the pleasure and enjoyment of artistic forms.

The weakest link of this theory is its definition of artistic form. Psychoanalysts have no satisfactory answer to this problem, and their attempts at solving it have so far been inadequate. Dreams, they say, awake the desires of which we are ashamed; thus only in art are expressed those desires which cannot be satisfied in a direct fashion. This is why art always has something to do with criminal, shameful, or rejected phenomena. In dreams these repressed desires appear in a strongly distorted form, and in works of art they reveal themselves in a disguised form.

"After scientific research has been able to determine the distortion of dreams," says Freud, "we shall easily see that dreams represent the same realization of desires as 'dreams in the state of wakefulness,' or the fantasies that we know all too well." [12] Similarly, the artist must give his suppressed desires an artistic form in order to satisfy them. From the psychoanalytic viewpoint, this imposed artistic form has two fundamental meanings.

First, the form must give a shallow and superficial pleasure, strictly sensory in nature, to serve as a decoy, a preliminary enjoyment which lures the beholder into the difficult, and occasionally painful, exercise of reacting to the subconscious.

Second, the form must produce an artificial disguise, a compromise which makes it possible for the artist both to reveal the forbidden desire and simultaneously deceive the censorship of the conscious.

From this viewpoint, the form performs the same function as does distortion in dreams. Rank states that aesthetic pleasure for the artist reader, or spectator, is nothing but the anticipation (*Vorlust*) which conceals the true source of pleasure and both ensures and enhances its basic effect. The form lures the reader or the spectator and deceives him, for he assumes that this is all, so to speak. Deceived by the form, the reader is given the chance to get rid of his suppressed impulses and desires.

Thus, the psychoanalysts distinguish two elements of pleasure in a work of art: the preliminary enjoyment and the real pleasure. According to them, an artistic form functions by giving preliminary enjoyment. Let us now take a close look at exactly how thoroughly this theory deals with the psychology of artistic form. Freud says, "How does the writer succeed in doing this? This is his most intimate secret. In the technique of overcoming what repels us . . . we find true *poetica*. We can imagine two kinds of techniques: the writer tones down the character of his egotistical 'dreams in a state of wakefulness' by certain changes and filterings and admits us to the purely formal, i.e., aesthetic, enjoyment that he produces by representing the images of his fantasies. . . . I am of the opinion that any aesthetic enjoyment given us by a writer has the character of this 'threshold of pleasure,' and that the true pleasure issuing from a work of poetry can be explained as the release of psychic forces from stress." [13]

Freud, too, stumbles over the problem of artistic enjoyment, and, as he explains in his last works, "although art, as tragedy, generates in us a whole series of painful experiences, its final effect is nonetheless subordinated to the pleasure principle, as in the similar phenomenon of child's play." [14]

But as we analyze this concept of pleasure, the theory appears to fall into an incredible eclecticism. In addition to the two sources of pleasure already mentioned, there are a whole series of others. Rank and Sachs, for instance, speak about an economy of the affect. The artist does not permit affect to consume itself instantly and uselessly, but forces it to build up gradually, following a plan. They claim that this economy of affect is a source of pleasure. Yet another source is the economy of thought, which, by saving the energy required to perceive a work of art again generates pleasure. And, finally, a purely formal source of sensory enjoyment is seen in the rhyme, the rhythm, the play of words, all of which psychoanalysts reduce to a child's joy. But we discover that even this pleasure is composed of a whole series of different forms and shapes. The pleasure derived from rhythm is also accounted for by the fact that, since time immemorial, it has been used to alleviate work; also, the most important aspects of sexual activity, and the sex act itself, are rhythmic. "In this way, a given activity acquires with the aid of rhythm, a certain resemblance to sexual processes. It becomes sexualized." [15]

All these sources are put together in a meaningless way and, as a whole, are totally incapable of explaining the significance and effect of artistic form. It is interpreted as a mere façade behind which true pleasure is hidden, while the effect of this pleasure is based, in the final analysis, on the content rather than on the form of a work of art. "It is taken to be an incontestable truth that the question, 'Will Johnny get his Jane?' is the leading theme of poetry with infinite variations and repetitions which never wear out nor bore the poet or his public." [16] Psychoanalysis reduces the distinction and difference between various types of art to different forms of child sexuality. Thus, the visual arts are interpreted and explained as the sublimation of the instincts of sexual observation, while landscape painting is the direct result of inhibiting this desire. The psychoanalysts tell us that ". . . in the artist, representation of the human body replaces interest in the maternal body, and the intensive repression of this incestuous desire transfers the artist's interest from the human body to nature. In the writer who is not interested in nature and its beauty we find a strong repression of the passion for viewing." [17]

Other types and forms of art are explained in the same way by different forms of infantile sexuality, the common basis of any art being the childhood sexual desire known as the Oedipus complex, which is "the psychological foundation of art. A particular place is held by the Oedipus complex from whose sublimated instinctive force the masterpieces of all times and peoples have sprung." [18]

If sexualism underlies art and determines the fate of the artist and the character of his work, then the effect of artistic form remains totally unexplained. It appears to be an irrelevant and rather meaningless appendage without which one could manage quite easily. Enjoyment is but a simultaneous combination of two opposite awarenesses: we see a tragedy and experience it emotionally, but we immediately realize that such events do not happen in reality and are purely fictitious. This transition from one awareness to the other is the main source of enjoyment and pleasure. Why, then, can any account, even a nonartistic one, fulfill the same role? A legal account, a murder mystery, gossip, or long pornographic discussions can serve this purpose for unfulfilled and unsatisfied desires. This is why Freud, when he talks about the similarities of novels and fantasies, must take trash literature as a model, even though its authors appeal to mass tastes and satisfy hidden and forbidden desires rather than aesthetic emotions and requirements.

It is incomprehensible why "poetry releases . . . various caresses, exchanges of motives, transformation of opposites, the breaking up of one image into several, the doubling of processes, the poeticizing of material, especially symbols." [19] It would be much simpler to do away with all this complex activity of the form and live the corresponding desire in a simple and frank way. Such an interpretation of art reduces its social role; art begins to appear as an antidote whose task it is to save mankind from vice, but which has no positive tasks or purposes for man's psyche.

Rank says that artists "are the leaders of mankind in the struggle for the domination and improvement of instincts inimical to civilization," and that they "deliver men from evil without depriving them, at the same time, of enjoyment and pleasure." [20] He states outright that "in our civilization the value of art as a whole is overstated." [21] An actor is but a physician, and art only saves us from sickness. Such an approach reveals the fundamental misunderstanding of the social psychology of art. The effect of a work of art and of the creativity of the poet is drawn entirely from ancient instincts which remain unchanged over the entire duration of a culture, and the effect of art itself is entirely limited by the narrow sphere of individual perception. This, obviously, most blatantly contradicts all the simple facts concerning the true position of art and its true role. Suffice it to say that the very problems of repression and inhibition (what is repressed or inhibited and how it is repressed or inhibited) are contingent upon the social environment in which the poet or the reader must live. Thus, psychoanalysis fails to explain the reasons for the historical evolution of art and changes in its social functions, since art has remained constant from its very beginning and has served as an expression of the oldest and most conservative instincts. Unlike dreams and symptoms of illness or neurosis, works of art are both social and socially conditioned. This, as pointed out by Rank, is the difference between art and the dreams or neuroses. However, he fails to draw any conclusions from this fact and evaluates it on its own merit only. He does not explain what makes art socially valuable and how, through the social values of art, the social gets hold of our subconscious. The poet is nothing but a hysteric who absorbs the feelings and emotions of a majority of strangers, and he is unable to get out of the narrow circle created by his own infantilism. Why must all the characters in a drama be regarded as the incarnation of various psychological traits of the author? [22] This might be understood in the case of a dream or a neurosis, but it is incomprehensible in a social manifestation of the subconscious as art. The conclusions that have resulted from their speculations have grown too big for psychologists to handle. What they have found has essentially only one important meaning for social psychology. They claim that art, by its nature, is a transformation of our subconscious into certain social forms, i.e., forms of behavior that have a social meaning and purpose. But they have failed to describe and explain these behavior forms in terms of social psychology. The reason for this failure is quite simple. The psychoanalytical theory of art has two main flaws from the viewpoint of social psychology. The first is the psychoanalytic compulsion to reduce, at any cost, all manifestations of the human psyche to sexual urges or instincts. This pansexualism is completely irrational, especially if applied to art. It may be reasonable, or even correct, for a man outside society, confined to the narrow circle of his own instincts and drives. But how can it be that a social man (*homo socialis*) who participates fully in the extremely complex forms of social activity has no other instincts, inclinations, or drives which, no less than the sexual ones, can determine his behavior or even dominate it? The exaggerated importance of sex becomes obvious as soon as we step from individual psychology into social psychology. But the assumptions made by psychoanalysts appear to be exaggerated and far-fetched even for the individual psyche. "Some psychoanalysts claim that whenever an artist draws the portrait of his mother, or represents his love for his mother in some poetic image, he expresses a fearfully concealed incestuous desire (Oedipus complex). Whenever a sculptor creates statues of boys or a poet sings the joys of friendship with young men, psychoanalysts immediately see the extreme forms of homosexuality. . . . Reading these authors, we get the impression that emotional life consists only of alarming prehuman instincts and urges, as if all concepts, exercises in will, and so on, were dead marionettes with strings pulled by dire instincts." [23]

Indeed, by excessively emphasizing the role of the subconscious, psychoanalysts reduce the role of the conscious to zero according to Marx. Yet, it is the primeval distinction between man and animal: "The early distinction between man and a sheep is the fact that in man conscience replaces instinct, or that man is aware of his instincts." While the old school of psychologists exaggerated the role of the conscious and proclaimed it omnipotent, psychoanalysts now exaggerate the opposite position by bringing the role of the conscious to naught and asserting that it is nothing but an impotent tool in the hands of the subconscious. The most elementary investigations show, however, that the same processes can also take place in the conscious. Lazurskii's experiments on the effect of reading on the course of mental associations have shown that "immediately after reading a passage there occurs in the mind of the reader a breaking up of the passage read, and a combining of its various components with the thoughts, concepts, and images already stored there." [24] We have in art an analogous process of breaking up and associating what has been read with the emotions previously stored in the mind. Ignoring the conscious element in experiencing art erases the boundary between art as an intelligent social activity and the senseless formation of pathological symptoms in neurotics or the disorderly accumulation of images in dreams.

These radical shortcomings of the theory under study are best exemplified by the practical applications of the psychoanalytical method published by investigators in the foreign and Russian literature. They reveal the inadequacy of the method and its inconsistency with social psychology. In his study of Leonardo da Vinci, Freud tried to explain the master's fate and work from his childhood experiences. Freud wanted to show "how artistic creativity issues from original emotional instincts." [25] At the end of his study, he expressed the fear that he might be criticized for having simply written a psychological novel. He also admitted that he himself did not overestimate the reliability of his conclusions. As far as the reader is concerned, this reliability equals zero, since from the first word to the last he engaged in guesswork, interpretation, surmise, comparisons between facts concerning creativity and items from da Vinci's biography, the connection between which cannot be established. It is as if psychoanalysis had a catalog of sex symbols, and these symbols remained the same at all times, for all peoples, and that it were enough to find the corresponding symbols in the artistic creativity of an artist to determine that he is suffering from an Oedipus complex, voyeurism, and so on. It appears, furthermore, that every person is inexorably chained to his Oedipus complex, and that in the most complicated and highest forms of our activity we are forced, again and again, to relive our childhood, so that even the most exalted forms of activity or creativity turn out to be connected with the remote past. Man emerges as the slave of his early childhood; all his later life he relives and is forced to solve the conflicts which arose during the first months of his life. Freud claims that "the key to Leonardo's varied mental activity and also to his failures is hidden in his childhood fantasies about the kite," [26] and that this fantasy, translated into erotic language, reveals the symbolism of the sexual act. Any serious investigator must rebel against this oversimplified interpretation, because he cannot fail to see that the story about the kite (Freud is talking about the bird, not the toy) reveals little about da Vinci's work. True, even Freud admits "a certain amount of arbitrariness which psychoanalysis cannot determine or pinpoint." [27] But, if we exclude this arbitrariness, all of life, activity, and creativity is enslaved to childhood sexuality. This flaw is clearly revealed in Neufeld's study of Dostoevsky. He says that "Dostoevsky's life and creativity were enigmatic . . . but the magic key of psychoanalysis unlocks the doors to the solutions of these riddles. . . . Psychoanalysis explains all the contradictions and enigmas: an eternal Oedipus lived in this man and created his works." [28] This is truly ingenious! Not a magic key, but a psychoanalytical passe-partout with which to penetrate any and all of the mysteries of artistic creativity! An eternal Oedipus lived and created inside Dostoevsky. But one of the fundamental tenets of psychoanalysis is that Oedipus lives in every person, without exception. Does this mean that we have solved the riddle of Dostoevsky? Why should we assume that the conflicts of childhood sexuality and of the child with his father exercise a greater influence on Dostoevsky's life than later traumas, experiences, and emotions? Why can't we assume that the experiences of awaiting execution, of forced labor, and so on are the sources of new and complex sensations and emotions? Even if we agree with Neufeld that "a writer cannot describe or represent anything but his own subconscious conflicts," [29] it is not clear why these subconscious conflicts can derive only from early childhood. "As we study the life of this great writer in the light of psychoanalysis, we see that his character, formed under the influence of his relationship with his parents, his life, and his fate depended entirely upon his Oedipus complex and were entirely determined by it. His perversity and neurosis, his sickness and his creative power, indeed all the qualities and peculiarities of his character can be explained by the Oedipus complex alone." [30] One can hardly imagine a stronger refutation of Neufeld's theory. The entire life appears to be nothing compared with early childhood, and all of Dostoevsky's novels seem to be derived from the Oedipus complex. But then all writers would be alike, because Freud teaches that the Oedipus complex is a common heritage. It takes a total rejection both of reality and social psychology to state that a writer in his work pursues only subconscious or unconscious conflicts without ever confronting any conscious social problem or task. This extraordinary flaw of the psychological theory of art becomes most evident when it is applied to the study of the nonfigurative arts. How can it explain music, ornamental painting, or architecture, where the language of form cannot be translated simply and directly into the erotic language of sexuality? This gaping void helps us reject the psychoanalytical approach to art and leads us to believe that through psychological theory we will be able to combine the elements common to poetry and music, and that these elements will turn out to be those of artistic form, which psychoanalysis regards only as masks or auxiliary methods of artistic expression. But nowhere else are the monstrous exaggerations of psychoanalysis as evident as in the works of Russian art critics. When Professor Yermakov claims that *The Little House in Kolomna* has to be understood as "I am sick of the house;" [31] * or that the Alexandrine verse signifies Alexander (Pushkin's first name), while Mavrusha signifies Pushkin himself, who is the descendant of a Moor (Mavr is Moor in Russian), we can dismiss all this as absurd, senseless interpretation which explains nothing. As a further example we shall give Yermakov's comparison between the prophet and the little house:

> The prophet was lying in the desert like a dead man; the widow, when she beheld Mavrusha shaving, screamed, "Oh, oh" and fell to the ground.
>
> The tired prophet fell—and there were no seraphim; the widow fell—and there was no trace of Mavrusha. . . .
>
> God's voice calls upon the prophet and forces him to act: "By words burn the hearts of men!" The widow's "Oh, oh," results in Mavrusha's shameful flight.
>
> After his transfiguration the prophet circles the oceans and continents and goes to the people; after the deception was discovered, there was nothing left for Mavrusha to do but flee as far as he could, away from people.[32]

The complete absurdity and arbitrariness of such comparisons only undermines any confidence in Yermakov's method. But when he explains that "Ivan Nikiforovich is close to nature, because he is Dovgochkhiun, i.e., he is a long sneezer, while Ivan Ivanovich is artificial, he is Pererepenko, and he has grown higher than the turnip," [33] † he completely destroys any confidence we might have in this method by preposterously interpreting the surnames, one as being close to nature,

---

* A free translation of a play on words, in which Yermakov engages in explaining the Russian of Pushkin's poem: *Domik v Kolomne* (The Little House in Kolomna) as *Domik kolom mne* (I am sick of the house).

† Ivan Nikiforovich Dovgochkhiun, and Ivan Ivanovich Pererepenko are the two principal characters in Gogol's short story "On How Ivan Ivanovich Quarreled with Ivan Nikiforovich." The ridiculous translation of their surnames corresponds to the literal meaning of the names in Russian, and Yermakov obviously plays on that absurdity.

and the other to mean artificial. Another classic example is Peredonov's interpretation of a Pushkin verse during a philology class: " 'Together with his hungry she-wolf, the wolf begins to roam the field . . .' This has to be understood properly. There is a hidden allegory here. Wolves roam and hunt in pairs. The wolf with a hungry she-wolf: the wolf is satisfied, but the she-wolf is hungry. The wife must always eat after the husband, since in everything the wife has to be subordinate to her husband." There are no more psychological reasons for this interpretation than there are for Yermakov's. Disregard for form analysis appears to be the general weakness of psychoanalytical investigations; we know of only one investigation which is near perfect in this respect. This is Freud's study of humor, where he compares humor to dreams. Unfortunately this study is on the borderline between general psychology and the psychology of art, because humor and wit belong more to general psychology than to the specialized psychology of art. Nonetheless it can be regarded as a classic example of analytical investigation. Freud begins with an extremely thorough analysis of the techniques of wit and humor, and from these techniques, i.e., from the form, he goes on to the impersonal psychology and notes that, despite all similarities, wit and humor differ fundamentally from dreams. "One of the prime distinctions rests in their social relationship. Dreams are completely asocial products of the soul; they cannot tell anything to another person . . . conversely, wit and humor are among the most social of all emotional mechanisms directed to obtain pleasure or enjoyment." [34] With this subtle analysis, Freud is unable to lump all works of art into one pile, but he determines three different sources of pleasure for such closely related forms as wit, comic, and humor. His only mistake is his attempt to interpret fictitious dreams, dreamt by literary characters, as real ones. This is as naive as trying to study actual avarice from *The Covetous Knight.*

Once the psychoanalytical method is fully applied in practice, it will bring out the tremendous theoretical values contained in it. Essentially, these values are the involvement of the subconscious in expanding the scope of investigation and the explanation of how the subconscious becomes social in art [23].

We will deal with the positive aspects of psychoanalysis when setting up a system on which to base a psychology of art. A practical application can be fruitful only if it will give up some of the "original sins" of the theory itself; if, along with the subconscious, it will also consider the conscious not as a purely passive but as an independently active factor; if it will explain the effect of the artistic form not as a façade but as an extremely important mechanism and technique of art; if, finally, giving up pansexualism and infantilism, it will include in the sphere of its investigation the sum total of human life and not just its primary and schematic conflicts.

One last point: It will have to give a correct sociopsychological interpretation to the symbolism of art and its historical evolution, and it will have to understand that art can never be fully explained from the limited viewpoint of one's own life but requires a wider approach of social life.

Art as the subconscious is a problem; art as the social solution for the subconscious is its likely solution.

NOTES

1. O. Rank and H. Sachs, *Significance of Psychoanalysis to the Mental Sciences,* translated by C. R. Payne, New York, Johnson Reprints, 1916.

2. O. Rank, *Der Künstler; Ansätze zu einer Sexualpsychologie,* Leipzig, 1918, p. 53.

3. *Ibid.*

4. S. Freud, *Psychological Essays.* Obsessive Actions and Religious Rites. The Poet and Fantasy. "Cultural" Sex Morals and Modern Neuroses, Macmillan, New York, 1964.

5. *Ibid.*

6. O. Rank and H. Sachs, *Significance of Psychoanalysis to the Mental Sciences.*

7. S. Freud, *Beyond the Pleasure Principle,* translated by J. Strachey, New York, Liveright, 1970, chap. 2.

8. S. Freud, *Psychological Essays.*

9. *Ibid.,* pp. 26–27.

10. O. Rank and H. Sachs, *Significance of Psychoanalysis to the Mental Sciences,* pp. 132–134.

11. *Ibid.,* p. 17.

12. S. Freud, *Psychological Essays.*

13. *Ibid.*

14. S. Freud, *Beyond the Pleasure Principle,* chapter 2.

15. O. Rank and H. Sachs, *Significance of Psychoanalysis to the Mental Sciences.*

16. *Ibid.*

17. I. Neufeld, *Dostoevsky. Psikhoanaliticheskii (Dostoevsky: a Psychoanalytical Sketch),* edited by S. Freud, Leningrad-Moscow: Petrograd, 1925, p. 71.

18. O. Rank and H. Sachs, *Significance of Psychoanalysis to the Mental Sciences.*

19. *Ibid.*

20. *Ibid.*

21. O. Rank, *Der Künstler,* p. 55.

22. *Ibid.,* p. 78.

23. R. Müller-Freienfels, *Psychologie der Kunst,* vol. 2, Leipzig-Berlin, 1923, p. 183.

24. A. F. Lazurskii, "Effect of Various Reading on the Course of Associations," *Nevrologicheskii vestnik (Neurological News)* 8:3:100, 1900.

25. S. Freud, *Leonardo da Vinci and a Memory of his Childhood*, translated by A. Tyson, New York: Norton, 1964, p. 111 *passim*.

26. *Ibid.*, p. 118.

27. *Ibid.*, p. 116.

28. I. Neufeld, *Dostoevsky*, p. 12.

29. *Ibid.*, p. 28.

30. *Ibid.*, pp. 71–72.

31. I. D. Yermakov, *Etiudi po psikhologii tvorchestva A. S. Pushkina* (*Essays on the Psychology of Pushkin's Art*), Moscow-Petrograd, 1923, p. 27.

32. *Ibid.*, p. 162.

33. I. D. Yermakov, *Ocherki po analizu tvorchestva N. V. Gogolia* (*Essays on the Analysis of Gogol's Creativity*), Moscow-Petrograd: GIZ, 1923, p. 111.

34. S. Freud, *Wit and Its Relation to the Unconscious*, New York: Moffat, Yard & Co., 1917, p. 241 *passim*.

III ANALYSIS OF THE AESTHETIC REACTION

5 ANALYSIS OF THE FABLE

FABLE, SHORT STORY, AND TRAGEDY. LESSING'S AND POTEBNIA'S THEORIES
OF THE FABLE. FABLES IN PROSE AND IN VERSE. STRUCTURAL ELEMENTS OF
THE FABLE: ALLEGORY, USE OF ANIMALS, THE MORAL, ANECDOTE, LYRICAL
STYLE, AND TECHNIQUE.

As we move from the critical to the positive portion of our investigation, we find it appropriate to eliminate a few studies in order to establish the salient points of our theoretical development. Preparing the
psychological material for subsequent generalizations, it appears most
convenient to proceed from simpler matters to more complex ones. We
have decided, therefore, to examine the fable, the short story, and the
tragedy as three literary forms which show a progression in complexity
and literary eminence.

We begin with the fable. Scholars have always considered it the most
elementary literary form, illustrating better than any other all the
properties peculiar to poetry. Most theoreticians proceed, in their commentaries and interpretations of poetry, from a specific interpretation of
the fable. They regard higher-level literary works as literary forms
which are more complex, but fundamentally similar to the fable. We
may therefore say that once we know how an investigator interprets
and understands the fable, we will have a pretty good idea of his general concept of art.

There exist only two completely elaborated psychological theories of the fable: Lessing's and Potebnia's. Both regard the fable as the most elementary literary form and base their explanation of all literature upon it. If, according to Lessing's definition, we apply a general moral statement to a specific story, narrated as if it were real—that is, not as a mere example or a comparison—and in such a way that the story explain the general moral statement, then this story is a fable.

The idea that a work of art is an illustration of a well-known general idea is a widespread aesthetic approach. In a novel or painting, the reader (or viewer) looks first for the artistic main intent. He tries to determine what the artist wants to express, what the work of art conveys, and so on. The fable, then, is but a more tangible, perceptible form of illustrating a general idea.

Potebnia criticizes this approach, particularly Lessing's theory. He concludes that the fable should be "a constant affirmation of different subjects taken from the domain of human life." [1] He sees it as a quick answer to a question, a way of perceiving, elucidating, or understanding intricate, everyday, political, or other matters. The fable is, for him, the key to solving the riddle of poetry itself. He claims that "any work of poetry, and in fact any word, at some instant of its existence consists of parts that correspond to those we discover in the fable. I shall try to prove that allegory is a necessary and indispensable feature of poetry." [2] ". . . The fable is one of the means of apprehending human relations, the character of people, and to put it briefly, anything that relates to the moral aspects of human life." [3] Curiously enough, despite sharp differences between Potebnia's over-all views and those of the supporters of the formalistic theory of art, the latter readily agree with Potebnia's formula and, while criticizing him in nearly all other areas, admit that he is completely right regarding the fable. Thus, the fable, a creation seemingly on the borderline of poetry, which to some is the prototype of poetry itself, while to others it is a striking exception from the entire domain of art, becomes an exceptionally compelling subject for formal psychological analysis. "Potebnia's theory," says Shklovskii, "is least controversial when dealing with the fable, which, as a matter of fact, was thoroughly investigated by him. He never addressed his theory to artistic, 'substantial' works, and consequently, never finished his book. . . ." [4]—"Potebnia's formula of art turned out to be well substantiated only in a very narrow field of poetry: in the fable and in the proverb. This is why Potebnia managed to finish this portion of his work. The fable and the proverb indeed proved to be a 'quick answer to a question.' Their images turned out to be a 'way of thinking.' However, the concepts of the fable and the proverb coincide very little, if at all, with the concepts of poetry." [5] Tomashevskii also shares this view: "The fable evolved from the apologue, a system of proving general statements by means of examples (anecdotes or tales). . . . The fable, built around a story, gives the narrative as an allegory from which a general conclusion, the moral of the fable, is then drawn. . . ." [6]

This definition of the fable takes us back to Lessing's, or even older theories, such as those of de La Motte and others. Theoretical aesthetics also considers the fable in this fashion and compares it with the art of advertising. "All the fables," says Haman, "in which the aesthetic interest of the fascinating story is adeptly used for the moral of that story must be regarded as advertising poetry; all tendentious poetry belongs to the aesthetics of advertisement; all rhetoric belongs in the same category. . . ." [7]

After the theoreticians and philosophers come the critics and the general public, who have a very low opinion of the fable and consider it an inferior poetic product. Krylov is known as a moralist who expresses the ideas of the man in the street. He is the bard of everyday practicality and common sense. One's opinion of the author is transferred to the fable; there are many who follow Eichenwald's opinion that once one has read these fables "he can well condition himself to reality. But reality is not what the great teachers are teaching us. Indeed this need not be taught at all . . . which is why the fable is shallow and trite. . . . The fable is only an approximation which glides over the surface." [8] Gogol, alone, quite casually and without really knowing its meaning, once remarked on the "deep, unfathomable spirituality of Krylov's fables," although he shared the general view of Krylov himself as a pedestrian and mundane artist.

It is a very instructive exercise to resort to a theory of the fable that explains it as above, to see what in fact distinguishes the fable from poetry, and then to determine the nature of those peculiarities of poetry which are obviously lacking in the fable. It would be futile to examine Lessing's or Potebnia's theories, as they point in completely different directions. Both authors have in mind two kinds of fables which differ in origin and artistic functions. Both history and psychology teach us the nice distinction between the poetic fable and the prosaic fable.

Let us deal first with Lessing. He states that the ancients placed the fable in the philosophic domain rather than the poetic and chose the philosophical fable as the subject of his study. "For the ancients, the fable belonged in the domain of philosophy, whence it was borrowed by the teachers of rhetoric. Aristotle discusses it, not in his *Poetica,* but in his *Rhetoric.* What Aphthonius and Theon have to say about the fable also belongs to rhetoric. Until La Fontaine's time, all that was said about

Aesop's fables was said in terms of rhetoric. La Fontaine succeeded in transforming the fable into a pleasant poetic toy and soon everyone began treating the fable as if it were only for children. . . . Anyone belonging to the ancient school, which taught the unaesthetic, artless representation of the fable, would not be able to understand in Batte, for instance, the long list of ornaments and frills that were claimed as characteristic of the fable. Full of surprise, he might ask, 'Could it be that for the modern authors the meaning of things has changed completely? All these ornaments and frills contradict the true essence of the fable.' " [9] Of course, Lessing is talking about the fable prior to La Fontaine as a subject of philosophy and rhetoric, not of art.

Potebnia takes a similar position: "To understand what a fable is, one must not study it as it is on paper, in the book of fables, or in the process of getting from the book of fables into the mouth of the narrator when its very narration is insufficiently motivated, as in the case of an actor who reads it to show his skill in reciting, or on occasions when a small child recites, 'How many times have I advised the world that flattery is vile and bad. . . .' Divorced from real life, a fable can easily become an accumulation of empty, meaningless words. But this poetic form is frequently used in cases where the subject matter is not at all funny, where the fate of man and society is discussed, where no jokes or empty words are involved." [10]

Potebnia refers to the passage we quoted from Lessing and says that "all the embellishments and frills were added by La Fontaine because people did not really want to know how to appreciate fables. There is the fable, which was once used in a powerful political pamphlet, or as a powerful publicity technique and which, despite its purpose (or even because of it), remained a full-fledged product of poetry that played an important role in the thinking of the times. Now it is reduced to almost nothing, to a virtually useless toy." [11] To corroborate his statement, Potebnia refers to Krylov to show how fables should not be written.

Both Potebnia and Lessing reject the lyrical fable, the fable of the book of fables, which to them seems only a child's toy. Instead they deal with apologues, and their analyses refer more to the psychology of logical thinking than to the psychology of art. We could formally challenge the opinions and theories of both, since they, consciously and intentionally, investigate the prosaic and not the lyrical fable. We could say to both that "all of what you say is quite correct, but it applies only to the rhetorical and prosaic fable." That the zenith of the fabular art reached by La Fontaine and Krylov appears to both Lessing and Potebnia as its nadir, proves that their theories refer to the fable not as a phenomenon in the history of art but as only one argument in a system of empirical truths. We know that the fable has a dual origin, that its didactic and descriptive parts, in other words, its prosaic and poetic parts, have frequently opposed one another, with either one or the other prevailing. In Byzantine civilization the fable almost completely lost its artistic character and become a moral-didactic product. Latin literature, on the other hand, produced a lyrical fable, written in verse. But the two parallel tendencies of the fable, the prosaic and the lyrical, have continued to coexist as two distinct literary trends.

Prosaic fables include those of Aesop, Lessing, Tolstoy, and others. Lyrical fables include those of La Fontaine and Krylov. This statement alone suffices to reject Potebnia's and Lessing's theories, but it would be a strictly formal argument, not one of merit or substance, and would be closer to juridical rejection rather than psychological investigation. We intend to go to the roots of both systems, to investigate their arguments, proofs, etc. It may be that the arguments which they use against the distortion of the prosaic fable can shed light on the very nature of the lyrical fable if we use them in an inverted fashion. According to the psychological thesis, with which both Potebnia and Lessing agree, the rules of art which govern the novel, the poem, and the drama, are not applicable to the fable. We have seen why this is so and how the authors manage to prove their point by dealing solely with the prosaic fable.

We shall now proceed with a diametrically opposite thesis. Our task will be to prove that the fable belongs entirely to the art form known as poetry and that all the rules and laws of the psychology of art, which we discover in the higher forms of art in a more complex form, can also be applied to the fable. We shall follow a different path and pursue a different aim. Both Potebnia and Lessing proceeded from the bottom up, from the fable to the higher forms of literature. We shall operate in the reverse manner and begin our analysis at the top, applying to the fable all the psychological rules governing the higher forms of poetry.

Let us begin by investigating the structural elements of the fable as studied by Lessing and Potebnia. The first is the allegory. Although Lessing disputes de La Motte's view that the fable is but a lecture concealed under the cloak of an allegory, he does introduce allegory into his argument, but in a slightly different fashion. As a matter of fact, in European literature the concept of the allegory has gone through quite a few changes in its evolution. Quintilian regarded allegory as an inversion that expresses one thing in words and something else—which may be directly opposite—in its meaning. Later writers substituted for the concept of the opposite that of similarity and, beginning with Fossius, excluded the concept of the opposite from the allegory entirely. Thus the allegory says, "not what it expresses in words, but something *similar*." [12]

We have here a radical contradiction of the true nature of the allegory. Lessing sees in the fable only the particular case of a general rule, and claims that a single case cannot resemble the general rule by which it is governed. He asserts that "a simple fable cannot in any event be allegorical." [13] It becomes allegorical only when applied to a specific case, and when for each action and each character of the fable we understand another action and another character. In that case everything becomes allegorical.

Thus, according to Lessing, allegory is not an original property of the fable, but a secondary, adopted property acquired only if the fable is applied to reality. Potebnia, proceeding from the same point of view, claims that the fable is essentially a scheme applied to all sorts of events and relationships in order to explain them. Therefore, the fable in its very essence is an allegory. His own examples, however, blatantly contradict this view. He refers to the passage in Pushkin's *The Captain's Daughter* where Grinev advises Pugachev to come to his senses and to hope for the Empress's pardon. " 'Listen,' said Pugachev with some sort of a wild inspiration. 'I'll tell you a story which an old Kalmuck woman told me in my childhood. The eagle once asked the raven, "Tell me, raven, why do you live in this world for three hundred years, while I live here only thirty-three years?" Replied the raven, "Because, my friend, you drink live blood, while I feed on carrion." And the eagle thought to himself, let me try his way. So, the eagle and the raven flew off. They saw a dead horse and flew down. The raven began to peck at and praise his food. The eagle pecked once, pecked twice, then shook his wings and said to the raven, "No, brother raven, rather than live three hundred years and eat carrion, it is far better to drink live blood once, and after this God will provide!" ' " Potebnia distinguishes two separate parts of the fable: ". . . one part represents the fable in the form in which it entered the book of fables, if we tear it from the roots on which it grew; the other part is made up of the roots themselves. The first part may be a fantasy or an imaginary situation (a raven talking with an eagle), or a situation which has nothing unreal about it. . . . What is the subject and what is the predicate in this fable? The subject in this case is the problem of why Pugachev preferred the outlaw's life he chose to the peaceful life of an ordinary Cossack. The predicate is the answer to that question, namely, the fable which, consequently, is an explanation of the subject. . . . The example shows quite clearly that Pugachev's decision is a consequence of his nature and may have no direct connection with will power." [14]

Here Potebnia interprets the fable as a perfect allegory: the eagle is Pugachev himself, and the raven is a peaceful Cossack, or Grinev. The dialogue of the fable is similar to actual talk between the two. But in Pushkin's description we can detect two psychological oddities that make us wonder about the correctness of the given explanation . . . The first, obviously, is: Why did Pugachev tell this fable "with some sort of wild inspiration"? If a fable is a perfectly common manifestation of a thought, the mere combination of a subject with a predicate, the explanation of certain everyday relationships—why, then, the "wild inspiration"? Could this not indicate that for Pugachev the fable was something exalted, something more than just a simple answer to a simple question?

The second oddity is the effect produced by the fable. According to the explanation given above, one would expect that it cleared up the difficulty and, by brilliantly dealing with the problem that brought it forth, stopped any argument. In Pushkin's tale, however, things are different. Grinev listened to the fable, interpreted it his own way, and turned it against Pugachev. He said that feeding on carrion implies brigandage and banditry. This effect should have been expected. It is, indeed, immediately clear that a fable can be used as a technique for expanding the thought of the speaker, but it can never explain complex relationships or deep thoughts and meanings. If a fable is at all convincing, the story would have had the same result without it. But if, as in this case, the fable misses the target, it is evidently incapable of shifting the idea toward the point to which it was directed by weightier and more substantial arguments. We are faced here with Quintilian's definition of allegory, in which the fable unexpectedly acquires a meaning completely opposite the one expressed in its own words. If we take a common similarity as the basis for an allegory, we will see that the stronger this similarity, the more trite the fable becomes. Here are two examples taken from Lessing and Potebnia: the first is Aesop's fable about the chicken and the greedy housewife. "A widow had a chicken which laid an egg every day. 'I'll try to give barley to the bird. Maybe it will lay an egg twice a day,' thought the woman. No sooner said than done. But the chicken became fat and stopped laying even one egg a day. He who for greediness runs after more, loses what he has." [15]

The other is Phaedrus' fable about a dog with a piece of meat. "A dog swimming in a river with a piece of meat in his mouth, saw his own reflection in the water and wanted to take the piece of meat from the other dog he thought he saw there. But he dropped the piece he was carrying in his own mouth and ended up with nothing." The moral is the same in both instances; therefore the category to which this fable may be assigned allegorically is the same for both versions. Which of the two fables then is more allegorical and which is more lyrical? There is no doubt that the fable about the dog is immeasurably more interesting and poetic, since it is hard to imagine anything more trite and reminiscent of dull, everyday events than the story told by the first fable. We could think of innumerable stories of this kind, and give them a special allegorical meaning. The first fable tells us only that the chicken laid eggs, became fat, and then stopped laying eggs. How can this interest anyone, even a child? What more than an unnecessary moral corollary can we gather from reading this fable? It is irrefutable, however, that, as an allegory, it is considerably superior to the second fable, and this is why Potebnia selected it to illustrate the fundamental law of fables. Indeed the first fable is considerably closer to all those everyday-life occurrences to which it can be applied, while the second fable has very little resemblance to them.

Lessing criticizes Phaedrus for having the dog that carries the meat swim in a river. "This is impossible, says Lessing, for if the dog were swimming in the river, it would certainly stir up the water around it so that it could not possibly see its own reflection. The Greek fable mentions that the dog, carrying the meat, walked through the river; this, of course, means that it crossed the river." [16]

Lessing considers such a small infraction of credibility a violation of the rules governing the fable. What, then, should he say about the essence of a plot which, strictly speaking, cannot be applied to any example of human greed? The whole point of this story about the dog is that it saw its own reflection, leaped after the phantom illusion of the meat it was carrying in its mouth, and therefore lost it. Without this point, we could tell the same story thus: "A dog carrying meat in his mouth saw another dog with meat in his mouth and pounced on him to take his meat. In so doing, he dropped the meat from his own mouth and, as a result, was left with nothing." It is obvious that in its logical construction this fable fully coincides with Aesop's fable. Greed makes the protagonist of each fable strive for two eggs, or two pieces of meat, and deprives him of both. But then the story loses all its poetic inspiration and becomes dull and trite.

As a slight diversion, a few words about the technique, or device, used here: This is the technique of *experimental deformation* (i.e., changing an element in the whole of the fable and investigating the result to which this leads). This is one of the most fruitful psychological devices to which many investigators resort quite frequently. Its significance is similar to comparing the treatment of the same subject of a fable by different authors and studying the changes introduced by each as well as studying the variations within all the fables of one author.

As any experimental method, however, it has the great advantage of extraordinary conclusiveness. We shall have to resort more than once to similar experiments with form, and also to comparative study of the formal composition of the same fable.

This brief analysis already shows that allegory and the poetic inspiration of a subject are diametrically opposed. The closer the similarity on which the allegory is based, the flatter, more trite, and duller becomes the subject itself. It reminds more and more of life's banality, deprived of the brilliance and glitter which Potebnia considers the greatest vitality of the fable. But is this so? Doesn't he confuse the parable with the fable while strictly distinguishing between them theoretically? Doesn't he transfer to the fable the psychological technique and handling of the parable? "What makes the fable survive? how can we explain that it has endured for millennia? The explanation is simple: the fable continues to find new applications." [17] Once again it is obvious that this refers only to the nonlyrical fable or to the fable's subject. So far as the fable as a work of poetry is concerned, it is governed by the rules and laws of any work of art. It does not live for millennia. The fables of Krylov and many others had a substantial meaning and significance in their time; then they began to die out. Did Krylov's fables fail to survive because no new applications for the old themes could be found? Potebnia speaks of only one cause for the demise of a fable—when it becomes unintelligible because the image contained in it is no longer in general use and needs to be explained. Krylov's fables, however, are understood by everyone even today. Therefore, they must have died for some other reason, for there is no doubt that as a whole they are outside today's reality of life and literature. Once again, this rule of the influence and death of the lyrical fable appears to be in full contradiction with the allegoricity to which Potebnia refers. Allegory can be preserved while the fable dies, and vice versa. Furthermore, if we take a close look at the fables of La Fontaine and Krylov, we see that they perform a function diametrically opposed to the one indicated by Potebnia. He feels that fables are applied to real events in order to explain them. However, analysis of the so-called composite, or complex, fable leads us to exactly the opposite conclusion. The poet uses a case from life, or one closely resembling life, in order to explain the whole fable with its aid. Thus, in Aesop's and Krylov's fable of the peahen and the crow, as used by Potebnia as a specimen of a composite fable, we read, "I shall explain this fable with fact." It turns out that facts explain fables, and not vice versa, as Potebnia assumed. Therefore, he saw in the composite fable a false and illegitimate type, because whereas Lessing assumed that the fable thus becomes allegorical, confusing the general idea contained in it, Potebnia pointed out that because of its composite portion such a fable is confined or narrowed to the application that can be given it, since this second kind of fable should be viewed as but one particular case of its possible applications. Such a composite fable has the significance of a label. "It can be compared in language by the following operation: To express better our idea we accumulate words that mean approximately the same thing." [18] Potebnia feels that this parallelism is excessive, because it limits the scope of the basic fable. He likens the author of such a fable to a toy merchant "who tells the child that with this particular toy one can play, somehow. . . ." [19] But if we carefully analyze the composite fable we can readily see that the second part of the fable is always a complement, an ornament, or an explanation of the first part of the fable, never the other way around. In other words, here also the theory of allegory suffers a defeat.

The second element with which one has to deal when composing a fable is the unusual selection of heroes or characters. Why is it that the fable prefers to deal with animals, and may even introduce some inanimate object, but hardly ever introduces people? What is the rationale, if any? Different writers give different answers to these questions. Breitinger thought that animals and other lower creatures are made to talk in fables in order to cause surprise and astonishment.[20]

Lessing was quite right to criticize this statement. He pointed out that astonishment and surprise in life and in art do not coincide at all: a talking animal would surprise us in actual life, but in art all depends on the way the talk is introduced. If it is introduced as a stylistic convention to which we immediately accustom ourselves as we do to a literary technique, and if the author, as asserted by ancient theoreticians, tries to minimize the effect of the amazing, then in reading about the most extraordinary events we are no more surprised or astonished then by any commonplace, average, or banal event in life. Lessing cites a brilliant example "When I read in the Scripture, 'And the Lord opened the mouth of the ass, and she said unto Balaam, . . .' I read of something astonishing. But when I read Aesop 'At the time when animals knew how to talk, the sheep said to the shepherd, . . .' it is perfectly obvious that the fabulist does not want to tell me anything astonishing, but rather, that at the time when, with the reader's permission, all this happened, it was consistent with the laws of nature." [21]

Lessing also points out (and quite correctly) that psychologically the use of animals in the fable may surprise us once or twice, but when it becomes a habit and when the author regards it as something perfectly normal and natural, it no longer causes any astonishment or bewilderment. Nonetheless, this practice has a very deep significance, so much so that when we substitute man for the animal the fable loses its meaning. "Owing to the use of these commonplace heroes, the fable acquires a surprising nuance. It would be a passable fable if we told the following story: 'A man noticed beautiful pears in a tree and wanted to eat them. He labored hard to climb the tree, but in vain. He had to abandon his efforts. As he was leaving he said 'It will be much healthier for me if I let the pears hang for a little while. They are not quite ripe yet.' But this little story would have a very poor effect on us, it is much too trite and banal." [22]

No sooner did we substitute a man for the fox in this well-known fable, that it lost its entire meaning. According to Lessing there are two reasons for using animals in fables: First, animals are steadier and more determined in their character. It suffices to name an animal, and we immediately identify it with the concept of strength, valor, and so forth, that it may represent. Mention a wolf in a fable and we immediately imagine a strong and rapacious person. Say fox, and we see a sly and cunning person. But if the fabulist replaces the wolf or the fox with a person, then he has to explain quite exhaustively the features and character of this person, lest the fable lose its expressivity. Because Lessing believes that animals are used in fables because of their "well-known character of steadiness and determination," [23] he reproaches La Fontaine for explaining the characters of his dramatis personae. When in three verses La Fontaine defines the character of the fox, Lessing considers it an unpardonable violation of the lyricism of the fable. He says, "the *fabulist* needs the fox to describe with one word the total image of a clever, cunning, sly person; the *poet* prefers to forget this convenience, to surrender it, for the sole purpose of giving an able and deft description of the object, which has the unique advantage at this point of requiring no description." [24]

Let us mention here in passing that Lessing juxtaposes the fabulist and the poet. This, of course, will subsequently explain why animals have a completely different importance for the prosaic and for the lyrical fable.

Potebnia is also inclined to believe that animals are used in fables because of their definitive characters. "The third property of the fable," he says, "which issues from its purpose, is that it does not dwell for any length of time on the characterization of the participants, and takes such personages whose names alone suffice to characterize them to the reader. We know that animals serve this purpose appropriately. . . . The practical advantages for the fable can be compared with certain games, chess for instance, where each man can make only specific moves—the knight moves one way, the king and queen differently; this is known to every player, and it is extremely important that it be so, because otherwise they would have to agree on the moves every time they start a game." [25]

No less important for Lessing is the fact that animals prevent the fable from having any emotional effect upon the reader. He supports this statement quite well by saying that he would never have come across this thought had not his feeling pushed him toward it. "The purpose of a fable is to give a clear and lively grasp of a moral rule; nothing confuses our perception and knowledge more than emotions; consequently, the fabulist must avoid evoking emotions as much as possible. Is there a better way to avoid emotions (such as compassion or sympathy) than by making their potential objects quite imperfect, by using animals and other lower creatures, instead of people? Let us consider . . . the fable about the wolf and the sheep as transformed . . . into the fable of the priest and the pauper. We sympathize with the sheep, but our sympathy is so weak that it does not do any noticeable harm to our objective perception of the moral rule. Exactly the opposite happens with the pauper, irrespective of whether the story is fictitious or real. We would have too much sympathy for the pauper and too much hostility toward the priest; so that the objective recognition of the moral rule could not be as clear as in the first case." [26] Here we reach the very core of Lessing's reasoning. He replaced the animals with the priest and the pauper to show that the fable loses its meaning only if its characters lose their determined and steady characteristics. If instead of the animals we use not just any persons but specific persons, say, a pauper and a priest (whose greed is well known to us from many stories about the clergy), the fable loses nothing in the characterizations of its protagonists; but, as Lessing shows, the second reason for using animals is revealed—the fable would generate in us much too strong an emotional reaction, one which could confuse and obscure its true meaning. Thus, the animals are necessary to efface or conceal emotions. Again we are faced with a sharp distinction between the lyrical and the prosaic fable. These two considerations have nothing to do with the tasks and purposes of the former. Let us look into the examples given by Lessing and Potebnia. Potebnia says, "If the characters of a fable were to draw our undivided attention, or evoke compassion, displeasure, or sympathy to a degree common in a regular work of literature, such as a short story, a novel, or an epic poem, the fable would fail to achieve its purpose. It would no longer be faithful to itself. It would no longer be the quick answer to a question. . . . Take the *Iliad* or perhaps not the epic itself but only that cycle of events not completely included in it. . . . The story told in this form could become the subject for a fable, i.e., in the broad sense, the reply to the question or theme contained in the Latin proverb *Delirant reges, plectuntur achaei* (The kings go mad, but the plebeians are punished). But if this cycle of events is told with all the details that make these events so attractive in the poem itself, then our attention will be taken up at every step by minor details and images requiring a definition or an explanation—and a fable would become a matter of impossibility.

. . . The fable, to be fit for application, must not dwell upon the roles of its characters, the detailed representation of actions, scenes, and so on." [27]

Here Potebnia is clearly talking about the fable as the subject of a work of literature. If we remove from the *Iliad* its prosaic part, the cycle of events included in the poem, and if we eliminate everything which makes these events attractive, then we will have nothing but a fable on the theme *Delirant reges, plectuntur achaei* (or, as the Ukrainians say, the masters quarrel, but the peasants get their skulls cracked). In other words, deprive a work of poetry of its lyricism, and it becomes a fable. All we do here is to equate the fable to a prosaic work.

This, of course, somewhat broadens the problem and shifts the argument from the characters to another element in the fable, the story. Before we start investigating this element, we should say a few words about the role played by animals in the lyrical fable, as contrasted with the prosaic one. The poet's intentions are obviously diametrically opposed to those of the prosaist. The poet, as clearly shown by Lessing, wants to concentrate our attention on the hero, to awaken our sympathy or displeasure, even if to a lesser degree than in a novel or epic poem. Intensity apart, the feelings are the same as those generated by a novel, an epic poem, or a drama.

We will try to show that the fable contains the seeds of the lyric, epic, and drama, and that the heroes of the fable are the same prototypes of epic and dramatic heroes as are all the other elements in the structure of fable prototypes. Thus when Krylov narrates the story of the two doves, he is indeed counting on stirring our compassion and sympathy for their mishaps. When he tells us about the mishaps of the crow, he wants us to laugh. We can see that here the selection of animals is determined less by their character than by their emotional qualities. Thus, a closer look at any of La Fontaine's or Krylov's fables reveals that neither the author nor the reader is indifferent toward the characters of these fables. We also see that they generate strong emotions in us, although these are quite different from those provoked in us by people.

We can say that one of the main reasons poets resort to the representation of animals and inanimate objects is the possibility of isolating and concentrating one affective element in such a hero.

We shall discover that animals and inanimate objects are used in the loftiest lyric for exactly the same reasons. Lermontov's "The Sail," "Mountains," "The Three Palms," "The Cliff," and "Clouds," or Heine's "The Fir and the Palm" are heroes of the same order, who grew out of these very same fabular animals.

The other reason for using animals in the fable is that they are suitable conventional figures that provide the isolation from reality indispensable for any aesthetic perception [24]. Haman mentioned this isolation as the first and foremost requirement for any aesthetic effect. Indeed, when we are told the story of the housewife who overfed her chicken, we really do not know what to do with it, whether to take it as a true story or as fiction, because the missing isolation from reality deprives us of the aesthetic effect. This lack of isolation is equivalent to taking the frame away from a picture on the wall and allowing the picture to blend into the surrounding environment, so that the viewer will not be able to decide at once whether he sees a representation or reality.

Thus the literary and conventional features of these protagonists isolate them from reality and produce the artistic effect. This is a property common to all protagonists of literary works. It is closely related to the third element of the fable, the story itself and its character.

As he continues to develop his thoughts about protagonists, Potebnia flatly states that "there exist two schools: One, known to us from childhood, is the school of La Fontaine and his imitators, to which Krylov belongs. It is characterized by the fable 'The Ass and the Nightingale. . . .' Many . . . found this method of narration, with the introduction of detail and picturesque descriptions, to be quite appropriate and poetical." [28] Potebnia, however, feels that this fable can be used as proof that people did not know, nor want to know, how to use the fable. He feels that the details and poetical descriptions completely destroy the fable and deprive it of its intrinsic properties. Lessing holds the same view when he compares La Fontaine, who introduced the wide use of lyrical fables, with a hunter who ordered an artist to carve a hunting scene on his bow. The artist did a beautiful job, but when the hunter wanted to use his bow, it broke.[29] Lessing therefore speculates that if Plato (who excluded Homer from his *Republic* but admitted Aesop without ranking him among the poets or creators of plots) were to see Aesop in the shape given him by La Fontaine, he would say: "My friend, we no longer know each other. Go thy way." [30] Thus Lessing also assumes that the lyrical beauty and practical usefulness of a fable are inversely related: the more poetic and picturesque the description, the more formally perfect the treatment of the story, the less the fable fulfills its original task. Nowhere does the contrast between the lyrical and prosaic fable become more obvious than here.

Lessing contradicts Richet, criticizes his definition of the fable as a small poem, and says, "If he feels that the only indispensable features of a poem are poetic language and a certain meter, I cannot share his view." [31] According to Lessing, all that characterizes poetry is incompatible with the fable. Lessing also objects to Richet's assertion that the rules governing the fable are stated in the form of pictures or images. This, Lessing feels, is completely incompatible with the true task and purpose of the fable. He reproaches Batte for "greatly confusing the effects of Aesop's fables with the effects of an epic or drama . . . The final aim of a heroic or dramatic writer is to stir passions, but he can do so by imitation only if he devises for the passions certain aims toward which they strive, or which they try to avoid . . . Conversely, the fabulist deals only with our perception, not with our passions." [32]

The fable is in great contrast with any other work. It no longer belongs to the realm of poetry, and all the qualities considered positive in a work of art are therefore bound to become negative in the fable. In accordance with the ancient viewpoint, Lessing assumes that "the soul of the fable is its brevity." Phaedrus was the first to abandon this principle when he began to write Aesop's fables in verse; he was forced to deviate from Aesop's rules only on account of "the meter and poetic style." [33] Lessing holds that Phaedrus chose the middle road between the lyrical and the prosaic fable and narrated it with the elegant brevity of the Romans, but in verse form.[34] Again, according to Lessing, the greatest crime committed by La Fontaine is his use of lyrical style and form. "The story in a fable must be much simpler. It must be brief and concise, satisfy clarity alone, and avoid, as much as possible, any ornaments, frills, and niceties." [35]

But the fable evolved in a completely opposite direction. It asserted itself as an independent poetic genre, with nothing to differentiate it from other forms of poetry. In his introduction to his fables, La Fontaine refers with touching ingenuousness to Plato's story about Socrates whom the gods allowed to study music before his death; so he began to transpose Aesop's fables into meters. He tried to combine the fable and poetry by means of musical rhythms, or in other words began the work which later was completed by La Fontaine, Krylov, and others. "As soon as the fables attributed to Aesop appeared, Socrates decided to dress them in the garments of the muses. . . . Socrates was not alone in regarding poetry and the fable as sisters. Phaedrus stated that he also was of the same opinion."

La Fontaine stated that he did not intend to make his fables as exceptionally short as those of Phaedrus, but he did want to make them somewhat more entertaining. La Fontaine's argument goes like this: "I assume that since these fables are known to everyone, no harm will be done if I add something new to them, some traits that would give them a certain literary flavor that they need. Everyone wants novelty and gaiety. Gaiety to me is not what excites laughter but what provides a certain charm, a certain pleasant form which we may give to any subject, even the most serious one." [36]

The significant story about Socrates who took the permission of the gods to study music to mean studying poetry, and who was afraid to touch poetry because it required subterfuge and untruth, sheds light on the two trends in the fable's evolution: one led to poetry, and the other to sermons and didactics. Almost from the very beginning the lyrical and prosaic fable followed separate paths. Each was governed by different rules, and each required completely different psychological techniques for its interpretation. While we cannot agree with Lessing and Potebnia that the use of animals in the prosaic fable is due mainly to their determined character and serves reasoned and unemotional purposes, we must admit that this very same fact acquires a totally different significance for the lyrical fable. If we take the swan, the lobster, and the pike, the tomtit, the crane, the horse, the ant, the lion, the mosquito, the fly, or the chicken, we see that these "heroes" have no specific character, and that even such classic fable personages as the lion, the elephant, and the dog have no specific and permanent character. Therefore, there must be other reasons to induce a poet to resort to these animals. We have already mentioned that the choice of these animals in the lyrical fable is determined, to a certain extent, by emotional considerations. What, then, are the reasons that induced the writers of lyrical fables to resort to animals?

We see that, in the lyrical fable, the limelight is shared with such household items as razors, barrels, paper, combs, axes, cannons, sails, money or coins, flowers, etc. It is also shared with mythological heroes, or with persons who have a specific purpose and activity, such as the peasant, the philosopher, the merchant, the nobleman, the liar, and so on. This leads us to a very important conclusion. Animals are used in the lyrical fable not for their known specific character (it is more likely that this character has already been derived by the reader on the basis of the fable and is therefore a secondary factor), but for a completely different reason. Each animal represents a specific, well-known pattern of activity. It is in the fable not because of its character but because of the properties and characteristics of its life. Now it can be understood why a razor, an ax, or a barrel can also become personages: they, too, are "actors," they are the chessmen mentioned by Potebnia, whose action is very precisely defined. This is why persons like the peasant, the liar, the philosopher, and the nobleman, or tools like an ax, or a hammer, can successfully replace animals in the fable.

If we take the fable of the swan, the lobster, and the pike, we wonder about the character of these three and also wonder for which previously known character traits the author selected them, to what life situations they can be referred, and which classes of human nature they symbolize. It is quite obvious that they have no specific character traits, and also that they were selected to illustrate the action, or rather the impossibility of action, which arises from their mutual efforts. Everyone knows that the swan flies, the lobster moves backward, and the pike swims. Therefore all three can be used for developing a certain action, to construct a story, in particular a fable story. But it will be impossible to show that greed and rapacity, the only character traits attributed to any of the three (to the pike), have any significance in the structure of this fable. This poetically ideal fable has run into a barrage of stern objections from a number of critics. It was pointed out in Krylov's version (as distinguished from La Fontaine's) that "the action, so important in any fable, is utterly incredible, so much so that no illusion is possible in this respect. How is it possible for a pike to go on a mouse hunt with a cat, for a peasant to hire an ass to guard his orchard, for another peasant to take snakes to raise his children, for a pike, a swan and a lobster to be harnessed together to a cart?" [37]

An Italian critic objected to the absurdity of taking a swan, a lobster, and a pike to pull a cart, since all three are aquatic animals and therefore would be more fit to pull a boat. Whoever argues this point does not understand the task of a poetic fable which in this particular case forced the author to use all those means which are objectionable from the viewpoint of a writer of prosaic fables.

The Introduction tells us that it is the purpose of the fable to show us an impossible situation with absurd contrasts. In fact, the author says, "When the companions lack agreement, their job cannot succeed and will become a torture rather than a job." To illustrate this thought in a prosaic fable, we would have to choose animals whose character would preclude any possible agreement and emphasize the quarrels and conflicts that could arise from their attempted cooperation. In other words, the fable would have to be written according to Lessing's prescription. This would eliminate some of the oddities and absurdities mentioned above. Izmailov's opinion is quoted by Kenevich: "Izmailov feels it is unnatural to put these three on a single job at the same time: 'if the load were really light, then the swan could have lifted the cart, pike, and lobster into the air.' " [38] It is not the final consideration of the critic which is important here, but his fundamental idea that the combination of these three individuals performing a common job is unnatural. Consequently, the story does not tell us about the lack of agreement among the three companions; on the contrary, we find no hint in the fable of any disagreement. All we see is that they try hard, exceedingly hard, and it is impossible to establish who among them is right and who is wrong. The fable therefore does not satisfy Lessing's prescription (to show the correctness of the general moral statement) but goes against it and shows, in agreement with Quintilian's definition, a blatant contradiction between its words and its meaning. We shall show that this element of impossibility and contradiction is an indispensable condition in the composition of fables. If we need a good fable to illustrate the general rule, we can easily compose such a fable by inventing a case in which two or more companions are unable to complete a job because they are quarreling with each other. The poet, however, proceeds in a completely different way. He stretches to a breaking point the chord of total agreement. He brings to a hyperbolic apex the motive of an exceptionally firm intent ("they lay themselves out"), intentionally eliminates any interference ("the load seemed light for them"); at the same time, he also stretches to a breaking point another chord which deals with disorder, lack of coordination, and incongruity in the action of the three. The fable balances itself on this contrast, which we shall try to explain at a later stage. This contrast, as a matter of fact, is inherent not only in this particular fable, but, as we shall show, is the psychological basis of any lyrical fable.

This is the way to understand all literary heroes that have developed from fabular animals. Initially a protagonist was not just some characteristic; we shall see later on that the dramatis personae of Shakespeare's tragedies, which for some reason are regarded as "character tragedies," lack this characteristic. We shall also see that the hero is nothing but a chessman [25] with a specific capacity, and in this respect the fabular personages are no exception to those of all the other literary genres. We have seen, from many examples, that this applies also to the rest of the story, and that the fable resorts everywhere to exactly the same techniques and devices as do other literary works. The fable describes its characters, violates the rule of laconic brevity, introduces frills and stylistic embellishments, verses, and rhymes.

If we enumerate Lessing's accusations against La Fontaine, and Potebnia's against Krylov, we get a precise list of the poetic techniques and devices used in writing a fable. We will try to determine the basic tendencies of all these and present a final formulation. The prosaic fable is set off against the lyrical fable, its characters are somewhat ignored, its story is not supposed to cause any emotional reaction or involvement, and its language must be absolutely prosaic. The lyrical fable, according to the tradition of Socrates' times, tends toward music and, as we shall try to prove, uses the logical thought from which it originates only as a material or as a poetic device.

To prove this point, we have to take a look at the so-called moral of the fable. The problem of the moral has a very long history. For some reason, everyone, from the time of the very first fables down to our day, believes that the moral is an indispensable, indeed, the most important part of the fable. It was said that the moral is the fable's soul, and the story is its body. Lessing, for instance, categorically rejects the view that the moral of a fable must be hidden behind an allegorical image. He is even opposed to de La Motte's idea that the moral must be woven into the story,[39] and is convinced that the moral must be absolutely clear and obvious, not hidden behind the story, because the moral is the final aim of the fable's action.

We also see, however, that once the fable becomes lyrical, it begins to distort the moral. There are some, like Tomashevskii, who believe to this day that the moral is also an intrinsic part of the lyrical fable. However, they are misinformed and have not taken into consideration the fact that the path of the historical development of the fable has split into two divergent directions.

Lessing had already discovered that even the ancient authors had trouble with the moral. He quotes Aesop's fable about the man and the satyr. "A man blows onto his cold fist in order to warm it with his breath, and then blows on hot food in order to cool it. 'You blow hot and cold from the same mouth?' says the satyr. 'Go away, I do not want to have anything to do with you.' This fable teaches us to avoid friendship with two-faced people." [40]

According to Lessing, this fable has difficulty in coping with the moral. It does not show that the person who breathes hot and cold from the same mouth even remotely resembles a two-faced or insincere person. Actually, the moral should be the other way around, and we ought to be surprised at the satyr's lack of perspicacity. As we can see, there is a contradiction between the general moral statement and the story that purportedly illustrates it.

Lessing finds exactly the same impasse in Phaedrus' fable of the wolf and the lamb. He cites Batte's opinion: "The moral which we gather from this fable is that the weak are frequently harassed by the powerful. How trite! How insincere! If this fable taught us nothing else, it would seem perfectly useless for the poet to have invented the 'insincere' arguments of the wolf. His fable would tell us more than he wanted to say. In sum, it would be a bad fable." [41] We shall see later that this verdict is true for any fabular moral. A fable tells us more than what its moral actually says. We shall always find superfluous elements, such as the invented accusation of the wolf, which are completely unnecessary for the expression of a commonplace idea. We have already shown these extraneous elements in the fable of the dog who saw his reflection in the water. Were we to relate a straightforward story which would completely exhaust the moral of a fabular situation and add nothing to it, we would have to compose a completely nonlyrical story which, as a simple fact of life, would exhaustively explain the case.

Lessing, in analyzing ancient fables, finds ridiculous incongruities between the story in the fable and the moral it is supposed to preach. He asks, "Is there anything one cannot express as an allegory? Name a story, an insipid tale, an ugly parody, into which I cannot instill some moral sense by means of an allegory. . . . 'Aesop's friends took a liking to the excellent figs of their host and ate them all up, but when questioned they claimed that Aesop was the culprit. To rid himself of the blame, Aesop drank a large glass of warm water, and ordered his friends to do the same. Soon the warm water had its effect, and the gourmands were exposed.' What does this story teach us? Essentially nothing but the fact that warm water taken in certain quantities is an emetic. A Persian poet, however, made much better use of this fact. 'On the day of judgment,' he said, 'you will be made to drink warm water, and it will reveal everything you have so carefully concealed during your entire life. And the hypocrite, whose simulations have made him become honorable, will stand naked, crushed with shame and embarrassment.' " [42]

This example reveals the weakness of the positions which Lessing tries so desperately to defend. If any story, even the most trite, can be given a moral meaning, then the moral has nothing to do with a lyrical story. Lessing himself establishes the two main points of the lyrical fable: (1) the moral never covers the entire story, for there is always a part of it which is unnecessary to the moral; and (2) since any story can have a moral, we are never sure of how strong and convincing the link between the particular story and the moral is.

Both Lessing and Potebnia pursue the critique of this theory. They resort to Phaedrus' fable "The Thief and the Lamp" to show that the author considers three moral issues in the story. "The moral lecture is so complicated that the author himself has to explain it: first, it means that our worst enemy is frequently someone we have nurtured; second, the criminal is punished—not when the gods are angry but when fate so decides; and third, the fable warns the good and virtuous never to ally themselves with criminals, no matter what the advantages might be. The author himself found too many applications for the reader to agree with any of them." [43]

Potebnia reaches the same conclusion by analyzing Phaedrus' fable of the man and the fly. "We know the purpose of a fable: it must be a steady predicate for changeable subjects. How can this fable answer one question when it contains various and different answers? Sometimes the fabulist himself (and this is what Phaedrus does) emphasizes quite innocently the complexity, or rather, the practical inadequacy, of his fable." [44] The analysis of the Indian fable about the ruff (a small bird) and the sea shows the same phenomenon. "The fable is famous because it has left a tremendous heritage. It [the fable] is divided into two parts. In the first part the sea steals the bird's eggs (there are other fables which preach that it is useless to fight nature); in the second part the weak fights the strong and wins. Thus the two parts of the fable are not in conflict with each other because of the content (the sea steals the eggs of the bird; the male bird decides to take vengeance on the sea and does so). But if we try to use the fable as a fixed predicate for changeable subjects, as mentioned earlier, we will discover that the nature of the cases applicable to the fable's first part is diametrically opposed to that of the cases applicable to its second part. The cases matching the first part are those that show the uselessness and impossibility of opposing nature; those applicable to the second part show the apparently weak person standing up to nature, fighting and winning. Consequently our fable has a logical flaw, and it also lacks the unity of action which we find in many other stories." [45]

Here again Potebnia defines a feature typical of the lyrical fable as a flaw of the prosaic fable: the contradiction that exists, not so much in the content as in our attempts to explain and interpret the fable. Any fable that comprises more than one action and more than one plot is bound to lead to several conclusions, and therefore contains a flaw in logic. Potebnia disagrees with Lessing only in that he believes that the fable applies to specific cases in life and not to general rules of morality which evolve as a result of the generalization from those cases in day-to-day life. He also requires, however, that some of these cases be defined beforehand during the construction of the fable. If these cases are numerous, and if the same fable can be applied to contrasting or contradictory cases, it is imperfect. But in complete contradiction to his own idea, Potebnia also shows that a fable may hold not one, but several, moral positions, and that it can be applied to different cases without being deemed imperfect or defective.

Thus, in analyzing the fable, "The Peasant and the Stork," by Babrius, he says that "the question concerning the general position to which the fable is reduced, or what generalization results from it, can be answered depending on the application of the fable or on the position taken by Babrius, such as 'you will be responsible for what you have been taught,' or 'human justice is unreasonable and blind,' or 'there is no truth in the world,' or 'there is a supreme justice; it is just that when observing superior interests, no attention should be paid to any particular evil resulting from it.' In other words, one gets what one wants from the fable, and it is extremely difficult to prove that any of these generalizations is either erroneous or correct." [46]

Potebnia also points out that "if one takes the fable in its abstract form, as one usually finds it in a book, then he should give it more than one generalization and indicate the one closest to its purpose, since the generalization may go very far." [47]

Therefore it is a foregone conclusion that the generalization cannot precede the fable, since we frequently encounter wrong conclusions drawn by fabulists, and "the image . . . described in a fable is poetry, while the generalization applied to it by the fabulist is prose." [48]

But this solution to the problem, which apparently is in contrast with Lessing's, is just as wrong for the lyrical fable as the preceding solution. La Fontaine said that although he added form only to Aesop's fables, they must be evaluated not for this form but for their intrinsic usefulness. "Not only do they lead us to morality, but they also provide us with other knowledge. They express the peculiarities of animals, their various characters, and so forth."

As we compare these scientific data on the characteristics of animals with the morals, we see that in the lyrical fable they have the same position (as correctly pointed out by La Fontaine) or, rather, they have no position at all.

After making this point in self-defense, and establishing the moral as the soul of the fable, La Fontaine is forced to admit that frequently he has to prefer the body to the soul. Occasionally he must even do away with the soul when it does not fit the story and disrupts the grace of the form, when it contrasts with the form, or, in simpler terms, when it is superfluous. He recognizes his violation of the ancient rules. "In Aesop's time, fables were told in a simple way: the moral was always separated and placed at the end. Phaedrus no longer followed this rule. He expanded and embellished the story and occasionally shifted the moral to the beginning of the fable."

La Fontaine goes even further by including the moral in the story only when he can find a place for it. He refers to Horace's advice to the writer to fight neither the inadequacy of his mind nor the clumsiness of the subject. Thus the writer is justified in abandoning what seems to have no useful purpose—the moral. Does this mean that the moral was confined only to prosaic stories and had no place in the lyrical fable? As a first step, we have to establish that a lyrical story does not depend on the moral in its logical trend and structure. We may then be able to find the significance of the moral which occasionally does appear in lyrical fables. We mentioned earlier the moral in the fable of "The Wolf and the Lamb," and it might be useful to recall Napoleon's statement that it "violates the principle of morality. . . . it is unfair *que la raison du plus fort fût toujours la meilleure,** and if this is really the case, then it is bad . . . it is abuse, worthy of censure. The wolf should choke as he devours the lamb." [49]

This statement clearly expresses the idea that were the fable really to follow the moral rules, it could not evolve according to its own internal mechanics, and the wolf would of course choke as he devours the lamb. But if we investigate the aims and purposes of this lyrical fable, we find that such an addendum destroys its poetic meaning. The story follows its own rules and obviously the laws of morality. Izmailov ends the fable "The Ant and the Grasshopper" in the following way: "The ant said this to teach him a lesson, but then she took pity and gave the grasshopper some food." Obviously, Izmailov was a kindhearted man who agreed to let the grasshopper have food and forced the ant to act according to the rules of morality. He was, however, a mediocre fabulist who failed to realize the requirement of the story. He failed to see that the moral and the story diverge completely and that, for the sake of the story, someone is bound to remain dissatisfied. Something similar happens in Khemnitser's famous fable "The Metaphysic." All of us know the crude and unsophisticated moral drawn by the author from the joke about the silly philosopher who had fallen into a ditch. Odoevskii, however, interpreted this fable in a different way. "With this fable, Khemnitser, despite his genius and ability, was a slave of the impudent philosophy of his time . . . It is the philosopher who is worthy of deep respect. He did not see the ditch into which he was tumbling, and once in it up to his neck, he forgets about his own safety, asks for a chart to help all

* . . . that the judgment of the strongest always prevails (quotation from La Fontaine's fable, "The Wolf and the Lamb").

those who are perishing, and makes some remarks about the nature of time." [50] The moral here is quite flexible, depending on how we interpret the fable. The story as given can easily contain two completely opposite moral judgments.

Thus we see that poets and fabulists use the moral in the fable in different ways. Sometimes it is absent altogether. Sometimes we find it spelled out in words or expressed by an example from everyday life. More frequently, we find it in the general tone and atmosphere of the story, as when we find a moralizing old man who tells us that the fable has a didactic and moralistic point. But Phaedrus, who embellished his stories and transferred the moral from the fable's end to its beginning, disrupted the existing equilibrium between the story and the moral. The story itself began to produce its own requirements which led it away from the moral, and the moral, in turn, once shifted to the introduction, began to play a completely different role. Thus, in La Fontaine's and Krylov's lyrical fables, the moral is almost completely dissolved and assimilated. According to Vodovozov, their fables have become so independent of the moral implications that even children understand them in a most unmoral way, against all the rules of morality. Most of the time, however, the moral is used as a poetic technique, as a jocular introduction, an intermezzo, a finale, or, most frequently, as what is called a "literary mask." This is a particular style of narration [26], through which the author speaks not on his own behalf, but on behalf of some fictitious personage and reflects all the actions and events in a particular conventionalized manner. Pushkin narrates in Belkin's name, or acts as both author and direct acquaintance of the protagonist in *Eugene Onegin*. Gogol's stories are frequently narrated on behalf of someone else; Turgenev has an I. I., who invariably lights a pipe and begins to tell a story. The moral in the fable is just such a literary mask. The fabulist never speaks for himself but always on behalf of a moralizing, teaching, or preaching old man. Frequently the fabulist flaunts this technique and plays with it. In Krylov's fable "The Lamb," for instance, more than half of the story is taken up by a long sermon reminiscent of conventional dissertations and "narrative" introductions. Krylov introduces fictitious conversations with beautiful women and tells the fable to an imaginary girl:

My sweet Aniutochka!
For you and your gay playmates
A fable have I invented. While still a child,
Learn it by heart; it may be of some use
To you now, or at some time to come.

Hear, then, the story of the Lamb.
Put your nice dolly in the corner,
My fable won't be long.

Earlier he said:

Should we not look around? Should we not smile?
This is not what I say; but every step,
Every word must be considered, pondered,
So that malignant tongues won't have a chance to cajole.

Here the fable is narrated with the technique of the literary mask, and if we take the moral which the author draws from the fable we shall see that it does not really issue from the story itself but appears as a humorous addition. Furthermore, the fable is told in a witty and humorous style, despite its tragic content. Thus, neither the fable's content nor its moral determines the character of the generalization, which, instead, clearly reveals itself as a mask.

In another fable, Krylov says:

Here, my dear friend, a comparison and a lesson:
It's good for an adult as well as for a child.
You ask, "Is this the entire fable?" Wait,
This is but a prelude to it,
The fable's still ahead,
And I shall give the moral to it now.
I see your eyes are filled with doubt again:
First of its brevity you were afraid, and now
You dread its length.
Well now, my friend, be patient!
My dread is just like yours.
But what can I do? I am not growing younger:
The autumn weather brings us fog and rain,
And man gets wordy as he's growing older.

Again the play with the literary technique, an obvious hint that the fable is one of a well-known literary convention of style, tone, approach, etc. According to Lessing, the final element in the composition of a fable (or, more precisely, the property of its story) requires that the story be a unique case and not a general or generalized one. Here, too, as in the preceding cases, we are faced with the duality of the subject under discussion. We get a completely different interpretation, depending on whether we take a poetic or a prosaic approach.

Both Lessing and Potebnia require that the story in the fable always refer to a particular and unique case. "Take the fable of Nathan. Notice that Nathan says, 'A person.' Why not 'some people' or 'everybody'? If he really couldn't say this because of the special characteristic of the fable, the image or the story in the fable must be unique." [51]

Potebnia admits that he has some difficulty in explaining this requirement because "here we leave the area of poetry and deal with works which are called prose. . . ." [52] He therefore holds that this requirement is a part of our logical thought, inasmuch as any generalization leads to particulars inherent in this one generalization, but not to particulars belonging to another one. Lessing has no better explanation. According to him, Aristotle's famous example of the election of a magistrate carried out in the same way as the appointment of a helmsman by a ship owner, according to his own choice, differs from a fable only in that in the case of the magistrate we are dealing with the possibility, and in the case of the ship owner with reality. "This is the point. The unique case of which a fable consists must be real. Were I to be satisfied only by a possibility, this would be an example, a parabole." [53] Consequently, a fable must be narrated as if it were a particular, unique case. "A fable requires a case that has actually happened, because we can then determine more readily the reasons for reactions and because reality gives a livelier, more vivid proof than speculation." [54] It is obvious that this statement has no foundation. There is no fundamental difference here between a unique and a general case, and any general scientifically based position or opinion narrated as a fable can be used as a basis for a given moral position. It is equally difficult to see why reality must necessarily underlie a fable, and to ascertain what kind of reality must be involved. There are, in fact, many cases in which the fable creates its own reality, and frequently refers to "what is told in a fable." Generally speaking, a fable describes actual happenings as realistically as any other literary genre:

A river, I forget its name,
Gave shelter to the fishermen,
Those villains of the ocean's realm.

Frequently the author refers to the fantastic aspect of the event he is about to tell the reader, and contrasts it with reality:

That for the powerful the weakling is always wrong,
Is shown to us by History in thousands of examples.
But History is not narrated here:
Here we report what fables tell us.

Here we have a contrast between fabular history and actual history. Although both Lessing and Potebnia correctly assume that a fable always has to deal with a unique case and that, in addition, that case has to be told as if it were real, they are unable to provide a satisfactory explanation for this rule. Let us take as an example a fable attributed to Aesop: "It is said that monkeys give birth to two little ones. The mothers adore one and hate the other. They smother and pet and choke the loved ones in their hairy arms, so that only the hated ones live to grow up." For this realistic account to become a fable, we would have to narrate it thus: A monkey once gave birth to two little monkeys. She loved one, and hated the other, and so on. Why does this manipulation change the story into a fable, and what do we add to the story to change it into a fable? According to Potebnia, "this generalization about monkeys must somehow be made to apply to each individual monkey by being told thus. Otherwise, there is no incentive for the mind to project from monkeys to something else. And this is exactly what we need in a fable." [55]

It is quite obvious that the fable of the monkey, told as a unique case, leads to an analogy with human parents who frequently adore their children and spoil them excessively.

According to Lessing, the transformation of a generality into a particular case makes a parabole into a fable, because this transformation makes the story clearer and more precise. Potebnia holds, however that this transformation also involves logic. In the case of lyrical fables, however, it gives the poetic story a completely different direction, changes the focal point of the reader's attention, and provides him with the protection against irritating realities which is so necessary for any true aesthetic reaction. When I am told the general story of the monkeys, my mind reverts quite naturally to reality, and to wondering whether or not the story is true. I process and evaluate it according to an intellectual technique which I always use to acquaint myself with a new idea. But the story about one single monkey works in a different way. I perceive it in a different fashion, immediately isolate this case from everything else, and relate to the case in such a way as to make an aesthetic reaction possible. We have seen that a lyrical story generally tries to emphasize the body and form of a fable at the expense of its soul (as stated by La Fontaine). Consequently such a narration emphasizes the authenticity and tangibility of the event by which it acquires its affective quality for us. However, this authenticity and tangibility of a story must not be confused with reality, as usually understood. We are dealing here with a special, strictly conventional reality or, to put it paradoxically, a voluntary state of hallucination into which the reader chooses to place himself.

NOTES

1. A. A. Potebnia, *Iz lektsii po teorii slovestnosti. Basnia, Poslovitsa. Pogovorka* (*Lectures on the Theory of Literature, The Fable, The Proverb, The Saying*), Kharkov, 1894, p. 12.

2. *Ibid.*, p. 73.

3. *Ibid.*, p. 11.

4. V. Shklovskii, "Art as Technique," *Poetika* (*Poetics*), a collection on the theory of poetic language 3: 106, 1919.

5. V. Shklovskii, "Potebnia," *Poetika* (*Poetics*), a collection on the theory of poetic language 3: 5–6, 1919.

6. B. Tomashevskii, *Teoriia Literatury* (*Poetika*) (*Theory of Literature: Poetics*), Leningrad: GIZ, 1925, p. 195.

7. R. Haman, "Aesthetics," *Problemy estetiki* (*Problems of Aesthetics*), Moscow, 1913, pp. 80–81.

8. I. Eichenwald, *Siluet russkikh pisatelei* (*Portraits of Russian Writers*), no. 1, Moscow: Nauchnoe slovo. 1908, p. 7.

9. G. E. Lessing, *Gesammelte Werke,* edited by Paul Rilla, vol. IV, Berlin, 1955, pp. 73–74.

10. A. A. Potebnia, *Lectures on the Theory of Literature,* p. 4.

11. *Ibid.*, pp. 25–26.

12. G. E. Lessing, *Gesammelte Werke,* vol. IV, p. 16.

13. *Ibid.*, p. 18.

14. A. A. Potebnia, *Lectures on the Theory of Literature,* pp. 9–11.

15. *Ibid.*, p. 12.

16. G. E. Lessing, *Gesammelte Werke,* vol. VI, pp. 77–78.

17. A. A. Potebnia, *Lectures on the Theory of Literature,* pp. 34–35.

18. *Ibid.*, p. 47.

19. *Ibid.*, p. 54.

20. G. E. Lessing, *Gesammelte Werke,* vol. VI, p. 48.

21. *Ibid.*, p. 50.

22. *Ibid.*, pp. 52–53.

23. *Ibid.*, p. 50.

24. *Ibid.*, p. 74.

25. A. A. Potebnia, *Lectures on the Theory of Literature,* pp. 26–27.

26. G. E. Lessing, *Gesammelte Werke,* vol. VI, p. 55.

27. A. A. Potebnia, *Lectures on the Theory of Literature,* pp. 22–24.

28. *Ibid.*, pp. 24–25.

29. G. E. Lessing, *Gesammelte Werke,* vol. VI, p. 75.

30. *Ibid.*

31. *Ibid.*, p. 22.

32. *Ibid.*, pp. 35–36.

33. *Ibid.*, p. 70.

34. *Ibid.*, p. 70.

35. *Ibid.*, p. 72.

36. J. de La Fontaine, *Fables, précédées de la Vie d'Ésope*, Tours, 1885, pp. 12–13.

37. V. Kenevich, *Bibliograficheskie i istoricheskie primechaniia k basnyam Krylova (Bibliographical and Historical Notes on Krylov's Fables)*, St. Petersburg, 1868, pp. 265–266.

38. *Ibid.*, p. 144.

39. G. E. Lessing, *Gesammelte Werke*, vol. VI, p. 22.

40. *Ibid.*, p. 20.

41. *Ibid.*, p. 33.

42. *Ibid.*, p. 21.

43. A. A. Potebnia, *Lectures on the Theory of Literature*, p. 18.

44. *Ibid.*, p. 17.

45. *Ibid.*, p. 20.

46. *Ibid.*, p. 55.

47. *Ibid.*, p. 55.

48. *Ibid.*, p. 58.

49. V. Kenevich, *Notes on Krylov's Fables*, p. 41.

50. V. F. Odoevskii, *Russkie nochi (Russian Nights)*, Moscow: Put, 1913, pp. 41–42; translated by Olga Koshanski-Olienikov and Ralph E. Matlaw, New York: E. P. Dutton, 1965.

51. A. A. Potebnia, *Lectures on the Theory of Literature*, p. 28.

52. *Ibid.*, p. 28.

53. G. E. Lessing, *Gesammelte Werke*, vol. VI, p. 39.

54. *Ibid.*, p. 43.

55. A. A. Potebnia, *Lectures on the Theory of Literature*, p. 31.

6 THE SUBTLE POISON,
A SYNTHESIS

He poured a subtle poison on his works.

THE SOURCE OF LYRIC, EPIC, AND DRAMA IN THE FABLE. KRYLOV'S FABLES. SYNTHESIS OF THE FABLE. AFFECTIVE CONTRADICTION AS THE PSYCHOLOGICAL BASIS OF THE FABLE. CATASTROPHE OF THE FABLE.

As we examined the structural elements of the fable, we were forced to take issue with earlier theories. We tried to prove that, in its historical evolution and psychological substance, the fable is divided into two completely different genres. We also tried to show that Lessing's arguments apply only to the prosaic fable, so that his attacks on the lyrical fable merely pointed up those elementary properties of poetry acquired by the fable as a poetic genre. These are separate elements, and we demonstrated the meaning and significance of each of them. Their meaning as a whole is not really understood, nor have we been able to understand the essence of the lyrical fable. Since it cannot be derived from any single set of elements, we must now turn from analysis to synthesis and study a few fables, and then we may be able to explain the meaning and significance of their individual parts. We shall deal with the same elements, but the meaning and significance of each will be determined by the over-all structure of the fable. We have chosen to devote the present chapter to the study of Krylov's fables [27].

THE CROW AND THE FOX

Vodovozov[1] points out that children usually cannot agree with the moral of this fable:

How often has the World been told
That flattery is vile and evil!
To no avail.
The adulator always finds
A cozy corner in man's heart.

Indeed, this moral, which comes to us from Aesop, Phaedrus, and La Fontaine does not fit the story in Krylov's fable. Surprisingly enough, according to some sources Krylov likened himself to the fox in the fable because of his relationship with Count Khvostov. He is said to have listened patiently to the Count's poems, praised them, and then asked the delighted Count to lend him some money.[2] Whether this anecdote is true is not important, but it is important that it is possible. For it is unlikely that in the fable the fox's action is vile and evil. If it were so, no one would expect Krylov to liken himself to the fox. Indeed the fox's adulation is extremely light and witty while the derision and scorn of the crow could not be more frank or biting. The crow is depicted as an utter fool, so that the reader, contrary to the fable's moral, is bound to believe that flattery is anything but vile. He is bound to feel that the crow fully deserves his punishment, and that the fox has taught it a very pertinent lesson. Such a change, of course, is a result of the lyrical narration. Our feelings would be completely different if the same story were told in prose, according to Lessing's prescription, without the words of adulation used by the fox, without the remark that the crow nearly choked from joy as he listened to the fox, and so on. The graphic description of the encounter, the characters of the participants, all that Lessing and Potebnia rejected in the fable—these are the mechanisms which induce us to perceive and feel the poetic atmosphere created by each word, verse, and rhyme. In Sumarokov's Russian version of this famous fable, the slight change from the raven of ancient times to the crow has contributed to a complete change in the style of the fable, but it is unlikely that a change in gender brought about any substantial change in the individual animal's character.* Our feeling is polarized between the two contrasting directions in which the author develops the story. We are immediately influenced by the statement that flattery is vile and

---

* In Russian, raven is a masculine noun and crow, feminine; hence the implication that one is a male bird and the other a female. *Translator's note.*

evil, and we expect to see in the fox the quintessence of an adulator. We know that adulation comes from those who are weak, those who are vanquished, or those who are begging. But our feeling is thrown in an opposite direction, because the fox is not adulating but scoffing, ridiculing, and deriding the crow. The fox is the master of the situation at all times, and each word he utters has for us a double meaning of adulation and mockery:

My dear, how beautiful you are!
And what a neck, what eyes! . . .
What feathers! What a beak! . . .

The story of the fable moves continually between these two extremes and keeps our interest alive. This duality makes the fable attractive, charming, and witty. All the other poetic devices, images, and choices of words, for example, are an essential part of the fable's over-all effect. Thus, Sumarokov's rewording of the fox's speech[3] misses the point:

A parrot is nothing compared to you, my dear;
Your feathers are a thousand times more beautiful than the
peacock's. . . .

The arrangement of the words, the description of the positions of the characters, their tone of voice, and so forth, emphasize this fundamental aim of the fable. With this aim in mind Krylov boldly eliminates the concluding part of the fable, when the fox says as he leaves, "Oh if you also had a mind, Crow." With this statement the struggle between the reader's two opposing feelings ends, and the fable loses its wittiness and becomes flat and trite. La Fontaine's fable ends like this, with the fox running away and at the same time deriding the crow, saying that he is a fool to believe adulators. The crow swears that he will never again listen to, or believe, any flattery. Here, again, one of the two feelings prevails, becomes too obvious, and causes the fable to miss its mark.

La Fontaine also described the fox's flattery in a manner different from Krylov's: "How pretty you are! How beautiful you seem to me!" And the fox's speech is introduced by La Fontaine thus: *". . . lui tint à peu près ce langage"* (he then held approximately the following speech.) This deprives the fable of the "counterfeeling" effect, so that it is completely lost as a work of poetry.

THE WOLF AND THE LAMB

We mentioned earlier that Krylov begins this fable by juxtaposing its story with the real story; so that his moral disagrees with the moral in the first verse, "For the strong, the weak are always wrong."

We also quoted Lessing who said that with such a moral the essential part of the story, the accusation of the wolf, becomes irrelevant.

This fable, too, runs in two different directions. If the purpose of the story were to show that the strong and the powerful frequently oppress the weak, it would suffice to tell how the wolf tore the lamb to pieces. Apparently, however, the whole point of the story is in those false accusations moved by the wolf against the lamb. Thus, the action in the fable moves continually on two levels. One is the "juridical oppression," and there, the odds are obviously in favor of the lamb. Every new accusation of the wolf is promptly and successfully countered. Finally, when the lamb reaches the apex of his juridical position and clears himself of all accusations, the wolf has no further arguments. He is defeated, and the lamb triumphs.

But the struggle between the two also evolves on another level. We remember that the wolf wants to devour the lamb, and we realize that the accusations are but a pretext. Now the game goes the other way. The wolf steps up his verbal attacks, but with each reply, the lamb, in justifying his position, moves closer to his doom. At the point of culmination the wolf runs out of arguments, both trends join, and victory on one level results in defeat on the other. In this carefully devised system, feelings are evoked on one level which are diametrically opposed to those evoked on the other. The fable seems to tease our emotions. With each new justification of the lamb we hope that his fate will be averted, while in reality he comes ever closer to his death. We realize, recognize, and feel the contradiction, and the technique of the fable reveals itself in the final combination of these contrasting emotions. When the lamb has completely demolished the arguments of the wolf, when reason tells us that he is finally safe, then fate strikes inexorably. All the devices used by the author prove this point. How politely, for instance, the lamb addresses the wolf:

"With the permission of Thy Majesty, oh Wolf,
May I report that by the brook downstream
Some hundred steps or more below Thy Highness I quench my thirst;
Thus Thy anger would appear to be in vain . . ."

The lamb's self-effacing attitude and the wolf's arrogant power are eloquently described. With every new argument the wolf becomes increasingly furious, and the lamb more dignified. The drama stirs conflicting emotions in us. It either rushes toward its inevitable end or seems to pause with hope, thus playing with these contradictory feelings.

THE TITMOUSE

This story is based on the fable of the ruff which Potebnia mentioned. He refers to the contradictions inasmuch as they involve two opposing concepts: weak people should not fight the elements, and weak people may sometimes defeat the elements. Kirpichnikov also compared the two fables.[4] A trace of this contradiction can be found in Krylov's fable as well, so much so that critics could easily tear it apart for its improbable and absurd paradoxicality. The whole fable is in disagreement with the moral given at the end:

Here we can draw the following conclusion,
And say without involving any person:
A deed should not be praised
Until it's done and finished.

But this moral does not at all follow from the story. The titmouse started an operation which it didn't know how to begin, much less finish. The purpose of the story (about the titmouse who wants to burn up the ocean) is to show the impossibility of the grandiose and extravagant enterprise on which it has embarked, not to blame the bird for bragging before it has completed the job. This is clear from the following verses which were deleted from the final version:

How to construe this fable?
It might be better not to try
A job beyond our strength . . .

The story itself shows that this task is impossible, and the point of the fable is that, while this whole endeavor is described in vivid and extremely realistic terms, the reader is constantly told of its impossibility. The phrase "to burn up the ocean" reveals this deep contradiction. But despite the apparent nonsense Krylov goes ahead, develops the subject, and forces the reader to experience it emotionally as if it were real and to expect the miracle. Here is how Krylov describes the behavior of animals which apparently have no connection with the fable:

The birds flew here in flocks;
Out of the forest came the animals to watch
How all the oceans would be burnt and how the flames would rise.
The word was passed around, and rumor has it
That some impatient party-goers
Were 'mongst the first to appear along the shores,
With drooling mouths and greedy eyes, to taste

A fish broth, rich and savory,
So palatable and delicious as they had ne'er yet sampled.
And there they are, in crowds and herds they stand,
Or sit, or lie, in silence, looking
At the ocean and awaiting the miraculous event.
From time to time you hear a whisper:
"Now it will burn! It is about to boil!"
Far from it though, the ocean does not burn;
Nor does it boil; not even that. . . .

Krylov describes all this nonsense as vividly and realistically as he
would a perfectly commonplace event. The event itself and its description are in obvious contradiction with each other. They stir in us contrasting and contradictory emotions which lead to a surprising result.
Almost imperceptibly, in a way of which we are not quite conscious, the
weight of our mockery and derision is led away from the titmouse and
falls on—whom? Of course, the animals who whispered to one another,
"The ocean is about to burn. It is already boiling." In fact, in the concluding verses the author states quite earnestly:

The titmouse stirred up a commotion,
But never got to burn the ocean.

Krylov described this absurd endeavor so seriously and so realistically
that he felt it necessary to explain that it was doomed to failure. The
subject of his fable is, of course, the "Pompous and Exalted Enterprises," not the modest corollary, the injunction not to brag about deeds
before they have been accomplished. . . .

THE TWO DOVES

This fable combines various styles and genres in one, and it is one
of the few that show some sympathy for their characters. Instead of
gloating with malicious joy at the moral conclusions, this fable bases its
teaching on such sentimental feelings as sympathy, pity, and grief. The
author wants the reader to be sympathetic to the adventures of the male
dove; for, strictly speaking, this is the only love story ever told us in a
fable. It is narrated in the style of a sentimental novel or short story,
dealing with the parting of two lovers:

Wait till the spring before you fly away so far,
Then I shan't hold you back, I promise.
Right now the feed is poor and scarce, and . . .
Hark! Do you not hear the raven's caw
Foreboding evil and calamity?

According to some critics and scholars, La Fontaine took this fable from an ancient tale where a vizier tells the story to his king who is about to take off in search of treasures revealed to him in a dream. This explains the romantic and sentimental basis of the fable and also shows how the seed of the sentimental novel begins to sprout from this fable. Here are the first verses:

Where you see one, the other is not far.
The joys, the sorrows, all these shared in full.
Time flew by fast, they did not even notice.
Now they were sad, now wistful, never bored.
Why run away, why separate?
Why leave one's love, one's sweetheart?

This looks like the beginning of a sentimental novel in verse. Zhukovskii points out that these verses, "are so charming because they are simple and express the tenderest feeling and emotions with ingenuity." [5]

The story has nothing of a fable; Zhukovskii quotes the verse, "Below him, like an ocean, the steppe was surging," as an example of a graphic description of a storm, a description which, from Lessing's point of view, would be out of place, unnecessary, and detrimental in a fable.

THE GRASSHOPPER AND THE ANT

We have already mentioned Vodovozov who pointed out that children reading this fable feel that the ant's moral is hard, tough, and unattractive; they are on the side of the grasshopper, who lived a gay and gracious life during the summer, and reject the ant who is repulsive and tiresome. It may very well be that the children's evaluation of the fable is not so wrong after all. In fact, if the deeper meaning and significance of the fable is to be sought in the ant's moral, why does Krylov devote so much effort and skill to the description of the grasshopper's life, rather than the ordered and well-organized life of the wise ant? A child's emotion may be a response to the composition of the fable when he sees the hero of the story as the grasshopper, not the ant. It is significant, if not convincing, that Krylov, who hardly ever deviated from the iambus, suddenly switches to the trochee, which of course rhythmically symbolizes the grasshopper and not the ant. "Thanks to the trochee, said K. Grigoriev, the verses seem to bounce around and brilliantly describe the leaping grasshopper." [6] Once again the power and impact of the fable lies in the contrast caused by the opposing images of the thoughtless gaiety of the grasshopper's life in the summer, and those of the troubles ahead. In this fable, also, the action runs on two different levels: the grasshopper shows us alternately one face and then the other. Grief and worry switch easily to graceful playfulness, and the antithesis on which the fable is based evolves in full. As soon as one image is developed, the one opposing it appears as well. The ant's questions, brought about by the present predicament, are immediately answered by the contrasting and enthusiastic accounts of the grasshopper. The ant is needed in the story to push the contrast to its apex and then reverse it with subtle and poignant ambiguity.

"So that you . . ." (the ant prepares to surprise the grasshopper)
"Oh with joy I sang,
I sang all summer long" (the grasshopper answers but out of context and again mentions the summer)
"Is that so? You sang?
Well then, go and dance, now!"

The ambiguity culminates in the phrase "Go and dance" which combines both of the levels on which the story evolved. As a follow-up of the question "You sang?" it belongs to one level and therefore has the obvious meaning; on the other hand, it also implies death, and thus reveals the other plane, that of final disaster. Both levels are thus brilliantly combined in one phrase which means simultaneously "die" and "have a good time," and this is obviously the essence of the fable.

THE ASS AND THE NIGHTINGALE

Krylov's description of the song of the nightingale in this fable is so precise, picturesque, and beautiful that many critics have taken it as a model description and considered it superior to anything that was written on the subject in all Russian literature up to his time. According to Potebnia this fable is the best example of the techniques used by the so-called new school of La Fontaine and Krylov: the detailed description of the characters, actions, events, and so forth. All this is the essence of the poetic fable, but as far as Potebnia is concerned, it is wrong. "Such flights of fantasy," says Lobanov, "occur in the minds of people like Krylov. Total charm and fascination, nothing to be added; but our poet turns out to be a painter." [7] It is obvious that these descriptions had to push the moral of this fable into the background, cunningly disguised in the traditional interpretation, according to which the sole purpose is to expose the stupidity of the ass. Why, then, such a detailed description of the song of the nightingale? Would the fable not gain in expressivity if it would say that the ass, after listening to the nightingale's song, decided that it was not good enough? Krylov, instead, finds it necessary to give a detailed description of the song of the nightingale, and almost forces us, in Zhukovskii's words, to witness the scene. He tells us not only that the nightingale sang well, but makes us feel with high-pitched emotionality how sweet the nightingale's voice was. Krylov's description of this lovely song and the sweet voice of the nightingale follows the pattern of a sentimental pastoral, with saccharine tones, words, and phrases, which lead to an outright monstrous exaggeration of the languor and bliss of the idyllic scene. When we read that the nightingale's song "made herds lie down," we cannot but marvel at the subtle poison so artfully introduced by Krylov in his description of this charming song: the trills, the passages, the jugs, and the whistles. The older critics attacked Krylov for the verses dealing with the shepherd and the shepherdess. Galakhov, for instance, wrote that with the song of the nightingale "Krylov has spoiled the whole picture and the effect produced by it." As for the verses,

Hardly breathing, the shepherd feasts his eyes,
And only now and then a fleeting smile he casts
Onto his shepherdess, enraptured
In the sweet music of the nightingale . . . ,

he says, "We may assume that the first four verses are an embellishment, although they attribute a certain mythical value to the voice of the nightingale. The last three, however, tear the reader away from the Russian milieu and, rather unpleasantly, transport him into the pastorals of Fontenelle. With this, of course, we cannot agree." [8]
Here the critic was able to discover the real significance of the whole scene. He is right when he complains about Krylov's saccharine description of the pastoral scene, and the juxtaposition of the cock and the nightingale is a discordant note that interrupts, or even disrupts, this sugary image. But it does not, of course, prove the stupidity and boorishness of the ass. Although Stoiunin upholds in the main lines the traditional interpretation of this fable, he points out with remarkable perspicacity: "The cock reveals here, without too many words, the real taste of the ass. Indeed, is there any greater contrast than the one between the song of the nightingale and the crow of the cock? This is where most of the poet's irony comes out." [9]
There is no doubt that Krylov had something greater in mind than just an exposé of the stupidity and boorishness of the ass. The whole picture in the fable changes abruptly, when with careful, cunningly chosen words, the ass mentions the cock. Stoiunin rightly says that there is no contrast greater than the songs and voices of these two birds and that

the point of the fable is made in the mere mentioning of the cock, which makes this contrast apparent. Again we find that the feeling in this fable evolves on two different levels: One involves a pastoral scene of grandiose breadth and scope. Toward the end of the fable the light changes, and with it changes the picture. It is as if we really heard the strident crowing of the cock brutally disrupting the idyllic scene. This "vulgar" level was pushed into the background only temporarily; we were prepared for it from the very beginning by certain nicknames, such as "old thing," "chief," and so forth, which are obviously quite unbecoming for a nightingale. This loud and vulgar music contrasts with the inspired and sweet song of the nightingale, which pushes it out of sight for some time. But toward the end of the fable it returns with the effect of a blast. The singing of the nightingale is exaggerated to the utmost limits of our tolerance. Equally exaggerated are the answers of the ass who does not frankly and openly admit that he does not understand this kind of singing or music. But behind the mask of understanding and appreciation (and therefore fully corroborating the pastoral level of the fable) he suddenly disrupts and destroys it on a completely different level.

So far as the symbols of the nightingale and the cock and their use in world literature are concerned, both are frequently contrasted with each other. The ass in the fable is nothing more than some sort of an official figure which, behind the mask of stupidity, must pronounce the judgment required by the author. Incidentally, the crowing of the cock is mentioned even in such stylistically elaborate pieces of prose as in the story of St. Peter's denials in the Gospel, or in scenes of such powerful tragedies as *Hamlet.* The song of the nightingale would be absurd and out of place in the Gospel scene or in *Hamlet,* whereas the crowing of the cock is quite appropriate [28], because from an emotional viewpoint it suits the tone and mood of the events, and therefore lies in their plane.

There has been a recent attempt in Russian literature to juxtapose these two symbols (the ass and the nightingale). This is Blok's poem "The Grove of Nightingales" where the bliss of love life is symbolized by the nightingale, and life and its harsh reality, by the ass. We do not intend to compare Krylov's fable with Blok's poem, but merely wish to point out that the true significance of this fable lies in the contrasting levels on which the action evolves, and in the way each level enhances the effect of the other. The more sophisticated and sweeter the chant of the nightingale, the shriller and more piercing is the crowing of the cock.

This fable, like the others, is based on antithesis, or "counterfeeling," only here its evolution and culmination take a slightly different form.

DEMIAN'S FISH SOUP

This is an example of pure comical writing in fable form. The psychological structure of this fable is the same as that of all the others. Here too the action evolves on two levels. Demian invites his neighbor, smothers him and chokes him with friendliness and hospitality, and thus becomes his torturer, as is perfectly obvious to the reader. With every plate of fish soup that Demian almost literally rams down the throat of his neighbor, the pains of the latter increase, but so does Demian's kindness and generosity. Everyone of Demian's invitations to eat more reveals some sort of hyperbolic and pathetic goodness, but it also reveals something very like a streak of cruelty. The reader, of course, is fully aware of this paradox, and this is why the fable is so comical. At the very end, when Demian flees, panic-stricken, the two contrasting levels fuse into one, and this is where we notice the psychological absurdity of the two motives which compose the fable.

TRISHKA'S OVERCOAT

Vodovozov complains about this fable, because he was unable to explain to children that the author intended to show troubled landowners and foolish farmers. For children, the hero is Trishka, an adroit, clever, and cunning tailor who continually gets into mischief but also continually finds new ways out which are both witty and clever.[10] The two levels in the fable are quite obvious, so much so that they are part of the subject. Every new patch that Trishka applies to his overcoat is also a new tear, so that the more he mends it the more it disintegrates. We witness the overcoat going through two diametrically opposed operations, which are, however, tied into a solid unity, despite the fact that their meanings are contradictory. Trishka mends the sleeves of his overcoat by cutting its tails; as he does this, we rejoice because he has such a bright idea, but at the same time we are sad because we know that there is more trouble ahead for him.

The final scene again combines the two levels of action and seemingly gets everyone's approval, despite the absurdity of the situation: "But Trishka is happy, although he wears an overcoat that is shorter than a vest." We know now that the overcoat has been finally mended, but also definitely ruined, so that both operations have been conducted to their expected conclusion.

THE FIRE AND THE DIAMOND

In this fable Krylov contrasts the sinister and harmful glow of a fire with the benign glitter of a diamond. Its significance, of course, points toward the merits of the calm and harmless gleam of the diamond. However, some commentaries on this fable contain information that might arouse a psychologist's suspicion. "It is known that Krylov was very fond of fires. This is why he describes them with particular care. He considered fires extremely entertaining spectacles. He never missed one if he could help it, and thought very fondly of them. There is no doubt," says Pletnev, "that due to this peculiar pyromaniac streak in his nature, Krylov's descriptions of fires are strikingly exact, original, and realistic." [11]

All this is true. Krylov loved fires; thus, his own passion is diametrically opposed to the meaning and moral significance he gives his fable. This alone, if nothing else, should make us suspicious. We should realize that the moral may not be quite the one expressed so cunningly, and that there may even be another moral which destroys the obvious one. The fire is described in a superb fashion, with the enthusiasm of an artist and a lover of such scenes. None of the features of that fire is belittled or destroyed by the subsequent arguments brought forth by the diamond. The fable is construed in the form of a dialogue, or even a dispute, between the fire and the diamond.

"You, with all your glitter, play, reflections,
Are a nonentity compared with me! . . ." thus quoth the fire,

And the diamond replies:

". . . The wilder, more impetuous your flames,
The closer are you to your end."

This expresses the meaning and significance not only of this fable but of any other fable in which action evolves simultaneously in two opposite directions. Figuratively speaking, the more intensely one level of the fable burns, the closer it comes to its end; at the same time, the other level approaches with glitter and reflections, and succeeds in its own right.

THE PLAGUE AMONG THE BEASTS

With this lovely fable, Krylov came close to reaching the height of epic poetry. Zhukovskii's remark about the description of the plague can be applied to the entire fable: "This is a beautiful description of pestilence . . . Krylov borrowed the art of mixing true poetic images with simple, light-hearted statements from La Fontaine.

'Death scars the plains, the woods, the mountains.
The victims of its wild ferocity are scattered everywhere . . .'

These lines could have adorned the description of an epidemic in any epic poem." [12]

The true meaning comes to us in extremely serious, almost grandiose, pictures and images. This fable is indeed a small epic poem with a slight touch of moralism at the very end:

And also among people, it is said,
The quiet ones are those who take the blame.

Of course this brief statement does not exhaust the moral significance of the fable.

The two levels on which the action in this fable evolves are both psychological and extremely complex. First we have terrifying pictures of death's wild ferocity which establish the tragic background for all further events. The beasts are frightened and make penitence. The lion sounds like a cunning and double-faced Jesuit, and, as a matter of fact, all the animals hit a note of hypocrisy in their speeches as they try to understate their sins which, nonetheless, have tremendous weight. For instance:

. . . and then, Milord!
The honor is sublime for us poor sheep
When Thou deignest to devour us . . .

Or the lion's penance:

. . . Let us make penance, friends!
Oh, I confess, as painful as it is for me,
That I was wrong!
The blameless sheep got it from me, for nothing;
And they were killed;
But then, sometimes,—who's free from sin?
The shepherd got the kill . . .

The gravity of the sins is apparent, but the lion, a true hypocrite, tries to lighten the burden of his confession. The other level of the fable reveals itself in the remarkable speech of the ox. There is nothing equal to it, in its kind, in Russian poetry:

The humble ox thus spoke,
"We, too, are sinners.
Five years ago winter was fierce,
And feed was poor and scarce.
The devil tempted me, and I succumbed to sin.
I tried, but no one lent me sustenance and so
I stole some hay from our priest's stack."

"We, too, are sinners" is in complete contrast with everything that has been said before. Grave, mortal sins were belittled in the guise of hypocritical self-defense; but here, a small, insignificant sin is presented in the pathetic guise of self-incrimination, and the reader feels that the ox has laid his soul bare before him.

Russian schoolbooks have long praised these verses as Krylov's masterpiece of onomatopoeia. Krylov, of course, had a bit more in mind. He had introduced an interesting stylistic change into La Fontaine's fable which proved that the meaning and significance of the fable lie in the contrasts between these two levels, developed in all seriousness and in an inverse proportion. In La Fontaine's fable the ox's speech is given by the ass. The ass's speech is fairly stupid and lacks the gravity and epic depth which we find in Krylov's verses, in the highly poetic images used by him, and possibly in the "we," in which the ox chooses to express himself.

Lobanov says, "In La Fontaine's fable the ass's confession is written in beautiful verses; but Krylov has substituted an ox for the ass; he is not stupid but merely a simple-minded animal. This change is all the more perfect as we hear in the ox's speech the lowing sounds which are as truly irreplaceable as are the words for their poetic meaning; this beauty, which our poet dispenses sparingly, always gives the reader the greatest delight." [13]

Here is a translation of La Fontaine's version of the ass's speech: "I remember, passing a monastery meadow I was driven by hunger, or the good opportunity, or the tender grass, and probably by some devil: I pinched a mouthful of grass from the meadow. I had no right to do this, but I have to say the truth." This demonstrates how serious and deep the change introduced by Krylov is and how much this change has affected the emotional structure of the story. It now has everything required in an epic poem, elevated language, exalted feelings and emotions, and true heroism, contrasted with something of the opposite, so that it may lead to a catastrophe. And as this catastrophe approaches, both levels meet again, as illustrated in the fable's closing words:

Sentence was passed,
And on the pyre the ox was thrown.

Thus we have the highest heroism and sacrifice on the part of the ox, and the abysmal hypocrisy of the other creatures.[14]

It is remarkable how artfully the moral contradiction is concealed. At first sight there is no contradiction. The ox pronounced his own death sentence in his speech, and the other animals merely corroborated his self-accusation. Thus, there seems to be no argument or struggle between the ox and the other beasts; but it is this apparent identity of views that conceals the contradiction in the fable. It exposes the two contrasting psychological levels: one in which the animals are motivated exclusively by their wish to live, and the other in which one animal is seized by the unexpected desire to perform a heroic deed of courage and self-sacrifice.

THE WOLF IN THE KENNEL

This is the most noteworthy of Krylov's fables. There is nothing equal to it in terms of emotion, form, or style. It has no moral and no conclusion. Its stern verses have hardly any space for jokes or jibes. A faint joke in the mouth of the huntsman acquires such a contradictory and sinister meaning that it no longer seems funny.

Here we have, strictly speaking, not a fable but a small drama. This is what Belinskii frequently called Krylov's style. In terms of its psychological meaning in this fable, we are dealing with the true seed of tragedy.

We agree with Vodovozov, who says that " 'The Wolf in the Kennel' is one of the most surprising and remarkable fables of Krylov. There are not many (if any) like it. Without fear of contradiction, we may call this fable one of the greatest works of the art of the narrative; no fabulist, in Russia or elsewhere, has ever created anything like it." [15]

Vodovozov's evaluation is correct, as is his deduction. But if we want to find out what motivated the critic to give such a high rating to this fable, we learn that Vodovozov followed more or less in the footsteps of other critics. "If you want to see the deep and extraordinary significance of Krylov's fable, you must read it along with the history of the war of 1812."

This tells the whole story. In fact, the fable has long been interpreted with reference to the historical events which it allegedly represents. Kutuzov is said to have recognized himself in the huntsman, and taking off his hat he passed his hand over his hair saying "and I, my friend, am grizzled." The wolf, of course, is Napoleon, and the entire situation described in the fable supposedly represents the predicament in which he found himself after his victory at Borodino.

We will not go into the complicated problem of determining whether or not this speculation is true, and if true, to what extent the fable depends upon the historical facts said to be described in it. All we will say is that no historical event or motive will explain anything in the fable. A fable created for any reason or purpose follows its own rules and is governed by its own requirements; and these rules and requirements can never be explained by a mirror image of historical fact or reality. At best, history may be a starting point for our speculations, it may help us to proceed in our thinking, but it will never be anything more.

However, let us use this starting point. Comparison of the fable with the tragic situation in which Napoleon found himself after his victory at Borodino reveals its serious dual character and points to the inner contradiction of the subject on which the fable is based. We will try to determine this contradiction and to distinguish the two levels on which the action of the fable evolves, probably in opposite directions. The first thing that strikes us is the extraordinary state of alarm, close to panic, that takes up the first part of the fable and is so masterfully described by the poet. The first impression of the wolf's mistake becomes apparent by the incredible confusion in the kennel itself:

> The kennel was in an uproar as everyone
> Sensed the intruder. The dogs were howling
> And tearing at their leashes for a fight.
> "Boys, there's the thief!" the huntsman yelled
> And slammed the kennel gate.
> And then all hell broke loose—
> Some ran around with guns;
> Some ran around with clubs.
> "Light! Give us light!" they screamed.

Each word in this section shows that hell had indeed broken loose. Then this loud, yelling, bouncing, confusing noise, which comes down on the wolf like an avalanche, suddenly changes to another level: it becomes long, slow, and calm, as the wolf is described.

> There was the wolf, pressed in a corner,
> Gnashing his teeth, his hair abristle,
> Rolling his eyes as if he wanted
> To devour everyone in sight.
> He saw that this was different from
> The fields and woods. He saw
> The reckoning before him for all the sheep
> He'd killed, and he decided, cunningly,
> To start discussions . . .

The wolf, cornered, sets a specific mood. We realize that a struggle is impossible; the wolf has been brought to bay, his end is imminent and is taking place before our eyes. But instead of losing his head and panicking, he begins to speak in majestic verses, like an emperor: "And he began: 'Friends, why all this noise?' " The wolf speaks as if it were a festive occasion. He addresses the mob that is running with sticks and guns as "friends," and adds a highly ironical note with, "why all this noise?" It takes unusual poetic daring to reduce to a mere "noise" all the hellish turmoil unleashed against the wolf. It is hard to find another example of such bold artistic technique in Russian poetry. This statement completely upsets the atmosphere and mood created at the beginning; it changes the entire situation and abruptly introduces the other level, so necessary for the further development of the fable. The words uttered subsequently by the wolf develop this plane with unusual poetic courage.

". . . I came to you in peace, not for a fight.
Let us forget the past and set up a joint order!
Not only will I henceforth not attack your herds,
But I shall fight for them against all common foes.
I am prepared to swear the oath of wolves
That I . . ."

The exalted tone of the speech is in open contradiction to the actual situation. The wolf's eyes want to devour everyone, but his words promise protection. They say that he came to seek peace and graciously offer protection for the herds, but in fact he is pressed into a corner, trembling. The dogs are ready to tear him to pieces, yet his words offer them protection. We are really looking at a thief, but his words offer an oath in which he majestically expresses the word "I." The contrast and contradiction between the two levels, as expressed in the experiences and emotions of the wolf and the true and false images, continue. The huntsman interrupts the wolf and answers him in a completely different tone. The wolf uses a lofty, slightly exalted popular language (as correctly pointed out by one critic), quite unique in its way. The huntsman, in contrast, uses rather pedestrian, common language, applicable to everyday facts and events. His familiar interjections, like "neighbor," "buddy," and "guts," are of course in violent contrast to the solemnity of the wolf's words. The huntsman, however, is ready to talk; he accepts the wolf's proposition and answers him in this sense. He is willing to reach an agreement and make peace. But at the same time his words may have a completely opposite meaning. In the clever contraposition "You're grizzly, buddy; I, instead, am grizzled," the distinction between the sounded *r* and the dull *d* is particularly significant.*

---

* The Russian word for gray is *serii*, with the stem *ser*, and for gray-haired, *sedoi*, with the stem *sed*. The sounded *r* in the former gives the word, in the context of the fable, a slightly sinister sound or meaning, which can be rendered with *grizzly*. There is an obvious reference to a growl. *Translator's note*.

We have stated that the emotional "shade" of sounds depends on the context in which these sounds are used. Sounds acquire an emotional expression from the meaning of their total context. We must interpret the difference between two sounds and sense their distinction in the light of all the preceding contrasts.

The catastrophe of this fable combines the two contradictory levels, while at the same time they are revealed by the words of the huntsman:

". . . Therefore I hold the view
That peace with wolves is made in one way only—
After they have been stripped of hide and hair."
This said, a pack of wolfhounds he unleashed.

The last line tells us that the discussions have ended in an "agreement," and that the hunt has resulted in death.

This fable, like the others, develops its action on two contrasting, and frequently opposing, emotional levels. It is obvious from the very beginning that the swift attack on the wolf is equivalent to his destruction. The threat of death is present at all times throughout the entire fable. But alongside it another theme develops. It is one of discussions, where one party wants to make peace and the other is at least agreeable to talking about it. The roles of the characters are inverted. The wolf promises to give protection to the herds and is willing to take a wolf's oath. These two levels are described with the utmost poetic realism, so much so that the author gives a dual characterization to the participants. No one can say that the wolf is pitiful in his majestic and solemn speech, as he displays utter disconcern and sublime courage. It is the dogs and the huntsman who are afraid and panic-stricken, not the wolf. The traditional critique ambiguously compares the nobles and merchants of the Kaluga district with the huntsman and dogs in Krylov's fable. Vodovozov says, "Kaluga's merchants collected 150,000 rubles in two days. Kaluga's nobles put up an army of 15,000 men in a month's time." Now we understand in Krylov's words:

And then all hell broke loose—
Some ran around with guns;
Some ran around with clubs.

This is the image of a popular uprising: some take pitchforks, others axes, sticks, or scythes." And even if we should agree with the contention that artistically the fable describes Napoleon's invasion of Russia and the superb struggle of our people against him, it does not detract from the prevailing mood of heroism.

We feel that we can consider this fable a true tragedy because the

combination of the two levels of the story causes emotions characteristic
of those provoked by a tragedy. In a tragedy the two levels, or themes,
finally meet in the general catastrophe which represents simultaneously
the death or destruction of the hero and his sublime triumph. Scholars
of psychology and aesthetics say that an impression or emotion is tragic
when the moments of sublime triumph coincide with those of unavoidable destruction or death. The words of one of Schiller's tragic characters, "You are elevating my spirit, but debasing me," are applicable to
this fable. No one can say that the edge of mockery and derision is
turned against the wolf. Our feelings and emotions are organized and
directed in the opposite direction. We now can understand the words of
the critic who said that Krylov, as he leads his wolf to his death, could
easily paraphrase the text of the Gospel and Pilate's words, *Ecce homo,* as
he presented Christ to his accusers, by saying *"Ecce lupus."*

In summarizing the results of our synthetic study of the fables, we shall
proceed by the following three steps: We shall first summarize our ideas
about Krylov's poetry as a whole and determine its character and general significance. On the basis of these results we shall then state our
ideas on the nature and substance of the fable. And finally we give a
psychological analysis of our reaction to the poetic or lyrical fable, study
the general mechanism of man's psyche set in motion by the fable, and
determine the action man takes as a result of reading a fable.

In the first place we label as incorrect the ideas about Krylov and his
poetry that were mentioned earlier in this chapter. Even Krylov's opponents have to admit that his poetry has "beautiful and poetic landscapes" and an "inimitable form and brilliant humor." [16] However, our
critics are unable to understand what, exactly, these features contribute
to the fable itself (which in their opinion is small, trite, and prosaic).
Gogol claims that "Krylov's verses are resounding where his subject is
resounding. They move where his subject moves. They become stronger
and more powerful when his idea and intent are stronger and more
powerful, or else become light and irrelevant when he describes the
light and irrelevant talk of a fool." Even the most malicious, ill-intentioned critic cannot but admit that a conspicuous, if not overwhelming,
number of Krylov's verses are far from trite and vulgar. But not one of
them, ill-intentioned or not, was ever able to account for the contradiction in Krylov's poetry. They praised the exquisite lyricism of his writings, but were stunned by the prosaic matter-of-factness of his fables.
One of Krylov's biographers suspected the existence of a riddle or mystery in the writer which has not been solved to this day and is therefore
not understood. In fact, it has been proven more than once that Krylov

had a sincere, wholehearted aversion to the fable. It is also a fact that his life was the exact opposite of what could be considered the existence of a wise, well-intentioned, average person. He was an extraordinary and exceptional individual in all respects: in his passions, his torpor, his scepticism. It is therefore surprising and astonishing that he has become "everybody's grandfather," to borrow Eichenwald's description, and has conquered, if not subdued, the nursery. It is surprising and astonishing that his writings are to everyone's taste and have become the incarnation of life's wisdom. The transition from a satirical writer to a fabulist was anything but painless. Pletnev, who knew Krylov well, writes: "It may be that the narrow horizon of ideas, beyond which it is impossible to see the wide spaces at first sight, generated in him the aversion for apologetic poetry, of which he never rid himself. When he reminisces, it is interesting to hear that it was one of his predecessors, the famous fabulist Dmitriev, who was the first to push him to writing fables after he had read three La Fontaine fables which Krylov had translated during his spare moments. Krylov overcame his aversion and silenced his early passion for dramatic poetry. He began to write fables, occasionally imitating or reworking them." [17]

If we assume that Krylov's original aversion for fables and early passion for dramatic poetry were never reflected in his fables, and if we assume that the painful transition from satirical writer to fabulist left no trace in his poetry, then we must conclude that poetry and life, artistic creativity and the psyche, are two completely separate and unconnected entities or areas. Of course, both were reflected in Krylov's poetry. In fact, they are hidden in that dual meaning of his fables which we have tried to reveal and explain. There is a good psychological reason for our assumption that this double meaning overcame the narrow horizon of the prosaic fable which Krylov detested, and helped him penetrate the wide field of dramatic poetry, which was his passion and which in the end is the true essence of any poetic, or lyrical, fable. Be it as it may, we may apply to Krylov the superb line which he himself wrote in reference to writers:

He poured a subtle poison on his works.

It is this subtle poison that we have tried to uncover as the second level, or the second meaning. It is present in every fable written by Krylov, makes its sense deeper, adds wit and humor to it, and turns his stories into true works of poetry.

We do not insist, however, that this was Krylov. We lack sufficient data to corroborate this theory. But we can affirm that this is the nature of the fable. Interestingly enough, for Zhukovskii the contrast between the poetic and the prosaic fable was perfectly clear. "More likely than not, it was always the domain of orators and philosophers, rather than verse makers and poets. . . . The history of the fable is divided into three main periods. During the first period, the fable was merely an exercise in rhetoric, intended to present examples and comparisons. During the second period, it became independent and was used as one of the most effective methods for orators or philosophers to preach the message of moral truths (such are the fables known to us through Aesop, Phaedrus and, in our times, Lessing). Finally, during the third period, the fable switched from the domain of eloquence to that of poetry; that is, it acquired the form which it inherited from Horace in antiquity, and from La Fontaine and his school in our time." [18]

Zhukovskii also feels that the ancient fabulists are simple moralists rather than poets. "Once it became the domain of poets, the fable changed its form. What was then an accessory—I am speaking of action—became the main subject. . . . What do I require of a fabulist? That he capture my imagination with the accurate and precise representation of characters; that his narration force my feelings and emotions to participate in these characters' tribulations; that he completely arrest my attention, my feelings, and my emotions, and force them to act and react according to the moral properties given them; that he carry me with him on the wings of his poetry into the imaginary world created by his fantasy and make me, for a limited amount of time at least, one of the inhabitants of this world. . . ." Translating these poetic words into a simpler language, we find that the action in fables must capture the feelings and attention of the reader, that the author must force the reader to participate actively in the joys and sorrows of the grasshopper, or in the grandeur and death of the wolf. "It follows from all this that the fable . . . can be either prosaic, that is, one in which the simple, unadorned story, told in plain words, serves as a transparent cover for the moral truth; or else poetic, or lyrical, that is, one in which the plot is adorned with all the riches of poetry and in which the main purpose of the author is to appeal to the imagination and to stir feelings and emotions."

The segregation of fables into prosaic and poetic ones becomes a necessity obvious to everybody, and the rules applicable to the prosaic fable turn out to be completely different from, if not opposite to, those applicable to the poetic fable. Zhukovskii also states that the poet must "narrate the story in a poetic language, that is, express the simple story in inspired poetic terms, analogies, and images." He adds: "Find in the fable of the 'Hawks and the Doves'. . . . the description of a battle; as you read it, you can see the Romans fighting the Teutons. It is filled with poetry, and the language of the poet seems to be quite suited to the subject. Why? Because the poet's imagination resides in the event which he describes, since the poet is convinced of its importance; he does not intend to deceive us. He himself is deceived." We begin to see quite clearly how the poetic style is to be applied to the fable. When we read the description of the battle between the hawks and the doves, our feelings and emotions must be stirred just as if we were reading about a battle between the Romans and the Teutons. The fable can, and must, generate strong and compelling feelings, and the poetic skill of all writers must be directed toward this purpose. "The reader's mind must be directly involved in the action described by the poet."

If the two levels, or parallel themes, in the fable are supported and described with all the skill of poetic technique, that is, if they exist not only as a logical contradiction, but especially as an affective contradiction, the reader of the fable will experience contradictory feelings and emotions which evolve simultaneously with equal strength. For the psychologist, the praise heaped by Zhukovskii and other literary critics on Krylov's verses has but one meaning: The power and inspiration of that verse guarantee the emotion generated by the very organization of the poetic material. Zhukovskii concludes: "The very sounds are picturesque! Two long words beautifully describe stirrings in the swamp . . . in the last verse, instead, there is a beautiful and artful combination of monosyllabic words which, in their harmony, describe leaps and bounds. . . ." Here is what he says about another fable: "The verses flutter around with the fly. They are immediately followed by others, which represent exactly the opposite, the slowness of the bear; here we find long words, long phrases. . . . All these words . . . beautifully express procrastination and caution. Five long, rather heavy verses are followed by a hemistitch, 'whang a stone on the friend's forehead.' This strikes like lightning! It is truly picturesque; and how different and contradictory is the last image from the first."

It follows, therefore, that when we read a poetic fable we are not governed by the rules which Potebnia considered mandatory: "When a fable is presented to us, not concretely as I mentioned but in an abstract form, in a book, then the listener or reader must find in his own imagination a certain number of possible applications of the fable in order to understand it. Otherwise he will be unable to explain the fable either to himself or to anyone else. However, the selection of appropriate cases requires time. This is why, incidentally, Turgenev suggested that fables be read slowly. . . . The point, however, is not in the slow reading of the fable but in the proper selection of cases and their application to the fable which I have just mentioned." [19]

This is not the main point, as far as we are concerned; there is yet another. It is wrong to assume that anyone reading a fable in a book will try to remember those cases from everyday life which could be applied to the fable, or to which the fable could be applied. Anyone reading a fable is completely enthralled by what he reads. He abandons himself to the feelings and emotions stirred by the fable and will not try to remember anything else. This much we gathered from the study and analysis of each fable.

There is, therefore, no contrast or contradiction between the fable and other forms of poetry, as was claimed by Lessing and Potebnia. On the contrary, the fable is a basic, elementary form of poetry and therefore contains the seeds of lyric, epic, and drama. Some of Krylov's fables were considered short dramas by Belinskii, who correctly determined not only their dialogic style, but also their psychological essence. Other critics, including Zhukovskii, have spoken of fables as if they were small epic poems. It is a cardinal mistake to assume that a fable must be mockery, satire, or a joke. It has an infinite variety of psychological genres, and it is perfectly true that it contains the seed of all other forms of poetry. We refer here to Croce's position, according to which the problem of genre is the problem of psychology par excellence. Along with such fables as "The Cat and the Nightingale" or "The Dance of the Fishes," which are nothing but hard social or even political satires, we have discovered in Krylov the psychological seed of tragedy in "The Wolf in the Kennel," that of the heroic epic in "The Plague Among the Beasts," and that of lyricism in "The Grasshopper and the Ant." We already had occasion to mention that lyrical poems, such as Lermontov's "The Sail," "Clouds," and so forth, that is, poems dealing with inanimate objects, have evolved from the fable. Potebnia is thus right only when he compares these poems with fables; and even then he reaches the wrong conclusions.

We have thus essentially reached the same definition of the nature of the fable that we can find in an encyclopedia. The fable, according to the encyclopedia, "may be distinguished by an epic, lyrical, or satirical style." [20] This is a poor conclusion, not worth the effort. Nothing new has been added to the truth that was accessible to everyone from the very beginning. But, by comparing the fable to poetry and its general laws and by contradicting the traditional teachings developed by Lessing and Potebnia, we have managed to come to other conclusions, and we may claim that our analysis has added some new content to the old, simple truth. Here is an example. Lessing tells us of the fable of the fisherman. "The fisherman pulled his net from the sea. He had caught some large fish, while the small fish managed to escape through the meshes back into the ocean. . . . We find this story among Aesop's fables, but it is not a fable, or at best a very mediocre one. It contains no action. It is spun around one single fact which can be easily represented by a drawing; but even after I have enriched this single fact [that only the large fish remained in the net while the small ones had slipped out] with a number of other circumstances, the moral of the story will still be found in the one, original fact and not in the additional circumstances." [21]

A study of this fable, brings us to a completely different conclusion. The story is an excellent plot for a fable and can easily be developed on two levels. We expect the large fish to have a better chance of survival than the small fish who appear to be much more helpless in this precarious situation. If the course of action were developed in such a way that, by building up the helplessness of the large fish, the chances for survival of the small fish would increase simultaneously, a fairly good fable could be made. This shows that a fable can be approached from two completely different, if not opposite, psychological viewpoints.

But there is more. We are inclined to believe that, in the form given, the fable is not poetic. It will become so only if the poet will develop the contrast and contradiction comprised in it, force us to participate mentally in this process, which occurs on both levels at the same time, stir in us two stylistically opposite emotions either with verses or other stylistic devices, and then destroy them in the denouement in which both themes of the fable connect as if by short circuit.

We must now formulate the psychological generalization of our aesthetic reaction to the fable. Any fable, and our reaction to it, evolves on two levels that develop simultaneously so that they represent a unit and are tied in one single action, even though they remain dual and separate. In "The Crow and the Fox," the stronger the flattery, the more biting the mockery; adulation and mockery are comprised in the same phrase which is adulation and mockery at the same time and which combines the two contradictory meanings into one entity.

In "The Wolf and the Lamb," the more strongly the lamb proves his rights (which should protect him from destruction), the closer he comes to the final point of his death. In "The Grasshopper and the Ant," the greater the light-heartedness, the more imminent is death. The whole point of the story is in the formal relationship between the two parts of the fable: first the period of carefree singing, then trouble; first the summer, and then the winter. The fable is composed in such a way that the gay and light part is the summer: the gayer the grasshopper is at this time, the more tragic the destiny awaiting it in the winter. Every word, every sentence the grasshopper utters in his conversation with the ant develops with equal intensity on both levels of the story. The fact that he sang with inspiration all summer long shows the joy he experienced during the summer, but it also makes us aware of his imminent destruction. The same happens in "The Wolf in the Kennel," where the serious and solemn negotiations forebode a terrible disaster: when agreement has been reached, the wolf is torn to pieces. The same happens in "Trishka's Overcoat," and in all the other fables; this proves that the affective contradiction engendered by the two levels in the fable is the true psychological basis for our aesthetic reaction.

In addition to this, every fable includes a characteristic element which we have called the catastrophe, in analogy with the corresponding element in tragedies. According to the rules of the narrative, this element should be called *pointe*, or punch-line; it is usually a short sentence or phrase, the main characteristic of which is its poignancy and surprise. In terms of the rhythm of the story, the *pointe* is "the end at an unstable, fluctuating moment, as a piece of music ending with a dominant chord." [22]

The catastrophe (or *pointe*) of a fable is its concluding phase, in which the contrasts and contradictions are driven to the extreme, and the emotions that built up in the course of the fable are discharged. There occurs a short-circuiting of the two opposing currents. The contrast explodes, burns, and dissolves. We have already mentioned several of these catastrophes in different fables. At this point, the fable gathers itself together in a last, supreme effort and in one blow solves the conflict of sensations and emotions. "You are guilty," says the wolf to the lamb, "because I am hungry." This statement proves that the lamb is completely right, that his arguments have led him to a complete victory, but it also marks his final and inescapable doom. The two levels on which the fable's action moves are now completely exposed. On the one hand, the lamb will be saved if he justifies his position; he has managed to do so, the wolf has no further arguments. Therefore the lamb should be safe. On the other hand, the stronger the lamb's justifications, the closer he approaches his doom; he exposes the irrelevance and insignificance of the wolf's accusations and, at the same time, reveals the true cause of his death, which becomes unavoidable the moment the lamb has completely justified himself.

The catastrophe in "The Crow and the Fox" comes when the crow sings. This is the culminating point of adulation. But it is also the apex of mockery; the crow loses the cheese, and the fox triumphs. Flattery and mockery are short-circuited, and the finale explodes.

The same happens in "The Grasshopper and the Ant," when the concluding "go and dance" again produces a short-circuit between the bouncing gaiety and joy and the final despair. We have already mentioned that the single phrase, "go and dance," means both "have a good time," and "die." It also represents the catastrophe and the short-circuit of feelings about which we have been speaking.

Summing up, we have found that the "subtle poison" is most likely the very essence of Krylov's poetry, that the fable contains the seeds of the lyric, the epic, and the drama and that it forces us, by the strength and inspiration of its poetry, to react emotionally to its story. Finally, we have found that the affective contradiction and its solution, by means of short-circuiting contrasting sensations and emotions, represent the true nature of our psychological reaction to fables. This is the first step in our investigation. Looking ahead, we have to mention the surprising concordance between the psychological law found by us for the fable and the laws which many other investigators have already discovered for higher forms of poetry.

NOTES

1. V. Vodovozov, "The Pedagogical Significance of Krylov's Fables," *Zhurnal Ministerstva narodnogo prosveshcheniia* (*Journal of the Ministry of Education*) 12:72–73, 1862.

2. V. Kenevich, *Bibliograficheskie i istoricheskie primechaniia k basnyam Krylova* (*Bibliographical and Historical Notes on Krylov's Fables*), St. Petersburg, 1868, p. 19.

3. From *Russkaia basnia XVIII–XIX veka* (*Russian Fables of the Eighteenth and Nineteenth Centuries*), Leningrad: Sovetskii pisatel, 1949, p. 54.

4. A. I. Kirpichnikov, *Ocherki po istorii novoi russkoĭ literatury* (*Essays on the History of the New Russian Literature*), St. Petersburg, 1896, p. 194.

5. V. Kenevich, *Notes on Krylov's Fables*, p. 56.

6. N. G. Priluko-Prilutskii, ed., *I. A. Krylov. Zhizn' i tvorchestvo* (*I. A. Krylov, His Life and Works*), St. Petersburg-Warsaw: Oros, p. 13.

7. V. Kenevich, *Notes on Krylov's Fables*, p. 82.

8. *Ibid.*, p. 83.

9. N. G. Priluko-Prilutskii, *I. A. Krylov*, p. 83.

10. V. Vodovozov, *Krylov's Fables*, p. 74.

11. V. Kenevich, *Notes on Krylov's Fables*, p. 139.

12. V. A. Zhukovskii, *Works*, Moscow: Goslitizdat, 1954, p. 513.

13. V. Kenevich, *Krylov's Fables*, p. 65.

14. V. Pokrovskii, ed., *I. A. Krylov, Evo zhizn' i sochineniia* (*I. A. Krylov, His Life and Works*), 3rd ed., Moscow, 1911, p. 129. This is a collection of historical and literary articles.

15. *Ibid.*

16. I. Eichenwald, *Siluety russkikh pisatelei* (*Portraits of Russian Writers*), no. 1, Moscow: Nauchnoe slovo, 1908, pp. 6, 10.

17. V. V. Kallash, *Liricheskie stikhotvoreniia i basni Krylova* (*Lyric Poems and Fables of Krylov*), St. Petersburg: Prosveshchenie, 1905, p. XII.

18. V. A. Zhukovskii, *Works,* p. 509ff.

19. A. A. Potebnia, *Iz lektsii po teorii slovestnosti. Basnia. Poslovitsa. Pogovorka* (*Lectures on the Theory of Literature: The Fable, The Proverb, and The Saying*) Kharkov, 1894, pp. 81–82.

20. *Brockhaus and Efron Encyclopedic Dictionary,* vol. III, St. Petersburg, 1891, p. 150.

21. G. E. Lessing, *Gesammelte Werke,* vol. IV, edited by Paul Rilla, Berlin, 1955, p. 26.

22. A. A. Reformatskii, *Opyt analiza novellisticheskoĭ kompozitsiĭ* (*Essay on the Analysis of the Composition of the Novella*), Moscow, 1922, p. 11.

7 BUNIN'S "GENTLE BREATH"

"ANATOMY" AND "PHYSIOLOGY" OF THE NARRATIVE. DISPOSITION AND COMPOSITION. CHARACTERISTICS OF THE MATERIAL. THE FUNCTIONAL SIGNIFICANCE OF COMPOSITION. AUXILIARY METHODS. AFFECTIVE CONTRADICTION AND REJECTION OF THE CONTENT OF FORM.

From the fable we proceed to an analysis of the short story. In this immeasurably more complex and sophisticated art form we come across all the aspects of the composition of material; yet, at the same time, the short story is more suited to analysis than the fable.

In the past decade, the basic elements of the short story have been dealt with in morphological investigations of Western European and Russian poetry and literature [30]. The analysis of any short story deals with two fundamental concepts, which we shall call the *material* and the *form*. We already mentioned that the material is what is readily available to the poet for his story, namely the events and characters of everyday life, or the relationships between human beings—in brief, all that existed prior to the story can exist outside of it or is independent of it. The form of this work of art is the arrangement of this material in accordance with the laws of artistic construction.

We have already established that these terms must not be understood to mean the external, audible or visual, or any other sensorial form accessible to our perception. The form is not a shell which covers the substance. On the contrary, it is an active principle by which the material is processed and, occasionally, overcome in its most involved, but also most elementary, properties. In the short story or novella, form and material are usually taken from certain everyday human relationships. The event, or events, upon which a story is based, comprise the *material* of that story. When we discuss the way this material is arranged and presented to the reader and *how* the event is told, we deal with its *form.* In the existing literature there is no agreement in the matter of terminology. For Shklovskii and Tomashevskii, the plot is the material of the story, the events from everyday life upon which it is based; the subject, for them, is the formal treatment of the story. Others, such as Petrovskii, use these terms in the opposite sense: the subject is the event that triggers the story, and the plot is the artistic treatment of that event. "I am inclined to use the term 'subject' to indicate the material of a work of art. The subject is a system of events, or actions (or else a single event, simple or complex in composition) in a form which is not the result of the artist's individual creative or poetic work. The treated subject, in my opinion, should be called the 'plot.' " [1]

However we understand them, it is necessary to distinguish between these two concepts. We shall use the terminology of the formalists, who call the plot, in accordance with literary tradition, the material upon which the work of art is based. The relationship between material and form in the story is, of course, identical to that between the plot and the subject. If we want to know the direction in which the poet's work evolves, we must investigate the techniques he uses: how he treats the material in the course of the story and how he transforms it into the poetic subject. The plot (material) of a story is in the same relationship to the narrative of which it is a part as individual words to a line of verse, the scale to music, colors to painting. The subject (form) is in the same relationship to the narrative as verses to poetry, a melody to music, a picture to the art of painting. In other words, we are dealing with the relationships between individual portions of the material, which means that the subject is in the same relation to the plot in a narrative as the form to its material.

This concept evolved with great difficulty, because the extraordinary rule of art, according to which authors usually treat their material in a fashion concealed from the reader, long misled the theorists when they tried to distinguish between these two aspects of the narrative in order to set up rules for its creation and perception. Writers have long known that the arrangement of the events in a story, the author's method of introducing the reader to the plot, and the composition of the literary work are extremely important tasks in the art of writing. Composition has always been the subject of particular conscious and subconscious care on the part of the poet or novelist. But only in the novella, which evolved from the narrative, did composition achieve its highest development. The novella can be regarded as a pure form of writing, whose main purpose is the formal treatment of a plot and its transformation into a poetic subject. There are a number of sophisticated and complex forms of construction and treatment of the plot. Some writers were quite aware of the role and significance of the techniques they used. The height of this awareness was achieved by Sterne who, as Shklovskii showed, explained the technique of subject composition, and in his *Tristram Shandy* gave five curves for the course of the novel's plot.[2]

"I am now beginning to get fairly into my work; and . . . make no doubt but that I shall be able to go on with my uncle Toby's story and my own in a tolerable straight line.

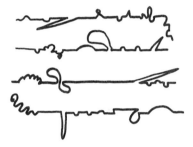

Now, these were the four lines [31] I moved in through my first, second, third, and fourth volumes.—In the fifth volume I have been very good, —the precise line I have described in it being this:

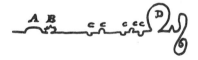

By which it appears that except at the curve, marked *A,* where I took a trip to Navarre,—and the indented curve *B,* which is the short airing when I was there with the Lady Baussiere and her page,—I have not taken the least frisk of a digression, till John de la Casse's devils led me around you see marked *D.*—for as *c c c c c* they are nothing but parentheses, and the common ins and outs incident to the lives of the greatest ministers of state; and when compared with what men have done,—or with my own transgressions as the letters, *A B D*—they vanish into nothing."

If we take any event of life in a chronological succession, we can represent it as a straight line, where every successive moment replaces the preceding one and is in turn superceded by the next. In exactly the same way we can graphically represent the sequence of sounds in a scale, or the syntactic distribution of words in an average phrase, and so on. In other words, the evolution and development of a material with natural properties can be graphically represented as a straight liine. But the artificial (or artistic) distribution of words which determines a verse [32] changes the normal order of their syntactic arrangement. The artificial (or artistic) distribution of sounds which transforms a simple series of sounds into a melody, again changes their order in a scale. The artificial (or artistic) arrangements of events determines an artistic subject and disrupts chronological succession. This artistic distribution, or arrangement, can be graphically represented as a curve traced around a straight line. Thus, we will have curves for verses, melody, or plot. All these curves illustrate the artistic form. The curves which describe the various volumes of Sterne's novel make this point very well.

Before we proceed, we must answer a question that is quite clear when we talk about such well-known artistic forms as melody and verse, but becomes quite intricate when we talk about the narrative. It can be formulated as follows: Why does the artist deviate from the chronological succession of the events in his story, why does he deviate from the rectilinear progression of his story, and prefer to describe a curve rather than move along the shortest distance between two points? Such a preference might easily be taken for a writer's whim, devoid of any rational foresight. If we take the traditional approach to the composition subject, we see that these curves were always wrongly interpreted by the critics. In Russian literature, for instance, the opinion long prevailed that *Eugene Onegin* was an epic poem, adorned with a large number of lyrical deviations. These were regarded as having been separated by the author from the main subject of the story. They were understood to be lyrics or lyrical fragments that had sneaked into the body of the poem without any organic connection to its fabric. These lyrics were believed to have an independent existence and to play the role of an epic interlude, a sort of lyrical entr'acte between the two acts of the story. This view is of course completely wrong. It neglects the purely epic role played by these "digressions." If we take a close look at the economy of the whole story of *Eugene Onegin*, we find that these digressions are a very important technique used by the poet in his development and treatment of the subject. It is just as absurd to consider these devices as digressions as it is to regard as digressions the ups and downs of a melody which, after all, are deviations from the normal course of a scale. Similarly, these so-called digressions in *Eugene Onegin* form the very essence and basic stylistic technique of this work of art. They are the melody of its subject. "One witty painter [Vladimir Miklashevskii]," says Shklovskii, "suggested drawing the main digressions (for instance, as legs); from a compositional viewpoint this would be quite correct." [3] Let us now explain the significance of a subject curve. We know that the dynamic ratio between sounds is the basis of a melody. A verse is not only the sum total of the sounds composing it, but also their dynamic sequence, their specific relationship to one another. Two sounds, or two words, in a specific order, form a definite relation which can be determined by the order of succession of elements. Similarly, two events, or actions, when put together, yield a certain new dynamic relation that is entirely determined by the order and disposition (arrangement) of these events. For instance, the sounds a, b, and c, or the words a, b, and c, or the events a, b, and c, totally change their significance and emotional meaning if we present them in a different order, say, b, c, and a; or b, a, and c; etc. Let us imagine that we are talking about a threat, then about the execution of such a threat, which could be a murder. If we acquaint the reader beforehand with the fact that the protagonist is in danger but keep him in the dark concerning the actual execution of the threat and only after a certain amount of suspense tell him about the killing, we will have achieved one kind of effect. A totally different effect is achieved if we begin our story with the discovery of the corpse, and then, in reverse chronological order tell the reader of the murder and the threat. Disposition and arrangement of events in a story, the combination of phrases and sentences, of concepts, ideas, images and actions is governed by the same rules of artistic association as are the juxtapositions of sounds in a melody, or those of words in a poem.

One last remark on the nature of the method before proceeding with the analysis of the novella: It is useful to distinguish (as many authors do) the static scheme of the construction of a narrative, which we may call its anatomy, from the dynamic scheme, which we may call its physiology. We have already said that every story has a specific structure that differs from the structure of the material upon which it is based. It is also obvious that every poetic technique of treating the material is purposeful; it is introduced with some goal or other, and it governs some specific function of the story. By studying the teleology of the technique (the function of each stylistic element, the purposeful direction, the teleologic significance of each component) we shall understand the very essence of the story and witness how a lifeless construction is transformed into a living organism.

We have selected for this purpose Bunin's short story "Gentle Breath," the complete text of which is reproduced starting on page 161. It is convenient for our analysis for many reasons. First, it can be regarded as a typical specimen of the classic as well as modern short story, which clearly reveals the fundamental stylistic elements characteristic of this genre. Artistically, it is most likely one of the best short stories ever written, and by general consensus, it stands as a true model of its genre. Finally, it has not fallen prey to commonplace and vulgar interpretation, the prejudices of which have to be dealt with every time one studies a familiar text, such as Krylov's fables or Shakespeare's tragedies. It is essential to our study to include a work of art that generates an impression which is in no way predetermined by established judgments. We wanted to find a literary stimulant that would be completely fresh and new, unspoiled, not yet reduced to triteness, and therefore unlikely to provoke a preconditioned aesthetic reaction in us.

Now let us take a look at the story.

We begin the analysis by establishing the melodic curve which we find implemented by the words of the text. To this end, it is best to compare the actual events upon which the story is based (events that are certainly possible and probably modeled on real events), which make up its material of the story, with the artistic form into which this material has been molded. This is a method followed by critics of verse when they try to establish the rules of rhythm [33] that govern certain word arrangements. We shall attempt the same with this story. The material on which it is based is the following: Olia Meshcherskaia, a highschool girl, lives a life which differs in nothing from the usual life of pretty, well-to-do girls living in provincial Russian towns. Then something happens. She has a love affair with Maliutin, a much older landowner and friend of her father's, and then a liaison with a Cossack officer whom she promises to wed. Thus, she "is led astray." The Cossack officer, betrayed yet still in love with Olia, shoots her in a crowded railway station. Olia Meshcherskaia's schoolteacher chooses the deceased as the subject of an almost passionate worship and frequently visits her grave. This is the entire *content* of the story. Let us now list all the events in the story in the chronological order in which they actually occurred, or might have occurred, in actual life. These events must be divided into two groups, since one is connected with Olia's life and the other with the story of her schoolteacher:

Disposition Scheme

I. Olia Meshcherskaia
  A. Childhood
  B. Adolescence
  C. Episode with Shenshin
  D. Conversation about gentle breath
  E. Arrival of Maliutin
  F. Liaison with Maliutin
  G. Writing in the diary
  H. Last of the winter
  I. Episode with the officer
  J. Conversation with the school principal
  K. Murder
  L. Funeral
  M. Subsequent investigation
  N. The grave
II. The schoolteacher
  a. Schoolteaching
  b. Daydreams about brother
  c. Daydreams about great works
  d. Conversation about gentle breath
  e. Daydreams about Olia
  f. Walks to the cemetery
  g. At the grave

Composition Scheme

N. The grave
A. Childhood
B. Adolescence
C. Episode with Shenshin
H. Last of the winter
J. Conversation with the principal
K. Murder
I. Episode with the officer
M. Subsequent investigation
G. Writing in the diary
E. Arrival of Maliutin
F. Liaison with Maliutin
f. Walks to the cemetery
g. At the grave
a. Schoolteaching
b. Daydreams about brother
c. Daydreams about great works
e. Daydreams about Olia
d. Conversation about gentle breath

This chronological enumeration is known as the *disposition* of the story, i.e., the natural sequence of events, which we may also call the graphic straight line. If we list the order in which the events actually occur in the story *as written*, we have the *composition* rather than the disposition of the material. We notice immediately that the events in the disposition list follow the order of the alphabet, the chronological order, while in the composition list the chronological sequence is completely disrupted. The letters are rearranged in a series without any apparent order. This new series contains all the events we labeled alphabetically. If we denote the progress of the story by two parallel lines, plotting on one of them the individual events, in succession, of Olia's story, and on the other the events in the schoolteacher's story we shall have two straight lines symbolizing the entire disposition of our story.

We will now show what the author has done with this material in order to give it an artistic form. To show this graphically in the composition diagram, we connect the points on these lines in the order in which they occur in the narrative. The bottom curve represents transition to chronologically earlier events (when the author moves backward) and the top curves represent transition to chronologically advanced events (when the author leaps forward). Thus we get two curves. The confused diagram reveals, at first glance, that the events do not evolve in a straight line [34] as would happen in real life, but in leaps and bounds. The story quite unexpectedly drifts from one event to another, connecting the most remote events of the chronologically arranged material. In other words, the curve represents the analysis of the plot and the subject of the story quite faithfully. Referring to the composition diagram, and following the order of succession of the individual elements, we see that our curve, from beginning to end, shows the action of the story as written. This is the "melody." Instead of narrating the content in chronological order, (how Olia Meshcherskaia was a schoolgirl, how she grew up, how she turned into a beautiful woman, how her moral degradation occurred, how her liaison with the officer took place, how she was murdered, how she was buried, and what her grave looked like), the author begins with the description of her grave, switches to her early childhood, suddenly talks about her last winter, describes the conversation she had with her school principal concerning her moral degradation the previous summer. Then he speaks of her death and, at the very end of the story, of an apparently irrelevant episode in her school life which goes back to a more remote past. Our curve reflects this progression or, as some might call it, this deviation from the straight path. The diagrams show what we earlier called the static structure, or "anatomy," of the story. Now we must establish its dynamic composition, or "physiology." We have to find out *why* the author treated the material as he did, for what obscure reason he begins his story at the end, and why he ends it as he does.

In other words, to determine the function of this rearrangement we must find the significance and purpose of the apparently meaningless, confused curve which symbolizes the composition of the story. To do this we must turn from analysis to synthesis to try to gain an understanding of the physiology of the story from its purpose and dynamics.

If we take a look at the content of the story, its material taken per se and the system of events in it, we find that it all comes under the category "troubles of life." There is not a single bright spot in the entire story. There is nothing but the insignificant and rather senseless life of a schoolgirl in a provincial Russian town. It is a life that springs from obviously diseased roots; its outcome is inevitably unhealthy and sterile. Could it be that this troubled life has been idealized, or somewhat adorned, in the story? Could it be that its darker aspects have been made somewhat lighter so that it may appear to be as a "pearl of creation," or could it be that the author represents them in a rosy light? Could it be that the author himself grew up in similar circumstances, and finds a certain charm in these events? Could it be that our evaluation differs from the one given these events by the author?

As we analyze the story, we find that none of these conjectures is justified. Not only does the author not attempt to conceal the gloom of life, he exposes it whenever he can, describes it with graphic precision, lets our sensations and emotions almost touch these events, and, figuratively, allows us to put our hand right into life's festering sores. He underscores the senseless emptiness of this life. This is what he says of the girl: ". . . her fame at school spread almost imperceptibly, and rumors began to circulate that she was frivolous, that she could not live without admirers, that the schoolboy Shenshin had lost his head over her, that she was also in love with him but was so capricious in her behavior toward him that he attempted suicide. . . ." Bunin uses harsh and brutal terms when he speaks of her liaison with the officer and reveals a truth of life which otherwise might have been somewhat concealed. ". . . Olia had seduced him, had had an affair with him, had promised to become his wife. But on the day of her murder, at the railway station, as she was seeing him off to Novocherkassk, she suddenly announced that she had never loved him, that all the talk about marriage was but a joke. . . ." Then there is the cruel revelation of the truth as it appears in Olia's diary. Here, she describes her encounter with Maliutin: "He is fifty-six, but still quite handsome and always well dressed—only I didn't like the cape he arrived in—it smells of English cologne, and his eyes are quite young and black, and his beard is carefully divided into two flowing parts and is entirely silver."

There is nothing in this scene, as recorded in Olia's diary, that makes us feel the existence of any feeling, or somehow brightens the dark and gloomy picture formed in the reader's mind. The word *love* is neither mentioned nor hinted at; one may well think that there is no word more alien to these lines than *love*. Thus, the entire material, all the circumstances of life, all the everyday events, concepts and emotions are described in a subdued tone, without a single bright spot. Thus, as we have stated, the author does not conceal the facts of life but exposes them with a brutality that makes us realize the full impact of the truth upon which his short story is based. We say once again: The essence of the story, viewed from this angle, can be defined as life's troubles, or its turbid waters. Surprisingly, however, the effect of the story, as a whole, is somewhat different.

The story is, after all, called "Gentle Breath." It produces in us an effect that is almost diametrically opposed to the impression caused by the events themselves. The true theme of this story is the gentle breath, not the muddled life of a provincial schoolgirl. Its fundamental trait is the feeling of liberation, lightness, the crystal transparency of life, none of which can be derived from the literal events. The duality of the story becomes particularly obvious in the part concerning Olia's school-teacher, which serves as a frame for the entire narrative. This teacher who goes into a stuporlike trance as she beholds Olia's tomb, this teacher who is ready to give half her life if only the funeral wreath would disappear, this teacher who is basically as happy as anyone in love or possessed by a dream,—it is she who suddenly gives a completely different meaning to the story. For a long time she has been living under delusions which she believes to be life. The author is bold enough to name three of them. The first was her brother, a poor, insignificant noncommissioned officer (this is reality) whom she expected to change miraculously her life and fate (this is the delusion). Then, she deluded herself that she was performing some sort of great work, or sacrifice, for an ideal; this served her as a substitute for life for some time. "Olia Meshcherskaia's death provided her with a new dream," says the author, and ranges this third self-deception beside the other two. With this technique, Bunin splits our emotions. He holds up a mirror to the story as he describes the new protagonist and breaks it up into several beams, as with a spectrum. As we read along, we are not only aware, but fully convinced that the story reflects both reality and dreams. From here our mind proceeds easily to the structural analysis mentioned earlier. The straight line is reality as it appears in the story, and the complex structural curve of reality, which we called the composition of the novella, is its light breath. We realize that the events are connected in such a way that they lose their turbidity. They are associated as in a melody, and in their crescendos, diminuendos, and transitions they untie the threads connecting them. They free themselves of the conventional bonds in which they are presented to us in actuality. They divorce themselves from reality, and associate in the same way as words associate and combine into a verse. Now we can formulate our idea and say that the author's reason for tracing such an extremely complex curve is his intent to undo life's turbidity and transform it into a crystal transparency. He did this to make life's events unreal, to transform water into wine, as always happens in any real work of art. The words of a story or verse carry its meaning (the water), whereas the composition creates another meaning for the words, transposes everything onto a completely different level, and transforms the whole into wine. Thus, the banal tale of a frivolous provincial schoolgirl is transformed into the gentle breath of Bunin's short story.

The story itself proves this beyond any doubt. If we take the first step in the composition, we see why the author begins with a description of the grave. We have to simplify matters here and try to reduce complex feelings to elementary emotions. If the story of Olia Meshcherskaia's life were told us in chronological sequence, suspense would be almost intolerable until the moment of her death. The poet would have created that special suspense, the damming up of our interests, which German psychologists like Lipps call a psychological dam, and literary theoreticians call *Spannung*, or suspense. The term means that tension, or suspense, rises exactly at the point where we have encountered the obstacle. The suspense of our interest, which each new episode of the story stresses and directs toward the next solution, would have filled this short story to excess: as stated earlier, the suspense would have been intolerable. The narrative would run somewhat as follows: We would learn how Olia seduced the officer, how she began a liaison with him, how she swore she loved him and talked about marriage, and how she began to make fun of him. We would witness the scene at the railway station, and with almost unbearable suspense would be there watching her for those last moments when the officer, her diary in his hands, steps onto the platform and shoots her. This is the effect this action in the disposition of the story would have on us. It is the culmination, the climax of the narrative around which all the other actions and events gravitate. But, at the very beginning the author places us before Olia's grave and we learn about her life after she is dead. We learn first that she was killed and only later how it happened; we realize that the composition already gives the solution of the tension inherent in the events, if we take them per se. We read of the killing and the writing in the diary with completely different feelings than if the events had been developed rectilinearly, in chronological sequence. Thus, step by step, from episode to episode, from one phrase to another, we can show that the events were selected and connected in such a way that through the suspense they caused, all the dark, confused feelings are released to produce an effect completely different from the one we would have felt if the action had been narrated in its natural sequence. Following the structural diagram of the narrative, we can show that all the artificial leaps of the story have but one purpose, the neutralization of the first impression provoked by an event and its transformation into another, in contrast to the first.

This destruction of content by form can be illustrated with individual scenes and episodes from the narrative. For example, we learn of Olia's tragic death in a very peculiar fashion. The author has already brought us to her grave, we have learned of her depravation from the talk with the school principal, Maliutin was named for the first time. "A month after this conversation took place, a Cossack officer, ugly and coarse in appearance and having nothing in common with the class of people to which Olia Meshcherskaia belonged, shot her on the platform of the railway station, in the midst of a large crowd which had just arrived on a train." The structure of this sentence reveals the teleology of the author's style. Notice how the main word is lost in the agglomeration of descriptions which apparently have nothing to do with the narrative. The word "shot" is completely lost; and yet, it is the most terrible, sinister word not only of this sentence, but of the entire story. It is lost in the middle of the long, calm, placid description of the Cossack officer and the railway platform, and the large crowd just arrived on a train. We can say that the structure of this sentence damps the sound of this terrible shot to near imperceptibility, deprives it of its impact, and transforms it into an imitative sign or symbol. The emotional stress of this event is released, pushed aside, and destroyed. Note how we learn for the first time of Olia's moral depravation: in the cozy office of the school principal, filled with fresh lilies of the valley, amidst talk of expensive slippers and hairdos. And the terrible, or, as the author says, "the incredible confession which stunned the school principal" is described thus: "At this point Olia, without losing her calm and simplicity, suddenly but politely interrupted her: 'Excuse me, Madame, but you're making a mistake. I *am* a woman. And do you know who is to blame? A friend and neighbor of Papa's, your brother Aleksei Mikhailovich Maliutin. It happened last summer, in the country. . . .' "

The shot is described as a minor detail in the scene of the arrival of the train. The shocking confession is placed as an insignificant detail in a conversation about slippers and hairdos. The purpose of the meticulous detail, "a friend and neighbor of Papa's, your brother Aleksei Mikhailovich Maliutin," is to eradicate the impact caused by the confession. But the author does not fail to emphasize the realistic aspects of both the shot and the confession. In the cemetery scene Bunin describes in plain words the true significance of the events. He tells us of the state of mind of Olia's teacher, who cannot associate with this pure, innocent look all the horror now connected with Olia Meshcherskaia's name. Yet this horror, undiminished, follows us throughout the narrative. The story, however, does not strike us as a horror story; the horror is transposed to another level where we experience it differently. For some reason, this narrative of a dreadful event has the strange title "Gentle Breath," and for some reason the entire story is permeated with the breath of a cold, clear spring.

Let us look at the title. A title is given a story for the purpose of disclosing its most important theme, the dominant which in turn determines the structure of the narrative. This concept, which Christiansen introduced into aesthetics, is an extremely useful one, without which no serious analysis is possible. A work of art—a narrative, painting, or poem— is a complex whole which consists of heterogeneous elements organized in different ways and according to different hierarchies. In such a whole there exists always some dominating element which determines the structure of the entire story, as well as the significance of each of its parts. The dominant of our narrative is, of course, the *gentle breath* [35]. It appears at the very end, the schoolteacher's reminiscence of a conversation she once overheard, between Olia Meshcherskaia and her girl friend. It is a conversation about feminine beauty, and it proceeds in a semicomical style with reference to funny antique books. It happens to be the *pointe* of the story, the catastrophe which reveals its true significance. The "funny antique book" places the greatest emphasis on "gentle breath." "A gentle breath! I have it, don't I? Listen, how I sigh. It's there, isn't it?" It is as if we heard the sigh. . . . And in this trivial description, we suddenly discover its other significance, as we read the concluding words of the author: "And now this gentle breath is again dissipated in the world, in this cloud-covered sky, in this cold spring wind . . ." These words complete the circle and bring the end back to the beginning. Frequently, one small word in an artist's hands can have great significance and tremendous impact. Such a word in this context is "this." It carries the outcome of the story, *this* gentle breath. We are talking about the sigh, we are talking about the gentle breath that Olia Meshcherskaia asked her girl friend to listen to. Further on we again meet significant words, ". . . in this cloud-covered sky, in this cold spring wind. . . ." The very last three words establish the whole idea of the narrative, which begins with a description of a cloudy sky and cold spring wind. Bunin uses the same mood in the beginning and end of his narrative, thus summarizing all that has happened, all that amounted to the life, love, and death of Olia Meshcherskaia (all this, in essence, is but one single event). And now *this* gentle breath has again dissipated in the world, in *this* cloud-covered sky, in *this* cold spring wind. All the earlier descriptions of the grave, the April weather, the gray days, the cold wind, all this is suddenly compressed at one point and introduced into the narrative. The story acquires a new significance, a new meaning. This is no longer a Russian provincial landscape, this is no longer a

Russian provincial cemetery, this is no longer the sound of the wind in the porcelain wreath. No, it is the gentle breath, all the gentle breaths dissipated in the everyday world of the shot, Maliutin, and the horror associated with the name of Olia Meshcherskaia. Literary theoreticians characterize the *pointe* as the finale of a story at an unsettled point, or the finale in music ending with a dominant chord. At the very end of the narrative, when we know everything, when the story of the life and death of Olia Meshcherskaia has passed before our eyes, when we know all that could possibly interest us about the schoolteacher—at this point an unusually bright new light is cast upon the entire story. The transition from the tomb to the gentle breath is decisive for the composition of the narrative, inasmuch as it suddenly shows us the whole story in a completely different light.

The concluding sentence, which we called catastrophic, resolves this unsteady finale with a tonic chord. This unexpected and rather flighty confession of the light breath brings together the two levels of the narrative. Bunin does not conceal reality here, nor does he confuse it with invention. What Olia tells her friend is funny in the precise sense of the word. When she quotes from the book, ". . . black eyes, of course, gleaming like boiling pitch, that's the way it was written: gleaming like boiling pitch! Eyelashes as black as night . . ." and so on. It is amusing, it is simple, and it is true. And the real sigh ("listen, how I sigh"), so long as it is a part of reality, is but a small detail of this strange conversation. Taken in another context, however, it makes it possible for the author to bring together the scattered parts of his story, so that in its catastrophic concluding lines we see with unusual conciseness the whole story once again, from *this* gentle sigh to *this* cold spring wind on the tomb. And we are satisfied that the story is about gentle breath.

The author has used quite a number of auxiliary devices and techniques in this narrative. We have mentioned only one, that of the artistic treatment, or subject composition. It appears to be the most obvious and clear-cut of all the techniques used by Bunin. But there are of course many others, such as the manner in which the author narrates the events, the language he uses, the tone, the mood, his choice of words, his construction of sentences, whether he describes scenes or gives only a brief summary, whether he transcribes the dialogues of his characters or just tells us what they have said, and so forth. All of this is quite important and has a great bearing on the artistic treatment of the subject. Of similarly great importance is the choice of facts. For the sake of our argument we proceeded from a comparison between disposition and composition, assuming that disposition is the natural element and composition the artificial, or art one. We did not mention, however, that disposition in itself, that is, the choice of the facts to be treated, is already a creative act. In Olia Meshcherskaia's life there were thousands of events, thousands of dialogues. Her liaison with the officer included dozens of quarrels. Among her school loves, Shenshin was not alone. She mentioned Maliutin more than once to the principal. But, for some reason, the author chose precisely some of these facts and episodes, and rejected thousands of others. This selection and screening, is, of course, a creative act. A painter portraying a tree cannot paint its every leaf, but gives a general impression by means of spots of color and draws a few leaves here and there. In the same fashion, the writer selects only those events that characterize best and most convincingly the real life material with which he is dealing. Strictly speaking, we already step outside the limits set by this selection when we begin to apply our own viewpoints about life to this material.

Blok has quite successfully described this rule in a poem:

Life has no end and no beginning.
Chance waits for us at every step. . . .

On the other hand Blok says:

Erase sometimes the chance—
And thou shalt see:
The world is beautiful.

Particular attention must be paid to the organization of the writer's language, rhythm, and melody. In the calm, flowing, almost classic phrasing used by Bunin in his short story we find all the elements of power, strength, and eloquence necessary for an artistic treatment of the subject. To determine the importance of the effect produced on our breathing by the language used by the writer, we have made experimental recordings of our breathing while reading excerpts of prose and poetry with different rhythms, in particular while reading Bunin's story. Blonskii claims that we feel the way we breathe, and he is right. We can determine the emotional effect of a work of literature from the breathing that corresponds to it [36]. When the author makes us breathe in short intervals, he creates a general emotional atmosphere corresponding to a sad and somewhat withdrawn mood. When he makes us exhale all the air we have in our lungs and then take another deep breath to refill them, he creates a completely different emotional mood for our aesthetic reaction.

At some later stage we shall discuss the meaning of these recordings of our breathing. It is significant, however, that the pneumographic recording made during the reading of the story under discussion shows a *gentle* breathing, which means that we read about the murder, the death, the troubles, and the horrors associated with Olia Meshcher-skaia's name and breathe as if every new sentence brought us release from these horrors. Instead of painful tension and suspense, we experience an almost pathological lightness. This illustrates the affective contradiction, the collision between two contrasting emotions which apparently makes up the astonishing psychological rules of the aesthetics of the story. Astonishing, because traditional aesthetics prepared us for a diametrically opposite understanding of art. For centuries, scholars of aesthetics have told us of the harmony of form and content. They have told us that the form illustrates, completes, or accompanies, the content. And now we suddenly discover that this was an error, that the form may be in conflict with the content, struggle with it, overcome it. We discover in this dialectic contradiction between content and form the true psychological meaning of our own aesthetic reaction. It would seem that to represent gentle breath Bunin should have chosen a lyrical, calm, peaceful, and untroublesome event in life. Why did he not tell us about some transparent, airy, and lofty first love, pure and untouched? Why did he choose terrifying, vulgar, turbid, and troublesome events to develop his theme of gentle breath?

We seem now to have reached the point where we can say that a work of art always contains a certain amount of contradiction, a certain inner incongruity between the material and the form. We can say that the author intentionally chooses a difficult, brittle material which will resist his efforts to say what he wants to say. The more brittle and hostile the material, the more suitable will it be for the author. The form given by the author to this material is not intended to reveal the feelings hidden in the material itself. It is not intended to expose the life of a Russian schoolgirl in a provincial town in all its depth. On the contrary, its purpose is to overcome these properties, to compel the horror to speak the language of gentle breath, and to induce the trouble, the pain, and the turbidity of life to breathe and move like the cold spring wind.

NOTES

1. M. Petrovskii, "Morphology of Pushkin's 'The Shot,'" in *Problemy poetiki* (*Problems in Poetry*), a collection of articles edited by V. I. Briusov, Moscow-Leningrad: Zemlia i fabrika, 1925, p. 197.

2. V. Shklovskii, *'Tristram Shendi' Sterna i teoriia romana* (*Sterne's 'Tristram Shandy' and the Theory of the Novel*), Opoyaz (Petrograd), 1921, pp. 38–39.

3. *Ibid.*, p. 39.

"GENTLE BREATH,"
by I. BUNIN*

In the cemetery, on a fresh pile of earth, there is a new cross. It is made of oak, it is heavy and smooth—a pleasure to look at.

It's April, but the days are gray. In the spacious country-town cemetery the monuments are visible in the distance through the branches of barren trees, and the cold wind rings through the leaves of the porcelain wreath at the foot of the cross.

The cross holds a fairly large bronze medallion; on it is the photograph of an elegant and lovely high-school girl with joyful, uncommonly lively eyes.

This was Olia Meshcherskaia.

As a girl she did not stand out in the noisy crowd of schoolgirls, all dressed in brown, who filled the halls and classrooms of the school with laughter and noise. Nothing much could be said about her except that she was a pretty, well-to-do, and happy girl, that she was gifted but mischievous, and totally unconcerned with the admonitions given her by her teachers. Suddenly she began to blossom, by the day, by the hour. At fourteen she had a thin waist, handsome legs, well defined breasts, and all those contours of the body, the grace of which human words have been unable to express. At fifteen everyone said she was a beauty. Her schoolmates took pains to comb their hair frequently and meticu-

* Russian original reprinted from: I. Bunin, *The Gentleman from San Francisco*, Works 1915–1916. (Moscow: Writers' Publishing House, 1916) pp. 105–112.

lously, to move gracefully—but not Olia; she was worried about nothing! Not of ink stains on her fingers, nor of a flushed face, disheveled hair, or of scraping her knee in a fall. Everything that distinguished her from all the others during her last two years at school—grace, elegance, a lively and intelligent look in her eyes—came to her without any effort on her part, unnoticed, as a blessing. No one danced as well as Olia Meshcherskaia. No one skated as gracefully as she. No one was courted as much at dances as she. And for some reason, the younger grades liked her better than anyone else. Imperceptibly she became a young lady, and her fame at school spread almost imperceptibly, and rumors began to circulate that she was frivolous, that she could not live without admirers, that the schoolboy Shenshin had lost his head over her, that she was also in love with him but was so capricious in her behavior toward him that he attempted suicide. . . .

During the last winter of her life Olia Meshcherskaia's schoolmates said that she threw herself into the pursuit of pleasure. The winter was sunny, cold, with plenty of snow. The sun set early behind the tall fir trees of the snow-covered school park. Every evening there was a serene sunset that promised another sunny, cold day for tomorrow. To say nothing of strolling down Cathedral Street, skating in the city park on a rose-tinged evening, music, the throng gliding over the ice; in this Olia Meshcherskaia seemed to be the most elegant, carefree, and happy person. Once, during a recess at school, when she was dashing about in the main hall with the first-graders chasing her with happy screams, she was unexpectedly summoned to the principal's office. Olia stopped dead, took one deep breath, smoothed her hair with a habitual gesture, pulled up her pinafore, and ran upstairs, her eyes radiant. The principal, a small, young-looking, but gray-haired lady, was sitting under the Tsar's portrait, quietly knitting behind her desk.

"Good morning, Mlle Meshcherskaia," she said in French without lifting her eyes. "Unfortunately, this is not the first time that I have had to summon you here to talk to you about your behavior."

"I am listening, Madame," replied Olia as she approached the desk, looking at the principal with bright and lively eyes, but with a demure expression on her face, and sitting down with her customary ease and grace.

"You'll listen quite carelessly, as bitter experience has taught me," the principal said, pulled the thread, making a swirl on the polished floor, which Olia watched with curiosity; she raised her eyes and said, "I shan't repeat myself. I'll be brief."

Olia liked the unusually neat and spacious study, which was particularly warm and cozy during cold winter days, with its shiny tile stove and lilies of the valley on the desk. She looked at the young Tsar painted life-size, standing in some glittering hall, and at the principal's white hair, carefully parted in the middle and carefully curled, and sat in silence and expectation.

"You're no longer a little girl," said the principal, significantly, and she was secretly beginning to grow irritated.

"Yes, Madame," Olia answered simply, almost gaily.

"But not yet a woman," added the principal even more significantly, and her pale face flushed slightly. "First of all, what kind of a hairdo is this? This is a woman's hairdo!"

"It isn't my fault, Madame, that I have nice hair," replied Olia, as she smoothed her beautifully groomed hair with both hands.

"So now it's not your fault!" said the principal. "The hairdo is not your fault! The expensive combs are not your fault! The twenty-ruble slippers you made your parents buy you are not your fault! But let me repeat, you seem to forget that you're only a schoolgirl. . . ."

At this point Olia, without losing her calm and simplicity, suddenly but politely interrupted her.

"Excuse me, Madame, but you're making a mistake. I *am* a woman. And, do you know who is to blame? A friend and neighbor of Papa's, your brother Aleksei Mikhailovich Maliutin. It happened last summer, in the country. . . ."

A month after this conversation took place, a Cossack officer, ugly and coarse in appearance and having nothing in common with the class of people to which Olia Meshcherskaia belonged, shot her on the platform of the railway station, in the midst of a large crowd which had just arrived on a train. Olia's incredible confession, which had stunned the school principal, was fully corroborated. The officer told the investigator that Olia had seduced him, had had an affair with him, had promised to become his wife. But on the day of the murder, at the railway station, as she was seeing him off to Novocherkassk, she suddenly announced that she had never loved him, that all the talk about marriage was nothing but a joke, that she had been making fun of him, and then she had let him read the page in her diary where she mentioned Maliutin.

"I ran through these lines, stepped up onto the platform where she was strolling, waiting for me to finish reading, and shot her," testified the officer. "The diary is in the pocket of my overcoat. Take a look and see what it says on the page marked the tenth of July of last year."

The investigator read what follows.

"It's two o'clock in the morning. I had fallen asleep, but woke up before long. . . . Today I had become a woman! Papa, Mama, and Tolia had all gone to town, and I had remained alone. I was so happy to be alone. There are no words to express how happy! In the morning I walked in the garden, in the fields, in the woods, all by myself. I felt as though I were alone in the entire world, and I had never felt so good. I had lunch all by myself, then I played the piano for an hour, and the music made me feel as if I would live forever, happy as no one else! I had a nap in Papa's study; Katia woke me at four to tell me that Aleksei Mikhailovich had arrived. I was very glad and quite pleased to receive and entertain him. He came with his pair of Vyatka colts, very beautiful ones. They stood all the time near the porch, but he stayed on because it was raining and he didn't want to get wet. He was sorry that he had missed Papa, carried on a lively conversation with me, was very *galant*, and said jokingly that he had fallen in love with me long ago. When we walked through the garden before tea, the weather had become fine again and the wet foliage was glittering in the sun. It had become chilly, and as he took my arm he said that he was Faust with Marguerite. He is fifty-six, but still quite handsome, and always well dressed,—only I didn't like the cape he arrived in,—it smells of English cologne, and his eyes are quite young and black and his beard is carefully divided into two flowing parts and is silver. We had tea on the glass-enclosed veranda, I felt faint for a moment and lay down on a low couch, while he smoked; then he sat by me, paid me compliments, took my hand and kissed it. I covered my face with a silk handkerchief, but he kissed me several times on the lips through the handkerchief. . . . I don't understand how it could have happened. I must have lost my mind. I never thought I could be like that! Now there's only one way out for me . . . I feel such disgust for him, that I cannot live with it!"

During those April days the town has become clean and dry. The stones are white. and it is pleasant to walk on them. Every Sunday, after Mass, a little woman dressed in black for mourning, with black kid gloves and a black umbrella, walks along Cathedral Street, which leads outside the town. She walks by the fire station and crosses a dirty square, where there are many sooty smithies. Further, between the monastery and the jail, the spring fields are gray and the cloudy sky is white. She treads through the puddles along the monastery wall; turns left into a large garden enclosed by a white fence with a gate on which is painted, "The Assumption of the Mother of God." The little woman crosses herself several times and walks along the main path like someone who knows her way. She reaches a bench in front of the oaken cross, sits down in the wind and spring chill for an hour or two, until her feet in their light shoes and her hands in their kid gloves are frozen. She listens to the birds singing in the cold and to the wind softly whistling in the porcelain wreath, and she thinks that she would give half her life not to see that dead wreath. The idea that Olia Meshcherskaia lies there, buried in the frozen earth, throws her into a state of mind that borders on stupor. How can one associate that sixteen-year-old school-girl, so full of life, grace, and joy only two or three months ago, with this earthen mound and oaken cross? Is it possible that they hide the girl, whose eyes sparkle, as if they were alive, in the bronze medallion? How can one combine this pure and innocent look with all the horror associated with Olia Meshcherskaia's name? But deep down in her heart the little woman is happy, as are all those in love, or devoted to some ardent dream.

The little woman is Olia Meshcherskaia's schoolteacher, a maiden lady of thirty, who for a long time has been living under delusions which to her are a substitute for life's reality. The first was her brother, a poor, commonplace noncommissioned officer. She had tied her soul to his, to his future, which she believed would be brilliant. She had lived in the strange expectation that her fate would miraculously change on account of him. Then, when he was killed in the battle of Mukden, she convinced herself (to her great relief apparently) that she was different from the others, that for her, beauty and femininity would be replaced by superior qualities of the mind. She believed she was a martyr to the world of ideas. Olia Meshcherskaia's death provided her with a new delusion; and now Olia is the object of her ceaseless thoughts, admiration, and delight. Every holiday she visits the grave. The habit of wearing black goes back to her brother's death. She stares at the oaken cross for hours, thinks of Olia's pale face in the coffin among the flowers, and remembers what she once overheard during school recess. Walking in the schoolyard with her closest friend, the stout, tall Subbotina, Olia had breathlessly told her: "In one of my father's books,—he has so many funny antique books—I read a description of what a woman's beauty should be. . . . You understand, there is so much in it that you can't remember everything: well, black eyes, of course, gleaming like boiling pitch, that's the way it was written: like boiling pitch! Eyelashes as black as night, a gentle glow of color, a slender figure, hands longer than usual—you know, longer than usual!—a small foot, a moderately large bosom, a nice round calf, knees the pink color of a seashell, fairly high shoulders. I've learned all this by heart. It's all so true! And most important, you know what? A gentle breath! I have it, don't I? Listen, how I sigh. It's there, isn't it?"

And now this gentle breath is dissipated again in the world, in this cloud-covered sky, in this cold spring wind. . . .

8 THE TRAGEDY OF HAMLET, PRINCE OF DENMARK

THE RIDDLE OF *Hamlet*. "SUBJECTIVE" AND "OBJECTIVE" SOLUTIONS. THE PROBLEM OF HAMLET'S CHARACTER. STRUCTURE OF THE TRAGEDY. FABLE AND SUBJECT. IDENTIFICATION OF THE HERO. CATASTROPHE.

The tragedy of *Hamlet* is generally considered an enigma. It differs from Shakespeare's other tragedies as well as from the works of others in that its course of action never fails to surprise and bewilder the spectator. This is why the essays and critical studies on the play are more like commentaries. They have one trait in common: all try to solve the riddle set by Shakespeare. After his first encounter with the ghost, Hamlet is expected to kill the king—why is he unable to do this? And why does the play reflect nothing but his failure to act? Shakespeare does not explain the reasons for Hamlet's inertia, and thus the critics approach the riddle from two different angles: the first, from the character and personal experiences of Hamlet, and the second, from the environmental obstacles in his path. According to one viewpoint, the problem lies in Hamlet's personality. Critics of this persuasion attempt to show that the reason for Hamlet's delay in taking revenge is that his feelings rebel against an act of violence, that he is irresolute and weak-willed, or that, as Goethe claimed, too heavy a task was placed on his weak shoulders. Since none of these interpretations allows for an exhaustive explanation of the tragedy, we can positively say that they are devoid of any scientific significance, for exactly opposite views may exist just as rightfully. Other critics explain Hamlet's lingering as a manifestation of his state of mind, as if he were a real person. These critics usually argue from true life experience and human nature, not from the artistic structure of the play. They go so far as to say that Shakespeare intended to show the tragedy of the weak-willed person called upon to perform a task for which he is not properly equipped. They regard *Hamlet* as a tragedy of weakness and the absence of will, despite the scenes in which the hero exhibits just the opposite character traits and appears as a man of extraordinary determination, courage, valor, and implacability in the face of moral considerations.

Another school of critics seeks to explain Hamlet's procrastination by the objective obstacles that lie on the path to his goal. The king and his courtiers exert opposition against Hamlet, who does not kill the king at once, because it is impossible for him to do so. These critics, who follow Werder's view, claim that Hamlet's task is not to kill the king but to expose his guilt and chastise him. We can, of course, find as many arguments in favor of this view as opposed to it. These critics are badly mistaken, because they miss two fundamental points. First, nowhere in the tragedy does Shakespeare formulate such a task for Hamlet, either directly or by implication. The critics, therefore, are attempting to write for Shakespeare by inventing new, complicated tasks, again proceeding from common sense and life experience rather than from the aesthetics of tragedy. Also, they are shutting their eyes and ears to many scenes and monologues in which Hamlet, aware of the subjective character of his procrastination but unable to understand the reasons for it, attempts some explanations, none of which suffices fully to support his actions.

Both groups of critics agree, however, that the tragedy is highly enigmatic; this admission takes most of the substance out of their arguments. Indeed, if their considerations were correct, the tragedy would have no riddle. How could the play be mysteriously enigmatic if Shakespeare intended merely to portray a weak and undecided person? It would be clear from the outset that the hero's procrastination is due to his irresolution. A play about a weak-willed character would be a bad one if his weakness were concealed in a riddle. If the critics of the second group, those who claim that the main difficulties arise from external causes, were correct, then *Hamlet* would fail because Shakespeare, unable to represent with clarity the real meaning of the tragedy (this very struggle with external obstacles), would disguise it, too, with a riddle. The critics are trying to solve Hamlet's mystery with arguments irrelevant to the tragedy itself. They approach it as if it were a case from actual life which must be explained and understood on the basis of common sense. According to Berné's very pertinent remark, a veil has been thrown over the picture, but in trying to lift it in order to examine the picture beneath we discover that the veil is painted into the picture itself. This observation is quite accurate, for it is easy to show that the riddle has been intentionally built into the tragedy. The tragedy is structured as a riddle which cannot be explained nor solved by strictly logical means. By depriving the tragedy of its riddle, the critics deprive the play of its most essential element.

Let us now consider the enigma of the play. Despite differences in approach, critics unanimously note the obscurity and ambiguity of the play. Hessner speaks of *Hamlet* as a tragedy-mask. According to Kuno Fischer, we stand before Hamlet and his tragedy as if we were standing before a curtain. We expect the curtain to rise and reveal the image, but we discover that the image concealed is none other than the curtain itself. Berné says that *Hamlet* is an absurdity, worse than the death of one that has not yet been born. Goethe refers to some somber mystery associated with the tragedy. Schlegel compares it to an irrational equation. Baumgardt mentions the complexity of a fable that contains a long series of diverse and unexpected events. "The tragedy *Hamlet* indeed resembles a labyrinth," writes Kuno Fischer. *"Hamlet,"* says Brandes, "is not permeated by a 'general meaning' or by the idea of unity. Certainty and definition were not the ideals which Shakespeare was striving to reach. . . . The play is laden with riddles and contradictions, but its charm and attractiveness are due mostly to its obscurity." [1] Speaking of "obscure" books, Brandes claims that *Hamlet* is one such: "At times a gulf opens between the action that envelops the play like a mantle, and the core of the play." [2] "Hamlet remains a mystery," says ten Brink, "but an infinitely attractive one, because we know that it is not artificially construed but draws its origin from nature's wisdom." [3] —"But Shakespeare created a mystery," to quote Dowden, "which remains a question, forever exciting, but never fully explained. Therefore one cannot assume that an idea or a magical formula can solve the difficulties presented by the drama or suddenly shed light upon all. Obscurity is characteristic of a work of art concerned, not with a specific problem, but with life; and in that life, in the story of a soul that treads the shady boundary between dark night and bright day there are . . . many things that defy or confuse investigation." [4]

We could continue forever with these excerpts and quotations, since almost all critics dwell on this subject. Even such deprecators of Shakespeare as Tolstoy and Voltaire state essentially the same view. Voltaire, for example, in the introduction to his tragedy *Semiramis* states that "the course of events in the tragedy *Hamlet* is a huge mess." Rümelin describes the play as a whole as incomprehensible." [5]

All these critics see in the obscurity a mantle that conceals a center, a curtain that hides an image, or a veil that prevents our eyes from seeing the picture beneath. But if *Hamlet* is what the critics claim it to be, why is it shrouded in so much mystery and obscurity? Frequently the mystery is greatly exaggerated, and even more frequently it is based on utter misunderstanding. Such misunderstanding underlies Merezhkovskii's view that "the ghost appears to Hamlet in an atmosphere of solemnity and romanticism, with claps of thunder and earthquakes . . . The ghost tells Hamlet of the secrets of the dead, of God, blood, and vengeance." [6] This might be read in some operatic libretto, but certainly not in the actual *Hamlet*.

We can therefore disregard all criticism which tries to separate the enigma from the tragedy and take the veil from the picture. However, it may be of some interest to see how this criticism deals with the inscrutability of Hamlet's character and behavior. Berné says that "Shakespeare is a king who does not obey laws. Were he like anyone else, we could say that Hamlet is a lyrical character who defines dramatic processing." [7] Brandes also notes this incongruity: "We must not forget that this dramatic phenomenon—an inactive hero—is required to some extent by the technique of the play. If Hamlet were to kill the king immediately upon receiving the ghost's message, the play would have to be restricted to one act. Hence, it becomes imperative to find delaying tactics." [8] But this need to delay would imply that the subject is not suited to tragedy, that Shakespeare artificially delays an action that could be completed instantly, and introduces four superfluous acts into a play capable of being resolved in a single act. Montague notices this, too, and provides an excellent formula: "Inaction is the action of the first three acts." Beck comes to a similar interpretation. He explains everything by the contradiction between the plot of the play and the character of the protagonist. The plot belongs to the chronicle into which Shakespeare has woven his subject, and Hamlet's character belongs to Shakespeare himself. Between the two there is an irreconcilable contradiction. "Shakespeare was not fully the master of his own play and was not completely free to use all its component parts," a deficiency which can be attributed to the chronicle. This view, however, is so simple and self-evident that it is pointless to look elsewhere for solutions or explanations. Thus we turn to a new group of critics who seek the solution to Hamlet either in the requirements of dramatic technique (as mentioned by Brandes) or in the historic and literary roots of the tragedy. In this case, however, it is obvious that the author's talent is defeated by the rigid rules of technique, or that the historic background of the subject exceeds the possibilities of artistic treatment. In either case we must regard *Hamlet* as a failure because Shakespeare was unable to select a suitable subject for his tragedy. Then Zhukovskii would be correct in saying that "Shakespeare's masterpiece, *Hamlet,* looks like a monstrosity to me. I don't understand its meaning. Those who find so much in Hamlet exhibit the wealth of their own thought and imagination rather than prove the superiority of the play. I can't believe that Shakespeare, when composing this tragedy, thought in exactly the same way as Schlegel and Tieck did, when they read into its incongruities all the unsolved riddles of human life . . . I asked him* to read Hamlet to me and then tell me in detail his thoughts on this *monstrosity.*"

Goncharov holds the same view. He claims that Hamlet cannot be played on stage. "Hamlet is not a typical role. No one can play it; there has never been an actor who could play it . . . He would lose himself in it as if he were the Wandering Jew. . . . Hamlet's character is a phenomenon which anyone in a normal state of mind simply cannot comprehend." [9] Not all the literary critics who seek to explain Hamlet's wavering by technical or historical means think that Shakespeare has written a bad play. Many of them point to the positive aesthetic aspects of Hamlet's procrastination. Volkenshteyn, for instance, holds a different view, which is the opposite of Heine's, Berné's, Turgenev's, and many others, who believe that Hamlet himself is weak-willed and spineless. The opinions of this group are reflected in Hebbel's words: "Hamlet is a corpse, long before the curtain rises. What we see are the roses and thorns which sprung from his corpse." Volkenshteyn feels that the true essence of a drama, particularly a tragedy, is the tension and stress of passions; he also feels that a tragedy is always supported by the hero's inner strength. This is why he believes that the view of Hamlet as a weak-willed and spineless person, "is based on the blind trust in semantics which characterizes some of the most profound literary criticism. . . . A dramatic hero cannot be taken for what he says he is. He must be judged for his *acts.* Hamlet's acts are energetic. He alone carries on a long and bloody fight with the king and the entire Danish court. In his tragic striving for the restoration of justice, he attacks the king three times: the first time he kills Polonius by mistake; the second time he spares the king because the latter is praying; and the third time, at the end of the play, he succeeds. With superb ingenuity he sets a trap to corroborate the statements of the ghost. He deftly eliminates Rosen-

---

* Here Zhukovskii refers to a critic who is left unnamed by Vygotsky. *Translator's note.*

crantz and Guildenstern from his path. Indeed, he conducts a titanic struggle. . . . Hamlet's versatile, strong character corresponds to his physical fitness: Laertes is the best fencer in France, yet Hamlet defeats him because he turns out to be more adroit (how this contradicts Turgenev's assertion of Hamlet's physical weakness!). The protagonist of the tragedy shows a *maximum* of will. . . . We would not feel the tragedy in *Hamlet* if its hero were irresolute and weak." [10] There is nothing new in outlining those traits in Hamlet which denote his strength and courage. This has been done many times before as has the demonstration of the obstacles facing Hamlet. What is new is the treatment of the material which deals with Hamlet's irresolution and weakness. According to Volkenshteyn, all the monologues in which Hamlet reproaches himself for his lack of resolution are but instruments to whip up his will; they do not illustrate his weakness, but rather his strength.

Thus, according to Volkenshteyn, Hamlet's self-accusations are yet another evidence of his extraordinary strength of character. His titanic struggle requires a maximum of effort and fortitude, but he is not satisfied with himself and he demands still more of himself. This interpretation proves that the contradictions are not accidental but have been introduced intentionally and that, moreover, they are only seemingly fortuitous. Any mention of weakness and irresolution is evidence of exactly the opposite—Hamlet's formidable will. But even this attempt to solve Hamlet's problem is not entirely successful. As a matter of fact, it repeats, only in slightly different terms, the earlier view of Hamlet's character, without explaining why he procrastinates, why he does not kill the king in the first act, immediately after the revelations of the ghost (as suggested by Brandes), or why the tragedy does not end with the first act. We are thus forced to side with Werder, who claims that the exterior obstacles represent the true cause of Hamlet's procrastination. This view, however, is in complete contradiction with the meaning of the play. We may agree, though, with the fact that Hamlet is conducting a titanic struggle, if we proceed from Hamlet's own character. Let us assume that tremendous forces are concentrated within him. But with whom does he conduct his struggle, against whom is it directed, and how does it express itself? No sooner are these questions asked than it becomes obvious that Hamlet's opponents are nonentities and the forces preventing him from murder are insignificant; he himself blindly gives in to the machinations directed against him. The critic cannot but note that although prayer saves the king's life once, there is hardly any indication that Hamlet is devout or that he spares the praying king because of any deep personal conviction. On the contrary, this reason crops up as if by accident and is almost incomprehensible to the spectator. The accidental killing of Polonius proves that Hamlet's decision to kill was made immediately after the players' performance before the court. Why, then, does his sword smite the king only at the very end of the tragedy? Finally, no matter how premeditated or accidental, no matter how limited by outward circumstances his struggle may be, most of the time Hamlet is parrying blows directed against him rather than carrying on his own attack. The murders of Guildenstern and all the rest are nothing but self-defense, and we cannot possibly term such self-defense a titanic struggle. We will show that Hamlet's three attempts to kill the king, to which Volkenshteyn refers, are evidence of exactly the opposite of what that critic sees in them.

Equally poor interpretation was the staging of *Hamlet* by the Second Moscow Art Theatre, a production which followed Volkenshteyn's line closely. The directors proceeded from the clash of two distinct aspects of human nature. "One is protesting, heroic, fighting to assert its own sense of life. This is our Hamlet. In order to emphasize this aspect of our hero we had to shorten the text of the tragedy considerably and eliminate from it all that could possibly interfere with the whirl of events. . . . As early as the middle of the second act Hamlet takes his sword in his hand and does not let it go until the end of the tragedy. We have also underscored Hamlet's activity by condensing all the obstacles which he encounters in his path. This was our guideline in the treatment of the king and the other characters. King Claudius personifies everything that attempts to thwart the heroic Hamlet. . . . And our Hamlet dwells continuously in an impassioned state of struggle against all that is personified by the king . . . To emphasize the shades and colors in the play we found it necessary to transfer the action to the Middle Ages." Thus spoke the directors of the play in their announcement of plans for the staging of *Hamlet*. They admit quite openly that for stage requirements and for better understanding of the tragedy they had to perform the following three operations on the play: to discard from it everything that prevents such an understanding; to condense the obstacles that lie in Hamlet's way; and to accentuate the shades and colors in the play, while transferring the action to the Middle Ages (despite the fact that the play is usually seen as taking place during the Renaissance). After three such operations it is obvious that any and all interpretations of the drama are possible. It is also obvious that these three operations transform the tragedy into something diametrically opposed to the author's intent. The fact that such radical surgery was required to produce a particular interpretation of Shakespeare's work is the best evidence of the immense discrepancy between the true meaning of

Hamlet's story and the meaning attributed to it by the critics. To illustrate the almost colossal contradictions which beset this staged version of *Hamlet*, it suffices to mention that the king, who has a fairly modest role in the original play, suddenly becomes the heroic counterpart to Hamlet [37]. If Hamlet, as the focal point of heroic, enlightened will, is one of the tragedy's poles, then the king, as the focal point of the anti-heroic, dark power, is its other pole. But to reduce the role of the king to the personification of all the negative principles of life would require the writing of a new tragedy with a purpose different from that pursued by Shakespeare.

Much closer to the truth are those explanations of Hamlet's irresolution which, while also proceeding from formal considerations, try to solve the riddle without performing major surgical operations on the original text. One such attempt is an explanation of some of the peculiarities of Hamlet based on the technique and design of the Shakespearean stage [38]. Its importance, cannot be denied; indeed study of the subject is vital to a proper understanding of the tragedy. In this regard, significance is acquired by Prels' law of temporal continuity in the Shakespearean drama which requires from both audience and author a concept of staging totally different from that of our modern theaters. We divide a play into acts, each involving only the brief time interval during which the events represented in it occur. Important events, and their effects, take place between acts, and the audience learns about them subsequently. Acts may be separated by intervals of several years. All this requires specific stylistic techniques. Things were totally different in Shakespeare's day: the action was continuous, a play apparently was not divided into acts, the performance was not interrupted by intermissions, and everything happened before the eyes of the audience. This important aesthetic convention was bound to have a considerable bearing upon the composition and the structure of any play. Many things become clear once we acquaint ourselves with the technique and aesthetics of the stage of Shakespeare's time. But if we overstep the boundary and assume that by establishing the necessity of some technical measure we have solved the problem of the play, we commit a grave error. We must be able to discern the extent to which each device is really due to the stage technique of that time. This, however, is not sufficient, for we must also show the psychologic significance of the device. We must explain why from among many such devices Shakespeare chose this one, since to admit that a device can be explained only by its technical indispensability is tantamount to a declaration of the supremacy of bare technique over art. There is no doubt that the structure of a play greatly depends upon its technique, but it is also true that each and every technical device acquires its own aesthetic significance. Here is a simple example. Silverswan says: "The poet was greatly hampered by a specific stage arrangement. Among the cases that show the inevitability of the exit of the actors from the stage, or the impossibility of having the play or scene end with a group of persons on stage, we have those in which there are corpses on stage. They cannot be made to rise and walk out. But in *Hamlet,* for instance, Fortinbras appears at the end (he is otherwise totally superfluous), with many other people, for the sole purpose of exclaiming:

Take up the bodies: such a sight as this
Becomes the field, but here shows much amiss.
Go, bid the soldiers shoot.

Exeunt all, bearing off the dead bodies.
The reader can find a great number of such instances if he reads Shakespeare's plays carefully." [11] Here we have an example of an interpretation of the final scene of *Hamlet* based solely upon technical considerations. It is obvious that without a curtain, with the action unfolding before the audience on an open stage, the playwright must end his play in such a way as to allow someone to carry away the corpses. Someone has to remove the bodies in the final scene of Hamlet; however, this could be done in several different ways. The bodies could be taken by the courtiers, or simply by the Danish guard. Thus, even from this strictly technical necessity, we should never conclude that Fortinbras appears *only* for the purpose of removing the corpses, that he is otherwise totally superfluous. Let us look at Kuno Fischer's interpretation of the tragedy. He sees the theme of revenge embodied in three different characters: Hamlet, Laertes, and Fortinbras, all avengers of their respective fathers. Thus, it becomes immediately evident that Fortinbras' final appearance acquires a deep artistic significance, since the revenge theme reaches its final resolution. The procession of the victorious Fortinbras before the bodies of the other two avengers, who have been constantly juxtaposed to him, is highly significant. Here a strictly technical device acquires an aesthetic meaning. We shall be forced more than once to resort to such an analysis, and the rule established by Prels will prove very helpful in explaining Hamlet's procrastination. This, however, is only the beginning of the investigation. The principal task consists in arriving at an understanding of the aesthetic expediency of a device once its technical necessity on stage has been established. Otherwise we shall have to conclude, with Brandes, that technique wholly dominates the poet, not vice versa, and that Hamlet procrastinates during four

acts merely because Elizabethan plays were written in five acts rather than one. We shall never understand why the same technique that confines and restricts Shakespeare exactly as it does other authors creates one aesthetic in Shakespeare's work and another in the tragedies of his contemporaries; or moreover, why the same technique compels Shakespeare to write *Othello, King Lear, Macbeth,* and *Hamlet* in completely different ways. Obviously, within the limits allowed the poet by his technique, he retains freedom of creation and composition. The same inadequacy is found in attempts to explain *Hamlet* entirely from formal requirements, which establish perfectly correct rules that may help to understand the tragedy but are totally inadequate for its explanation. This is how Eichenbaum casually speaks about Hamlet: "As a matter of fact, it is not because the action in the tragedy is delayed that Schiller has to analyze the psychology of procrastination; quite the contrary, Wallenstein [one of Schiller's tragic heroes] procrastinates because action in the tragedy must be held back, and the delay must be concealed. The same happens with Hamlet. It is not in vain that there exist directly contradictory interpretations of Hamlet as a personality. All of these are correct in their own way, because all of them are equally mistaken. Both Hamlet and Wallenstein represent two aspects indispensable for the treatment of tragic forms: a driving force and a delaying force. Instead of a simple movement forward on the path of the subject, or plot, we have something like a dance with complex movements. From a psychological point of view we run into contradictions. This is inevitable, because psychology serves only as a motivation: the hero only seems to be a personality; in reality he is a mask.

Shakespeare introduces the ghost into his tragedy and makes a philosopher out of Hamlet, thus motivating both movement and procrastination. Schiller forces Wallenstein to become a traitor almost against his will in order to create movement in the tragedy; then he introduces astrology as a factor to bring about procrastination. . . ." [12]

Here a number of perplexing questions arise. Let us agree with Eichenbaum that for the proper treatment of art forms, the protagonist must simultaneously develop and delay the action. Can this insight explain *Hamlet?* No more than the need to remove the corpses at the end of the play can explain the appearance of Fortinbras. This is true for both Shakespeare and Schiller. Why, then, has one written *Hamlet,* and the other *Wallenstein?* Why have an identical stage technique and identical formal requirements led once to the creation of *Macbeth* and another time to *Hamlet,* two plays which are completely opposed in their composition? Let us assume that the protagonist's psychology is nothing but the audience's illusion and is introduced by the author only as a

motivation. But then, is the motivation chosen by the author of any significance to the tragedy? Are the motivation and its selection arbitrary?
Does motivation mean anything in itself, or is the effect of the rules of
tragedy identical no matter what the motivation or the concrete form of
its manifestation, just as the correctness of an algebraic formula remains
constant, no matter what arithmetic values are substituted in it?

Thus, formalism, which began with a healthy respect for concrete
form, degenerates to the point of reducing certain individual forms to
algebraic formulae. No one will contradict Schiller when he says that a
tragic poet "must drag out the torment of feelings;" but we cannot understand why this torment is dragged out in *Macbeth* where the action
develops at a breath-taking pace, and again in *Hamlet,* where the action
is very slow. Eichenbaum believes that his formula explains Hamlet
completely. Shakespeare introduces the ghost as a motivation for movement. He makes Hamlet into a philosopher in order to bring about
delay. Schiller uses other motivations—astrology in place of philosophy
and treason in place of a ghost. Why, then, do we have two completely
different consequences from one and the same cause? Or must we admit
that the cause given here may not be the true one or that it may not explain everything sufficiently? Indeed, it may not even explain the most
superficial events. Here is an example: "For some reason," says Eichenbaum, "we love 'psychologies' and 'characteristics.' We naively believe
that a writer wants to 'express' or 'represent' a psychology or a character. We rack our brains about *Hamlet*—did Shakespeare really *want* to
express procrastination, or did he *want* to express something else? In
point of fact, however, the artist does not represent or express any such
thing, for he is not concerned with psychology. Nor do we go to see
Hamlet to study psychology." [13]

All this is true, of course, but does it follow that the choice of the character or the psychology of the protagonist makes no difference to the author? It is true that we do not see *Hamlet* in order to study the psychology of procrastination, but it is equally true that were we to change
Hamlet's character, the play would lose its entire effect. Of course the
author has not written the tragedy for the purpose of giving a treatise
on psychology or human character. Nevertheless, the hero's psychology
and character are neither meaningless, random, nor arbitrary elements;
they are extremely important aesthetically, and to explain Hamlet in
one sentence the way Eichenbaum does is not satisfactory. If we claim
that action is delayed in *Hamlet* because the hero is a philosopher, then
we must accept and repeat the opinion of the dull books and articles Eichenbaum tries to disprove. Indeed the traditional approach to psychology and the study of character asserts that Hamlet fails to kill the king

because he is a philosopher. The same shallow approach claims that the ghost is introduced in order to force Hamlet into action. However, Hamlet could have gotten the information from other sources. All we have to do is turn to the tragedy itself to realize that action is not delayed by Hamlet's philosophy but by something else.

Those who want to study *Hamlet* as a psychological problem must abandon criticism. We have tried to show how little guidance it gives the scholar, and how it can occasionally lead investigators astray. The first step toward a psychological study of *Hamlet* is to discard the 11,000 volumes of commentary that have crushed the hero under their weight, and of which Tolstoy speaks with horror. The tragedy must be taken as it stands if we are to understand what it reveals, not to the sophisticated commentator but to the honest beholder; it has to be taken in its unexplicated form [39] and looked at as it is. Otherwise we run the risk of interpreting a dream rather than studying the play. Only one such attempt to look at Hamlet with unsophisticated simplicity is known to us. It was made by Tolstoy who, with ingenious boldness, wrote a brilliant article on Shakespeare which, for some unfathomable reason, is generally considered stupid and uninteresting. This is what he writes:

> None of Shakespeare's characters shows, in such a striking fashion, the playwright's—I don't want to say inability—complete disregard for proper characterization as does Hamlet. None of his other plays reveals as much as *Hamlet* the blind worship of Shakespeare, the unreasoning hypnosis which does not even admit the thought that a work of Shakespeare's can be anything but brilliant or that one of his main characters can be anything but the expression of some new, deeply involved idea.
>
> Shakespeare takes a reasonably good story or drama written some 15 years earlier, writes his own play from it, putting into the mouth of the principal character, quite inopportunely (as he always does), all those ideas of his own which he thinks worthy of consideration. But, in doing so . . . he is totally unconcerned about when and under what circumstances these ideas are uttered. Thus the character who expresses all these ideas becomes Shakespeare's mouthpiece and loses his own essence to the extent that his deeds do not correspond to his words.
>
> Hamlet's personality is quite understandable in the story from which Shakespeare drew his play. He is outraged by his uncle's and mother's deed, wants to take vengeance on them, but is afraid his uncle might kill him as he did his father, and therefore feigns insanity. . . .
>
> All this is clear, and it follows from Hamlet's character and position. But by putting into Hamlet's mouth those ideas which Shakespeare wants to tell the world, and by forcing him to perform those actions which Shakespeare needs

for preparing the most effective scenes, the author destroys the character of the Hamlet of the legend. For the entire duration of the play Hamlet does not act the way he might want or might like to, but the way the author requires him to act: at one time he is terrorized by his father's ghost, and another time he chaffs at him, calling him an old mole; first he loves Ophelia, later he teases her cruelly, and so forth. It is impossible to find an explanation for Hamlet's actions or words, and it is therefore impossible to assign to him any character at all.

But since it is generally accepted that the great Shakespeare could not possibly write anything bad, scholars and critics have racked, and are racking their brains to discover some unusual beauty in an obvious defect, which is particularly evident and quite irritating in *Hamlet,* where the protagonist has no character. The wise critics now proclaim that Hamlet expresses, with extraordinary power, a completely new and profound character, whose distinguishing feature is the absence of character, and that only the genius of a Shakespeare could create such a profound characterless character. Having established this, the scholarly critics proceed to write volume upon volume to praise and explain the greatness and significance of the characterization of a person without character. It is true that some of the critics occasionally produce timid remarks that there might be something odd about that character, that Hamlet is an unsolvable riddle; but no one finds the courage to say that the emperor is naked, that it is perfectly plain that Shakespeare was either unable or unwilling to give Hamlet a specific character. Nor did he understand that it was at all necessary. And so the scholarly critics continue to study, investigate, and extol this mysterious literary production. . . .[14]

We defer to Tolstoy's opinion, not because we believe his conclusions to be correct or absolutely trustworthy. The reader will understand that Tolstoy's final judgment of Shakespeare issues from nonartistic motivations; the decisive factor in his moral condemnation of Shakespeare is the fact that he regards the latter's morals as irreconcilable with his own moral ideals. We must bear in mind that this moralistic approach has led Tolstoy to disapprove not only of Shakespeare but of many other authors and their works. Toward the end of his life he considered even his own writings harmful and unworthy, proving that this moralistic view reaches beyond the boundaries of art, is too broad and universal to take account of details, and cannot be applied in the psychological investigation of art. However, Tolstoy supports his moralistic conclusions with purely aesthetic arguments; these appear to be so convincing as to destroy that unreasoning and unreasonable hypnosis which surrounds Shakespeare and his opus. Tolstoy looks at Hamlet with the eyes of the child in Andersen's fairy tale of the emperor's new clothes; he is the first who has the courage to say that the emperor is naked, i.e., that all the merits, such as profundity, precision of character, penetration of the depths of the human psyche, and so forth, exist only in the spectator's imagination. Tolstoy's greatest merit lies in his statement that the emperor is naked, with which he exposes not primarily Shakespeare but the preposterous and false concept of the Bard, with which he compares his own opinion which he considers diametrically opposed to the one accepted by the entire civilized world. Thus, pursuing a moralistic aim, Tolstoy destroys one of the most absurd prejudices in the history of literature. He was the first to express boldly what now has been confirmed by many, namely, that Shakespeare fails to give convincing psychological motivation to quite a few of the intrigues and actions in his plays, that his characters are often implausible, and that frequently there are serious incongruities, unacceptable to common sense, between the protagonist's character and his actions. Stoll, for instance, bluntly asserts that in *Hamlet* Shakespeare is more interested in the situation than in the hero's character, that *Hamlet* should be viewed as a tragedy of intrigue in which the decisive role is played by the sequence of events and not by the disclosure of the hero's character. Rügg holds the same view. He speculates that Shakespeare does not entangle the action in order to complicate Hamlet's character, but that he complicates the character to make the hero fit more easily into the traditional dramatic concept of the fable [40]. Such commentaries are by no means unique, nor do they stand alone among other conflicting opinions. In other Shakespearean plays, quite a few facts have been found which prove incontestably that Tolstoy's assertion is basically correct. We will show how Tolstoy's opinion can be properly applied to such tragedies as *Othello*, and *King Lear*, how convincingly he has proved the irrelevance of character in Shakespeare's works and how precisely he has understood the aesthetic significance of Shakespeare's language.

We take, as the starting point for our discussion, the obvious view, according to which no specific character can be assigned to Hamlet, for he is made up of contradictory traits, and it is impossible to find a credible explanation for his words and actions. However, we will dispute Tolstoy's views on Shakespeare's complete inability to represent the artistic progress of the action. Tolstoy fails to understand, or perhaps does not want to accept, Shakespeare's aesthetics. By narrating the latter's artistic devices in plain language, he transposes the author's poetic language into a language of prose, removes the devices from the aesthetic functions which they perform in the drama—and reaches a nonsensical conclusion. This, of course, is bound to happen if we perform a similar operation on the work of any other poet and deprive his text of its proper sense by narrating the story in plain language. Tolstoy proceeds to recount *King Lear,* scene by scene, to show the preposterousness of their concatenation. Were we to do the same to his *Anna Karenina,* we would reduce that novel to a similar bundle of absurd nonsense. What Tolstoy says about *Anna Karenina* can also be applied to *King Lear.* It is impossible to retell the facts of a novel or a tragedy and express its meaning, because meaning can only be found in the combination of ideas. Tolstoy claims that this combination is not made up of thoughts but of "something else" which cannot be expressed in words but only through images, scenes, situations, and so forth. To retell *King Lear* in one's own words is as impossible as putting music into words. This is why narration is the least convincing method of artistic critique. His basic mistake, however, did not prevent Tolstoy from making a number of brilliant discoveries which will supply students of Shakespeare with many interesting problems for years to come and which of course will be interpreted in a way different from Tolstoy's. While we agree with Tolstoy that Hamlet has no character, we persevere in our argument: Could this lack of character be an artistic intention of the author rather than just a mistake? Of course Tolstoy is right when he points out the absurdity of those arguments that maintain that the depth of Shakespeare's character lies in this absence of character. We cannot dismiss the idea, however, that in this tragedy, Shakespeare had no intention of revealing, describing or studying a character per se, and that he may intentionally have used a character totally unfit for the particular events of the play in order to obtain a specific artistic effect from the paradox.

We shall show the fallacy of the idea that Shakespeare's *Hamlet* is a tragedy of character. At this point, however, we shall merely assume that the lack of character is the author's intention, and that he uses it as a device for specific artistic purposes. We shall begin by analyzing the structure of the tragedy.

We can proceed with our analysis in three different ways: First, we have the sources used by Shakespeare, the original treatment of the material; then, the plot of the tragedy; and, finally, a new and more complex artistic feature—the dramatis personae. We shall now try to determine the interrelationship between these three elements.

Tolstoy rightly begins his investigation by comparing the original saga of Hamlet with Shakespeare's tragedy. In the saga everything is clear and understandable. The motives behind the prince's acts are obvious. The action is well coordinated, and each step is justified both psychologically and logically. Many of the earlier studies of the play have elaborated this point sufficiently. The riddle of Hamlet could hardly have sprung up if the story had been confined to the old sources, or at least to its older pre-Shakespearean dramatic forms, since there is absolutely nothing mysterious or obscure in them. This fact enables us to draw a conclusion diametrically opposed to Tolstoy's view that all is clear and obvious in the legend but muddled and unreasonable in *Hamlet* and that consequently Shakespeare has spoiled the legend. It is more correct to follow an opposite trend of thought: since everything is logical and understandable in the saga, Shakespeare had available to him ready-made logical and psychological motives. If he chose to process this material so as to ignore all the obvious ties which hold the original saga together, he must have had a special intention. We are inclined to believe that Shakespeare created Hamlet's enigma for stylistic reasons and that it is not the result of the author's inability. We therefore choose to approach the problem from a different angle. As a matter of fact, we no longer consider it to be an unsolved riddle or a difficulty to be overcome; we consider it an intentional artistic device that we must try to understand. The question we ask is, "Why does Shakespeare make Hamlet delay," rather than, "Why does Hamlet delay?" Any artistic method, or device, can be grasped much more easily from its teleological trend (the psychological function it performs) than from its causal motivation, which may explain a literary fact but never an aesthetic one.

To find an answer to the question of why Shakespeare makes Hamlet delay, we must compare the Hamlet legend with the plot of the tragedy. We have already mentioned that the treatment of the plot follows the law of dramatic composition, prevalent in Shakespeare's time, known as the law of temporal continuity. Action on stage was considered continuous, and consequently the play proceeded according to a time concept completely different from that of contemporary plays. The stage was never empty, not even for an instant. While a dialogue took place on stage, some lengthy events of perhaps several days' duration occurred backstage, as the audience learned several scenes later. The spectator thus did not perceive the passing of real time, for the playwright operated with a fictitious stage time of totally different proportions. Consequently, there figures a tremendous distortion of the concept of time in the Shakespearean tragedy. The duration of events, everyday occurrences, and actions are distorted to fit the requirement of stage time. How absurd then it is to talk of Hamlet's temporizing in terms of real time! By what real time units could we measure his procrastination? The real time periods are in constant contradiction in the tragedy and there is no way of determining the true duration of events in the tragedy. We are unable to estimate how much time elapses between the first apparition of the ghost and the killing of the king. Is it a day, a month, a year? It is therefore evident that the problem of Hamlet's procrastination cannot be solved psychologically. If he kills the king only a few days after the first appearance of the ghost, then there is no delay, no procrastination, in terms of the course of our everyday life. But if it takes him longer, we must seek different psychological explanations for different periods of time; that is, there is one explanation if it takes him a month and another if it takes him a year to kill his uncle. In the tragedy, Hamlet is not in any way bound by these units of real time, since all the events of the play are measured and related to one another in terms of conventional [41] stage time units. Does this mean that the question of Hamlet's delaying no longer arises? Could it be that the author allocated to the action exactly the amount of time it requires on stage and that therefore everything happens on schedule? We shall see that this is not the case. Indeed, all we have to do is remind ourselves of the monologues in which Hamlet reproaches himself for procrastinating. The tragedy apparently emphasizes the temporizing of its hero and, surprisingly enough, gives several quite different explanations for this procrastination.

Let us follow the main plot of the tragedy. Immediately upon the revelation of the ghost's secret, when Hamlet learns that he has been charged with the duty of revenge, he says that he will fly to revenge on wings as swift as love's desire. From the pages of memory he deletes all the thoughts, feelings, and dreams of his entire life, to devote himself entirely to the secret behest. Already at the end of this scene he sighs under the unbearable burden of the discovery that has befallen him. He bemoans the fact that he was born to perform a fateful exploit. After his talk with the actors, Hamlet reproaches himself for the first time for his inaction. It astonishes him that an actor is carried away by passion and inflamed by a meaningless plot, while he himself remains silent and inactive in the face of the crime which has destroyed the life and the reign of a great sovereign—his father. The remarkable thing in this famous monologue is Hamlet's inability to understand the reason for his delay. He reproaches himself by speaking of shame and dishonor, but he alone knows that he is no coward. Here we are given the first motive for delaying the death of the king: perhaps the words of the ghost are not to be believed. Indeed, the accusations must be thoroughly verified. So, Hamlet sets his famous "mousetrap," and only after it snaps are all his doubts gone. Since the king has given himself away, Hamlet no longer doubts the veracity of the ghost. When Hamlet's mother calls him, he convinces himself not to lift his sword against her:

'Tis now the very witching time of night,
When churchyards yawn and hell itself breathes out

Contagion to this world: now could I drink hot blood,
And do such bitter business as the day
Would quake to look on. Soft! Now to my mother.
O heart, lose not thy nature; let not ever
The soul of Nero enter this firm bosom:
Let me be cruel, not unnatural;
I will speak daggers to her, but use none;
My tongue and soul in this be hypocrites;
How in my words soever she be shent,
To give them seals never, my soul, consent! (III, 2)

Hamlet now is ready to kill, and he fears that he might even harm his own mother. Oddly enough, this realization is followed by the prayer scene. Hamlet enters, takes his sword, and places himself behind the king whom he could kill on the spot. We have left Hamlet ready to avenge, ready to kill, we have left him as he was convincing himself not to raise arms against his mother; now we expect him to perform his act. But instead we hear

Now might I do it pat, now he is praying;
And now I'll do't: and so he goes to heaven . . . (III, 3)

A few verses later Hamlet sheathes his sword and gives a completely new reason for his procrastination: he does not want to kill the king while the latter is praying or atoning.

Up, sword; and know thou a more horrid hent:
When he is drunk asleep, or in his rage,
Or in the incestuous pleasure of his bed,
At gaming, swearing, or about some act
That has no relish of salvation in't,
Then trip him, that his heels may kick at heaven,
And that his soul may be as damn'd and black
As hell, whereto he goes. My mother stays:
This physic but prolongs thy sickly days. (III, 3)

In the next scene Hamlet kills Polonius, who is hiding behind a tapestry, by unexpectedly making a pass with his sword through the arras and calling out "A rat!" From this, and from his words to the dead Polonius it is obvious that he intended to kill the king, who is precisely the rat caught in the mousetrap; it is the king to whom Hamlet refers as "thy better" and for whom he mistook Polonius. The motives that have stopped Hamlet in the preceding scene have disappeared, so much so that it appears irrelevant. One of the two scenes must include an obvious contradiction if the other is correct. Kuno Fischer says that most critics consider the scene of Polonius' killing to be proof of Hamlet's unplanned, thoughtless actions. Many productions, and quite a few critics, omit the prayer scene because they fail to understand how it is possible to introduce a new motive for procrastination without prior preparation. Nowhere in the tragedy, either earlier or later, does this new condition for killing the king (to kill him while he is sinning in order to destroy his soul after death) appear. During Hamlet's scene with his mother the ghost appears again, and Hamlet thinks that he has come to reproach him for putting off the revenge. Hamlet does not resist being exiled to England; in the monologue after the scene with Fortinbras he compares himself to that courageous leader, and once again reproaches himself for his weak will and inactivity. He feels that his procrastination is a disgrace, and finishes his monologue resolutely:

. . . O, from this time forth
My thoughts be bloody, or be nothing worth! (IV, 4)

Later when we find Hamlet in the graveyard, or again talking to Horatio, or finally during the duel, there is no mention of revenge. Not until the very end of the play is Hamlet's promise that he will think only about blood kept. Before the duel he is full of premonitions:

Not a whit, we defy augury; there's a special providence in the fall of a sparrow. If it be now, 'tis not to come; if it be not to come, it will be now; if it be not now, yet it will come: the readiness is all: since no man has aught of what he leaves, what is't to leave betimes? (V, 2)

He feels that his death is approaching, and so does the audience. Not until the very end of the duel does he think about revenge. The final catastrophe seems to be contrived for completely different reasons. Hamlet does not kill the king to fulfill his promise to the ghost. The spectator learns that Hamlet is virtually dead because the poison is already in his blood and he has less than half an hour to live. Only now, with one foot in the grave, does he kill the king.

The final scene leaves absolutely no doubt that Hamlet kills the king for his latest crime: the poisoning of the queen, and the killing of Laertes and Hamlet himself. Not a word is said about Hamlet's father, and the audience has completely forgotten about him. The denouement is astonishing and inexplicable—nearly all the critics agree that the killing of the king leaves us with the feeling of duty unfulfilled, or, at best, fulfilled by default.

The play, it would appear, was obscure and enigmatic because Hamlet had not killed the king. Now that he has performed the killing, the enigma should vanish; instead it has really only now become apparent. Mezières quite correctly states: "Indeed, everything in the last scene surprises us; everything from the beginning to the end is unexpected. Throughout the play we have been waiting for Hamlet to kill the king. Finally he strikes—but no sooner does he perform the deed than we are again astonished and bewildered. . . ." Says Sokolovskii, "The last scene of the tragedy is based on a collision of accidental circumstances that happen so unexpectedly and so suddenly that some commentators with old-fashioned views have accused Shakespeare of blundering. . . . The intervention of an external force had to be invented. . . . It is purely accidental, and in the hands of Hamlet it functions like those sharp weapons which we occasionally allow children to handle but all the while guide their grip on the hilt. . . ." [15]

Berné is correct in saying that in killing the king Hamlet avenges not only his father but his mother and himself as well. Johnson reproaches Shakespeare for having the king killed not according to a premeditated plan but as a totally unexpected accident. Alfonso states, "The killing of the king is due to events totally beyond Hamlet's control; it is not the result of a well-prepared plan. Had it been left entirely to Hamlet, the king would never have been killed." If we take a closer look at this new line of plot, we see that Shakespeare at times emphasizes Hamlet's procrastination and at other times conceals it. He composes several scenes in a row without ever mentioning the task set before the prince, and then he has Hamlet reveal his weakness once more in statements and monologues. The audience is reminded of Hamlet's procrastination in sudden, explosionlike spurts, rather than being apprised of it in a continuous, uniform fashion. After the sudden explosion of a monologue, the spectator looks back and vividly realizes the existence of procrastination. But the author rapidly covers it up until the next explosion, and so on. In the spectator's mind are combined two fundamentally incompatible ideas. On the one hand, Hamlet must avenge his father and let no internal or external causes prevent him from going into action. The author even plays with the audience's impatience and makes it see Hamlet draw his sword but then, quite unexpectedly, not strike. On the other hand, the audience realizes that Hamlet is delaying, but fails to understand why. It observes the drama of Hamlet evolve, torn by contradictions, evading the clearly set task and constantly straying from the path which is so clearly outlined.

Given such treatment of the subject, we may plot our interpretational curve of the tragedy. The plot of our story runs in a straight line, and if

Hamlet had killed the king immediately after hearing the ghost's revelations, he would cover the distance between these two events in the shortest possible way. The author, however, proceeds in a different fashion. Because at all times he lets us see, feel, and be aware of the straight line which the action should follow, we are even more keenly conscious of the digressions and loops it describes in actual fact.

It appears as if Shakespeare had set himself the task of pushing the plot from its straight path onto a devious and twisted one. It is quite possible to find in these the series of events and facts indispensable for the tragedy, on account of which the play describes its oblique orbit.

We must resort to synthesis, to the physiology of the tragedy, in order to understand this fully. We must try to guess the function assigned to this curve from the significance of the whole. We must try to find out why the author, with such exceptional and in many respects unique boldness, forces the tragedy to deviate from its straight path.

Let us consider the end of the tragedy. Two things immediately strike the critic's eye. First of all, the main line of development of the tragedy is fuzzy and obscured. The king is killed in the course of a melee; he is but one of four victims, whose deaths occur as suddenly as a bolt from the blue. The audience is caught by surprise, for it does not expect events to proceed in this fashion. The motives for the king's death are so obviously implicit in the final scene that the audience forgets that it has finally reached the point to which the tragedy had been leading without actually reading it. As soon as Hamlet sees the queen die, he shouts:

O villany! Ho! let the door be lock'd:
Treachery! Seek it out.

Laertes reveals to Hamlet that these plots are all the king's. Hamlet then exclaims:

The point envenom'd too!
Then, venom, to thy work.

Finally, as he gives the king the poisoned goblet,

Here, thou incestuous, murderous, damnéd Dane,
Drink off this potion. Is thy union here?
Follow my mother.

Nowhere is there any mention of Hamlet's father, and all the motivations are based on the events of the last scene. Thus the tragedy reaches its catastrophe, but it is concealed from the spectator that this is precisely the point to which the plot development has been directed. Yet, in addition to this direct camouflage another, exactly opposing one, reveals itself, and we can easily show that the scene of the killing of the king is treated on two diametrically opposed psychological planes: On the one hand, the king's death is overshadowed by a series of immediate causes, as well as other deaths; on the other hand, it is distinguished from the series of killings in a way that has no comparison in any other tragedy. All the other deaths come to pass almost unnoticed. The queen dies, and no one seems to take note. Only Hamlet bids her farewell, "Wretched queen, adieu!" Even Hamlet's own death seems to be blurred and overshadowed. Once dead, nothing is said about him anymore. Laertes dies inconspicuously and, significantly, he exchanges forgiveness with Hamlet before his life leaves him. He forgives Hamlet Polonius' death and his own, and begs Hamlet to forgive him for having killed him. This sudden and quite unnatural change in Laertes' character has no motivation in the tragedy. It is necessary only to calm the audience's reaction to these deaths and make the king's death stand out more clearly against this dimmed background. As mentioned earlier, the king's death is made to stand out by means of a highly exceptional device that has no equal in any other tragedy. What is so unusual about this scene is the fact that for some unexplained reason Hamlet kills the king twice, first with the tainted sword, then with the poisoned potion. Why? The action does not call for it. Both Laertes and Hamlet die from the effect of one poison only, that on the sword. It would appear that the killing of the king has been split into two separate actions, to emphasize it and to impress upon the audience the fact that the tragedy has reached its conclusion. We can easily find a reason for this double killing of the king, which would appear to be absurd from a methodological viewpoint and futile from a psychological viewpoint. The meaning of the tragedy is in its catastrophe, the killing of the king, which we have been expecting from the first act on, but which we reach by a totally different, unexpected path. In fact, the catastrophe comes as a result of a new plot, and when we reach that point we do not immediately realize that it is the point to which the tragedy has been carrying us all along.

It now becomes clear that at this point (the king's double death) converge two distinct lines of action, each of which we have seen go its own way, and each of which must end in its own, separate death. But no sooner does the double killing happen then the poet begins to blur this device of short-circuiting the two lines of the catastrophe. In the brief epilogue in which Horatio, in the manner of all Shakespearean narrator-players, briefly retells what has happened in the play, the king's death is once again obscured:

And let me speak to the yet unknowing world
How these things came about: so shall you hear
Of carnal, bloody, and unnatural acts,
Of accidental judgments, casual slaughters,
Of deaths put on by cunning and forc'd cause,
And, in this upshot, purposes mistook
Fall'n on the inventors' heads: all this can I
Truly deliver.

In this general mass of "bloody acts and casual slaughters" the catastrophe of the tragedy is once again diluted to the point of obliteration. In this climactic scene we come to realize the tremendous power of the artistic treatment of the subject, and witness the effects that Shakespeare manages to draw from it. A closer look into the sequence of these deaths reveals that Shakespeare perverts their natural order to obtain a satisfactory artistic effect. The deaths form a melody, as if they were individual notes. In actual fact the king dies before Hamlet, but in the artistically treated plot we do not hear about the king's death. All we do know is that Hamlet is dying and that he will not live for another half hour. Though we know that he is virtually dead and that he received his wound before anyone else, he outlives the rest of the victims. All these groupings and regroupings of the basic events serve to satisfy one requirement, that of the psychological effect. When we learn of Hamlet's imminent death we lose, once and for all, any hope that the tragedy will ever reach the point toward which it has been developed. We are convinced, indeed, that all events are running in the opposite direction. But at that very instant, when we least expect it, and are personally convinced that it is impossible, the catastrophe does finally come to pass. Hamlet, in his last words, points to some mysterious hidden meaning in all the preceding events. He asks Horatio to recount how everything happened, and why, and asks him to give an impartial description of the events, the one that the audience might also remember, and concludes, "The rest is silence." And it is indeed silence for the audience, since the rest happens in the unexpressed sequels that arise from this extraordinarily constructed play. More recent investigators quite willingly underscore that eternal complexity of the play which earlier critics neglected to notice. "We see here several plots running parallel: the story of the murder of Hamlet's father and Hamlet's vengeance, the story of Polonius' death and Laertes' vengeance, Ophelia's story, Fortinbras' story, the episodes with the actors, Hamlet's trip to England, and so on. The action changes location no less than twenty times. In each individual scene we witness rapid changes of theme, character, and location. An element of arbitrariness prevails. . . . There is much talk about intrigue . . . and many episodes that interrupt, or change, the course of action. . . ." [16]

However, Tomashevskii misses the point by claiming that these sudden changes are only a matter of the variety and diversity of the subject. The episodes that interrupt or change the course of action are closely connected with the basic plot. They include the episodes with the actors and with the gravediggers who in a grimly jocular way renarrate Ophelia's death, the killing of Polonius, and all the rest. The plot of the tragedy, in its final form, unfolds before us in the following way: the story on which the tragedy is based is conserved. From the very beginning, the audience has a clear view of the outline of the action and of the path along which it should develop. The action, however, constantly strays from the path set by the plot and meanders in quite complex curves. At some junctures, such as in Hamlet's monologues, the audience is informed, in spurts, that the tragedy has left the preset track. These monologues, in which Hamlet bitterly reproaches himself for procrastinating, are primarily meant to make us realize that things are not evolving the way they should and to keep us aware of the final point toward which all action is directed. After each monologue, we hope that the action will right itself and fall back into the preset path, until a new monologue reveals to us that the action has once more gone astray. As a matter of fact, the structure of the tragedy can be expressed by two very simple formulas. The formula of the story is that Hamlet kills the king to avenge the death of his father; that of the plot is that he does not kill the king. If the material of the tragedy tells us how Hamlet kills the king to avenge the death of his father, then, the plot of the tragedy shows us how he fails to kill him and, when he finally does, that it is for reasons other than vengeance. The duality of the story and the plot accounts for the action taking its course on two different planes. Constant awareness of the preset path, the deviations from it, and the internal contradictions, are an intrinsic part of this play. Shakespeare apparently chose the most suitable events to express what he wanted to say. He chose material that definitely rushed toward a climax, but at the same time forced him to deviate from it. Shakespeare used a psychological method quite appropriately called the "method of teasing the emotions" by Petrazhitskii, who wanted to introduce it as an experimental method. In fact, the tragedy does nothing but tease our feelings. It promises the fulfillment of the task set from the very beginning, but deviates again and again from this goal, thus straining our expectations to the utmost and making us quite painfully feel every step that leads away from the main path. When the target is reached at last, it turns out that we have been brought to it from a completely different direction; we also discover that the two paths which led away from each other in apparent conflict suddenly converge at one point during the final scene (when the king is killed twice). The same motives that prevent the killing of the king finally lead us to his death. The catastrophe reaches a point of extreme contradiction, a short-circuiting of two currents flowing in opposite directions. Add to this the fact that the evolving plot is continuously interrupted by completely irrational events, and we can see that the effect of mysteriousness and obscurity is one of the fundamental motives of the author. We think of Ophelia's madness, of Hamlet's intermittent insanity, of his deception of Polonius and the courtiers, of the pompous and rather senseless declamation of the actor, of the cynical conversation between Hamlet and Ophelia, of the clownish scene of the gravediggers—and we discover that all this material reworks the same events that occurred earlier in the play but exaggerates them to some extent and emphasizes their absurdity, as in a dream. Suddenly we understand the true meaning of these events. We may liken them to lightning rods of absurdity ingeniously placed by the playwright at the most dangerous points of his tragedy, in order to bring the affair somehow to an end and make the absurdity of Hamlet's tragedy plausible. However, the task of art, like that of tragedy, is to force us to experience the incredible and absurd in order to perform some kind of extraordinary operation with our emotions. Poets use two devices for this purpose. First, there are the "lightning rods of absurdity," as we called all the irrational and absurd parts of *Hamlet*. The action evolves in such an incredible way that it threatens to become absurd. The internal contradictions are extreme. The divergence between the two lines of action reaches its apogee and they seem to burst asunder, tearing apart the entire tragedy. It is at this stage that the action suddenly takes on the forms of paradox, pompous declamation, cynicism, recurrent madness, open buffoonery. Against this background of outspoken insanity the play's absurdity slowly becomes less marked and more credible. Madness and insanity are introduced in massive doses to save the play's meaning. Every time absurdity threatens to destroy the play's action, it is diverted by the "lightning rod" [42] which solves the catastrophe that is bound to happen at any moment. The other device used by Shakespeare to force us to put our feelings into the paradox of the tragedy is the following: Shakespeare operates with a double set of conventions [43], introduces a stage on stage, forces his characters to stand up against actors, presents one and the same event twice (once as the real event and then as one played by the actors), splits actions in two and with the fictitious part, the second convention, obliterates and conceals the absurdity of the first "real" part.

Let us take an example. The actor recites the pathetic monologue of Pyrrhus, becomes emotional, and weeps. Hamlet points out immediately that the tears are only an act, that the actor weeps for Hecuba (about whom he does not care), but that all the emotion and passion are fictitious. But when Hamlet juxtaposes these fictitious feelings to his own, we suddenly realize that Hamlet's emotions are true, and we are almost violently taken by them. Shakespeare uses the same device of introducing a fictitious action in the famous scene of the "Mousetrap." The player king and queen play the fictitious murder scene, while the real king and queen sit horrified by the representation. This juxtaposition of actors and spectators on two different planes of action makes us vividly realize that the king's discomfiture is quite real. The paradox on which the tragedy is based remains intact, because it is protected by two reliable guardians: outright lunacy on the one hand, compared to which the tragedy acquires an obvious sense and significance, and outright fictitiousness on the other; this is the second convention, next to which the actions occurring on the first plane appear real. It is as if another picture were superimposed on the first. In addition to this contradiction, there is another one in the tragedy which is of equal importance for the artistic effect of the play. The dramatis personae chosen by Shakespeare somehow do not quite fit the action; moreover, Shakespeare convincingly disproves the widespread belief that the individual characters of the dramatis personae must determine their own actions. It would appear, however, that if Shakespeare wanted to represent a killing that is somehow never carried out, he must either follow Werder's recommendation—to surround the execution of the task with as many complicated obstacles as possible in order to block the protagonist's way, or he must follow Goethe's prescription—show that the task assigned the hero exceeds his strength and requires of him a titanic performance, irreconcilable with human nature. But Shakespeare had a third way out. He could have followed Berné's formula and made Hamlet a coward. However, not only did he choose none of the three possibilities above, but he operated in the exactly opposite direction. He so thoroughly removed all objective obstacles from the hero's path that there is no indication in the tragedy of what prevents Hamlet from killing the king immediately after the ghost's revelations. Furthermore, he gave Hamlet a fully feasible objective (since in the course of the play, in totally incidental and unimportant scenes, Hamlet kills three times). Finally, he portrayed Hamlet as a man of exceptional energy and tremendous strength, making him into a character opposite to the one actually required by the plot.

To save the situation, the critics had to introduce the corrections mentioned earlier, and either adapt the plot to the hero or adapt the hero to the plot, for they proceeded from the incorrect assumption of a direct relation between the hero and the plot—that the plot must grow out of the characters of the play, just as these must be understood from the plot.

All this is refuted by Shakespeare. He proceeds from the opposite point of view, from the incompatibility between protagonist and plot, the fundamental contradiction between character and events. Being familiar with the fact that the subject was treated in contradiction to the story, we can readily find the significance of the contradiction that constantly arises in the play. There arises another unity from the structure of the play, that of the dramatis personae, or the protagonist. We shall show how the idea of the protagonist's character develops. At this point, however, we can assume that a poet who always plays with the intimate contradiction between the subject and story can very easily exploit this second contradiction between the character of his protagonist and the unfolding action. Psychoanalysts are right in asserting that the substance of the psychological effect of a tragedy consists in our identification with the hero. It is quite correct that the author forces us to view all the other characters, actions, and events from the protagonist's viewpoint. The hero becomes the point upon which our attention is focused [44], and simultaneously serves as a support for our feelings which would otherwise be lost in endless digressions as we evaluate, empathize, and suffer with every character. Were we to evaluate the king's and Hamlet's emotions or Polonius' and Hamlet's hopes in the same way, our feelings would suffer constant changes and oscillations in which one and the same event would appear to us to have completely contradictory meanings. The tragedy, however, proceeds in a different way. It shapes our feelings into a unity and forces them to follow the protagonist alone and to perceive everything through his eyes. It suffices to examine any tragedy, *Hamlet* in particular, to realize that all its characters are portrayed as the protagonist sees them. All the events are refracted by the lens of his soul. The author actually builds his tragedy on two planes: on the one hand, he sees everything with Hamlet's eyes; but then he also views Hamlet with his own—Shakespeare's—eyes, so that the spectator becomes at the same time Hamlet *and* his contemplator. This insight explains the important roles played by the characters of the tragedy, in particular Hamlet. We are dealing here with a completely new psychological level. In the fable we discovered two meanings within one and the same action. In the short story we discovered one level for the story (subject) and one for the plot (material). In the tragedy we uncover yet another level, the psyche and the emotions of the hero. Since all three levels refer in the last analysis to the same facts taken in three different contexts, it is obvious that they must contradict one another, be it only to show that they mutually diverge. We can understand how a tragic character is constructed if we use the analogies devised by Christiansen in his psychological theory of portraits. According to him, the problem of a portrait is primarily how the painter portrays life in his painting, how he animates the face, and how he obtains the effect characteristic only of portraits—the representation of living persons. We will never find a difference between a portraiture and nonportrait painting if we examine the formal and material aspects only. (A nonportrait painting may of course include faces just as a portrait may include a landscape or still life.) Only if we base our search on the characteristic that distinguishes the portrait, that is, the representation of a living person, will we be able to determine the difference between the two. Christiansen proceeds from the premise that "lifelessness and size are interdependent. As the size of the portrait grows, its life becomes fuller and more definite in its manifestations; motion becomes calmer and steadier. Portrait painters know from experience that a larger head talks better." [17]

Thus, our eyes detach themselves from one specific point in the portrait upon which they have been focused (and which therefore loses its immobile compositional center), and begin to wander about, "from the eyes to the mouth, from one eye to the other, and observe all those details which make up the expression of the face." [18]

At the various points at which the eye stops while examining the portrait, it takes in a different expression of the face, a different mood, a different feeling, and discovers the liveliness, the motion, the succession of unequal and disparate states which are the distinguishing mark of a portrait. Nonportrait paintings remain as they have been originally painted, while portraits change constantly, whence their liveliness. Christiansen devised the following formula for the psychological life of a portrait: "It is the physiognomic incongruity of the various factors that makes up the expression of a face. Of course it is possible, and, speaking in abstract terms, also more natural to have the corners of the mouth, the eyes, and other parts of the face express the same feeling or emotion or mood. . . . Then the entire portrait would resonate with the same tune. . . . But then, like any tune, it would be devoid of life. This danger of consistency is why the painter . . . makes the expression in one eye slightly different from that in the other, and makes the effect of the corners of the mouth different again, and so forth. However, it is not enough to paint different moods, expressions, and feelings; they must also harmonize with one another. . . . . The principal theme is given by the relationship between the eyes and mouth: the mouth talks and the eyes answer. Excitement, will, and tension are concentrated around the corners of the mouth, while the relaxed calm of the intellect prevails in the eyes. . . . The mouth reveals the instincts and the driving forces of a man. The eye shows what he has become in his victory, defeat, or tired resignation. . . ." [19]

Christiansen interprets portraits as if they were dramas. A portrait conveys not simply a face and an intimate feeling frozen into it, but far more. It tells us of the changing emotions of a soul; it tells us its history and its present life. A spectator approaches the problem of a tragic character in a similar fashion. Character, strictly speaking, can be expressed only in an epic, just as spiritual life can be expressed only in a portrait. In order to be really alive, the tragic character must be composed of contradictory traits and must carry us from one emotion to another. The physiognomic incongruency among the various details of the facial expression in a portrait is the basis for our emotional reaction; and the psychological noncoincidence of the various factors expressing the character in a tragedy is the basis for our tragic sympathy. By forcing our feelings to alternate continuously to the opposite extremes of the emotional range, by deceiving them, splitting them and piling obstacles in their way, the tragedy can obtain powerful emotional effect. When we see *Hamlet,* we feel as if we have lived the lives of thousands of persons in one night; indeed, we have experienced more than we would have in years of common, everyday life. And at the point when, together with the hero, we begin to feel that he no longer belongs to himself and no longer does the things he should do, the tragedy acquires its strength. Hamlet expresses this impuissance remarkably well in his love letter to Ophelia, "Thine evermore, most dear lady, whilst this machine is to him." Russian translators usually translate the word *machine* as *body* because they fail to understand that the essence of the tragedy lies in this one word. (Boris Pasternak, incidentally, translates this correctly.) Goncharov was quite right in saying that Hamlet's tragedy is to be a man, not a machine [45]. Indeed, we begin to feel together with the hero like a "machine of feelings," directed and controlled by the tragedy itself.

We now come to the results of our study. We can formulate our findings as a threefold contradiction on which the tragedy is based: the contradiction involving the story, the plot, and the dramatis personae. Each of these three factors develops in its own way, and it is perfectly clear that a new element is introduced into the tragic genre. We already dealt with split planes in the short story, when we experienced events from two opposite directions, one given by the subject and the other acquired in the plot. These two conflicting levels reappear in the tragedy—we have mentioned several times that *Hamlet* causes our emotions to move on two different levels. On the one hand we perceive the goal toward which the tragedy moves, and on the other we perceive its digressions as well. The new contribution of the protagonist is that *at any moment, he unifies both contradictory planes and is the supreme and ever-present embodiment of the contradiction inherent in the tragedy*. We have said that the tragedy is constructed from the viewpoint of the protagonist, which means that the tragedy is the force uniting the two opposing currents and combining in the protagonist, two opposing emotions. Thus the two opposite levels of the tragedy are perceived as a single unit, for they merge in the tragic hero with whom we identify. The simple duality which we discovered in the story is replaced in the tragedy by a much deeper and more serious one, because of the fact that not only do we view the entire tragedy through the protagonist's eyes, but we in turn look at the protagonist himself through our own eyes. This is as it should be; our analysis of the tragedy proves it. We showed that it is at this point of convergence that the two levels of the tragedy, which we had thought were leading in diametrically opposed directions, meet. Their unexpected convergence gives the tragedy its special character and shows its events in an entirely different light. The spectator is deceived. What he thought were deviations from the main thread of the tragedy have led him to its final goal, but when he finally reaches it he does not realize that it is the last stop on his trip. Now the contradictions have changed roles; they are united, in the final analysis, in the experiences of the protagonist which the spectator perceives as in a dream. He is not relieved by the killing of the king, he experiences no relaxation. Immediately after the killing of the king the audience's attention is attracted by another death, that of the protagonist, Hamlet. This death makes the spectator at last aware of all the conflicts and contradictions that besieged his conscious and unconscious self during the play.

And when in Hamlet's last words and Horatio's narrative the tragedy again describes its circle, the spectator is keenly aware of the duality upon which it is built. Horatio's narration returns him to the tragedy's external plane, to the "words, words, words." The rest, to speak with Hamlet, "is silence."

NOTES

1. G. M. C. Brandes, *Shakespeare: A Critical Study*, vol. II, translated by W. Archer, New York: The Macmillan Co., 1898.

2. *Ibid.*

3. B. A. K. ten Brink, *Five Lectures on Shakespeare,* translated by J. Franklin, New York: Holt & Co., 1895.

4. E. Dowden, *Shakespeare: A Critical Study of His Mind and Art,* 3rd ed., New York: Harper, 1880.

5. G. Rümelin, *Shakespeare-Studie,* Stuttgart, 1866, pp. 74–97.

6. D. S. Merezhkovskii, *Collected Works,* vol. X, Moscow, 1914, p. 141.

7. L. Berné, *Collected Works,* vols. II–III, St. Petersburg, 1899, p. 404.

8. G. M. C. Brandes, *Shakespeare.*

9. I. A. Goncharov, *Collected Works,* vol. 8, Moscow, 1955, pp. 202–204.

10. V. Volkenshteyn, *Dramaturgiia. Metod issledovaniia dramaticheskikh proizvedeniy* (*Dramaturgy: A Method of Studying Dramatic Works*), Moscow: Novaia Moskva, 1923, pp. 137–138.

11. *Teatr i stsena epokhi Shekspira* (*Theater and Stage in the Shakespearean Era*), a collection of theater history, 1918, p. 30.

12. B. M. Eichenbaum, *Skvoz' literaturu* (*Through Literature*), Leningrad: Academia, 1924, p. 81.

13. *Ibid.,* p. 78.

14. See *Tolstoy on Shakespeare,* translated by V. Tchertkoff, New York: Funk and Wagnalls Co., 1906.

15. See *Shakespeare,* translated and with comments by A. L. Sokolovskii, vol. 2, St. Petersburg, 1909, pp. 42–43.

16. B. Tomashevskii, *Teoriia literatury* (*Poetika*) (*The Theory of Literature: Poetics*), Leningrad: GIZ, 1925, p. 182.

17. Christiansen, *Filosofiia iskusstva* (*The Philosophy of Art*), p. 283.

18. *Ibid.,* p. 284.

19. *Ibid.,* pp. 284–285.

IV THE PSYCHOLOGY OF ART

9 ART AS A CATHARSIS

THEORY OF EMOTIONS AND FANTASIES. PRINCIPLES OF THE ECONOMY OF FORCE. THEORY OF EMOTIONAL TONE AND FEELING. THE LAW OF THE "DOUBLE EXPRESSION OF EMOTION" AND THE LAW OF THE "REALITY OF EMOTION." CENTRAL AND PERIPHERAL DISCHARGE OF EMOTIONS. AFFECTIVE CONTRADICTION AND THE BEGINNING OF ANTITHESIS. CATHARSIS. REJECTION OF THE CONTENT OF FORM.

The psychology of art involves two, or possibly three, branches of theoretical psychology. It depends upon findings from the study of perception, the study of the emotions, and the study of imagination and fantasy. Art, when studied in a psychology course, is considered under one, two, or all three of these topical umbrellas. These categories are of differential importance in the study of the psychology of art. The psychology of perception obviously plays a tertiary role because theorists long ago abandoned the naive sensualism according to which art is nothing but the enjoyment of beautiful things. The aesthetic response, at its most primitive, has long been distinguished from the perception of a pleasant taste, odor, or color. Although the problem of perception is an important consideration in the psychology of art, it is not the main one, because it depends on prior decisions about other questions which form the very heart of our problem. The response to art begins with sensory perception, but does not end with it. This is why the psychology of art must begin, not with a chapter on elementary aesthetic experiences, but with the other two problem areas—emotion and imagination. Indeed, all psychological systems which attempt to explain art are nothing but various combinations of the theories of imagination and emotion. In psychology there are no areas more obscure than these two. In recent times they have been the subject of a great many investigations, all of which have neglected to propose a generally acceptable system for study. Matters are even worse in objective psychology, where a system has been developed which conceptualizes the behavioral forms corresponding to processes of the will (to use the old mentalistic term), and represents intellectual processes, but continues to leave domains of emotion and imagination virtually untouched. "The psychology of feeling," says Titchener, "is to a large extent the psychology of personal opinion and conviction." [1] This view applies also to imagination, and, as Zenkovskii says, "psychology here is like a bad joke." Since little is known about imagination and emotion, the most mysteriously problematic question in modern psychology is the association between emotional facts and imagination. Emotions have many different characteristics, the first of which, according to Titchener, is indefiniteness. This indefiniteness is what distinguishes emotion from sensation. "Clarity is not one of the properties of emotion. Pleasure and displeasure may be intense and prolonged, but they are never clear. In terms of naive psychology, this means that we cannot concentrate our attention on an emotion. The more attention we pay to a sensation, the clearer it becomes and the better we remember it. But we cannot concentrate our attention on an emotion. As soon as we try, pleasure or displeasure immediately dissipates, and we find ourselves observing some irrelevant sensation or image which we had not intended to observe in the first place. If we want to enjoy a concert or a painting, we must carefully perceive what we hear or see; pleasure, however, disappears as soon as we try to focus our attention on it." [2]

Thus, in terms of empirical psychology, emotion is beyond the domain of consciousness, since everything that cannot be fixed within the attentional focus is pushed to the extreme limits of the conscious. Many psychologists, however, emphasize a different, contrasting characteristic of emotion. They claim that feeling is always conscious and that the concept of unconscious feeling is a contradiction in terms. Freud, the great champion of the unconscious, says, "The essence of emotional feeling is that it is felt, that is, consciously realized. Emotions, sensations, and affects can therefore never be unconscious." [3] At the same time, he tries to establish whether such a paradoxical term as *unconscious fear* is meaningful. He finds out that, although psychoanalysis speaks of unconscious affects, these differ from unconscious perception, since an unconscious affect corresponds to an affective embryo and a possibility of action left undeveloped. "Strictly speaking . . . unconscious affects, similar to unconscious (or subconscious) concepts, do not exist." [4]

The aesthetic psychologist Ovsianiko-Kulikovskii holds the same view. He differentiates between feeling and thought, in part because feelings cannot be unconscious. His solution of the problem is similar to James', but very different from Ribot's. He asserts that we have no memory for feeling. "First we must decide whether unconscious feeling exists, for there exists unconscious thought. I feel that a negative answer to this question is almost automatic. Emotional feeling, with all its nuances, remains such only as long as it is felt, or consciously realized. . . . It seems to me that the expression 'unconscious feeling' is a *contradictio in adjecto*, like *black whiteness*—there is no unconscious area in feeling." [5]

We seem to run into a contradiction here. On the one hand, emotions are necessarily deprived of conscious clarity, but on the other hand they cannot possibly be unconscious. This contradiction, established in empirical psychology, seems to reflect reality; but we must also apply it to objective psychology and attempt to find its true meaning. We will try to describe emotions in general terms as nervous processes and specify the objective characteristics of these processes.

Many writers agree that in terms of nervous mechanisms, emotions must be regarded as an output, or discharge, of nervous energy. Orshanskii states that our psychic energy can be expended in three ways: "First, by the motor nerves, in the form of a concept or a will stimulus of motion, amounting to a higher psychic activity. Second, by internal discharge. If this takes the form of irradiation, or the passage of a psychic wave, it forms the basis for an association of concepts. If it amounts to a further release of live psychic energy in different nervous waves, it represents the source of emotion. Finally, inhibition pushes part of the psychic energy into the hidden, the subconscious . . . this is why energy transformed by inhibition into a latent state becomes the basis for any function of logic. Thus, the three aspects of psychic energy, or work, correspond to the three aspects of nervous work; emotion corresponds to discharge, will corresponds to working energy, and intellectual energy, especially abstraction, is associated with inhibition or the economy of nervous and psychic strength . . . In higher mental activity, the transformation of live psychic energy into reserve energy prevails." [6]

Most authors agree with this view (according to which emotion is the output of energy). Freud says, for instance, that affects and feelings are expenditures of energy, the final expression of which is perceived as a sensation (feeling). "Affectivity is essentially expressed by motor energy outflow (secretory, regulating the cardiovascular system), that results in an (internal) bodily change unrelated to the external environment;

motor activity is expressed by actions, the purpose of which is to change the external environment." [7]

This view is shared by many art psychologists, including Ovsianiko-Kulikovskii, who considers the principle of the economy of energy as the fundamental principle of aesthetics, even though he makes an exception for feeling. He says, "Our sensate soul can truly be compared with the proverbial cart of which it is said 'whatever falls from it, is lost forever.' Our thinking soul, however, is like a cart from which nothing can fall. Its load is well-packed and hidden in the unconscious . . . If the feelings we experience lived and worked in our unconscious, continuously breaking into our conscious (as does thought), our emotional life would be such a mixture of heaven and hell that even the strongest constitution could not withstand the continuous succession of joys, sorrows, resentment, wrath, love, envy, jealousy, fears, regrets, hopes, and other emotions. No, feelings do not enter the unconscious; there is no such region in the feeling soul. Feelings, as all conscious psychic processes, expend rather than save psychic energy. The life of feelings is the expenditure of the soul." [8]

To corroborate this idea, Ovsianiko-Kulikovskii shows that the law of memory prevails in our thinking, while the law of oblivion prevails in our feeling. He bases his observations on the strongest and highest manifestation of feelings—affects and passions. "Affects and passions are an expenditure of psychic force—there is no doubt about it. If we take all the affects and passions in a given period of time, their expenditure will be enormous. Which components of this expenditure can be considered useful and productive is another question; indeed, most passions and some affects are a waste leading to bankruptcy of the psyche. Thus, if we take the higher processes of scientific and philosophical thought on the one hand, and the strongest affects and passions on the other, we will be fully apprised of the antagonism between the thinking and the feeling psyche. We will realize that these 'two souls' are inharmonious, and a psyche consisting of them is badly organized, unsteady, and full of internal contradiction." [9]

A fundamental problem for the psychology of art is whether emotion is only a waste of psychic energy or whether it has some value in an individual's psychic life. This problem is of basic importance for the psychology of emotion. On its solution depends the solution of another basic problem of the psychology of aesthetics, the principle of the economy of energy. Since Spencer's time we have based our understanding of art on the law of the economy of psychic forces, a law which Spencer considered the universal principle for function of the psyche. This principle was adopted by art historians, and in the Russian literature it was best understood by Veselovskii, who devised the well-known rule that "the merit of a style was the formulation of as many thoughts as possible, in as few words as possible." This view is also held by Potebnia's school, and Ovsianiko-Kulikovskii similarly reduces artistic feeling (as opposed to aesthetic feeling) to a feeling of economy. The formalists opposed this view with a series of quite convincing arguments which contradict this principle. Yakubinskii, for instance, showed that poetic language lacks a rule for the distribution of flowing sound; other scholars showed that poetic language is characterized by a combination of sounds difficult to pronounce, that one of the techniques used is that of hampering perception to deprive it of its customary automatism, and that poetic language is governed by Aristotle's rule that it should sound like a foreign language. The contradiction that exists between this principle and the theory that feeling is an expenditure of psychic energy is obvious. As a matter of fact, it induced Ovsianiko-Kulikovskii, who wanted to preserve both rules in his theory, to divide art into two completely distinct areas, the figurative arts and the lyrical arts. He quite correctly separates artistic feeling from other aesthetic feelings, but for him artistic emotion is emotion derived from thoughts, that is, emotion from a pleasure based on the economy of strength. Conversely, he regards lyrical emotion as an intellectual emotion, fundamentally distinct from the form. The distinction lies in the fact that lyrics actually call forth real emotions and must consequently be set apart in a special psychological grouping. But since emotion is an output of energy, there arises question of how the theory of lyrical emotion accords with the principle of the economy of energy. Ovsianiko-Kulikovskii is correct in separating lyrical emotion from any "applied" emotion caused by lyrics. Unlike Petrazhitskii, who claims that military music is intended to stir bellicose emotions, and church singing functions to arouse religious emotions, he points out that it is impossible to mix these emotions, because "if we admit the possibility of such a mixture, we find that the purpose of erotic poems is stimulation of the sexual appetites. The idea of 'The Covetous Knight' is to prove that avarice is a vice . . . and so on." [10]

If we accept this distinction between the immediate and secondary, or "applied," effect of art (its direct result and consequence), we will have to formulate two separate questions concerning the economy of strength: does the economy of strength (considered by many to be essential for experiencing and understanding art) occur in the secondary or primary effect of art? On the basis of the critical and practical studies we performed in the preceding chapters, the answer appears obvious. We have seen that everything in the primary, or direct, effect of art indicates difficulty with respect to nonartistic activity; consequently, the principle of the economy of strength, if at all applicable, should be applied to the secondary effect of art—to its consequences, but not to the aesthetic response to a work of art. This is the way Freud explains the principle of the economy of strength, as he points out that this economy is quite different from Spencer's naive version. It reminds Freud of the petty economy of the housewife who is ready to travel for miles to a distant market in order to save a few pennies on a purchase. "We have abandoned long ago this naive interpretation of economy," says Freud, "according to which it represents the desire to avoid the expenditure of psychic energy, with the economy occurring when there is a maximum limitation in the use of words and the construction of associations of thought. We have already said that a short, laconic statement is not necessarily a witty one. Brevity of wit is something special, it is 'witty' brevity . . . we may liken psychic economy to a commercial enterprise. So long as the volume is small, general expenses are small and overhead is low. Thrift can be applied to the absolute magnitude of expenditure. But as the business expands, the importance of overhead becomes secondary. Now it is important to increase the volume and the profits, rather than worry about the extent of costs. It would be risky and stupid for the enterprise to economize on costs now." [11]

We shall show that poets usually resort to an economy different from the trivial one proposed by Veselovskii. In fact, were we to retell a tragedy in a short and concise manner, as is done in theater program notes, the economy of words would be even greater than that proposed by Veselovskii. The poet, however, uses a different technique, which is essentially uneconomical with respect to the distribution of our mental forces. The poet intentionally attenuates the cause of the action, arouses our curiosity, plays with our ingenuity, makes our attention run to and fro; in other words, he wastes our strength and energies to the extent required by his work of art. An absolutely faithful and precise narration in prose of Shakespeare's *Hamlet* or Dostoevsky's *The Brothers Karamazov* saves much more psychic energy than the actual works of art. Dostoevsky, for instance, at one of the most climactic moments in his novel, inserts several dots rather than disclose who killed Fedor Karamazov— he lets our thoughts run in circles of suppositions, suspicions, and surmises, seeking the answer. It would have been far more economical (as regards the expenditure of psychic energy) to put down the facts, as in a court investigation or a scientific report. We must conclude, therefore, that the principle of the economy of strength, at least in its Spencerian interpretation, is inapplicable to art forms. Hence Spencer's reasons and arguments are useless here. He assumes that the English language

is economical (i.e., that it saves psychic energy), because adjectives usually precede substantives: "a black horse" is more economical for our
attention than "a horse black," because we meet with trouble concerning the kind of horse we are dealing with if its color is not previously specified. This psychologically naive argument might possibly be
applied to a prosaic distribution of thoughts [46]. In art, however, the
expenditure and utilization of nervous energy are governed by a completely different and opposite rule. The greater the expenditure of nervous energy, the more intense is the effect produced by the work of art.
We must remember that an emotion is an expenditure of psychic force;
we must also remember that art is indissolubly associated with a complex play of emotions; thus, we shall see that art violates the principle of
economy of strength, at least insofar as its immediate effect is concerned, and obeys an opposite principle in the construction of artistic
forms. Our aesthetic response, above all, is a response that annihilates
our nervous energy; it is an explosion, not a penny-pinching economy.

It may be that the principle of the economy of strength can be applied
to art in a completely different manner. To determine this, we must
have a clear idea about the nature of aesthetic reaction. There are
many views on this subject, but these are difficult to organize because
no generally accepted system, psychological or otherwise, exists to deal
with this problem. Every investigator is concerned with a specific problem, and there is no comprehensive psychological system to explain all
aesthetic behavior and response on a total scale. A theory usually deals
with but one aspect of this response; hence it is difficult to determine
whether it is true, because it may well solve a problem that had not
been hitherto formulated for investigation. In his systematic psychology
of art, Müller-Freienfels closes his theory of aesthetic response with the
remark that the position of the psychologist in this case resembles that
of the biologist who can decompose an organic substance into its chemical components but is unable to reproduce the whole from its parts.[12]

The psychologist may, at best, reach the stage of analysis; he has absolutely no access to the synthesis of an aesthetic response. The best proof
of his inability is his attempt to synthesize the psychology of art. He can
find sensorial, motor, associative, intellectual, and emotional factors for
a reaction, but he can say nothing about the relationships among them
nor about how a complete psychology of art may be constructed from
these factors, each of which can be found outside of art. He may obtain
results which are a step beyond the "dead sea of abstract concepts," but
which are of little importance for objective psychology.

These results could be expressed in many pages but, in essence, they
are as follows: this author firmly believes that artistic enjoyment is not

pure perception, but that it requires the highest psychic activity. Artistic emotions are not collected by the psyche as if they were a handful of seeds thrown into a bag. They require a process of germination and growth, and a psychologist may be able to discover the auxiliary and secondary needs of this process, such as warmth, moisture, chemical additives, and so forth.[13] But after his investigation, the psychologist will know no more about the process of germination than before he began.

Our purpose consists in leaving aside systematic analysis and the exhaustive absolute components of aesthetic responses in order to study the germination itself rather than the conditions which cause it. With the aid of synthetic theories of aesthetic emotions, we can group all that has hitherto been said on the subject around two basic arguments. The first was developed by Christiansen in a thorough but ordinary way. He claims that any action of the external world entails a special sensorial and moral effect. According to Goethe, this is the emotional impression, the differential in the mood we experience, which psychologists of the past called the sensorial tone of perception. The color blue calms us, yellow excites us, and so forth. Christiansen claims that art is based on these mood differentials; hence, aesthetic reaction can be represented as follows: an aesthetic object consists of different parts and comprises impressions of material, object, and form which are essentially different but have in common the fact that each element corresponds to a specific emotional tone. "The material of the object and its form are not comprised directly in the aesthetic object, but in the form of the emotional elements added to it," [14] which can be fused into what is generally known as an aesthetic object. The aesthetic response therefore reminds us of piano playing; each element of a work of art strikes a corresponding emotional key in our organism which produces a tone, and the entire aesthetic reaction is made up of emotional impressions arising in response to the "keys."

In a work of art no element is important in itself: it is merely a key. It is the emotional reaction it generates that is important. Such a mechanical concept, however, is in the end incapable of solving the problem of artistic response, because the emotional portion of an impression is quite small compared with the strong affects that make up an aesthetic response. In addition to the emotional impression generated by the individually existing elements of art, an aesthetic response consists also of certain emotional experiences which cannot be included among these mood differentials. Christiansen distinguishes his own theory from the banal theory of art as a mood; this distinction, however, is quantitative rather than qualitative, and in the end we retain the concept of art as a mood arising from various differentials. We cannot understand why there exists a connection between the aesthetic experience and the course of our everyday life, and why art is so important to us. Christiansen finishes by contradicting himself and his own theory when he determines art as embodied desire and an extremely important life activity. His psychological theory is unable to explain how, by the emotional nature of its elements, art can accomplish the tangible realization of the fundamental desires of our psyche. Given such a psychological interpretation, art becomes a very shallow matter that affects only the surface of our psyche because its sensorial tone cannot be separated from the emotion itself. This theory opposes sensualism and demonstrates that enjoyment of art does not occur in the eye or ear; it fails, however, to tell us precisely where it does occur, but places the experience at the approximate level of the eye and ear, closely associating it with the activity of our perceptive organs.

The other theory, known in the psychological literature as the theory of *Einfühlung* (empathy), is therefore more effective. This theory harks back to Herder and was developed by Lipps. It proceeds from an opposite concept of emotional feeling. According to this theory, emotions are not produced in us by a work of art, as are sounds by the keys of a piano. An artistic element does not introduce its emotional tone into us. It is we who introduce emotions into a work of art, emotions arising from the greatest depths of our being and generated not at the shallow level of the receptors but in the most complex activities of our organisms. "Such is the nature of our psyche," says F. T. Fischer, "that it insinuates itself into physical phenomena, or into man-made forms, attributing certain moods to these phenomena, moods which, by means of an unconscious act, enter into the objects. Aesthetics deals with this addition, this *Einfühlung* into inanimate objects."

Lipps has developed a brilliant theory of *Einfühlung* into both linear and three-dimensional forms. He showed that we rise with an ascending line, fall with a descending line, bend with a circle, and so on. If we take only the empirical facts uncovered by Lipps's theory, we can say that it will certainly become part of the future objective psychological theory of aesthetics. From an objective viewpoint, *Einfühlung* is a response to a stimulus. Lipps, who asserts that we introduce our responses into a work of art, is closer to the truth than Christiansen who believes that an aesthetic object introduces its emotional properties into us. But Lipps's theory has as many drawbacks as Christiansen's. First, it offers no criterion by which to distinguish aesthetic responses from other responses unrelated to art. We cannot deny that "*Einfühlung* is an omnipresent part of our perception; hence, it cannot have any specific aesthetic meaning. . . ." [15]

Equally convincing are Meiman's two other objections, that *Ein-fühlung*, such as generated by Faust's verses, sometimes moves to the fore but at other times is completely concealed by the content, and that in the interpretation of *Faust* it is a subordinate element of the aesthetic reaction, rather than its core. If we consider such complex artistic works as novels or architectural structures, we see that their main effect is based on different, very complex processes associated with our perceiving the whole, performing difficult and complicated intellectual operations, and so on.

Müller-Freienfels holds that a work of art generates two kinds of affect in us. Experiencing Othello's jealousy or Macbeth's terror at Banquo's apparition is a coaffect on our part; fearing for Desdemona before she realizes she is in danger is our own affect and should be distinguished from the coaffects.[16]

It is obvious that Christiansen's theory explains only our own, "the viewer's," affects and ignores the coaffects, because no psychologist will define the coaffect of Macbeth's terror or Othello's emotional pains as the emotional tone of these images (their emotional tone is different, and consequently Christiansen's theory ignores coaffects). Lipps's theory, on the other hand, deals exclusively with coaffects. It explains how, by means of *Einfühlung*, we can experience Othello's or Macbeth's passion, but it is unable to explain how we experience a feeling of fear for Desdemona while she still is unconcerned, suspecting nothing. According to Müller-Freienfels, the *Einfühlung* theory cannot explain the different kinds of affect. At most, it can be applied to coaffects, but for our own affects it is inadequate. Only in part do we experience the affects as they are given to the characters in a drama; most of the time we experience them not with, but because of, the characters. Compassion, for instance, is a very inappropriate term, because we very seldom experience a passion *with* someone. Usually, we experience a passion on account of someone else's feelings.[17] These remarks are fully corroborated by Lipps's theory of tragic perception. He introduces the law of the "psychic dam" according to which "a psychic event . . . held up in its natural course . . . forms a block, or dammed-up area," that is, it rises exactly to the point at which the impediment or interruption occurs. Thus, tragic delays increase the value of the suffering protagonist, and *Einfühlung* increases our own value. "When we see psychic sufferings," says Lipps, "what is heightened is the objective feeling of self-value; I feel, to a more intense degree, myself and my human value as reflected in someone else; I feel and experience to a more intense degree what it means to be a human being . . . The means to this end is suffering. . . ." The understanding of the tragic proceeds from the coaffect, while the affect of the tragedy itself remains unexplained.

We realize that none of the existing theories of aesthetic emotion can explain the intimate connection between our feeling and the objects we perceive. To arrive at this explanation, we must resort to psychological systems based on the association between fantasy and feeling. I am speaking here of the review of the problem of fantasy performed by Meinong and his school, Zeller, Meyer, and other psychologists in recent decades. This new approach can be described approximately as follows: The psychologists proceed from the irrefutable association that exists between emotion and imagination. We know that every emotion has a psychic expression in addition to a physical one. In other words, a feeling "is embodied, fixed in an idea, as is evidenced in cases of persecution mania," according to Ribot. Consequently, an emotion is expressed by the mimic, pantomimic, secretory, and somatic responses of our organism. It also requires some expression of our imagination. We find the best evidence for this view among the so-called objectless emotions. Pathological phobias, persistent fears, and so forth, are always associated with specific ideas, most of which are absolutely false and distort reality, but in so doing find their "psychic" expression. A patient who suffers from obsessive fear is emotionally sick, his fear is irrational; and so in order to rationalize it, he imagines that everyone is pursuing and persecuting him. For such a patient, the sequence of events is exactly the opposite of that of a normal person. For the latter, persecution is perceived first, then fear; for the sick man, it is first the fear, then the imagined persecution. Zenkovskii aptly called this phenomenon the "double expression of feelings." Most contemporary psychologists would agree with this view if it is assumed to mean that an emotion is serviced by imagination and expressed in a series of fantastic ideas, concepts, and images that represent its second expression. We might say that an emotion has a central effect in addition to a peripheral one, and that in this case we are discussing the former. Meinong distinguishes opinions from assumptions by establishing whether or not we are convinced of their correctness. If we accidentally take someone we meet for an acquaintance and do not realize our mistake, then this is a judgment (albeit a mistaken one); but if, knowing that the person is not our acquaintance, we persevere in our misjudgment and continue to take him for an acquaintance, we are dealing with an assumption. Meinong holds that children's games and aesthetic illusions are based on assumptions, which are the source of the "feelings and fantasies" that accompany both these activities. For some, these illusory feelings are identical to the real ones. It is quite possible, they say, that the differences (known to experience) between actual and imaginary feelings are based on the fact that the former stem from judgments and the latter from assumptions. We can illustrate this by the following example: If at night we mistake an overcoat hanging in our room for a person, our error is obvious, the experience is false and devoid of real content. But the feeling of fear experienced at the instant the coat was sighted is very real indeed. This means that, in essence, all our fantastic experiences take place on a completely real emotional basis. We see, therefore, that emotion and imagination are not two separate processes; on the contrary, they are the same process. We can regard a fantasy as the central expression of an emotional reaction. We now come to an extremely important conclusion. Psychologists of the past have pondered the relation between the central and peripheral expression of emotions, whether the external expression of feelings is enhanced or weakened by imagination. Wundt and Lehman gave contrasting answers to this question; Meyer postulates that both may be correct. Two distinct cases could well be involved. First, when the images of our fantasy function as the internal stimulus for our new response, they enhance the basic response. A very vivid imagination increases our amorous excitation, but in this case the fantasy is not the expression of the emotion it enhances but rather the discharge of the preceding emotion. Whenever an emotion finds its solution in images of fantasy, this "dreaming" weakens the true manifestation of the emotion; if we expressed our doubts in our fantasy, its external manifestation would be quite weak. We feel that, with reference to emotional responses, all those general psychological laws established with respect to any simple sensory-motor response remain valid. It is an irrefutable fact that our reactions slow down and lose intensity as soon as the central element of the emotion becomes more complicated. We discover that, as the imagination (the central element of the emotional reaction) increases, its peripheral part loses intensity. This has been established by Wundt's school with regard to time, and also studied by Kornilov. We think that it is applicable here. The law can be formulated as follows: It is a single-pole energy outflow characterized by the fact that nervous energy is expended at one pole, either at the center or at the periphery, and increases in energy outflow at one pole lead to a decrease at the other. This same law has been discovered, in a somewhat scattered fashion, by other investigators of emotion. The novelty that we introduce amounts to gathering these diverse thoughts into a single concept. According to Groos we are dealing, both in play and aesthetic activity, or response, with a *delay, but not with an inhibition of the response.* "I am more and more convinced that emotions as such are in extremely close connection with physical sensations. The internal or-

ganic state on which psychic motions and emotions are based is likely to
be impeded to some extent by the tendency toward continuation of the
initial concept, as it might be in the case of a child who plays that he is
fighting, but delays the motion of his arm ready to strike." [18]

I feel that this delay and weakening of inner organic and external
manifestations of emotions should be regarded as a particular case of
the general law of single-pole energy outflow due to emotions. As we
have seen, energy flows out from one of two poles, either at the periphery or at the center; and an increased activity at one pole leads immediately to a decrease at the other.

It seems to me that only from this viewpoint can we approach art
which appears to stir very strong feelings in us, which feelings are not
specifically expressed. The enigmatic difference that exists between artistic feeling and ordinary feeling may be explained as follows: Artistic
feeling is the same as the other, but it is released by extremely in-
tensified activity of the imagination. The contrasting elements of which
any aesthetic response is composed are thus joined into a unit. Psychologists have up to now been unable to establish a mutual relationship between contemplation and emotion. They could not establish the place
of each element in the framework of artistic emotion, so much so that
the most consequential art psychologist, Müller-Freienfels, suggested
the existence of two kinds of art and two kinds of spectators. One at-
taches greater significance to contemplation, and the other to feeling,
and vice versa.

Our assumption is supported by the fact that until now psychologists
have been unable to determine the difference between feeling in art and
conventional, or ordinary, feeling. Müller-Freienfels suggests that the
difference is merely quantitative, and says, ". . . aesthetic affects are
powerful, that is, they are affects which do not strive toward action, but
which nonetheless can attain the highest intensity of feeling." [19] This
statement agrees with what we have just stated. It also comes close to
Münsterberg's psychological theory, according to which isolation is an
indispensable condition for aesthetic experience. In the last analysis,
isolation is nothing but the condition in which it is possible to distinguish the aesthetic stimulus from other stimuli; this condition is indispensable because it guarantees a strictly central release of the affects
generated by art and ensures that these affects are not expressed by any
other external action. Hennequin recognizes the same difference between real and artistic feeling in the fact that emotions in themselves do
not lead to actions. "The purpose of a work of literature," he states, "is
to cause specific emotions that cannot be directly expressed in action. . . ." [20]

It is the delay in the external manifestation which is the distinguishing characteristic of an artistic emotion and the reason for its extraordinary power. We can show that art is a central emotion, one that releases itself in the cerebral cortex. The emotions caused by art are intelligent emotions. Instead of manifesting themselves in the form of fist-shaking or fits, they are usually released in images of fantasy. Diderot states that an actor weeps real tears, but the tears come from his brain; thus, he expresses the essence of his artistic reaction. But, we must realize that a similar central release is quite conceivable with conventional or ordinary emotions. Consequently, a single characteristic does not yet establish, or define, the specific distinction of aesthetic emotion.

But there is more. Psychologists frequently claim that mixed feelings exist. Although some authors, such as Titchener, deny their existence, others maintain that art always deals with mixed feelings, and that emotions, in general, have an organic character. This is why many authors regard an emotion as an internal organic response, which expresses the agreement or disagreement of our organism with the neural response released by an individual organ. The unity of our organism expresses itself in the emotion. Titchener explains, "When Othello is harsh toward Desdemona, she excuses his rudeness by saying that he is upset by affairs of state. '. . . Let our finger ache,' she says, 'and it induces our other healthful members even to that sense of pain.' " [21] Emotion is taken here as a general global organic response to events occurring in an individual organ. This is why art (which, rather than repelling us, attracts us even as it provokes unpleasant feelings) is bound to be associated with mixed feelings and emotions. Müller-Freienfels refers to Socrates' opinion, as stated by Plato, that the same person should write both comedies and tragedies[22] because the contrast of feelings is essential to an aesthetic impression [47]. In analyzing tragic feeling, he points out duality as its basis and shows that the tragic is impossible if taken objectively and without any psychological background, because this background is the contrast between inhibition and excitation.[23] Despite the depressing nature of the tragic emotion, "on the whole it is one of the loftiest heights to which human nature can attain, since the spiritual conquest of deep pain or sorrow generates a feeling of triumph which has no equal." [24]

For Schilder also, this emotion is based upon the duality of the tragic impression.[25] Indeed, every author has made some comment concerning the fact that a tragedy always involves contrasting feelings. Plekhanov cites Darwin's views of the principle of antithesis in our expressive emotions and attempts to apply them to art. According to Darwin, some moods cause certain habitual movements which may be regarded as useful; in an opposing intellectual mood there exists a strong, involuntary tendency to perform movements of an opposite nature which seem useless. This appears to be due to the fact that any voluntary movement invariably requires the action of certain muscles; by performing a diametrically opposite movement, we put opposite muscles to work (movement right or left, pushing or pulling, lifting and dropping, and so forth). Since the performance of opposite movements under the influence of opposing impulses has become habitual in us as well as in lower animals, when movements of one kind are closely associated with an emotion or feeling, it is perfectly natural to assume that movements of an opposite nature are performed involuntarily, as a consequence of a habitual association.[26]

This remarkable law discovered by Darwin is applicable to art, and it is no longer surprising that the tragedy which simultaneously generates in us opposing affects acts according to the principle of antithesis and sends opposite impulses to opposing muscle groups. It forces us to move simultaneously to the right and left, simultaneously to lift and drop weights, simultaneously to move one group of muscles and their opposites. This is how we can explain the delay in the external manifestation of affect that takes place in art. And this is where we may find the specific distinguishing marks of the aesthetic response.

We have seen from the foregoing that a work of art (such as a fable, a short story, a tragedy), always includes an affective contradiction, causes conflicting feelings, and leads to the short-circuiting and destruction of these emotions. This is the true effect of a work of art. We come now to the concept of *catharsis* [48] used by Aristotle as the basis for his explanation of tragedy, and repeatedly mentioned by him with regard to the other arts. In his *Poetica* he says that "tragedy imitates an important and finished action of a certain magnitude, with a speech whose every part has a different ornament, or with action, not narration, that performs a purification of such affects by means of pity and fear." [27]

No matter what interpretation we assign the enigmatic term catharsis, we must be sure that it corresponds to Aristotle's. For our purposes, however, this is irrelevant. Whether we follow Lessing, who understands catharsis to be the moral action of the tragedy (the transformation of passions into virtues) or Müller, for whom it is the transition from displeasure to pleasure; whether we accept Bernays' interpretation of the term as healing and purification in the medical sense, or Zeller's opinion that catharsis appeases affect,—we will imperfectly and incompletely express the meaning we assign to this term. Despite the indefiniteness of its content, despite our failure to explain the meaning of this term in the Aristotelian sense, there is no other term in psychology which so completely expresses the central fact of aesthetic reaction, according to which painful and unpleasant affects are discharged and transformed into their opposites. Aesthetic reaction as such is nothing but catharsis, that is, a complex transformation of feelings. Though little is known at present about the process of catharsis, we do know, however, that the discharge of nervous energy (which is the essence of any emotion) takes place in a direction which opposes the conventional one, and that art therefore becomes a most powerful means for important and appropriate discharges of nervous energy. The basis for this process reveals itself in the contradiction which inheres in the structure of any work of art. We have already mentioned Ovsianiko-Kulikovskii, who believes Hector's farewell scene stirs in us contrasting and conflicting emotions. On the one hand, these are emotions we would experience if the scene were described by Pisemskii; they are anything but lyrical since the description is not a poem; on the other hand, the emotion is stirred by the hexameters and a lyrical emotion par excellence. But then, in any work of art there are emotions generated by the material as well as the form; the question is: how do these two kinds of emotion interrelate to each other? We already know the answer, for it derives from our preceding arguments. This relation is one of antagonism; the two kinds of emotion move in opposite directions. The law of aesthetic response is the same for a fable as for a tragedy: *it comprises an affect that develops in two opposite directions but reaches annihilation at its point of termination.*

This is the process we should like to call catharsis. We have shown that the artist always overcomes content with form, and we have found a corroboration of this statement in the structures of the fable and the tragedy. If we study the psychological effect of individual formal elements, we find that they fit precisely the requirements set by the task. Wundt has shown that rhythm in itself expresses only "a method of expressing feelings in terms of time." An individual rhythmic form is the expression of a flow of feelings, but since the temporal placement of the flow of feelings is part of the affect, the representation of this method in rhythm causes the affect as such. "Thus, the aesthetic significance of rhythm is its function as a cause affect. In other words, rhythm generates the affect of which it is a part through the psychological laws of emotional processes." [28]

We see, therefore, that rhythm itself, as one of the formal elements, is capable of generating the affects represented by it. If a poet selects a rhythm whose effect is in contrast with, or opposite to, the effect of the content of his work, we perceive this phenomenon of contrast. Bunin has described murder, shooting, and passion with a rhythm of cold, detached calm. His rhythm generates an affect opposite to the one generated by his story's material. In the end the aesthetic response becomes a feeling of catharsis; we experience a complex discharge of feelings, their mutual transformation, and instead of the painful experiences forming the content of the short story, we experience the delicate, transparent feeling of a breath of fresh air. The same thing occurs in fables and tragedies. Such a contrast of feelings exists also in the case mentioned by Ovsianiko-Kulikovskii. Hexameters, if needed at all, and if Homer is at all better than Pisemskii, do enlighten and cathartically purify the emotions generated by the content of the *Iliad*. The contrast discovered by us in the structure of artistic form and that of artistic content is the basis of cathartic action in the aesthetic response. Schiller puts it like this: "The secret of a master is to destroy content by means of form; the more majestic and attractive the content, the more it moves to the fore, and the more the viewer falls under its spell, the greater the triumph of art which removes the content and dominates it."

A work of art always contains an intimate conflict between its content and its form, and the artist achieves his effect by means of the form, which destroys the content.

Let us now make some final statements. We can say that the basic aesthetic response consists of affect caused by art, affect experienced by us as if it were real, but which finds its release in the activity of imagination provoked by a work of art. This central release delays and inhibits the external motor aspect of affect, and we think we are experiencing only illusory feelings. Art is based upon the union of feeling and imagination. Another peculiarity of art is that, while it generates in us opposing affects, it delays (on account of the antithetic principle) the motor expression of emotions and, by making opposite impulses collide, it destroys the affect of content and form, and initiates an explosive discharge of nervous energy.

Catharsis of the aesthetic response is the transformation of affects, the explosive response which culminates in the discharge of emotions.

NOTES

1. See E. B. Titchener, *Experimental Psychology, A Manual of Laboratory Practice,* New York: Macmillan, 1901.

2. *Ibid.*

3. S. Freud, *Fundamental Psychological Theories in Psychoanalysis.*

4. *Ibid.*

5. D. N. Ovsianiko-Kulikovskii, *Collected Works,* vol. VI, St. Petersburg, 1914, pp. 23–24.

6. I. G. Orshanskii, *Mekhanizm nervnykh protsessov (The Mechanism of the Nervous Processes)*, St. Petersburg, 1898, pp. 536–537.

7. S. Freud, *Fundamental Psychological Theories.*

8. D. N. Ovsianiko-Kulikovskii, *Collected Works*, vol. VI, pp. 24–26.

9. *Ibid.*, pp. 27–28.

10. *Ibid.*, pp. 191–192.

11. S. Freud, *Wit and Its Relation to the Unconscious*, New York: Moffat, Yard & Co., 1917.

12. See R. Müller-Freienfels, *Psychologie der Kunst*, vol. I, Leipzig-Berlin, 1923, p. 242.

13. *Ibid.*, p. 248.

14. Christiansen, *Filosofiia iskusstva* (*The Philosophy of Art*), p. 111.

15. E. Meiman, *Sistema Estetiki* (*Aesthetic Systems*), Moscow, 1920, p. 149.

16. R. Müller-Freienfels, *Psychologie der Kunst*, vol. I, pp. 207–208.

17. *Ibid.*, pp. 208–209.

18. K. Groos, *Dushevnaia zhizn rebenka* (*The Mental Life of the Child*), Kiev, 1916, pp. 184–185.

19. R. Müller-Freienfels, *Psychologie der Kunst*, vol. I, p. 210.

20. E. Hennequin, "An Attempt to Create a Scientific Criticism: An Aesthetic Psychology," *Russkoe Bogatstvo* (*The Wealth of Russia*), 1892, p. 15.

21. E. Titchener, *Experimental Psychology*.

22. R. Müller-Freienfels, *Psychologie der Kunst*, vol. I, p. 203.

23. *Ibid.*, p. 227.

24. *Ibid.*, p. 229.

25. P. Schilder, *Medizinische Psychologie für Aerzte und Psychologen*, Berlin, 1924, p. 320.

26. Chas. R. Darwin, *The Expression of the Emotions in Man and Animals*, with a preface by K. Lorenz, Chicago: University of Chicago Press, 1965.

27. Aristotle, *Poetica*.

28. W. Wundt, *Grundzüge der physiologischen Psychologie*, Leipzig: W. Engelmann, 1902–1903.

10 THE PSYCHOLOGY OF ART

VERIFYING THE FORMULA. PSYCHOLOGY OF VERSE. LYRIC AND EPIC. HERO
AND DRAMATIS PERSONAE. DRAMA. THE COMIC AND THE TRAGIC. THEATER.
PAINTING, DRAWING, SCULPTURE, ARCHITECTURE.

We have ascertained that contradiction is the essential feature of artistic form and material. We have also found that the essential part of
aesthetic response is the manifestation of the affective contradiction
which we have designated by the term *catharsis*.

It would be very important to show how catharsis is achieved in
different art forms, what its chief characteristics are, and what auxiliary
processes and mechanisms are involved in it. However, such an investigation would lead beyond the scope of our present endeavor, since special research on the function of catharsis in each art form would have to
be undertaken. Our main purpose is to focus attention on the central
point of the aesthetic response, determine its psychological "weight,"
and use it as the fundamental explanatory principle in our further investigations. We must now check the accuracy of the formula we have
found and determine its general applicability and explanatory power.
This test, and the corrections which no doubt will be made as a consequence of its application, should be the subject of many further individual studies. Here we shall confine ourselves to making a brief survey to
determine whether or not our formula withstands the test. It is obvious

that we must abandon the idea of a systematic, empirical verification of our formula. We are only able to survey individual, random phenomena by taking typical examples from all fields of art and attempting to see whether, and to what extent, our formula applies to them. Let us begin with poetry.

If we take existing studies of verse, studies performed not by psychologists but by art critics, as an aesthetic fact, we immediately note the striking resemblance between the conclusions reached by psychologists on the one hand, and art critics on the other. The two sets of facts—psychic and aesthetic—reveal a surprising correspondence which corroborates and confirms our formula. This observation applies to the concept of rhythm in modern poetry. We have long since abandoned the naive interpretation of rhythm as meter, or measure. Andrei Bely's investigations in Russia and Saran's studies abroad showed that rhythm is a complex artistic structure that corresponds to the contradiction which we conceptualize as the heart of the artistic response. The Russian tonic system of versification is based on the regular sequence of stressed and unstressed syllables. If an iambic tetrameter [49] is defined as a verse consisting of four disyllabic feet, each consisting of a stressed syllable followed by an unstressed syllable, it is almost impossible to compose such a verse; for the tetrameter would have to consist of four two-syllable words (in the Russian language every word has but a single stress). In actual practice, however, verses are written in this meter. These verses contain three, five, or six words, that is, more or fewer stresses than required by theory. According to the academic theory of philology, any discrepancy between the requirements of the meter and the actual number of stresses in a verse is made up by subtraction or addition of stresses with correspondent adjustment of articulation and pronunciation. In poetry, however, we retain the natural stress of words, so that the verse frequently deviates from the required meter. The sum of deviations from the meter defines the rhythm, according to Bely. He proves his point as follows: if the rhythm of a verse consists in nothing but keeping the correct beat, then all the verse written in one meter should be identical, and such a regular beat should produce no emotional effect aside from reminding us of a rattle or a drum. It is the same with music, where rhythm is not the beat that can be marked with the foot, but the filling of the measures with unequal and uneven notes which give the impression of complex movement. These deviations observe certain regularities, engage in certain combinations, form a certain system; this system of irregularities is what Bely takes as the basis for his concept of rhythm.[1] His studies have been proved to be correct, for today we may find a precise differentiation between the concepts of meter and rhythm in any textbook. The need for such a differentiation arises from the fact that words resist the meter which attempts to adjust them into a verse. ". . . With the aid of words," says Zhirmunskii, "it is as impossible to create a work of art governed completely by the rules of musical composition without distorting the very nature of the words, just as it is impossible to create an ornament of the human body and still maintain its primary purpose. There is no pure rhythm in poetry, just as there is no symmetry in painting. Rhythm is the interaction of the natural properties of speech components with the rules of composition which cannot be fully applied because of the resistance of the material." [2]

We perceive a natural number of stresses in words, and at the same time we perceive the norm toward which verse strives but never approaches. The conflict between meter and words—the discrepancy, discord, and contradiction between them—this is rhythm. As we can see, this view coincides with the analyses we have already conducted. Here are the three parts of the aesthetic response which we mentioned at an earlier stage: the two conflicting affects and the catharsis which completes them in the three elements established by the theory of metrics for the verse. According to Zhirmunskii, these are "(1) the natural *phonetic properties* of the speech material, . . . (2) the *meter,* an ideal law governing the succession of strong and weak sounds in a verse; and (3) the *rhythm,* the actual succession of strong and weak sounds resulting from the interaction between the natural properties of the speech material used and the metric rules." [3] Saran holds the same view: "A verse form is the result of an intimate unification of, or a compromise between, two elements, the sound form characteristic of spoken language, and the orchestral meter . . . This is how the struggle, whose results are the various 'styles' of the same verse form, arises." [4]

We now must demonstrate that the three poetical elements in the verse coincide in their psychological meaning with the three elements of aesthetic action. To do this, we must establish that the first two elements are in mutual contradiction and provoke affects of contrasting nature; the third element, rhythm, is the cathartic resolution of the first two. Such an approach is supported by the latest studies which replace the old-fashioned teaching of the harmony of all the elements of a work of art and contrast it with the principle of the struggle and antinomy of certain elements. If we do not study static form, and if we reject the crude analogy according to which form contains content as a glass does wine, then, according to Tynianov, we must adopt a constructive principle and consider form to be dynamic. We must study the factors making up a work of art not in their static structure but in their dynamic flow. We shall then see that "the unity of the work is not a closed symmetrical entity but an unfolding, dynamic whole. There is no static sign of equality or multiplication between its elements, but the dynamic sign of correlation and integration exists always." [5] Not all factors in a work of art are equivalent. Form is the result of the constructive subordination of certain factors to others, rather than of their fusion into one. "We always perceive form as flow (that is, change), as the correlation of the subordinating, constructive factor and the subordinated one. There is no need to attach a temporal characteristic to this unfolding. The flow, the dynamics, can be taken per se, outside of time, and considered as pure motion. Art is this interaction, this struggle. Without this subordination, without the deformation of factors by the one factor playing the constructive role, there can be no art." [6]

Such reasoning is why modern scholars do not accept the traditional teaching of the relationship between the rhythm and the meaning of a verse. They show that the structure of a verse is not based upon the correspondence between rhythm and meaning, nor upon the uniform trend of all its factors; the exact contrary is true. Meiman distinguished two opposing tendencies in the declamation of verses, a time-beating one and a phrasing one. He assumed, however, that these two tendencies are characteristics of different individuals) when, actually, they are part of the verse itself—a verse which simultaneously contains two opposing tendencies. "The verse reveals itself as a system of complex interactions, a struggle rather than a cooperation between factors. It becomes obvious that the specific *plus* of poetry is to be found in this interaction, the basis of which is the constructive role of rhythm, and its deforming function with respect to the other factors . . . Thus, the acoustic approach to verse reveals the paradox of apparently balanced and even poetic work." [7] Proceeding from this contradiction and the struggle of factors, investigators were able to show how the very meaning of a verse or word changes, how the evolution of the subject, the selection of an image, and so on, change under the effect of rhythm as the constructive factor in a poem. The same is true in the case of meaning. Tynianov, paraphrasing Goethe, concludes that "great impressions depend mysteriously on various poetic forms. It would be tempting to transpose the content of several Roman elegies to the tone and meter of Byron's *Don Juan*." [8] A few examples may show that the meaningful construction of a verse necessarily includes an intimate contradiction in an instance where we expect harmony. One of Lermontov's critics writes about his remarkable poem, *I, the Mother of God*, "These ornate verses lack inspired simplicity and sincerity, the two main characteristics of prayer. In praying for a young, innocent woman, it is inappropriate to mention old age or death. Note: 'the warm patroness of a cold world. . . .' What a cold antithesis!" Indeed, it is difficult not to note the inner contradiction in the meaning of those elements which make up the poem. Evlakhov says, "Not only does Lermontov discover a new species in the animal kingdom (in addition to Anakreon's horned doe) in his description of a 'lioness with a curly mane around her head,' but in his poem *When the Yellow Cornfield Waves*, he changes nature to suit his case. Gleb Uspenskii remarks that 'for the sake of this special case, climate and feelings are confused, and everything is chosen so arbitrarily that one can only doubt the poet's sincerity' . . . This remark is very correct in essence, although not very intelligent in its conclusion." [9]

All of Pushkin's poetry involves two contradictory feelings. Let us take the poem *I Roam the Noisy Streets* as an example. It is traditionally understood to represent a poet persecuted by the notion of death. His preoccupation saddens him, but he adjusts to the idea of death's inevitability and ends by praising youth and life. Given such an interpretation, the last line of the poem contrasts with the entire work. We can easily show that this traditional interpretation is totally inaccurate. If the poet wanted to show how the environment leads to thoughts of death, he would have chosen a more appropriate environment. He would have led us to the usual haunts of sentimental poets: a cemetery, a hospital, to the dying, or perhaps to suicide. But Pushkin chose an ambient which creates a contradiction in every line. The poet is seized by the thought of death in noisy streets, in crowded churches, in busy squares —in places where death is definitely out of place. A lone oak, sovereign of the forests; a newborn child—these images again conjure the idea of death, and the contradiction becomes overwhelming. Thus we can see that the poem is built upon the juxtaposition of two extremes [50], life and death. We find this contradiction in every line, for it pervades the entire poem. In the fifth line, for example, the poet recognizes that death comes every day, but it is not really death—it is the anniversary of death, that is, death's trace in life. It is not surprising that the poem concludes with the statement that even the insensible corpse wishes to rest near its homeland. The last, catastrophic line is not in contrast to the whole poem but presents a catharsis of the two contrasting ideas by casting them in a new form: young life conjured death's image everywhere; it now plays at the threshold of death.

Pushkin habitually uses such sharp contradictions. His *Egyptian Nights*, his *Banquet during Pestilence*, and others are based on similar contradictions which are carried to the extreme. Pushkin's lyric poetry always follows the law of dualism. His words are simple in meaning, but his verse transforms this meaning into lyrical emotion. A similar pattern exists in his epics. The most striking examples are his *Tales of Belkin*. For a long time these tales were regarded as rather insignificant and quite idyllic works, until critics discovered two conflicting levels, a tragic reality hidden beneath a smooth and happy surface, so that *Tales of Belkin* suddenly became dramatic, full of strong and powerful effects. The artistic effect of the stories is based upon the contradiction between the core and the surface of the story. "The superficial course of events," says Uzin, "imperceptibly leads the reader toward a peaceful, calm solution of the problems, the most complex of which apparently unravel themselves in the simplest way. But the narration itself contains contradictory elements. As we carefully observe the complex ornamentation of the *Tales of Belkin* we find that the final resolutions are not the only ones possible." [10] "Life itself and its hidden meaning are here fused into a unit, so much so that we cannot distinguish them. The commonplace facts appear tragic because we feel along with them the action of hidden underground forces in action. Belkin's secret intention, which is so carefully concealed in the introduction of his anonymous biographer, shows us that beneath the peaceful and placid surface, fateful possibilities lie hidden . . . Let everything come to a happy ending: this is consolation for Mitrofan, because any thought of another solution fills us with terror." [11]

The merit of this critic consists in his success in showing convincingly that Pushkin's stories contain a hidden meaning, that the lines which seem to lead to happiness may lead to misery as well; he succeeded in showing that the interplay of these two directions in one and the same line represents the true phenomenon which we seek in the aesthetic experience of catharsis. "These two elements are joined together in every one of Belkin's stories with extraordinary, inimitable art. The slightest increase of one at the expense of the other would lead to a complete destruction of these marvellous works. The introduction creates the equilibrium among the elements." [12]

The same rule is applicable to the structure of the more complex epic works. Let us take *Eugene Onegin*. This work is usually understood as the portrayal of a young man of the 1820's and an idealized Russian girl. The heroes are conceptualized as static, completely finished entities that do not change during the course of the narrative.

Yet, we need only look at this work to see that Pushkin treats his heroes dynamically and that the constructive principle of his narrative in verse lies in the development of the characters as the story proceeds. Tynianov says, "Only recently have we abandoned the kind of criticism in which we discuss and condemn the protagonists of a novel as if they were live human beings . . . All such criticism is based upon the assumption of a *static protagonist*. . . . The static unity of the protagonist (as any static unity in a work of literature) is very unstable; depending entirely upon the principle of construction employed, it can oscillate in the course of a literary work in the way called for by the dynamics of each individual case. Suffice it to say that there exists a *sign* of unity, a category that justifies the most obvious cases of its violation and forces us to regard them as *equivalents of unity*. But this unity cannot be the naively conceptualized static unity of the protagonist; instead of the law of static unity we must consider the symbol of dynamic integration, of completion. There is no static protagonist, there can only be dynamic ones. And the name of the protagonist alone is enough of a symbol to prevent us from observing the hero himself at every juncture in the narrative." [13] Nothing corroborates this statement better than Pushkin's *Eugene Onegin*. In this verse narrative, Onegin's name functions only as the symbol of a hero; it is equally easy to show that the protagonists represented are dynamic and change in accordance with the structure of the work. Critics have always proceeded from the wrong assumption, namely, that the hero of this work is static. To corroborate their approach they pointed out Onegin's character traits, which were taken from his model in life. "The object of a study of art must be the specific matter that distinguishes art from other fields of intellectual endeavor and methods of employing these fields as material or as tools. A work of art is a complex interaction of many factors; consequently, the purpose of a study must be the determination of the specific character of this interaction." [14] This view clearly says that the material of the study must be nonmotivated in art, that is, something which belongs to art alone. Let us now take a look at *Eugene Onegin*.

The conventional characteristics ascribed to Onegin and Tatiana are derived entirely from the first part of the novel. The dynamics of the development and evolution of these characters are ignored, as are the extraordinary contradictions into which the hero and heroine run at the end of the work. Hence there appears a whole series of misunderstandings and misconceptions. Take Onegin's character first: we can easily show that Pushkin initially introduces certain conventional static elements with the sole purpose of making them function in contradictions at the end of the narrative. We are told about the unique, overwhelming, and hopeless love of Onegin and of its tragic end. The author should have here selected protagonists predestined to play a love role. Instead, we see from the very beginning that Pushkin stresses those traits in the character of Onegin which make it impossible for him to be the hero of a story of tragic love. In the first chapter, in which the poet describes in detail how Onegin was familiar with the science of sweet passion (stanzas X, XI, and XII) he is shown as a person who has wasted his heart on worldly people. From the first stanzas the reader is prepared for the fact that anything can happen to Onegin *except* death from unrequited love. It is remarkable that this very first chapter contains the lyrical digression on beautiful female legs, a digression which hints at the extraordinary power of unfulfilled love, and immediately introduces another, opposing, level which contrasts to the previous exposition of Onegin's character. Immediately afterward, however, the poet says that Onegin is incapable of love (stanzas XXXVII, XLII, and XLIII):

No feelings lived within his heart;
The worldly glamour bored him;
Beauties were but fleetingly
The subject of his thoughts . . .

We are absolutely certain that Onegin will not become the hero of a tragic romance when the narrative suddenly takes an unexpected turn. After Tatiana's profession of love, we see that Onegin's heart has hardened to the extent that involvement with her is out of the question. However, the other line of development manifests itself still. Onegin learns that his friend Lenskii is in love and says, "I'd take the other one [Tatiana], were I, like you, a poet." The true image of catastrophe finally emerges from the contrast between Onegin and Tatiana. The poet represents Tatiana's love as an imaginary love; he stresses everywhere that she loves not Onegin but a romantic hero whom she has invented.

"She began to read novels when she was very young": from this statement Pushkin develops the imaginary, dreamy character of her love. According to Pushkin's story, Tatiana does not love Onegin, or rather she does love, but her object is not Onegin; the poem tells us about her overhearing rumors that she will marry Onegin:

A thought was born within her heart;
And when time came when she fell in love.
A seed that falls onto the ground,
Takes life from spring's own ardor.
Her mind, consumed
By tenderness and desire, had
Long been hungry for forbidden fruit;
Her heart has long been
Beating with passion in her breast;
She yearned . . . for someone,

At last . . . she saw the light;
And then she said: It's he!

It is stated quite clearly here that Onegin is the "somebody" for whom
Tatiana yearns. From then on, her love evolves along an imaginary line
(stanza X). She fancies herself Clarissa, Julie, or Delphine, and

She sighs, she weeps, adopts
Someone else's joy and sorrow,
Becomes oblivious, whispers
The words she'll write her dearest one . . .

Her famous letter is written first in her mind, and then on paper. We
shall see that it has indeed all the features of a fictitious letter. It is remarkable that already in stanza XV Pushkin sets his novel on a seemingly false course when he bemoans Tatiana, who has placed her fate in
the hands of a superficial dandy, when in actual fact it is Onegin who
perishes of love. Before his encounter with Tatiana, Pushkin reminds us
that

His heart no longer burnt with love for beauty,
Although at times, indifferently, he would
Indulge in courting girls;
If they refused, he was at once consoled,
If they betrayed him, he was glad to rest.

His love, says Pushkin, is like the performance of an indifferent guest
who arrives to play whist.

Early in the morning he does not know
Where in the evening he will go.

When Onegin meets Tatiana, he immediately talks about marriage
and describes a torn, unhappy family life. It is hard to imagine duller or
more complex images than these, which are diametrically opposed to
the subject matter of their talk. The character of Tatiana's love reveals
itself when she visits Onegin's house, looks at his books, and begins to
understand that he is actually a sham. Her mind and feeling now find a
solution to the riddle that was haunting her. The unexpectedly pathetic
character of Onegin's last love becomes particularly obvious when we
compare Onegin's letter to Tatiana's. In the latter, Pushkin emphasizes
the elements of the French *roman* from which it is derived. In writing
this letter, he appeals to the bard of banquets and languid sorrow, because he is the only one who can sing its magic melody. Pushkin calls
his rendition of the letter an incomplete and poor translation. Interest-

ingly, he precedes Onegin's letter with the remark, "There is his letter, word for word." In Tatiana's letter, on the other hand, all is romantically indefinite, vague, and nebulous; in Onegin's reply all is clear and precise—word for word. It is remarkable that in her letter Tatiana, as if by accident, reveals the true purpose of the narrative when she writes: "To be a faithful wife and a good mother." Compared with this gentle carelessness and sweet nonsense (to quote Pushkin), the frank truthfulness of Onegin's letter is overwhelming.

> I know it well, my days are counted;
> But for my life to flow a while,
> I must be certain in the morning
> That I shall see you before the night . . .

The entire last part of the narrative down to the very last strophe is permeated with hints that Onegin's life is ended, that he is dying, that he can no longer breathe. Though Pushkin talks about this half jokingly, half seriously, the truth reveals itself with shattering force in the famous scene of their new encounter, which is interrupted by the sudden and unexpected clicking of spurs:

> Here, my dear friend, I shall abandon
> Our hero, when his luck
> Has turned against him,
> For long . . . forever. . . .

Pushkin ends his tale at a seemingly arbitrary point, but this strange and completely unexpected operation strongly emphasizes the artistic completeness of the work. When in the catastrophic stanza Pushkin speaks about the bliss of those who have left the festival of life at an early age without drinking the brimming cup to the very end, the reader wonders whether the poet speaks about his hero or about himself.

Lenskii's parallel romance with Olga is in direct contrast with the tragic love of Onegin and Tatiana. Pushkin claims that her faithful portrait can be found in any novel or *roman*. He chose her because she is by nature predestined to be the heroine of a love story. Lenskii, too, is presented as a person born for love, but is killed in a duel. Here, the reader is faced with a paradox: He expects the real love drama to unfold between the woman destined to be the true heroine of the narrative, and the man destined to play the role of Romeo; he expects the shot that destroyed their love to be crucially dramatic—but his expectations are cut short. Pushkin develops his story against the natural grain of the material, when he transforms Olga's and Lenskii's love into commonplace triteness (Lenskii's fate, he reveals, is that of "a country squire, happy and cuckolded, wearing a quilted dressing gown"), and makes the real drama occur where we least expect it. In fact, the entire work is built on an impossibility. The analogy between the first and the second part (although their meanings are opposite) shows this quite clearly: Tatiana's letter—Onegin's letter; the encounter of Onegin and Tatiana in the country garden—the talk at Tatiana's in Petersburg. The reader, misled by this parallelism, does not notice to what extent the hero and the heroine have changed; he does not notice that the Onegin of the end of the narrative is not only different from the Onegin of the beginning, but his complete opposite, and the concluding action at the end is the opposite of that at the beginning.

The character of the hero has changed dynamically, the narrative has taken an unexpected course, and, most important, the change in the hero's character is essential to the unfolding of the action. Pushkin prepares the reader to believe that Onegin cannot become the hero of a tragic love affair, but in the end transforms him into a tragic victim of love. A scholar very aptly once said that there are two kinds of works of art, just as there are two kinds of flying machines—those lighter and those heavier than air. A balloon rises because it is lighter than air. This is not really a triumph over nature, for the balloon floats in the air not by its own devices, but because it is pushed upward. Conversely, an airplane (a flying machine heavier than air) fights air resistance, overcomes it, pushes itself up, and rises despite its tendency to fall. A true work of art reminds us of a heavier-than-air machine. It is always made of material much heavier than air, and from the very outset seems to oppose any effort to make it rise. The weight of the material counteracts its rise and drags the structure to the ground. Flight can be achieved only by overcoming this tendency to fall.

This is the case with *Eugene Onegin.* How simple (and how trite) the story would be if we knew from the very beginning that Onegin would have an unhappy love affair. At best, this plot could be developed into a second-rate sentimental novel. But when he actually falls victim to the tragic love in spite of his own efforts, then we witness the artist's triumph over "material heavier than air" and experience the real joy of flying, the lift imparted by the catharsis of art.

The heroes of a drama, as well as an epic, are dynamic. The substance of drama is struggle, but the struggle contained in the principal material of a drama overshadows the conflict between artistic elements that results from conventional dramatic strife. This point is easy to understand if we regard a drama not as a finished work of art but as the basic material for a theatrical performance. A closer look at the problem of content and form, however, will make it possible to differentiate these two dramatic elements.

First, we must apply the concept of the dynamic protagonist to drama. The false notion that the purpose of drama is to represent characters could have been abandoned long ago, had scholars treated Shakespeare's dramas with the proper objectivity. Evlakhov calls the idea of Shakespeare's remarkable skill in representing characters "an old wives' tale." Volkelt says that "Shakespeare in many cases went much further than psychology properly admits." No one, however, has understood this fact better than Tolstoy (as we have already noted in our discussion of *Hamlet*). He states that his opinion is completely opposed to the one then prevalent in Europe and correctly points out that King Lear speaks a pompous, characterless language, as do all of Shakespeare's kings. He then shows that the events in the tragedy are unbelievable, paradoxical, and unnatural. "Perhaps this tragedy is absurd the way I retell it . . . but in its original version it is even more so." [15] As the main proof that there are no real characters in Shakespeare's plays Tolstoy adduces that "none of his characters ever speak their own language, but always talk in the same Shakespearian, stilted, unnatural language which not only does not suit the roles, but cannot be spoken by any person alive." [16] Tolstoy regards language as the principal tool for representing a character, and Volkenshteyn remarks that Tolstoy's view is ". . . the critique of a bellelettristic realist." [17]

But he corroborates Tolstoy's opinion when he proves that a tragedy cannot have a characteristic language and that "the language of a tragic hero is a resounding and pompous one, imagined by the author; there is no room in the tragedy for a detailed characterization of speech." [18] With this insight, he demonstrates that tragedy has no character because it represents man in the extreme, whereas character consists in proportions, correlations, and compromises between features and attitudes. Tolstoy is right when he says that "not only are Shakespeare's *dramatis personae* placed into impossible tragic situations that do not follow the course of events and are inappropriate in terms of time and place, but they act completely arbitrarily, not in accord with their own stated characters." [19] Tolstoy makes a great discovery here, as he points out the domain of the unmotivated, which is a specific distinguishing mark of art. He points to the real problem of Shakespearian studies when he says "Shakespeare's characters constantly do and say things that are not only against their nature, but serve no purpose." [20]

We take *Othello* as an example to show how correct this analysis is and how it can be used to uncover Shakespeare's merits as well as his faults. Tolstoy says that Shakespeare, who borrowed the subjects of his plays from older dramas or narratives, not only distorted, but weakened and frequently destroyed the character of his protagonists. "Thus, Shakespeare's characters in *Othello* (Othello, Iago, Cassio, or Emilia) are far less genuine and lively than those in the original Italian novella. . . . The reasons for Othello's jealousy are much more natural in the Italian original than in Shakespeare's tragedy. . . . Shakespeare's Iago is a villain, a cheat, a thief, an impostor. . . . The motives for his villainy, according to Shakespeare, are many and unclear. In the novella, however, there is but one motive, and it is simple and clear: Iago's passionate love for Desdemona has changed into hatred for her and Othello after she preferred the Moor to Iago." [21]

Tolstoy points out that Shakespeare intentionally omitted, changed, or destroyed the characters of the Italian story. The character of Othello himself is only a point of encounter for the two opposing affects. Let us take a look at the hero. If Shakespeare wanted to describe a tragedy of jealousy, he should have chosen a jealous man, put him together with a woman who would provide him with a motive, and finally would have established between them a relationship in which jealousy could become the inevitable and inseparable companion of love. Instead, he chooses characters and material which make the solution of his problem extremely difficult. "Othello is not jealous by nature; on the contrary, he is trustful," remarked Pushkin.[22] Indeed, Othello's trustfulness is one of the mainsprings of the tragedy. Everything proceeds because Othello is trusting and because there is not a streak of jealousy in his nature. In fact, his character is utterly opposed to that of a jealous person. Similarly, Desdemona is not the type of woman who would cause blind jealousy in a man. Many critics even find her too idealized and pure. Finally, the most important point—Othello's and Desdemona's love appears so platonic that one might think they never really consummated their marriage. The tragedy reaches its climax: the trusting Othello, now violently jealous, kills the innocent Desdemona. Had Shakespeare followed the first "prescription," he would have achieved the same banal effect as Artsybashev in his play *Jealousy*, in which a suspicious husband is jealous of a wife who is ready to give herself to any man, and where the relationship between husband and wife is shown only in terms of their problems. The "flight of a machine heavier than air," with which a work of art was compared, is triumphantly achieved in *Othello*, where the tragedy evolves in two opposing directions and generates conflicting emotions in us. Each step, each action, drags us lower, to abject treason and treachery, while at the same time lifting us to the heights of an ideal character, so that the collision and cathartic purification of the two opposite affects engendered becomes the basis of the tragedy. Tolstoy attributes Shakespeare's unsurpassed mastery to a specific technique: "His ability to write scenes expressing the movement of feelings. No matter how unnatural the situations in which he places his characters, how inappropriate the language they speak, how impersonal they are, the movement of their feelings, the combination of contradictory emotions is expressed with power and precision in most of Shakespeare's scenes." [23]

It is the ability to represent changes in feelings which is the basis for understanding the dynamic protagonist. Goethe remarks that at one point Lady Macbeth says she suckled her children with her breast, but at another point we learn that she has no children. This, according to him, is an artistic convention, for, Shakespeare "is concerned about the power and effect of each individual speech . . . The poet makes his characters say exactly what the situation requires and what produces the best effect, without worrying too much whether or not it contradicts a statement made elsewhere." [24] If we bear in mind the logic contradiction of words, we can agree with Goethe. There are innumerable examples from Shakespeare's plays that show that the characters always evolve dynamically, depending on the structure of the play, and that they always follow Aristotle's dictum that ". . . the plot is the basis, the soul, of the tragedy, and the characters follow it." [25] Müller points out that Shakespeare's comedies differ from the ancient Roman comedies (with their inevitable parasite, bragging warrior, pimp, and other stereotypes), but he fails to understand that the purpose of the free rendition of characters, which Pushkin admired so much in Shakespeare, is not to make them look like real people or to liken their situations to real life, but to complicate and enrich the plot and enhance the tragic setting. In the final analysis, a character is static, and when Pushkin says that Molière's "hypocrite runs hypocritically after the wife of his benefactor, hypocritically accepts the custody of the estate, hypocritically asks for a glass of water," he defines the very essence of a character tragedy. Thus, when Müller tries to determine the interrelationship between characters and plot in the English drama, he has to admit that the plot is decisive, while the characters are "of secondary importance in the creative process. In Shakespeare's case this may sound like nonsense. . . . It is therefore all the more interesting to show by examples that he too occasionally subordinates his characters to the plot." [26] When he tries to explain Cordelia's refusal to verbally express her love for her father as a technical requirement, he runs into the same contradiction as we did in the attempt to explain, from the technical viewpoint, a nonmotivated phenomenon in art which is in fact not only a sad necessity required by the technique, but also a joyous privilege afforded by form. The fact that Shakespeare's lunatics speak in prose, that letters are written in prose, that Lady Macbeth raves in prose, makes us realize that the connection between the language and the character of the dramatis personae can be purely fortuitous.

It is important to clarify the substantial difference that exists between the novel and the tragedy. In the novel the characters of the protagonists are also frequently dynamic and full of contradictions. They evolve as a constructive factor capable of changing events or, conversely, of being transformed by other, stronger or superior factors. We find this inner contradiction in Dostoevsky's novels, which evolve simultaneously on two levels (the most base and the most sublime), where murderers philosophize, saints sell their bodies on the streets, parricides save mankind, and so on. In the tragedy, however, character has a completely different meaning. To understand the peculiarity of the structure of a tragic hero we must bear in mind that drama is based on struggle, and, whether we consider a tragedy or a farce, we will see that their formal structure is identical. While a protagonist always fights objects, laws, or forces, the various types of drama are distinguished by what he actually opposes. In tragedy he fights inflexible, absolute laws; in comedy he usually fights social laws; and in farce he struggles against physiological laws. "The hero of a comedy violates sociopsychological norms, customs, and habits. The hero of a farce . . . violates sociophysical norms of social life." [27] This is why farce, as in Aristophanes' *Lysistrata*, frequently deals with eroticism and digestion. The farce plays at all times with the animality of man while his formal nature remains purely dramatic. Consequently, in any drama, we perceive both a norm and its violation; in this respect, the structure of a drama resembles that of a verse in which we have also a norm (meter) and a system of deviations from it. The protagonist of a drama is therefore a character who combines two conflicting affects, that of the norm and that of its violation; this is why we perceive him dynamically, not as an object but as a process. This becomes particularly obvious if we look at the various types of drama. Volkenshteyn considers a distinguishing feature of tragedy the fact that its hero is endowed with very great strength; he recalls that the ancients defined the tragic hero as a spiritual maximum. Hence, the prime characteristic of tragedy is maximalism, or the violation of absolute law by absolute strength of heroic struggle. As soon as tragedy steps down from this lofty level of struggle it becomes drama. Hebbel is mistaken when he explains the positive effect of tragic catastrophe by saying that "when a man is covered with wounds, to kill him is to cure him." This statement would mean that when a tragic poet leads his hero to destruction, he gives us a satisfaction similar to the one we experience when a suffering, mortally wounded animal is put to death. But this view is wrong. We do not feel that death gives relief to the hero; at the time of the catastrophe we do not see him covered with wounds. The tragedy performs a remarkable and astonishing catharsis whose effect is diametrically opposed to its content.

In tragedy, the sublime moment of the spectator coincides with the sublime moment of the protagonist's death or destruction. The spectator perceives not only what the protagonist is or represents but something more; this is why Hebbel says that catharsis in the tragedy is necessary for the spectator only and "it is not at all necessary . . . for the protagonist to achieve inner peace." A remarkable illustration of this point is given in the dénouement of all Shakespearean tragedies, most of which end in an identical manner. Once the catastrophe is accomplished, the protagonist dies unappeased, and one of the surviving characters takes the spectator once again through the events of the tragedy, and, in a manner of speaking, collects the ashes of tragedy consumed in the catharsis. When the spectator hears Horatio's brief account of the frightful events which have just passed before his eyes, it is as if he saw the same tragedy for a second time, only without its sting and venom. This narrated review gives him time to realize his own catharsis, to compare his own relationship to the tragedy, as given in the dénouement, with the immediately experienced impression of the tragedy as a whole. "A tragedy is an explosion of supreme human force; therefore it is in a major key. In viewing a titanic struggle, the spectator's feeling of horror is replaced by a feeling of cheerfulness which approaches enthusiasm. Tragedy appeals to and awakens the subconscious, mysterious original forces hidden in our souls. The playwright seems to tell us that we are timid, indecisive, obsequious to society and the state. Then he tells us to look at how strong people act: See what will happen if you surrender to your ambition, to your voluptuousness, to your pride. Try in your imagination to follow my hero and see if it is not tempting to give in to passion!" [28] Although this formulation is somewhat simplified, it contains a certain amount of truth, because the tragedy awakens our most hidden passions, forces them to flow within banks of granite, made of completely opposite feelings, and ends this struggle with a catharsis of resolution.

Comedy has a similar structure, with a catharsis which results in the spectator's laughter becoming directed at the protagonist. The distinction between the spectator and the protagonist of a comedy is obvious: the hero weeps, while the spectator laughs. An obvious dualism is created. The hero is sad and the spectator laughs, or vice versa; a positive hero may meet a sad end, but the spectator is happy just the same.

We will not dwell on the specific features that distinguish the tragic from the comic, or the drama from the comedy. Many authors (among them Croce and Haman) hold that in essence these categories are not aesthetic ones, since the comic and the tragic also exist outside the arts. They are quite right. At this stage it is important for us to show that whenever art uses the tragic, comic, or dramatic modes, it invariably obeys the law of catharsis. According to Bergson, the purpose of comedy is to show "the deviation of the *dramatis personae* from the conventional norms of social life." He feels that "only man can be ridiculous. If we laugh at an object or an animal, we take them for human beings and humanize them." Laughter requires a social environment. Comedy is impossible outside society and, consequently, again reveals itself as a dualism between certain societal norms and deviations from them. Volkenshteyn perceives this dualism in the comic hero and says, "A funny and witty reply given by a comic character obtains a particularly strong effect. Shakespeare's representation of Falstaff is successful because he is not only a coward, a glutton, a philanderer, and so on, but also a marvelous joker." [29] This is why the jokes destroy the trite and commonplace aspects of his nature in a catharsis of laughter. According to Bergson, the origin of fun lies in automatism; that is, when something live deviates from certain norms, it behaves as if it were mechanical, and this generates laughter.

The results of Freud's investigations into wit, humor, and the comic are far more interesting. We feel that his interpretation of these three forms of experience as purely energetic is somewhat arbitrary, but quite aside from this point we cannot but agree with the extreme accuracy of Freud's analysis. It is remarkable that it fully coincides with our formula for catharsis as a basis for aesthetic reaction. Wit for him is a Janus which can develop a thought simultaneously in two opposite directions. There is a discrepancy in our feelings and perceptions in the case of humor, and the laughter resulting from this discrepancy is the best proof of the relaxing effect of wit.[30] Haman holds a similar view: "Wit requires above all novelty and originality. A joke can hardly be appreciated twice, and most of the time creative people are also witty, since the jump from stress to discharge can be quite unexpected and unpredictable. Brevity is the soul of wit; its essence lies in the sudden transition from stress to discharge." [31]

This also applies to a field introduced into scientific aesthetics by Rosenkranz, author of *The Aesthetics of Ugliness*. A faithful follower of Hegel, he reduces the role of ugliness to a contrast (antithesis), whose purpose is to set off the positive element (thesis). But this view is basically wrong because, as pointed out by Lalo, the ugly may become an element of art

for the same reasons as the beautiful. An object described and reproduced in a work of art can by itself (that is, outside the work of art), be
both ugly and indifferent; in some cases it *must be* in reality either ugly
or indifferent. Characteristic examples are portraits and realistic works
of art. This fact is well known, and the idea is far from new. "There is
no snake [Lalo refers here to Boileau], there is no monster that could
not be pleasing in a work of art." [32] It is also Vernon Lee's view that the
beauty of objects frequently cannot be introduced directly into art.
"The most sublime art," she says, "for instance, the art of Michelangelo, frequently gives us bodies whose structural beauty is distorted by
conspicuous defects. . . . Conversely, any art exhibit or even the most
commonplace art collection can give us dozens of examples of the reverse; that is, they provide the possibility of easily and convincingly recognizing the beauty of the original model which may, however,
have inspired mediocre or bad paintings or statues." Vernon Lee sees
the fact that true art processes the original sensory impression introduced into it as the cause of this relationship between art and ugliness
[51]. It is hard to find a more suitable application for our formula than
the aesthetics of ugliness, for it discusses catharsis, without which the enjoyment of art would be impossible. It is much harder to fit the average
type of drama into this formula. But here, we can show by the example
of Chekhov's plays that this rule is quite correct.

Let us consider his plays *The Three Sisters* and *The Cherry Orchard.* The
former is usually (and quite erroneously) said to represent the melancholy yearnings of three provincial belles for the glamorous life of Moscow.[33] In actual fact, however, Chekhov eliminates all those traits that
could conceivably motivate the three sisters' desire to go to Moscow,
[52] and since Moscow is only an imaginary artistic construct for them,
not an object of real desire, the play has not a comical but a deeply dramatic effect on the spectator. After its first presentation, the critics
wrote that the play is somewhat ridiculous because for four entire acts
the sisters keep moaning, "To Moscow, to Moscow, to Moscow," even
though each of them could at any time simply buy a railway ticket and
go to that Moscow which, apparently, none of them needs. One of the
critics called the play the drama of a railway ticket; and in a way he
was more right about it than critics like Izmailov. Indeed, the author
who has made Moscow the center of attraction for the sisters should
somehow also motivate their urge to get there. True, he says, they spent
their childhood there; but none of them remembers the place. The idea
that they might be prevented by some impediment from going to Moscow turns out to be incorrect also. We cannot find any comprehensible
reason why the sisters cannot go. There are some critics who think that

the sisters want to go to Moscow because for them the city is the symbolic center of civilized and cultivated life. This view also is wrong because not a word, not a syllable mentions this fact. On the contrary, their brother's urge to go to Moscow contrasts with theirs: for him Moscow is not a dream but a reality. He recalls the university, he wants to sit in Testov's restaurant, and his real and realistic Moscow is intentionally contrasted with the Moscow of his three sisters. Theirs remains vague and without motivation, since there is no reason why they could not get there—and this lack of motivation, of course, is the basis for the dramatic effect of the play.

Something similar happens in *The Cherry Orchard*. It is hard to understand why the sale of the cherry orchard is such a terrible misfortune for Ranevskaia. Perhaps she lives permanently in this cherry orchard. But then we learn that she spends her entire life traveling abroad and that she never could or would be able to live on her estate. Perhaps the sale could mean ruin or bankruptcy for her, but this motive falls away, too, because it is not the need of money that places her in the dramatic situation. For Ranevskaia as well as for the spectator the cherry orchard is an unmotivated element of the drama, as is Moscow for the three sisters. The distinguishing feature of these plays is this unreal motive—which we accept as a psychological reality—and which paints itself onto the canvas of real everyday life. The struggle between the two irreconcilable motives ("real" and unmotivated) yields the contradiction which must necessarily be solved in the catharsis, and without which there is no art.

In conclusion we must demonstrate very briefly, by means of arbitrary examples, that this formula can be applied to all other art forms beside poetry. Our reasoning and arguments proceed from concrete examples from literature, but we can apply our conclusions to other domains of art. The closest one is the theatre, one half of which belongs to literature. We can show, however, that the other half, taken in its strict interpretation as the playing of actors and the staging of the spectacle, is also governed by our aesthetic rule. The basis for this view was established by Diderot in his famous *Paradox of the Actor* in which he analyzes the playing of an actor. He shows clearly that an actor not only experiences and expresses the feelings of the character he represents, but develops them into an artistic form. "But excuse me," someone will reply, "these mournful sounds, full of sorrow and sadness which an actor produces from the depth of his being, which upset my heart and soul, are they not caused by genuine feeling, by genuine despair? Not at all. And here is the proof: they, these sounds, are measured, they are a component part of declamation. Were they one twentieth of a quarter of a tone higher or lower, they would be false. They obey the law of unity. They have been selected in a specific way and are distributed harmonically. They contribute to the solution of a specific problem. . . . He knows with accomplished precision when to take out his handkerchief and when to shed tears. Expect this to happen when a specific word is said, when a specific syllable is pronounced, neither before, nor later." [34] Diderot calls the actor's creativity a pathetic grimace, a magnificent aching. This statement is paradoxical only in part; it would be true if we said that on stage the moan of desperation of a mother includes, of course, genuine desperation as well. The actor's ability and success depend on the measure he gives to this desperation. The task of aesthetics is, as Tolstoy facetiously wrote, "to describe capital punishment as if it were as sweet as honey." Capital punishment is capital punishment even on stage, and it is never as sweet as honey. Despair remains despair, but it is released by the action of artistic form, and therefore the actor may not himself fully experience the feelings attributed to the character he represents. Diderot tells us a wonderful story: "I would like to tell you how an actor and his wife, who hated one another, were lovers on stage, and very passionately taken with one another. Never had they played any other role so successfully and convincingly, or reaped such thunderous applause. No less than ten times did we interrupt their scene to shout our enthusiastic approval." Diderot then quotes a long dialogue in which the actors talk aloud to each other of passionate love, but then, under their breath, call each other unmentionable names. As an Italian proverb states, *Se non è vero, è ben trovato.*

For the psychology of art this is very significant, because it points out the duality of an emotion experienced and represented by an actor. Diderot claims that once an actor has finished playing his part, he does not retain any of the feelings he has represented; they are transferred to the audience. Unfortunately, this observation is today considered a paradox, and no sufficiently thorough study has yet been made of the psychology of acting, although in this field the psychology of art could solve this problem much better than in any other art form. There are good reasons to believe that, irrespective of its results, such a study would corroborate the fundamental dualism of an actor's emotion which, it seems to us, makes it possible to apply our formula of catharsis to the theatre [53].

The best way to show the effect of this law in painting is to study the difference in style that exists between the art of painting (in the proper sense of the word) and that of drawing. Klinger's studies have made this evident. We believe (as does Christiansen) that this difference is due to the different interpretations of space in painting and in drawing: painting does away with the flat, two-dimensional character of the drawn image and forces us to perceive everything in a new, three-dimensional fashion. A drawing may represent a three-dimensional space, but the character of the drawing remains two-dimensional. Thus, the impression generated by a drawing is always dualistic: on the one hand, we perceive the image as three-dimensional, but we also perceive the play of lines in the two-dimensional plane. This dualism places drawing in a special category of art. Klinger points out that, unlike painting, drawing uses impressions of disharmony, horror, etc., quite frequently; all of these are of positive significance. He claims that in poetry, drama, and music such features are not only permissible, but indispensable. Christiansen states that it is possible to produce such impressions because the horror produced is solved by the catharsis of form. "A dissonance must be *overcome;* there must be resolution and appeasement. I should like to say catharsis, had Aristotle's beautiful term not become meaningless because of the many attempts to interpret it. The impression of horror or fear must find its resolution and purification in an element of Dionysiac enthusiasm; horror is represented not for its own sake but as an impulse to be overcome . . . And this distracting element must signify overcoming and catharsis simultaneously." [35]

The potential of catharsis in values of form is illustrated by Pollaiolo's *Men Fighting*, "where the horror of death is completely obliterated by the Dionysiac triumph of rhythmic lines." [36]

Finally, a cursory look at sculpture and architecture reveals that here, too, the contrast between material and form is frequently the starting point for the artistic impression. To represent the human or animal body, sculpture almost exclusively uses marble or metal—materials that are among those least naturally suited to this purpose. But for the artist, this refractoriness of the material is the greatest challenge to the creation of a live figure. The famous Laocoön group best illustrates the contrast between form and material from which sculpture emerges.

Gothic architecture reveals this same contrast. It is remarkable that the artist forces the stone to take on the shape of plants—to sprout branches, to bear leaves and to blossom; it is astonishing that in a Gothic cathedral, where the experience of material massiveness reaches its zenith, the artist obtains the effect of a triumphant vertical which makes the viewer feel the whole edifice striving upward with tremendous force. The lightness and transparency that the Gothic architect manages to draw out from heavy, inert stone is the best corroboration of this idea.

We agree with the author who wrote about the Cologne cathedral, "In its slender and harmonious distribution of arches intersecting as if they were part of a filigree, the high vaults, and so on, we see the same bold-ness and courage that we admire in knightly exploits. In its soft and harmonious outlines we find the same warm feeling that emanates from the love songs of chivalry." As the artist produces boldness and delicate grace from stone, he obeys the same law as that which forces him to propel upward the stone that gravity pulls to the ground, and to create in a Gothic cathedral the effect of an arrow shot into the sky.

The name of this law is *catharsis*. This law, and nothing else, compelled the master of Notre Dame in Paris to place atop the cathedral ugly and horrifying monsters, the gargoyles, without which the cathedral is un-imaginable.

NOTES

1. A. Bely, *Simbolizm (Symbolism)*, a collection of articles, Moscow: Musaget, 1910.

2. V. Zhirmunskii, *Vvedenie v metriky. Teoriia stikha (Introduction to Metrics: A Theory of the Verse)*, Leningrad: Academia, 1925, pp. 16–17.

3. *Ibid.*, p. 18.

4. *Ibid.*, p. 265.

5. Yu. N. Tynianov, *Problema stikhotvornovo iazyka (Problems of Verse Language)*, Leningrad: Academia, 1924, p. 10.

6. *Ibid.*

7. *Ibid.*, pp. 20–21.

8. *Ibid.*, p. 120.

9. A. Evlakhov, *Vvedenie v filosofiiu khudozhestvennovo tvorchestva (Introduction to the Philosophy of Artistic Creativity)*, vol. I, Warsaw, 1910, pp. 262–263.

10. V. S. Uzin, *O povestiakh Belkina. Iz kommentariev chitatelia (A Reader's Comments on Belkin's Stories)*, Petrograd: Akvilon, 1924, p. 15.

11. *Ibid.*, p. 18.

12. *Ibid.*, p. 19.

13. Yu. N. Tynianov, *Verse Language*, pp. 8–9.

14. *Ibid.*, p. 13.

15. L. N. Tolstoy, *Collected Works*, vol. 35, Moscow, 1951, p. 236.

16. *Ibid.*, p. 239.

17. V. Volkenshteyn, *Dramaturgiia. Metod issledovaniia dramaticheskikh proizvedeniy (Dramaturgy: A Method of Studying Dramatic Works)*, Moscow: Novaia Moskva, 1923, p. 114.

18. *Ibid.*

19. L. N. Tolstoy, *Collected Works*, vol. 35, p. 238.

20. *Ibid.*, p. 251.

21. *Ibid.*, pp. 244–246.

22. A. S. Pushkin, *Collected Works*, vol. 12, Moscow, 1949, p. 157.

23. L. N. Tolstoy, *Collected Works*, vol. 35, p. 249.

24. *Goethes Gespräche mit Eckermann* (28 April 1827) Berlin, 1955, pp. 320–321.

25. Aristotle, *Poetica.*

26. V. K. Müller, *Drama i teatr epokhi Shekspira (Drama and Theater in Shakespeare's Time)*, Leningrad, 1925, p. 45.

27. V. Volkenshteyn, *Dramaturgiia*, p. 156.

28. *Ibid.,* pp. 155–156.

29. *Ibid.,* pp. 153–154.

30. S. Freud, *Wit and Its Relation to the Unconscious,* New York: Moffat, Yard & Co., 1917.

31. R. Haman, "Aesthetics," *Problemy estetiki (Problems of Aesthetics)*, Moscow, 1913, p. 124.

32. C. Lalo, *Introduction à l'esthétique,* Paris: Colin, 1912.

33. See the article by A. A. Izmailov, in A. P. Chekhov's *Collected Works,* vol. 22, Petrograd, 1918, pp. 264–265.

34. D. Diderot, *Paradoxe sur le comédien,* Cambridge University Press.

35. Christiansen, *Filosofiia iskusstva (Philosophy of Art)*, p. 249.

36. *Ibid.,* p. 251.

11 ART AND LIFE

THEORY OF CONTAMINATION. SIGNIFICANCE OF ART IN LIFE. SOCIAL SIGNIFICANCE OF ART. ART CRITICISM. ART AND TEACHING. THE ART OF THE FUTURE.

Now we must study the following questions: What significance does art acquire if we assume that our interpretation of it is correct? What is the relation between aesthetic response and all other forms of human behavior? How do we explain the role and importance of art in the general behavioral system of man? There are as many different answers to these questions as there are different ways of evaluating the importance of art. Some believe art is the supreme human activity while others consider it nothing but leisure and fun.

The evaluation of art depends directly on the psychological viewpoint from which we approach it. If we want to find out what the relationship between art and life is, if we want to solve the problem of art in terms of applied psychology, we must adopt a valid general theory for solving these problems.

The first and most widespread view holds that art infects us with emotions and is therefore based upon contamination. Tolstoy says, "The activity of art is based on the capacity of people to infect others with their own emotions and to be infected by the emotions of others. . . . Strong emotions, weak emotions, important emotions, or irrelevant emotions, good emotions or bad emotions—if they contaminate the reader, the spectator, or the listener—become the subject of art." [1]

This statement means that since art is but common emotion, there is no substantial difference between an ordinary feeling and a feeling stirred by art. Consequently, art functions simply as a resonator, an amplifier, or a transmitter for the infection of feeling. Art has no specific distinction; hence the evaluation of art must proceed from the same criterion which we use to evaluate any feeling. Art may be good or bad if it infects us with good or bad feelings. Art in itself is neither good nor bad; it is a language of feeling which we must evaluate in accordance with what it expresses. Thus, Tolstoy came to the natural conclusion that art must be evaluated from a moral viewpoint; he therefore approved of art that generated good feelings, and objected to art that, from his point of view, represented reprehensible events or actions. Many other critics reached the same conclusions as did Tolstoy and evaluated a work of art on the basis of its obvious content, while praising or condemning the artist accordingly. Like ethics, like aesthetics—this is the slogan of this theory.

But Tolstoy soon discovered that his theory failed when he tried to be consistent with his own conclusions. He compared two artistic impressions: one produced by a large chorus of peasant women who were celebrating the marriage of his daughter; and the other, by an accomplished musician who played Beethoven's Sonata opus 101. The singing of the peasant women expressed such a feeling of joy, cheerfulness, and liveliness that it infected Tolstoy and he went home in high spirits. According to him, such singing is true art, because it communicates a specific and powerful emotion. Since the second impression involved no such specific emotions, he concluded that Beethoven's sonata is an unsuccessful artistic attempt which contains no definite emotions and is therefore neither remarkable nor outstanding. This example shows us the absurd conclusions that can be reached if the critical understanding of art is based upon the criterion of its infectiousness. Beethoven's music incorporates no definite feeling, while the singing of the peasant women has an elementary and contagious gaiety. If this is true, then Yevlakhov is right when he states that " 'real, true' art is military or dance music, since it is more catchy." [2] Tolstoy is consistent in his ideas; beside folk songs, he recognizes only "marches and dances written by various composers" as works "that approach the requirements of universal art." A reviewer of Tolstoy's article, V. G. Valter, points out that "if Tolstoy had said that the gaiety of the peasant women put him in a good mood, one could not object to that. It would mean that the language of emotions that expressed itself in their singing (it could well have expressed itself simply in yelling, and most likely did) infected Tolstoy with their gaiety. But what has this to do with art? Tolstoy does not say whether the women sang well; had they not sung but simply yelled, beating their scythes, their fun and gaiety would have been no less catching, especially on his daughter's wedding day."

We feel that if we compare an ordinary yell of fear to a powerful novel in terms of their respective infectiousness, the latter will fail the test. Obviously, to understand art we must add something else to simple infectiousness. Art also produces other impressions, and Longinus' statement, "You must know that the orator pursues one purpose, and the poet another. The purpose of poetry is trepidation, that of prose is expressivity," is correct. Tolstoy's formula failed to account for the trepidation which is the purpose of poetry.

But to prove that he is really wrong, we must look at the art of military and dance music and find out whether the true purpose of that art is to infect. Petrazhitskii assumes that aestheticians are wrong when they claim that the purpose of art is to generate aesthetic emotions only. He feels that art produces general emotions, and that aesthetic emotions are merely decorative. "For instance, the art of a warlike period in the life of a people has as its main purpose the excitation of heroic-bellicose emotions. Even now, military music is not intended to give the soldiers in the field aesthetic enjoyment, but to excite and enhance their belligerent feelings. The purpose of medieval art (including sculpture and architecture) was to produce lofty religious emotions. Lyric appeals to one aspect of our emotional psyche, satire to another; the same applies to drama, tragedy, and so on. . . ." [3]

Apart from the fact that military music does not generate bellicose emotions on the battlefield, the question is not properly formulated here. Ovsianiko-Kulikovskii, for example, comes closer to the truth when he says that "military lyrics and music 'lift the spirit' of the army and 'inspire' feats of valor and heroic deeds, but neither of them leads directly to bellicose emotions or belligerent affects. On the contrary, they seem to moderate bellicose ardor, calm an excited nervous system, and chase away fear. We can say that lifting morale, calming nerves, and chasing away fear are among the most important practical functions of 'lyrics' which result from their psychological nature." [4] It is therefore wrong to think that music can directly cause warlike emotions; more precisely, it gives bellicose emotions an opportunity for expression, but music as such neither causes nor generates them.

Something similar happens with erotic poetry, the sole purpose of which, according to Tolstoy, is to excite lust. Anyone who understands the true nature of lyrical emotions knows that Tolstoy is wrong. "There is no doubt that lyrical emotion has a soothing effect on all other emotions (and affects) to the point that at times it paralyzes them. This is also the effect it has on sexuality with its emotions and affects. Erotic poetry, if it is truly lyrical, is far less suggestive than works of the visual arts in which the problems of love and the notorious sex problem are treated with the purpose of producing a moral reaction.[5] Ovsianiko-Kulikovskii is only partly correct in his assumption that sexual feeling, which is easily excited, is most strongly stirred by images and thoughts, that these images and thoughts are rendered harmless by lyrical emotion, and that mankind is indebted to lyrics, even more than to ethics, for the taming and restraining of sexual instincts. He underestimates the importance of the other art forms, which he calls figurative, and does not remark that in their case also emotions provoked by images are counteracted by the nonlyrical emotion of art. Thus we see that Tolstoy's theory does not hold in the domain of the applied arts, where he thought its validity to be absolute. As concerns great art (the art of Beethoven and Shakespeare), Tolstoy himself pointed out that his theory is inapplicable. Art would have a dull and ungrateful task if its only purpose were to infect one or many persons with feelings. If this were so, its significance would be very small, because there would be only a quantitative expansion and no qualitative expansion beyond an individual's feeling. The miracle of art would then be like the bleak miracle of the Gospel, when five barley loaves and two small fishes fed thousands of people, all of whom ate and were satisfied, and a dozen baskets were filled with the remaining food. This miracle is only quantitative: thousands were fed and were satisfied, but each of them ate only fish and bread. But was this not their daily diet at home, without any miracles?

If the only purpose of a tragic poem were to infect us with the author's sorrow, this would be a very sad situation indeed for art. The miracle of art reminds us much more of another miracle in the Gospel, the transformation of water into wine. Indeed, art's true nature is that of transubstantiation, something that transcends ordinary feelings; for the fear, pain, or excitement caused by art includes something above and beyond its normal, conventional content. This "something" overcomes feelings of fear and pain, changes water into wine, and thus fulfills the most important purpose of art. One of the great thinkers said once that art relates to life as wine relates to the grape. With this he meant to say that art takes its material from life, but gives in return something which its material did not contain.

Initially, an emotion is individual, and only by means of a work of art does it *become* social or generalized. But it appears that art by itself contributes nothing to this emotion. It is not clear, then, why art should be viewed as a creative act nor how it differs from an ordinary yell or an orator's speech. Where is the trepidation of which Longinus spoke, if art is viewed only as an exercise in infectiousness? We realize that science does not simply infect one person or a whole society with thoughts and ideas, any more than technology helps man to be handy. We can also recognize that art is an expanded "*social* feeling" or *technique of feelings*, as we shall show later. Plekhanov states that the relationship between art and life is extremely complex, and he is right. He quotes Taine who investigated the interesting question of why landscape painting evolved only in the city. If art were intended merely to infect us with the feelings that life communicates to us, then landscape painting could not survive in the city. History, however, proves exactly the opposite. Taine writes, "We have the right to admire landscapes, just as they had the right to be bored by it. For seventeenth-century man there was nothing uglier than a mountain. It aroused in him many unpleasant ideas, because he was as weary of barbarianism as we are weary of civilization. Mountains give us a chance to rest, away from our sidewalks, offices, and shops; we like landscape only for this reason." [6]

Plekhanov points out that art is sometimes not a direct expression of life, but an expression of its antithesis. The idea, of course, is not in the leisure of which Taine speaks, but in a certain antithesis: art releases an aspect of our psyche which finds no expression in our everyday life. We cannot speak of an infection with emotions. The effect of art is obviously much more varied and complex; no matter how we approach art, we always discover that it involves something different from a simple transmission of feelings. Whether or not we agree with Lunacharskii that art is a concentration of life,[7] we must realize that it proceeds from certain live feelings and works upon these feelings, a fact not considered by Tolstoy's theory.

We have seen that this process is a catharsis—the transformation of these feelings into opposite ones and their subsequent resolution. This view of course agrees perfectly with Plekhanov's principle of antithesis in art. To understand this we must look at the problem of the biological significance of art, and realize that art is not merely a means for infection but something immeasurably more important in itself. In his "Three Chapters of Historic Poetics," Veselovskii says that ancient singing and playing were born from a complex need for catharsis; a chorus sung during hard and exhausting work regulates muscular effort by its rhythm, and apparently aimless play responds to the subconscious requirement of training and regulation of physical or intellectual effort. This is also the requirement of psychophysical catharsis formulated by Aristotle for the drama; it manifests itself in the unsurpassed mastery of Maori women to shed tears at will, and also in the overwhelming tearfulness of the eighteenth century. The phenomenon is the same; the difference lies only in expression and understanding. We perceive rhythm in poetry as something artistic and forget its primitive psychophysical origins.[8] The best repudiation of the contamination theory is the study of those psychophysical principles on which art is based and the explanation of the biological significance of art. Apparently art releases and processes some extremely complex organismic urges. The best corroboration of our viewpoint can be found in the fact that it agrees with Bücher's studies on the origins of art and permits us to understand the true role and purpose of art. Bücher established that music and poetry have a common origin in heavy physical labor. Their object was to relax cathartically the tremendous stress created by labor. This is how Bücher formulated the general content of work songs: "They follow the general trend of work, and signal the beginning of a simultaneous collective effort; they try to incite the men to work by derision, invective, or reference to the opinion of spectators; they express the thoughts of the workers about labor itself, its course, its gear, and so forth, as well as their joys or sorrows, their complaints about the hardness of the work and the inadequate pay; they address a plea to the owner, the supervisor, or simply to the spectator." [9]

The two elements of art and their resolution are found here. The only peculiarity of these songs is that the feeling of pain and hardship which must be solved by art is an essential part of labor itself. Subsequently, when art detaches itself from labor and begins to exist as an independent activity, it introduces into the work of art the element which was formerly generated by labor: the feelings of pain, torment, and hardship (which require relief) are now aroused by art itself, but their nature remains the same. Bücher makes an extremely interesting statement: "The peoples of antiquity considered song an indispensable accompaniment of hard labor." [10] From this we realize that song at first organized collective labor, then gave relief and relaxation to painful and tormenting strain. We shall see that art, even in its highest manifestations, completely separate from labor and without any direct connection thereto, has maintained the same functions. It still must systematize, or organize, social feeling and give relief to painful and tormenting strain. Quintilian puts it this way: "And it appears as if [music] were given to us by nature in order to make labor bearable. For instance, the rower is inspired by song; it is useful not only where the efforts of many are combined, but also when it is intended to provide rest for an exhausted worker."

Thus art arises originally as a powerful tool in the struggle for existence; the idea of reducing its role to a communication of feeling with no power or control over that feeling, is inadmissible. If the purpose of art, like Tolstoy's chorus of peasant women, were only to make us gay or sad, it would neither have survived nor have ever acquired its present importance. Nietzsche expresses it well in *Joyful Wisdom*, when he says that rhythm involves inducement and incentive: "It arouses an irresistible desire to imitate, and not only our legs but our very soul follow the beat. . . . Was there anything more useful than rhythm for ancient, superstitious mankind? With its help everything became feasible—work could be performed magically, God could be forced to appear and listen to grievances, the future could be changed and corrected at will, one's soul could be delivered of any abnormality. Without verse man would be nothing; with it, he almost became God." It is quite interesting to see how Nietzsche explains the way in which art succeeded in acquiring such power over man. "When the normal mood and harmony of the soul were lost, one had to dance to the song of a bard—this was the prescription of that medicine . . . First of all, inebriation and uncontrolled affect were pushed to the limit, so that the insane became frenzied, and the avenger became saturated with hatred." Apparently the possibility of releasing into art powerful passions which cannot find expression in normal, everday life is the biological basis of art. The purpose of our behavior is to keep our organism in balance with its surroundings. The simpler and more elementary our relations with the environment, the simpler our behavior. The more subtle and complex the interaction between organism and environment, the more devious and intricate the balancing process. Obviously this process cannot continue smoothly toward an equilibrium. There will always be a certain imbalance in favor of the environment or the organism. No machine can work toward equilibrium using all its energy efficiently. There are always states of excitation which cannot result in an efficient use of energy. This is why a need arises from time to time to discharge the unused energy and give it free rein in order to reestablish our equilibrium with the rest of the world. Orshanskii says that feelings "are the pluses and minuses of our equilibrium." [11] These pluses and minuses, these discharges and expenditures of unused energy, are the biological function of art.

Looking at a child, it is evident that its possibilities are far greater than actually realized. If a child plays at soldiers, cops and robbers, and so on, this means, according to some, that inside himself he really becomes a soldier or a robber. Sherrington's principle (the principle of struggle for a common field of action) clearly shows that in our organism the nervous receptor fields exceed many times the executing effector neurons, so that the organism perceives many more stimuli than it can possibly attend to. Our nervous system resembles a railway station into which five tracks lead, but only one track leads out. Of five trains arriving at this station, only one ever manages to leave (and this only after a fierce struggle), while the other four remain stalled. The nervous system reminds us of a battlefield where the struggle never ceases, not even for a single instant, and our behavior is an infinitesimal part of what is really included in the possibilities of our nervous system, but cannot find an outlet. In nature the realized and executed part of life is but a minute part of the entire conceivable life (just as every life born is paid for by millions of unborn ones). Similarly, in our nervous system, the realized part of life is only the smallest part of the real life contained in us. Sherrington likens our nervous system to a funnel with its narrow part turned toward action, and the wider part toward the world. The world pours into man, through the wide opening of the funnel [54], thousands of calls, desires, stimuli, etc. enter, but only an infinitesimal part of them is realized and flows out through the narrowing opening. It is obvious that the unrealized part of life, which has not gone through the narrow opening of our behavior, must be somehow utilized and lived. The organism is in an equilibrium with its environment where balance must be maintained, just as it becomes necessary to open a valve in a kettle in which steam pressure exceeds the strength of the vessel. Apparently art is a psychological means for striking a balance with the environment at critical points of our behavior. Long ago the idea had been expressed that art complements life by expanding its possibilities. Von Lange says, "There is a sorry resemblance between contemporary civilized man and domestic animals: limitation and monotony. Issuing from the patterns of bourgeois life and its social forms, these are the main features of the individual existence, which lead everybody, rich and poor, weak and strong, talented and deprived, through an incomplete and imperfect life. It is astonishing how limited is the number of ideas, feelings, and actions that modern man can perform or experience." [12]

Lazurskii holds the same view when he explains the theory of empathy by referring to one of Tolstoy's novels. "There is a point in *Anna Karenina* where Tolstoy tells us that Anna reads a novel and suddenly wants to do what the heroes of that novel do: fight, struggle, win with them, go with the protagonist to his estate, and so on." [13] Freud shares this opinion and speaks of art as a means of appeasing two inimical principles, the principle of pleasure and that of reality. [14]

Insofar as we are talking about the meaning of life, these writers come closer to the truth than those who, like Grant-Allen, assume that "aesthetics are those emotions which have freed themselves from association with practical interests." This reminds us of Spencer's formula: he assumed that "beautiful is what once was, but no longer is, useful." Developed to its extreme limits, this viewpoint leads to the theory of games, which is accepted by many philosophers, and given its highest expression by Schiller. The one serious objection against it is that, in not recognizing art as a creative act, it tends to reduce it to the biological function of exercising certain organs, a fact of little importance for the adult. Much more convincing are the other theories which consider art an indispensable discharge of nervous energy and a complex method of finding an equilibrium between our organism and the environment in critical instances of our behavior. We resort to art only at critical moments in our life, and therefore can understand why the formula we propose views art as a creative act. If we consider art to be catharsis, it is perfectly clear that it cannot arise where there is nothing but live and vivid feeling. A sincere feeling taken per se cannot create art. It lacks more than technique or mastery, because a feeling expressed by a technique will never generate a lyric poem or a musical composition. To do this we require the creative act of *overcoming* the feeling, resolving it, conquering it. Only when this act has been performed —then and *only then* is art born. This is why the perception of art requires creativity: it is not enough to experience sincerely the feeling, or feelings, of the author; it is not enough to understand the structure of the work of art; one must also creatively overcome one's own feelings, and find one's own catharsis; only then will the effect of art be complete. This is why we agree with Ovsianiko-Kulikovskii who says that the purpose of military music is not to arouse bellicose emotions but, by establishing an equilibrium between the organism and the environment at a critical moment for the organism, to discipline and organize its work, provide appropriate relief to its feelings, to chase away fear, and to open the way to courage and valor. Thus, art never directly generates a practical action; it merely prepares the organism for such action. Freud says that a frightened person is terrified and runs when he sees danger; the useful part of this behavior is that he runs, not that he is frightened. In art, the reverse is true: fear per se is useful. Man's release per se is useful, because it creates the possibility of appropriate flight or attack. This is where we must consider the economy of our feelings, which Ovsianiko-Kulikovskii describes thus: "The harmonic rhythm of lyrics creates emotions which differ from the majority of other emotions in that such 'lyric emotions' save our psychic energies by putting our 'psychic household' into harmonic order." [15]

This is not the same economy of which we talked earlier, it is not an attempt to avoid the output of psychic energies. In this respect art is not subordinated to the principle of the economy of strength; on the contrary, art is an explosive and sudden expenditure of strength, of forces (psychic and otherwise), a discharge of energy. A work of art perceived coldly and prosaically, or processed and treated to be perceived in this way, saves much more energy and force than if it were perceived with the full effect of its artistic form in mind. Although it is an explosive discharge, art does introduce order and harmony into the "psychic household," of our feelings. And of course the waste of energy performed by Anna Karenina when she experienced the feelings and emotions of the heroes of the novel she was reading, is a saving of psychic forces if compared to the actual emotion.

A more complex and deeper meaning of the principle of economizing emotions will become clearer if we try to understand the social significance of art. Art is the social within us [55], and even if its action is performed by a single individual, it does not mean that its essence is individual. It is quite naive and inappropriate to take the social to be collective, as with a large crowd of persons. The social also exists where there is only one person with his individual experiences and tribulations. This is why the action of art, when it performs catharsis and pushes into this purifying flame the most intimate and important experiences, emotions, and feelings of the soul, is a social action. But this experience does not happen as described in the theory of contamination (where a feeling born in one person infects and contaminates everybody and *becomes* social), but exactly the other way around. The melting of feelings outside us is performed by the strength of social feeling, which is objectivized, materialized, and projected outside of us, then fixed in external objects of art which have become the tools of society. A fundamental characteristic of man, one that distinguishes him from animals, is that he endures and separates from his body both the apparatus of technology and that of scientific knowledge, which then become the tools of society. Art is the social technique of emotion, a tool of society which brings the most intimate and personal aspects of our being into the circle of social life. It would be more correct to say that emotion becomes personal when every one of us experiences a work of art; it becomes personal without ceasing to be social. "Art," says Guyau, "is a condensation of reality; it shows us the human machine under high pressure. It tries to show us more life phenomena than we actually experience." Of course this life, concentrated in art, exerts an effect not only on our emotions but also on our will "because emotion contains the seed of will." [16] Guyau correctly attributes a tremendous importance to the role played by art in society. It introduces the effects of passion, violates inner equilibrium, changes will in a new sense, and stirs feelings, emotions, passions, and vices without which society would remain in an inert and motionless state. It "pronounces the word we were seeking and vibrates the string which was strained but soundless. A work of art is the center of attraction, as is the active will of a genius: if Napoleon attracts will, Corneille and Victor Hugo do so too, but in a different way. . . . Who knows the number of crimes instigated by novels describing murders? Who knows the number of divorces resulting from representations of debauchery?" [17] Guyau formulates the question in much too primitive a way, because he imagines that art directly causes this or the other emotion. Yet, this never happens. A representation of murder does not cause murder. A scene of debauchery does not inspire divorce; the relationship between art and life is very complex, and in a very approximate way it can be described as will be shown.

Hennequin sees the difference between aesthetic and real emotion in the fact that aesthetic emotion does not immediately express itself in action. He says, however, that if repeated over and over again, these emotions can become the basis for an individual's behavior; thus, an individual can be affected by the kind of literature he reads. "An emotion imparted by a work of art is not capable of expressing itself in immediate actions. In this respect aesthetic feelings differ sharply from actual feelings. But, since they serve an end in themselves, they justify themselves and need not be immediately expressed in any practical activity; aesthetic emotions can, by accumulation and repetition, lead to substantial practical results. These results depend upon the general properties of aesthetic emotion and the particular properties of each of these emotions. Repeated exercises of a specific group of feelings under the effect of invention, imagination, or unreal moods or causes that generally cannot result in action do not require active manifestations, and doubtless weaken the property common to all real emotions, that of expression in action. . . ." [18] Hennequin introduces two very important corrections, but his solution of the problem remains quite primitive. He is correct in saying that aesthetic emotion does not immediately generate action, that it manifests itself in the change of purpose. He is also correct when he states that aesthetic emotion not only does not generate the actions of which it speaks, but is completely alien to them. On the basis of Guyau's example, we could say that the reading of novels about murder not only does not incite us to murder, but actually teaches us not to kill; but this point of view of Hennequin's, although it is more applicable than the former, is quite simple compared with the subtle function assigned to art.

As a matter of fact, art performs an extremely complex action with our passions and goes far beyond the limits of these two simplistic alternatives. Andrei Bely says that when we listen to music we feel what giants must have felt. Tolstoy masterfully describes this high tension of art in his *Kreutzer Sonata:* "Do you know the first place? Do you really know it?" he explains. Oh! . . . A sonata is a frightening thing. Yes, this part, precisely. Music, generally, is a frightening thing. What is it? I don't understand. What is music? What does it do? And why does it do whatever it does? They say that music elevates our soul. Rubbish, nonsense! It does work, it has a terrible effect (I am talking for myself), but it certainly does not lift the soul. It does not lift the soul, nor does it debase it, but it irritates it. How can I put it? Music makes me oblivious of myself; it makes me forget my true position; it transfers me into another position, not mine, not my own: it seems to me, under the effect of music, that I feel what I don't feel, that I understand what I actually don't understand, can't understand. . . .

"Music immediately, suddenly, transports me into the mood which must have been that of the man who wrote it. I become one with him, and together with him I swing from one mood into another, from one state into another, but why I am doing it, I don't know. That fellow, for instance, who wrote the Kreutzer Sonata, Beethoven, he knew why he was in that state. That state led him to certain actions, and therefore, for him, that state was sensible. For me, it means nothing, it is completely senseless. And this is why music only irritates and achieves nothing. Well, if I play a military march, the soldiers will march in step, and the music has achieved its purpose; if dance music is played, I dance, and the music achieves its purpose. Or, if Mass is sung and I take communion, well, here too the music has achieved its purpose; otherwise, it is only irritation, and no one knows what to do with this irritation. This is why music occasionally has such a horrible, terrifying effect. In China music is an affair of state, and this is how it should be . . .

"Otherwise it could be a terrifying tool in the hands of anybody. Take for instance the Kreutzer Sonata. How can one play its presto in a drawing room, amidst ladies in décolleté? Play it, and then busy oneself, then eat some ice cream and listen to the latest gossip? No, these things can be played only in the face of significant, important circumstances, and then it will be necessary to perform certain appropriate acts that fit the music. If it must be played, we must act according to its setting of our mood. Otherwise the incongruity between the place, the time, the waste of energy, and the feelings which do not manifest themselves will have a disastrous effect." [19]

This excerpt from *The Kreutzer Sonata* tells us quite convincingly of the incomprehensibly frightening effect of music for the average listener. It reveals a new aspect of the aesthetic response and shows that it is not a blank shot, but a response to a work of art, and a new and powerful stimulus for further action. Art requires a reply, it incites certain actions, and Tolstoy quite correctly compares the effect of Beethoven's music with that of a dance tune or a march. In the latter case, the excitement created by the music resolves itself in a response, and a feeling of satisfied repose sets in. In the case of Beethoven's music we are thrown into a state of confusion and anxiety, because the music reveals those urges and desires that can find a resolution only in exceptionally important and heroic actions. When this music is followed by ice cream and gossip amidst ladies in décolleté we are left in a state of exceptional anxiety, tension, and disarray. But Tolstoy's character makes a mistake when he compares the irritating and stimulating effect of this music to the effect produced by a military march. He does not realize that the effect of music reveals itself much more subtly, by means of hidden shocks, stresses, and deformations of our constitution. It may reveal itself unexpectedly, and in an extraordinary way. But in this description, two points are made with exceptional clarity: First, music incites, excites, and irritates in an indeterminate fashion not connected with any concrete reaction, motion, or action. This is proof that its effect is cathartic, that is, it clears our psyche, reveals and calls to life tremendous energies which were previously inhibited and restrained. This, however, is a consequence of art, not its action. Secondly, music has coercive power. Tolstoy suggests that music should be an affair of state. He believes that music is a public affair. One critic pointed out that when we perceive a work of art we think that our reaction is strictly personal and associated only with ourselves. We believe that it has nothing to do with social psychology. But this is as wrong as the opinion of a person who pays taxes and considers this action only from his own viewpoint, his own, personal budget, without bearing in mind that he participates in the huge and complex economy of the state. He does not reflect that by paying taxes he takes part in involved state operations whose existence he does not even suspect. This is why Freud is wrong when he states that man stands face to face with the reality of nature, and that art can be derived from the purely biological difference between the principle of enjoyment toward which all our inclinations gravitate, and that of reality which forces us to renounce satisfaction and pleasure. Between man and the outside world there stands the social environment, which in its own way refracts and directs the stimuli acting upon the individual and guides all the reactions that emanate from the individual. For applied psychology it is therefore of immense significance to know that, as Tolstoy puts it, music is something awesome and frightening to the average listener. If a military march incites soldiers to march proudly in a parade, what exceptional deeds must Beethoven's music inspire! Let me repeat: music by itself is isolated from our everyday behavior; it does not drive us to do anything, it only creates a vague and enormous desire for some deeds or actions; it opens the way for the emergence of powerful, hidden forces within us; it acts like an earthquake as it throws open unknown and hidden strata. The view that art returns us to atavism rather than projecting us into the future, is erroneous. Although music does not generate any direct actions, its fundamental effect, the direction it imparts to psychic catharsis, is essential for the kind of forces it will release, what it will release, and what it will push into the background. Art is the organization of our future behavior. It is a requirement that may never be fulfilled but that forces us to strive beyond our life toward all that lies beyond it.

We may therefore call art a delayed reaction, because there is always a fairly long period of time between its effect and its execution. This does not mean, however, that the effect of art is mysterious or mystical or that its explanation requires some new concepts different from those which the psychologist sets up when he analyzes common behavior. Art performs with our bodies and through our bodies. It is remarkable that scholars like Rutz and Sievers, who studied perceptual processes and not the effects of art, speak of the dependence of aesthetic perception on a specific muscular constitution of the body. Rutz was the first to suggest that any aesthetic effect must be associated with a definite type of muscular constitution. Sievers applied his idea to the contemplation of sculpture. Other scholars mention a connection between the basic organic constitution of the artist and the structure of his works. From the most ancient times, art has always been regarded as a means of education, that is, as a long-range program for changing our behavior and our organism. The subject of this chapter, the significance of applied arts, involves the educational effect of art. Those who see a relationship between pedagogy and art find their view unexpectedly supported by psychological analysis. We can now address ourselves to the last problems on our agenda, those of the practical effect of art on life and of its educational significance.

The educational significance of art and its practical aspects may be divided into two parts. We have first criticism as a fundamental social force, which opens the way to art, evaluates it, and serves as a transitional mechanism between art and society. From a psychological point of view, the role of criticism is to organize the effects of art. It gives a certain educational direction to these effects, and since by itself it has no power to influence the basic effect of art per se it puts itself between this effect and the actions into which this effect must finally resolve itself.

We feel therefore that the real purpose and task of art criticism is different from its conventional one. Its purpose is not to interpret or explain a work of art, nor is its purpose to prepare the spectator or reader for the perception of a work of art. Only half of the task of criticism is aesthetic; the other half is pedagogical and public. The critic approaches the average "consumer" of art, for instance, Tolstoy's hero in *The Kreutzer Sonata,* at the troublesome point when he is under the incomprehensible and frightening spell of the music and does not know what it will release in him. The critic wishes to be the organizing force, but enters the action when art has already had its victory over the human psyche which now seeks impetus and direction for its action. The dualistic nature of criticism obviously entails a dualistic task. The criticism which consciously and intentionally puts art into prose establishes its social root, and determines the social connection that exists between art and the general aspects of life. It gathers our conscious forces to counteract or, conversely, to cooperate with those impulses which have been generated by a work of art. This criticism intentionally leaves the domain of art and enters the sphere of social life, with the sole purpose of guiding the aesthetically aroused forces into socially useful channels. Everyone knows that a work of art affects different people in different ways. Like a knife, or any other tool, art by itself is neither good nor bad. More precisely, it has tremendous potential for either good or evil. It all depends on what use we make of, or what task we assign to, this tool. To repeat a trite example: a knife in the hands of a surgeon has a value completely different from that of the same knife in the hands of a child.

But the foregoing is only half the task of criticism. The other half consists in conserving the effect of art as art, and preventing the reader or spectator from wasting the forces aroused by art by substituting for its powerful impulses dull, commonplace, rational-moral precepts. Few understand why it is imperative not only to have the effect of art take shape and excite the reader or spectator but also to explain art, and to explain it in such a way that the explanation does not kill the emotion. We can readily show that such explanation is indispensable, because our behavior is organized according to the principle of unity, which is accomplished mainly by means of our consciousness in which any emotion seeking an outlet must be represented. Otherwise we risk creating a conflict, and the work of art, instead of producing a catharsis, would inflict a wound, and the person experiences what Tolstoy describes when his heart is filled with a vague, incomprehensible emotion of depression, impotence, and confusion. However, this does not mean that the explanation of art kills the trepidation of poetry mentioned by Longinus, for there are two different levels involved. This second element, the element of conservation of an artistic impression, has always been regarded by theoreticians as decisively important for art criticism but, oddly enough, our critics have always ignored it. Criticism has always approached art as if it were a parliamentary speech or a nonaesthetic fact. It considered its task to be the destruction of the effect of art in order to discover the significance of art. Plekhanov was aware that the search for the sociological equivalent of a work of art is only the first half of the task of criticism. "This means," he said when discussing Belinskii, "that evaluation of the idea of a work of art must be followed by an analysis of its artistic merits. Philosophy did not eliminate aesthetics. On the contrary, it paved the way for it and tried to find a solid basis for it. This must also be said about materialistic criticism. In searching for the social equivalent of a given literary phenomenon, this type of criticism betrays its own nature if it does not understand that we cannot confine ourselves to finding this equivalent, and that sociology must not shut the door to aesthetics but, on the contrary, open it wide. The second action of materialistic criticism must be, as was the case with many critic-idealists, the evaluation of the aesthetic merits of the work under investigation . . . The determination of the sociological equivalent of a given work of literature would be incomplete and therefore imprecise if the critic failed to appraise its artistic merits. In other words, *the first action of materialistic criticism not only does not eliminate the need for the second action, but requires it as a necessary and indispensable complement.*" [20]

A similar situation arises with the problem of art in education: the two parts or acts cannot exist independently. Until recently, the public approach to art prevailed in our schools as well as in our criticism. The students learned or memorized incorrect sociological formulas concerning many works of art. "At the present time," says Gershenzon, "pupils are beaten with sticks to learn Pushkin, as if they were cattle herded to the watering place, and given a chemical dissociation of H_2O instead of drinking water." [21] It would be unfair to conclude with Gershenzon that the system of teaching art in the schools is wrong from beginning to end. In the guise of the history of social thought reflected in literature, our students learned false literature and false sociology. Does this mean that it is possible to teach art outside the sociological context and only on the basis of individual tastes, to jump from concept to concept, from the *Iliad* to Maiakovskii? Eichenwald seems to believe this, for he claims that it is impossible as well as unnecessary to teach literature in the schools. "Should one teach literature?" he asks. "Literature, like the other arts, is optional. It represents an entertainment of the mind. . . . Is it necessary that students be taught that Tatiana fell in love with Onegin, or that Lermontov was bored, sad, and unable to love forever?" [22]

Eichenwald is of the opinion that it is impossible to teach literature and that it should be taken out of the school curriculum because it requires an act of creativity different from all the other subjects taught at school. But he proceeds from a rather squalid aesthetic, and all his weak spots become obvious when we analyze his basic position, "Read—enjoy, but can we force people to enjoy?" Of course, if "to read" means "to enjoy," then literature cannot be taught and has no place in the schools (although someone once said that the art of enjoyment could also be taught). A school that eliminates lessons in literature is bound to be a bad school. "At the present time, explanatory reading has as its main purpose the explanation of the content of what is being read. Under such a system, poetry as such is eliminated from the curriculum. For instance, the difference between a fable by Krylov and its rendition in prose is completely lost." [23] From the repudiation of such a position, Gershenzon comes to the conclusion: "Poetry cannot and must not be a compulsory subject of education; it is time that it again become a guest from paradise on earth, loved by everyone, as was the case in ancient times. Then it will once again become the true teacher of the masses." [24] The basic idea here is that poetry is a heavenly guest and it must be made to resume the role it played "in ancient times." But Gershenzon does not concern himself with the fact that these ancient times are gone forever, and that nothing in our time plays the same role it played then. He ignores this fact because he believes that art is fundamentally different from all the other activities of man. For him, art is a kind of a mystical or spiritual act that cannot be recreated by studying the forces of the psyche. According to him, poetry cannot be studied scientifically. "One of the greatest mistakes of contemporary culture," he says, "is the application of a scientific or, more precisely, a naturalistic method to the study of poetry." [25] Thus, what contemporary scholars consider to be the only possible way of solving the riddle of art is for Gershenzon the supreme mistake of contemporary culture.

Future studies and investigations are likely to show that the act of creating a work of art is not a mystical or divine act of our soul, but as real an act as all the other movements of our body, only much more complex. We have discovered in the course of our study that art is a creative act that cannot be recreated by means of purely conscious operations. But, by establishing that the most important elements in art are subconscious or creative, do we automatically eliminate any and all conscious moments and forces? The act of artistic creation cannot be taught. This does not mean, however, that the educator cannot cooperate in forming it or bringing it about. We penetrate the subconscious through the conscious [56]. We can organize the conscious processes in such a way that they generate subconscious processes, and everyone knows that an act of art includes, as a necessary condition, all preceding acts of rational cognizance, understanding, recognition, association, and so forth. It is wrong to assume that the later subconscious processes do not depend on the direction imparted by us to the conscious processes. By organizing our conscious, which leads us toward art, we insure a priori the success or failure of the work of art. Hence Molozhavy correctly states that the act of art is "the process of our response to the phenomenon, although it may never have reached the stage of action. This process . . . widens the scope of our personality, endows it with new possibilities, prepares for the completed response to the phenomenon, that is, behavior, and also has educational value . . . Potebnia is wrong to treat the artistic image as a condensation of thought. Both thought and image are a condensation either of the conscious with respect to the phenomenon involved or of the psyche, which issued from a series of positions preparatory to the present position. But this gives us no right to confuse these biological elements, these psychological processes, on the basis of the vague argument that both thought and artistic image are creative acts. On the contrary, we must emphasize all their individual peculiarities in order to understand each as a part of the whole. The tremendous strength that arouses emotions, inspires the will, fortifies energy, and pushes us to action lies in the concreteness of the artistic image which is in turn based upon the originality of the psychological path leading to it." [26]

These considerations need one substantial correction if we move from the field of general psychology into child psychology. When we determine the influence exerted by art, we must take into account the specific peculiarities facing one who deals with children. Of course this is a separate field, a separate and independent study, because the domain of child art and the response of children to art is completely different from that of adults. However, we shall say a few brief words on the subject and trace a basic line along which child psychology intersects this field. There are remarkable phenomena in the art of children. First, there is the early presence of a special structure required by art, which points to the fact that for the child there exists a psychological kinship between art and play. "First of all," says Bühler, "is the fact that the child very early adopts the correct structure, which is alien to reality but required by the fairy tale, so that he can concentrate on the exploits of the heroes and follow the changing images. It seems to me that he loses this ability during some period of his development, but it returns to him in later years. . . ." [27] Apparently art does not perform the same function in a child as it does in an adult. The best example of this is a child's drawing which in many cases is on the borderline of artistic creativity. The child does not understand that the structure of a line can directly express the moods and trepidations of the heart and soul. The ability to render the expressions of people and animals in different positions and gestures develops very slowly in a child, for various reasons. The principal one is the fundamental fact that a child draws patterns, not events or phenomena.[28] Some claim the opposite, but they seem to ignore the simple fact that a child's drawing is not yet art for the child. His art is unique and different from the art of adults, although the two have one very interesting characteristic in common. It is the most important trait in art and we shall mention it in conclusion. Only recently was it noticed that certain absurdities or amusing nonsense which can be found in nursery rhymes by inverting the most commonplace events play a tremendously important role in child art. Most frequently the required or desired absurdity is achieved in a nursery rhyme by assigning certain functions of object A to object B, and vice versa. . . . "The hermit asked me how many strawberries grow at the bottom of the ocean. I answered him: 'As many as there are red herrings in the forest.' To understand this nursery jingle the child must know the truth about life: herrings exist only in the ocean, and strawberries only in the forest. He begins to look for the absurd only when he is absolutely sure of the facts." [29] We, too, feel that the statement, that this aspect of child art comes very close to play, is true; as a matter of fact, it gives us a good explanation of the role and the significance of art in a child's life. "We still do not quite understand the connection which exists between nursery rhymes and child's play. . . . When evaluating books for small children, critics frequently forget to apply the criterion of play. Most folk nursery rhymes do not issue from games but are play, a game in themselves: a play of words, a play of rhythms, sounds; . . . these muddles always maintain some sort of ideal order. There is system in this folly. By dragging a child into a topsy-turvy world, we help his intellect work, because the child becomes interested in creating such a topsy-turvy world for himself in order to become more effectively the master of the laws governing the real world. These absurdities could be dangerous for a child if they screened out the real interrelationships between ideas and objects. Instead, they push them to the fore, and emphasize them. They enhance (rather than weaken) the child's perception of reality." [30]

Here, too, we observe the same phenomenon of the dualism of art. In order to perceive art, we must contemplate simultaneously the true situation of things and their deviation from this situation. We can also observe how an effect of art arises from such a contradictory perception. Since absurdities are tools for the child to use in understanding reality, it becomes suddenly clear why the extreme leftists in art criticism come up with a slogan: *art as a method for building life.* They say that art is building life because "reality is forged from the establishment and destruction of contradictions." [31] When they criticize the idea of art as the cognition of life and advance the idea of a dialectic perception of the world through matter, they reach agreement with the psychological laws of art. "Art is an original, chiefly emotional . . . dialectic approach to building life." [32]

Now we can envision the role of art in the future. It is hard to guess what forms this unknown life of the future will take, and it is even harder to guess what place art will take in that future life. One thing is clear, however: arising from reality and reaching toward it, art will be determined by the basic order of the future flow of life.

"In the future," says Friche, "the role of art is not likely to change substantially from its present role. Socialist society will not be the antithesis of capitalist society, but its organic continuation." [33]

If we regard art as an embellishment or ornament of life, such a viewpoint is admissible. However, it basically contradicts the psychological laws of art. Psychological investigation reveals that art is the supreme center of biological and social individual processes in society, that it is a method for finding an equilibrium between man and his world, in the most critical and important stages of his life. This view of course completely refutes the approach according to which art is an ornament, and thereby leads us to doubt the correctness of the above statement. Since the future has in store not only a rearrangement of mankind according to new principles, not only the organization of new social and economic processes, but also the "remolding of man," there seems hardly any doubt that the role of art will also change.

It is hard to imagine the role that art will play in this remolding of man. We do not know which existing but dormant forces in our organisms it will draw upon to form the new man. There is no question, however, that art will have a decisive voice in this process. Without new art there can be no new man. The possibilities of the future, for art as well as for life, are inscrutable and unpredictable. As Spinoza said, "That of which the body is capable has not yet been determined."

NOTES

1. L. N. Tolstoy, *Collected Works,* vol. 30, pp. 64–65.

2. A. Yevlakhov, *Vvedenie v filosofiiu khudozhestvennovo tvorchestva* (*Introduction to the Philosophy of Artistic Creativity*), vol. I, Warsaw, 1910, p. 439.

3. L. I. Petrazhitskii, *Vvedenie v izuchenie prava i nravstvennosti. Osnovy emotsionalnoi psikhologii* (*Introduction to the Study of Law and Morality: Fundamentals of an Emotional Psychology*), St. Petersburg, 1907, p. 293.

4. D. N. Ovsianiko-Kulikovskii, *Collected Works,* vol. VI, St. Petersburg, 1914 p. 193.

5. *Ibid.,* pp. 192–193.

6. H. A. Taine, *Philosophie de l'art,* 2nd ed., Paris: G. Baillière, 1872.

7. A. V. Lunacharskii, *K voprosu ob iskusstve, etyudy* (*Essays on the Problem of Art*), Moscow-Petrograd, 1922, p. 29.

8. See A. Veselovskii, "Three Chapters from Historical Poetics," *Collected Works,* vol. I, St. Petersburg, 1906.

9. K. Bücher, *Rabota i ritm* (*Work and Rhythm*), Moscow: Novaia Moskva, 1923, p. 173.

10. *Ibid.,* p. 229.

11. I. Orshanskii, *Khudozhestvennoie tvorchestvo* (*Artistic Creativity*), Moscow, 1907, p. 102.

12. J. C. F. W. von Lange, *Das Wesen der Kunst* (*Grundzüge einer realistischen Kunstlehre*), vol. II, Berlin: Grote, 1901, p. 53.

13. A. F. Lazurskii, *Psikhologiia obshchaia i eksperimentalnaia* (*General and Experimental Psychology*), Leningrad, 1925, p. 240.

14. See S. Freud, *Fundamental Psychological Theories in Psychoanalysis.*

15. D. N. Ovsianiko-Kulikovskii, *Collected Works,* vol. VI, p. 194.

16. M. Guyau, *Iskusstvo s tochki zreniia sotsiologii* (*Art from the Viewpoint of Sociology*), pp. 56–57.

17. *Ibid.,* p. 349.

18. E. Hennequin, "An Attempt to Create a Scientific Criticism: An Aesthetic Psychology," *Russkoe Bogatstvo* (*The Wealth of Russia*), 1892, pp. 110–111.

19. L. N. Tolstoy, *Collected Works,* vol. 27, pp. 60–62.

20. G. V. Plekhanov, *Literatura i estetika* (*Literature and Aesthetics*), vol. I, Moscow, 1958, pp. 128–129.

21. M. Gershenzon, *Videnie poeta* (*Introduction to Poetics*), p. 46.

22. I. Eichenwald, *Pokhvala prazdnosti* (*In Praise of Idleness*), a collection of articles, Moscow: Kostry, 1922, p. 103.

23. P. Blonsky, *Pedagogika* (*Pedagogics*), Moscow: GIZ, 1922, pp. 160–161.

24. M. Gershenzon, *Introduction to Poetics,* p. 47.

25. *Ibid.,* p. 41.

26. S. Molozhavy and E. Shimkevich, *Problemy trudovoi shkoly v marksistkom osveshchenii* (*Problems of Labor Schools in a Marxist Light*), Moscow: Rabotnik prosveshcheniia, 1924, pp. 78, 80–81.

27. K. Bühler, *Dukhovnoe razvitie rebenka* (*The Mental Development of the Child*), Moscow: Novaia Moskva, 1924, p. 369 (in Russian translation).

28. *Ibid.,* pp. 321–322.

29. K. Chukovskii, "Reasonable Absurdities," *Russkii sovremennik* (*The Russian Contemporary*) 4:180–181, 1924.

30. *Ibid.,* p. 188.

31. N. F. Chuzhak, "Under the Sign of Life-Building: How to Perceive Today's Art," *Lef,* 1:35, 1923.

32. *Ibid.,* p. 36.

33. V. M. Friche, *Ocherki sotsialnoi istorii iskusstva (Essays in the Social History of Art),* Moscow: Novaia Moskva, 1923, p. 211.

COMMENTARY
by V. V. IVANOV

COMMENTARY
by V. V. IVANOV

The celebrated Soviet psychologist Lev Semenovich Vygotsky (1896–1934) devoted the first decade of his research activity to the study of the problems of art and literary criticism, literary history, aesthetics, and the psychology of art. In 1915 he wrote the first version of his major work on *Hamlet,* and in 1925 he finished the present book.

During the early stages of his research (the scope of which is here illustrated by excerpts from the second version [1916] of his monograph on *Hamlet*), he explored a method of critical interpretation based solely upon the text of a literary work. This period was preceded by intensive preparatory investigation. In 1916, at the age of 20, Vygotsky referred to what he called "innumerable notes made over a long period of time while reading and rereading Hamlet and thinking about him for several years." His work on *Hamlet* was followed by many articles on literary criticism published between 1915 and 1922. From these Vygotsky developed the idea of the present book (see the author's introduction to this book).

From his early interest in the "reader's" criticism, which re-creates the general atmosphere of a text, Vygotsky proceeded to a more specific and detailed analysis, using principles of the formal school of poetics. However, he disputed many of the theoretical positions of the formalists (see the second chapter of the present book). In his early essays on literary criticism he dealt with the symbolic nature of the artistic image; this concern led him to develop a theory based on general socialistic ideas (as presented in the first chapter of the present book) and on the then most advanced psychological and physiological methods (cf. the "funnel" theory used to explain the functions and purposes of art). Gradually, Vygotsky's interests widened to include new aspects of psychology. A direct continuation of the aesthetic theory presented in this volume is his investigation of the role of signs in controlling human behavior, a topic to which Vygotsky devoted a series of theoretical and experimental psychological works. His output made him one of the most prominent of Soviet psychologists of the thirties. In his book *The Evolution of the Higher Mental Processes,* written in 1930 and 1931 but unpublished until 1960, he investigated behavioral patterns which have survived from human beginnings to the present and which can be included in a system of higher forms of behavior. This analysis (which Vygotsky himself compared to Freud's study of the psychopathology of everyday life) was conducted by means of the procedure known in contemporary linguistics as the "method of inner reconstruction." Vygotsky analyzed primitive mnemotechnical devices, such as tying a knot in a handkerchief, or counting with fingers, one of man's older cultural achievements. In these and similar instances, a person who is unable to carry out his behavior resorts to exterior signs which help him control it. Vygotsky pointed out that the signals on which these phenomena are based exist not only in man but in animals as well. However, it is characteristic of human behavior and human culture to use signs as well as signals. Vygotsky concentrated his efforts on language, the system of signs that has played the most important role in the evolution of man. His best-known work, *Thought and Language,* is devoted to an analysis of this subject. He refers to the Romans who divided instruments into three categories: *instrumentum mutum,* a mute, inanimate instrument (a tool or artifact); *instrumentum semivocale,* an instrument having the facility of semispeech (a domestic animal); and *instrumentum vocale,* an instrument with the gift of speech (a slave). He noted that "for the ancients the slave was a self-governing device, a mechanism with a special type of control." These ideas on the role of signs in behavioral control were at least ten years ahead of his time. Thus, Vygotsky is to some extent the father of contemporary cybernetics (the science of control, communication, and information) and semiotics (the science of signs). Significant for human culture, and particularly for the cultural development of the individual, are not only the existence of external signs which control behavior, but also the gradual transformation of these *external* into *internal* signs. This view was expressed for the first time by Vygotsky in his *Thought and Language,* published in 1934 (English translation in 1962).

According to Vygotsky there are three methods of human behavioral control: First, there are commands which are shaped outside the person and issue from the environment (for example, the orders of a parent to a child). Second, are the commands which take shape outside a person but issue from within him. (The "egocentric" speech of children studied by Vygotsky is an example, as well as similar phenomena occurring in societies where collective monologue or egocentric speech survive as a form of social behavior.) Third, there are commands which form within a person by the transformation of external into internal signs (for example, internal speech, which Vygotsky describes as "egocentric"). From this point of view, instruction or learning can be described in cybernetic terms as a turning inward of commands, or as the formation of a program within a person. In articles and lectures devoted to the analysis of perception, memory, and other higher mental processes, Vygotsky showed that very young children cannot control these functions. Perception in adults may be described as a translation into linguistic terms of standards formed or conserved in the memory. In young children, however, neither the linguistic terms nor the translation has yet been formed. Children up to a certain age have no control over perception, attention, or memory; similarly, many adults lack a program control over emotions (consider the various practical psychological systems, beginning with those of ancient India, which attempt to develop such a control). Although expressed in different terms from those used in cybernetics, Vygotsky's ideas are directly associated with the problems of teaching and learning discussed in recent cybernetic literature, and also with the comparison of mind and machine.

Much of Vygotsky's experimental work in the thirties dealt with diacronic analyses of the problems of the evolution and disintegration of the higher mental processes. He also studied child psychology, particularly the creativity of children, thus returning to the problems of creativity which had fascinated him during his first years of scientific activity. In addition, he studied teaching and learning, pedagogics, and defectology.* He made important discoveries in each of these fields. His analysis of the correlation between language and intellectual activity in the development of the child (and in the development of man as compared with the lower animals) was of particular significance. He discovered the fundamental difference between the complex word meanings characteristic of children's speech but conserved in adult language, and

---

* Defectology is defined as the study and treatment of retarded children. Defectologists assumed that any child who fell below a certain level of performance on intelligence tests was congenitally defective and incapable of profiting from instruction.

conceptual meanings, which form much later in the child's development and gradually supplant the originally formed meanings. This distinction is of fundamental importance for understanding the differences between the semantics of poetic speech and scientific speech, especially the formalized language of the technical sciences. Of particular significance in learning theory and general semiotics is Vygotsky's hypothesis that both recognition of the mother tongue (known or acquired subconsciously) and the beginnings of conceptual thinking belong to the period in which the child discovers other sign systems: the written language or a foreign language, and such sign systems as arithmetic or those belonging to other sciences. As in many other instances, Vygotsky anticipated the most recent scientific discoveries in his original treatment of the problems of language and intellect.

During the last years of his life, Vygotsky studied the structure of cognition and perception in defectology and psychiatry. He became so professionally competent in these and other related fields of medicine and experimental psychology that the test he introduced (the Vygotsky Block Test) has become known in the world literature by his name. He proceeded from the hypothesis that lower (primitive) functions and centers gain ascendance when the higher centers disintegrate. From the results of a vast amount of clinical work, Vygotsky suggested an original way of localizing brain damage (including aphasia and other speech disturbances). He made it possible "to determine the path that leads from focal disturbances of a certain type to specific changes in the whole personality and life style" (L. S. Vygotsky, "Psychology and the Teaching of Localization." In *Abstracts from the First All-Ukrainian Convention of Neuropathologists and Psychiatrists,* Kharkov, 1934, p. 41). Vygotsky's paper on the disintegration of concepts in schizophrenia is a classic example of social psychological analysis of intellectual speech disturbances. He showed that when the higher forms of logic and conceptual thinking disintegrate, structures arise which recall the early forms of complex thought. Vygotsky examined various aspects of conceptual grouping in children's speech and pathology. His studies are important both from a psychological and linguistic viewpoint, for he succeeded in avoiding intellectualization and the "logic" of language and personality which were to become a fad in subsequent years. Vygotsky's later years were devoted to the consideration of personality structure and the correlation between intellect and emotion. At that time he was also studying Spinoza's teachings on the passions. Completed written portions of this last work dealt first and foremost with Descartes and were to find a significant place in the history of philosophy.

An untimely death cut off the activity of this scientist who had the makings of a genius. He left an indelible mark on the subsequent development of the social and biological sciences (psychology, psychiatry, defectology, pedagogics, pedology, linguistics, aesthetics, and literary history), including several disciplines that did not exist in his lifetime, such as psycholinguistics, semiotics, and cybernetics. A number of his posthumous works, published in 1934 and 1935, proved to be of primary importance. These included *Thought and Language* and a collection of articles entitled "The Intellectual Development of Children during Teaching." After 1956 his influence and significance for the science of psychology became more and more apparent. Since the American publication of a translation of *Thought and Language* in 1962, Vygotsky has been rapidly recognized as one of the leading psychologists of the first half of the twentieth century. Eminent psychologists, such as Dr. Bernstein, professor of psychology at London University (who has published the works of several Soviet psychologists in English translation), have pointed out that Vygotsky's studies opened the way to a unification of the biological and social studies, and that their continuation may have at least as great a significance for science as the deciphering of the genetic code.

For literature on L. S. Vygotsky, the reader is directed to the following:

Leontiev, A. N., and Luria, A. R. "The Psychology of L. S. Vygotsky," in the book *Selected Psychological Studies by L. S. Vygotsky,* Moscow, 1956, pp. 4–36.

Kolbanovskii, V. N. "On the Psychological Views of L. S. Vygotsky," *Questions in Psychology* 5 (1956): 104–133.

Bruner, J. S., Introduction to *Thought and Language,* by L. S. Vygotsky, Cambridge, Massachusetts: The M.I.T. Press, 1962.

Piaget, J. "Comments on Vygotsky's Critical Remarks concerning *The Language and Thought of the Child,*" Cambridge, Massachusetts: The M.I.T. Press, 1962.

Weinreich, U. "A Review of *Thought and Language* by L. S. Vygotsky," *American Anthropologist* 65 (1963): 1401–1404.

Vygotsky's interests in the word and the sign, the relationship of the intellect to the emotions, and of the individual to the collective can be seen throughout his entire work. The present book, *The Psychology of Art,* which deals with these areas and proceeds from the art of the word, is of great interest, not only in itself but also as the illustration of a specific period in the intellectual evolution of a great scientist.

The present edition is based on a typescript which Vygotsky himself prepared for publication. The title page of the typescript gives the date of its completion as 1925, which happens to be the date of the establishment of the State Institute of Experimental Psychology. Vygotsky spent more than ten years on this monograph. In editing the text, only a few changes were made; these refer mostly to quotations from other authors and are of little importance to the substance of the book.

1. Vygotsky's early study, *The Tragedy of Hamlet, Prince of Denmark, by W. Shakespeare*, exists in two forms: a draft dated August 5–September 12, 1915 (written in Gomel); and a revised manuscript dated February 14–March 28, 1916 (Moscow). The final version amounts to 42 pages of introduction, 277 pages of handwritten text, and 64 pages of notes, for a total of 12 notebooks. Excerpts from it are given below in the comments on the chapter on *Hamlet*, starting on p. 279.

2. In his later works Vygotsky developed an original theory of the control of human behavior by means of signs (see L. S. Vygotsky, *The Evolution of the Higher Mental Processes*). The ideas formulated by him during the thirties coincide with contemporary ideas on the role of semiotics (sign systems) in human culture. But even in contemporary semiotics and cybernetics, despite the interest in problems of control and self-governing, no one underscored the leading role of sign systems with as much emphasis as did Vygotsky (see his endeavors in this respect): V. Ivanov, "La semiotica e le scienze umanistiche," *Questo e altro* 6–7:58, 1964.

3. A similar study of models of artistic creativity, independent of the individual psychology of the reader or author, is being undertaken by means of the most modern cybernetic methods (see for example, "The Machine Translation," in *Proceedings of the Institute of Precision Mechanics and Computation Technique*, USSR Acad. Sci. 2:372, 1964; and the *dhyana* philosophy in ancient Indian poetry).

4. To the end of his life, Vygotsky studied the works of Spinoza. His last monograph (on the emotions and the intellect) is devoted to this subject.

5. See a sociological investigation of the classic novel and the contemporary "new novel": *Problèmes d'une Sociologie du Roman*, Bruxelles: Editions de l'Institut de Sociologie, 1963.

6. Among the latest Soviet works devoted to the sociology of art, that of V. R. Grib on literary criticism should be mentioned (V. R. Grib, *Selected Works*, Moscow, 1956). Of related interest are the works of B. Asafev on musicology, written during the twenties (B. V. Asafev, *Musical Form as a Process*, 2d ed., Leningrad, 1963).

7. With reference to the production of poets like Pushkin, literary tradition has established objective methods for studying Russian verse. The influence of these has been shown in the dependence of each and every poet on the literary and versification rules of his time (see especially B. Tomashevskii, *The Verse*, Leningrad, 1929; G. A. Shengeli, Treatise on the Russian Verse, Moscow-Petrograd, 1923; K. Taranovskii, *A Collection of Russian Verse*, Belgrade, 1953; and also a series of articles by A. N. Kolmogorov and others: A. N. Kolmogorov, and A. N. Kondratov, "The Rhythm of Maiakovskii's Poetry," in *Voprosy yazykoznaniya* (*Problems in Linguistics*) No. 3, 1962; A. N. Kolmogorov, "A Study of Maiakovskii's Rhythm," in *Voprosy yazykoznaniya* No. 4, 1963; A. N. Kolmogorov, and A. V. Prokhorov, "The Dolnik in Contemporary Russian Poetry," *Voprosy yazykoznaniya* No. 4, 1963 and No. 1, 1964; also M. L. Gasparov, "Statistical Investigation of the Russian Three-stress Dolnik," *Teoriya veroyatnostei i yeye primeneniya* (*Theories of Probability and Their Application*) 8, 1963.

8. Vygotsky's notebooks include the following remark, which characterizes the essence of the analytical method:

As the basis of the investigation, or its starting point, the objective analytical method deals with the difference between the aesthetic and the nonaesthetic object. The elements of a work of art exist prior to its completion, and their effect has been studied. Art must now deal with the method of constructing these elements. Consequently, the difference between the artistic construction of these elements and their unification outside aesthetics represents the key to the solution of specific problems of art. The basic method of study is a comparison of the artistic with the nonartistic construction of the same elements. This is how the subject of analysis is formed; form is what distinguishes *art* from *non-art:* the content of a work of art can exist alone as a nonaesthetic fact.

9. We are dealing here with the often suggested connection between the ancient Indian word *mus* (mouse) and the verb *mus-na-ti* (he steals).

10. Etymologically, the Russian word *luna* is associated with the root *to give light* (cf. the Latin word *lux*, and the Ukrainian *luna*).

11. In more recent semiotic terminology we can speak of the relationship between the concept of a sign (i.e., the meaning or concept expressed by the sign) and its denotate (the object or class of objects to which it refers). Inner form is exemplified by cases in which the concept of a sign (e.g., *thief*) becomes the denotate of another sign (which has a different concept, *mouse*); this is a particular characteristic of natural languages (cf., A. Church, *Introduction to Mathematical Logic*, Moscow,

1960, p. 19). The concept of inner form was analyzed by G. G. Shpet and A. Marty (cf., G. Shpet, *Vnutreniaia forma slova: Etyudy i variatsiĭ na temy Gumbol'dta* [*The Inner Form of Words: Studies and Variations on Humboldt's Themes*]. Moscow, 1927, particularly the analysis of the aesthetics of the problem of inner form in poetic language on pp. 141 ff; O. Funke, "Innere Sprachform: Eine Einführung," in A. Marty, *Sprachphilosophie,* Reichenberg, 1924; A. Marty, "Concept and Method of the Drama and Philosophy of Language," in V. A. Zvegintsev [ed.], *Istoriia yazykoznaniia XIX i XX vekov v ocherkakh i izvlecheniiakh* [*History of Philology of the 19th and 20th Centuries in Sketches and Essays*], Part II, Moscow, 1960, p. 12. The structure of the sign ["symbol"] in language and in art was compared in E. Cassirer, Philosophie der symbolischen Formen, Berlin, Vols. I–III, Berlin, 1923–1929; and later by S. Langer, *Philosophy in a New Key,* Cambridge, Mass., 1942, and in works on semantics and semiotics, particularly in C. Morris's work in *A Modern Book of Esthetics,* edited by M. Rader, New York: Henry Holt and Co., 3rd ed., 1960).

12. The idea that art is a method of cognition similar to the scientific method is clearly expressed in B. Brecht's aesthetic viewpoints and in his concept of the "intellectual theater" and by S. M. Eisenstein in his concept of the "intellectual cinema." See, in particular, the articles by S. M. Eisenstein, "Perspectives," in *Selected Works,* Vol. 2, Moscow, pp. 35–44, 1964; and "Behind the Frame," pp. 283–296. Concerning problems in literary language, the interrelationship between art and science is studied in depth in A. Huxley's book, *Literature and Science,* London, 1963.

13. The estrangement technique, which corresponds to the "effect of alienation" in Brecht's aesthetic theory, was taken by V. B. Shklovskii and other followers of the formal school as a method for destroying the automatisms of perception. This technique makes sense for the theory of information, because it permits evaluation of the quantity of information contained in a communication. A communication that is fully known beforehand carries no information, and is therefore perceived automatically. Concerning the possibility of applying the theory of information to aesthetics, see A. A. Moles, *Théorie de l'information et perception esthétique,* Paris, 1958; J. Dorfles, "Communication and Symbol in the Work of Art," *Journal of Aesthetics and Art Criticism,* 1957; M. Porebski, "Teoria informacji a badania nad sztuka," *Estetyka* (Warsaw) 3: 23–43, 1962; H. Frank, *Grundlagenprobleme der Informationsästhetik und erste Anwendung auf die Mime pure,* Stuttgart, 1959; R. Gunzenhauser, *Aesthetisches Mass und ästhetische Information,* Hamburg, 1962; M. Bense, "Aesthetische Information" (*Aesthetica II*), Krefeld and Baden-Baden, 1956; A. A. Moles, "L'analyse des structures du message poétique aux differ-

ents niveaux de la sensibilité," *Poetyka* (Warsaw) 811–826, 1961; I. Fonagy, "Informationsgehalt von Wort und Laut in der Dichtung," *Ibid.*, pp. 563–569; J. Levy, "Teorie informace a literarni proces," *Česka literatura* 11:281–307, 1963; J. Levy, "Predbezne poznamkyz informacni analyze verse," *Slovenska literatura*, XI, 1964; N. Krasnova, "K teorii informacie v literarnej vede," *Slovenska literatura*, XI, 1964; I. Trzynadlowski, "Information Theory and Literary Genres," *Zagadnienia rodzajow literackich* 1:41–45, 1961; A. K. Zholkovskii, "Conference on the Study of Poetic Language," in *Mashinnyy perevod i prikladnaya lingvistika (Computer Translation and Applied Linguistics)* 7:88–101, 1962. I. I. Revzin, "Conference in the city of Gorky devoted to the application of mathematical methods to the study of the language of literature," in *Strukturnotipologicheskie issledovaniia (Structural and Typological Studies)*, Moscow, 1962.

14. The following passage in Vygotsky's notebooks apparently applies to this: "In his book *Abstruse Language* (published in Moscow by the All-Russian Poets' Association, 1925), A. Kruchenykh reaches the exact opposite conclusion concerning the fate of abstruse language. He registers 'the triumph of abstruseness on all fronts.' He finds it in Seifullina, V. Ivanov, Leonov, Babel, Pilniak, A. Veselyi, and even Demian Bednyǐ. But is this so? The facts cited by the author convince us of the contrary. Abstruseness triumphs in a meaningful text and becomes sensible from context in which the abstruse word is placed. Pure abstruseness is dead. And when the author himself 'imitates Freud in psychoanalysis' and practices 'psychology,' he does not prove the triumph of abstruseness: he forms quite meaningful and complex words by combining two elements in a word that are almost at opposite ends in terms of sense." Vygotsky's remark about the "triumph" of abstruseness in a meaningful text is remarkable; he talks about signs in artistic language which have *only* a syntactic significance and acquire it by becoming structural elements of a work of art. Vygotsky's remark shed light on the most varied trends in contemporary art (sculpture, painting, poetry, music); it is all the more valuable since the fact of the existence of signs with strictly syntactic significance in art put most of Vygotsky's contemporaries into a rather tight situation.

15. Further development of the formal school showed that its most talented representatives were aware of the inadequacy of the unilateral approach to art. Significant in this respect is the paper by Yu. N. Tynianov and R. O. Jakobson, "Problems in the Study of Literature and Language," *Novy Lef* 12:36–37, 1928, in which the necessity of combining philological and sociological analysis was emphasized: "The prob-

lem of a concrete choice of the part, or of the dominant, can be solved only by means of analyzing the correlation between the literary series and all other historical series. This correlation (a system of systems) has structural laws subject to investigation." The gradual inclusion of semantic problems (i.e., the study of the content of an object) in the investigations has become a characteristic feature in the development of scientists belonging to the formal school. This was pointed out by the author of the most complete study of that school (see V. Erlich, *Russian Formalism*, The Hague, 1954. Also important in this respect are the papers by R. O. Jakobson: "Randbemerkungen zur Prosa des Dichters Pasternak," *Slavische Rundschau* 8:357–374, 1935. Among the more recent literary criticisms by Jakobson, the following studies are particularly significant, since they deal with the study of individual poems on a formal, conceptual level: R. O. Jakobson and C. Lévi-Strauss, " 'Les chats' de Charles Baudelaire," *L'Homme*, January-April, 1962; R. Jakobson, "Màcha's Line on the Call of the Turtledove," *International Journal of Slavic Linguistics and Poetics* 3:1–20, 1960; R. O. Jakobson, "Comments of the Last Poem of Botev," *Language and Literature* 16:2, 1961; R. O. Jakobson, "Linguistics and Poetics," in *Style in Language,* edited by T. A. Sebeok, New York, 1960; R. O. Jakobson, "The Poetics of Grammar and the Grammar of Poetics," *Poetyka,* Warsaw, 1961.

As pointed out by B. M. Eichenbaum in 1927, the study of form as such, during the first decade of the development of the formal school, led to the study of the function of form (see B. M. Eichenbaum, "The Theory of the Formalistic Method," *Literatura. Teoria. Kritika. Polemika* [*Literature, Theory, Critique, and Polemics*], Leningrad, 1927, pp. 149–165.) A similar functional approach was developed by the Prague school. See I. Mukarovsky, "Strukturalismus v estetice a ve vede o literature," *Kapitoly z české poetiky* (Prague) vol. 1, No. 2, 1948. A general review of the problems associated with the study of structure and function in contemporary philology is given in the paper by R. Wellek, "Concepts of Form and Structure in Twentieth Century Criticism," *Neophilologus* 47:2–11, 1958. Concerning the structural analysis of artistic folklore, the following texts are particularly relevant: P. Bogatyrev and R. Jakobson, "Die Folklore als besondere Form des Schaffens," *Donum natalicium,* Schrijnen, Nijmegen-Utrecht, 1929, pp. 900–913; R. P. Armstrong, "Content Analysis in Folkloristics," *Trends in Content Analysis,* Urbana, 1959, pp. 151–170; T. A. Sebeok, "Toward a Statistical Contingency Method in Folklore Research," *Studies in Folklore,* edited by W. Edson, Bloomington, 1957; C. Lévi-Strauss, *Anthropologie structurale,* Paris, 1958; C. Lévi-Strauss, "La geste d'Asdiwal," Ecole pratique des hautes études, 1958–1959, pp. 3–43; C. Lévi-Strauss, "La structure et la forme,"

Cahiers de l'Institut de science économique appliquée, Recherches et dialogues philosophiques et économiques 29:7–36 (March), 1960.

The trend from a formalistic investigation of the textural structure to a semantic, historical interpretation may be followed in V. I. Propp's works on magical fairy tales. A first investigation in which the succession of motives in a formal fairy tale design is thoroughly analyzed (V. I. Propp, *Morfologiia skazki* [*The Morphology of Fairy Tales*], Leningrad, 1928) was followed by another work in which the structure of the fairy tale and its origin were given a sociological interpretation (see V. I. Propp, *Istoricheskie korni volshebnoi skazki* [*Historical Roots of the Magical Fairy Tale*], Leningrad, 1946). This is why a criticism concerning an insufficient use of semantics can be made only if the former paper is used and the latter ignored. In the thirties, the historical and literary works of its most prominent representatives were a direct continuation of the concerns of the formal school, on the one hand the literary-historical works of its most typical representatives (above all, Yu. N. Tynianov and B. M. Eichenbaum); on the other hand, the study of Dostoevsky's novels by M. M. Bakhtin (see M. M. Bakhtin, *Problemy tvorchestva Dostoevskovo* [*Problems of Dostoevsky's Works*], Leningrad, 1929, 2nd revised ed., Moscow, 1963), which represents a new step in the analysis of the formal and conceptual structure of the novel (see also his later work on Rabelais). The gradual inclusion of the semantics of a work of art (while maintaining all the most important achievements of formal analysis) is the distinguishing feature of S. M. Eisenstein's works, where the knowledge of the methods of contemporary science (including psychology) is combined with a deep insight into the substance of the work of art. This is why Eisenstein (as Vygotsky did in the present book) succeeded in avoiding involvement with the purely syntactic side of a work of art (i.e., the side that characterizes only its inner structure), which was characteristic of many theoretical and practical experiments in various art forms in the twenties. The development of theoretical investigations has coincided with trends in art itself. Purely formal constructions are more and more frequently replaced by artistic techniques used to express profound inner themes reflecting historical events (e.g., the first experiments in atonal music versus *The Witness from Warsaw* by Schönberg; Picasso's and Braque's early paintings, the beginning of cubism, versus Picasso's *Guernica*, which in 1937 coincided with Shostakovich's Fourth Symphony, etc.). The heritage of the formal school is evaluated by A. Zholkovskii and I. Shcheglov ("The Possibility of Constructing Structural Poetics," in *Simpozium po strukturnomu izucheniiu znakovykh sistem* [*Symposium on the Structural Studies of Symbolic Systems*], Moscow 1962, 138–141); and V. Strada, "Formalismo e neoformalismo," *Questo e altro* 6–7:51–56, 1964. See also the remarks in I. M. Lotman, "Lectures on Structural Poetics," *Uchenye zapiski Tartuskovo gosudarstvennovo universiteta* (*Proceedings of the Tartu State University*) No. 160 and *Trudy po znakovym sistemam* (*Collection of Works on Symbolic Systems*) (Tartu) 1:9, 1964.

16. The theory of elementary hedonism here criticized by Vygotsky was developed in V. B. Shklovskii's early works and therefore cannot be applied to all formalists.

17. The point here concerns various theories of synesthetic perception of individual sound units, their complexes and semantization, and, more generally, the semantization of the entire sound sequence of a work of poetry. The scientific consideration of these two interconnected problems (cf. a fairly complete review of them in P. Delbouille, *Poésie et sonorité*, Paris, 1961; also E. Brock, "Der heutige Stand der Lautbedeutungslehre," *Trivium*, 1944, No. 3, p. 199 ff.) could not be performed prior to the appearance of phonology, structural methods and the application of mathematics and information theory. During the twenties, scientific investigation of these problems had just begun. Previously, studies were conducted without a strict methodology; they involved unjustified and disproportionate generalization, the transition from observations of limited and specific texts (for instance, a given work of poetry) to the aggregate of texts in a given language.

For more detailed information on synesthetic reactions to various sound units (phonemes) noted by various authors, cf. S. M. Eisenstein, "Vertical Cutting" in *Selected works*, Vol. 2, Moscow, 1964, p. 200 ff., in which the author refers *inter alia* to the well-known sonnet by Rimbaud which served as the model for Balmont's remarks quoted by Vygotsky. Among modern Russian poets, Khlebnikov made many experiments dealing with the semantization of individual phonemes for his poem "Zangezi," and numerous practical and theoretical tests (cf., for instance, *Collected Works of Velimir Khlebnikov*, Vol. III, Leningrad, 1931, p. 325).

18. Cf., for instance, W. Wundt, *Völkerpsychologie*, I, 1904. In the more recent literature, cf., E. Sapir, "A Study in Phonetic Symbolism," *Journal of Experimental Psychology* 12, 1929 and *Selected Writings in Language, Culture and Personality*," Berkeley–Los Angeles, 1951; G. La Drière, "Structure, Sound and Meaning," in *Sound and Poetry*, edited by N. Frye, New York, 1957, pp. 85–108; W. Kayser, *Die Klangmalerei bei Harsdörffer*, 2nd ed, Göttingen, 1962; V. N. Toporov, "An Analysis of Several Poetic Texts" in *Programma i tezisy dokladov . . . po vtorichnym modeliruyushchim sisteman*" (*Program and Abstracts of Papers . . . on Secondary Modeling Systems*), Tartu, 1964, pp. 92–97.

19. The works of these scholars, representative of psychological aesthetics, were quite popular at the time (cf. abstracts by V. Shklovskii, *Sborniki po teori poeticheskovo yazyka* [*Collection on the Theory of the Poetic Language*] No. 1, Petrograd, 1916).

20. As for the phonetic organization of the verse, see the paper by E. D. Polivanov, "General Phonetic Principle of Any Poetic Technique," *Voprosy yazykoznaniya* (*Problems in Linguistics*) 1:99–112, 1963; the studies of S. I. Bernshtein on the phonetic structure of individual poems; and the works by R. O. Jakobson listed in note 15).

21. The importance of studying subconscious processes in connection with the cybernetic study of art has been recently emphasized by A. N. Kolmogorov (cf. A. N. Kolmogorov, "Automata and Life," in *Vozmozhnoe i nevozmozhnoe v kibernetike* [*The Possible and the Impossible in Cybernetics*], Moscow, 1963).

22. An interesting illustration of this trend of thought is given in the letters of R. M. Rilke written when he was considering the possibility of therapy by means of psychoanalysis. He indicated that for him therapy would only be possible if he stopped writing altogether (cf. letters to Emil von Gebsattel, dated January 24th, 1912 [Rainer Maria Rilke, *Letters*, Wiesbaden, 1950, p. 349] and Lou Andreas-Salomé, of the same date [R. M. Rilke, *Letters from 1907 to 1914*, Leipzig, 1933, p. 180]).

23. Critical remarks about psychoanalysis, to some extent similar to Vygotsky's, later led to a substantial change in the psychoanalytical concept of art. This was first expressed in C. G. Jung's works (cf. a brief exposition of Jung's aesthetic ideas in: M. Verli, *Obshcheye literaturovedenie* [*The Science of Literature*], Moscow, 1957, pp. 167–171; K. Gilbert and G. Kuhn, *History of Aesthetics*, Moscow, 1960, p. 596; Charles Baudouin, *L'oeuvre de Jung et la psychologie complexe*, Paris, 1963; and on the aesthetics of psychoanalysis; cf. also the anthology edited by M. Rader, *A Modern Book on Esthetics*, mentioned in Note 11). The attempt to get beyond Freudian pansexualism and set up a more general theory of the collective subconscious is also characteristic of many other scholars who tried to investigate language, art, and other sign systems from the viewpoint of the theory of the subconscious (cf., in particular, E. Sapir, *Selected Writings in Language, Culture and Personality*, Berkeley-Los Angeles, 1951).

24. The problem of isolation is discussed repeatedly in this book and becomes particularly acute in connection with the inclusion of the thing (object) as a fact (characteristic of various art forms of the twentieth century) without transformation into a work of art (cf. the inclusion in a painting of pieces of paper, posters, etc., as performed by Braque and

Picasso in their early periods; the use of a newspaper cutting in the "film-eye" of John Dos Passos; the cinéma-vérité of Dziga Vertov and his most recent western imitators, etc.).

25. The concept of the hero as a chessman, that is, as a point at which various structural relations intersect, agrees with a similar structural linguistic concept of the sign in natural language, beginning with Saussure (F. de Saussure, *Course in General Linguistics*, Moscow, 1933).

26. To analyze the fable, Vygotsky uses the theory of "narration" developed in the twenties by the formalists (above all, by B. M. Eichenbaum) and later by M. M. Bakhtin in his analysis of the word in an artistic text. It should be noted here also that the theoretical achievements of literary history went hand in hand with the practical achievements of literature, which in those years yielded samples of narration in the works of M. Zoshchenko, I. Babel, and others.

27. In addition to the old literature about Krylov referred to in the present book, see also N. L. Stepanov, *Krylov, His Life and Work,* Moscow, 1949; N. L. Stepanov, Introduction to *Russkaya basnia XVIII i nachala XIX veka* (*The Russian Fable of the 18th and Early 19th Centuries*), Leningrad, 1951; N. L. Stepanov, *Masterstvo Krylova-basnopistsa* (*The Mastery of Krylov, the Fabulist*), Moscow, 1956.

28. According to comparative historical mythology, the crowing of a cock is understood to be an ancient symbol encountered in many civilizations. The emotional interpretation given here cannot explain the origin of the symbol, although it might be correct in its application to certain later cases of its use.

29. As for the understanding of the term *form,* cf. the next chapter. The words *form* and *content* do not coincide with their contemporary interpretation. *Content* is identical here with *material,* that is, those elements of the work of art which existed prior to its complete realization. *Form* is identical with the processing, the *formation,* of this material. In regarding a work of art as a process, Vygotsky discovered the existence of two chains of evolution in this process which stand in a complex and contradictory relationship to one another. He illustrated this opposition with examples of the fable, the tragedy, and the short story.

30. Here and in the following discussion the author makes use of the results of his study of the structure of the short story by the formalists.

31. Curves reproduced from Laurence Sterne, *Tristram Shandy.*

32. The same idea, applied to syntax, can be expressed in more precise terms. In a sentence made up according to everyday syntactic norms, it is impossible to divide words which are grammatically con-

nected to each other by inserting other words not connected with them. This rule is not followed in poetic language.

33. This refers to the method demonstrated in the works of B. V. Tomashevskii and G. A. Shengeli (and recently developed by A. N. Kolmogorov) where the statistical study of the rhythm of words in common use is the basis for demonstrating which deviations are specific to a given poet (for instance, when one studies the distinction of a particular poet's iambus from a *calculated* or *ideal* iambus that can be constructed proceeding solely from the rhythmic rules of a language without any additional data).

34. Here Vygotsky introduces a distinction between real time and literary time, a distinction that was later the subject of many investigations of the artistic output of the twentieth century. Cf., in particular, the following remarkable studies: G. Müller, *Die Bedeutung der Zeit in der Erzählungskunst*, Bonn, 1946; E. Staiger, *Die Zeit als Einbildungskraft des Dichters*, Zürich, 1939; G. Poulet, *Etudes sur le temps humain*, Edinburgh, 1949; Paris, 1950; Paris, 1964. Regarding ancient Russian literature, a similar problem was recently studied by D. S. Likhachev ("The Time in Russian Folk Literature," *Russkaya literatura*, 4:32–47, 1962). An interpretation of the structure of a work of art close to Vygotsky's was later given by Eisenstein, who noted that "classical Russian examples of inconsequential narration are Pushkin's *The Shot*, where the story begins in the middle, Bunin's *Gentle Breath*, and a great many others" (S. M. Eisenstein, "The Non-Indifferent Nature," *Selected Works*, Vol. III, Moscow, 1964, p. 311).

35. The idea of the dominant, introduced here by Vygotsky, is one of the most important concepts of structural linguistics and philology (cf. B. M. Eichenbaum, *Melodika stikha* [*The Melody of Verses*], Petrograd, 1922.

36. In contradistinction to earlier works, in which he notes the association of breathing with aesthetic perception (cf. G. Santayana, *The Sense of Beauty*, New York, 1896, p. 56), Vygotsky later tried to check this hypothesis experimentally. However, the results cannot be regarded as final. One of the main difficulties was determining a mechanism capable of establishing that the rhythm of breathing depends on such totally different and diversified factors as the emotional effect of the work of art, its syntactic structure, etc.

37. Vygotsky's own view of the king's role in *Hamlet* can be found in the following excerpts from his early work:

The king, too, can hardly carry the heavy burden. He is also connected with the plot of the play. He is a fratricide, which makes him the principal character in the dénouement. Hamlet's passive struggle with him, as a result of which both die, is the main subject of the tragedy and the main path of the plot. They are the two strongest fighters, and between them all the others die or perish. The king is not a criminal. His crime was committed before the tragedy begins. Now he wants to live in peace with Hamlet. The play begins with the king's attempt to settle things between them. To all appearances he succeeds; at least their outward relationship, disturbed by the death of his brother, and their personal relationship are mended. As a final result, however, he perishes, and Fortinbras accedes to the throne . . . The king asks Hamlet to throw away the mask of mourning; he feels that it hides something evil; he feels that behind it is concealed an unusual, if not unnatural, sorrow of a son for his father, something truly horrible. All this time his soul is seized by terrible feelings. Although Hamlet takes no action against him, the king does not try to prevent his destruction, as witnessed clearly from his deeds and his words, and he gravitates toward it as if attracted by an invisible force. At the beginning of the play the king believed that everything might go well; Hamlet's agreement to remain at the court gives him joy, and he is also glad of the prince's desire to set up a stage performance and have a gay time. In an attempt to fight it, he enlists the help of Polonius, Guildenstern, and Rosencrantz to find out the reason for Hamlet's sorrow; thus they, without knowing it, are dragged into the ring, become instruments of the king (like Laertes), and perish with him. These three have much in common in their roles and in their characters . . . together with the king they are involved in his struggle, and from the very beginning of the play they try to drive Hamlet into a trap. This is why the king's destruction is theirs as well. Their role and fate in the play reveal to us the charged, fatal field between the fighters who have crossed their swords, a field fatal to everything that strays there. This is why Hamlet's sorrow and grief frighten the king so much . . . He appears to be exhausted all the time and is slowly perishing. Almost all the scenes of the tragedy (Hamlet's conversations with Ophelia, with the courtiers, with Polonius, with his mother, and even with the actors) are arranged by the king, including the last in which he himself perishes. The entire mechanism of the tragedy is propelled by those alarms and fears of the king which in the end lead to his destruction. We can therefore say that he himself prepares his own destruction. He is not drawn toward the catastrophe any more than Hamlet is. He rushes toward it in rushing toward Hamlet's armed hand. All hopes fade when, after the conversation with Ophelia, he states quite bluntly that the prince is not sick with love, but that a seed has fallen into his heart, the fruit of which will be dangerous . . . He decides to exile Hamlet to England, but agrees to Polonius' suggestion of allowing Hamlet to meet with his mother (these are *motives* for his actions—the conversation with Ophelia, the decision to send Hamlet to England, the play). His decision to exile his nephew is strengthened after Hamlet's conversation with his mother and the killing of Polonius. This is followed by the decision to destroy Hamlet in England, the return of the prince, and the king's conspiracy with Laertes. It is extremely important to point out that the *motion* of the action is with the king, not with Hamlet. Were it not for the king, the action of the play would go nowhere, because no one else does anything. Even Hamlet does nothing. Hamlet's role in the play is a static one; his actions are caused by the king's actions (the killing of the courtiers), so that the beginning of the story (the murder of Hamlet's father) and the *entire* mechanism of successive motion begin with the king and remain with the king; *he* is the main acting personage, not Hamlet. Since all action and motion are concentrated in and around the king, it is extremely important to establish (apart from a general outline of the image of a man crushed under an exceedingly heavy burden) the motives for his actions. They amount to one—a vague fear, a feeling of terror concerning Hamlet's sorrow and grief. All the king wants to do is prevent trouble and misfortune. It is he who begins the struggle, and all his actions unavoidably lead him to his own destruction. There is another important point to be made here. The king has no plan of action. His plans change, fail, combine with the reactions of others (Polonius, Laertes) and, as a result, it is revealed that there is no plan. Certainly the king has none. He does not lead the play; it (the plot) leads him. The play has its own design which governs and controls the king and uses him for its own purpose. It is this design of the play that drags the king to his inevitable destruction. No matter how he seems to counteract it, the king must carry out this design. Hamlet's wisdom, his own lack of planning, his prophetic *readiness* are achievements of the play's design and are totally subject to it.

38. With regard to the scene in the Shakespearean theatre, cf. A. A. Smirnov, *Shakespeare,* Leningrad-Moscow, 1963, p. 35.

39. Vygotsky's first attempts to take *Hamlet* in "an uninterpreted form" and look at the play "as it actually is" are given in his early work which is preceded by a rather vast introduction in which his approach is explained:

So many books have been written about the tragedy *Hamlet,* such a vast literature exists on this subject in virtually all languages of the world, so many critical analyses, so many philosophical, and scientific (psychological, historical, juridical, psychiatric, etc.) works have been devoted to it, that the tragedy is completely submerged by a mass of interpretations and comments. This is why a new work on the subject requires, as a categorical imperative, some preliminary explanation to clarify its tasks and subject. A work of art (like any phenomenon) can be viewed from many different approaches. There can be an unlimited number of comments and interpretations; these are, as a matter of fact, a guarantee of the permanent value of the work of art. This is why we feel that the polemics conducted by the various trends and schools of thought are useless. Historical, social, philosophical, and aesthetic critiques do not exclude each other; since they approach the subject of their research from different sides, they investigate one and the same thing at the same time. Therefore the question is not to determine which of these schools is closest to the truth and must therefore become the absolute master and sovereign of critique, but rather how to delineate the fields of competence in which each is fully justified. . . . *Hamlet* has been interpreted and criticized an infinite number of times. Such evaluations include psychiatric and juridical interpretations. The studies of the author's relation to his work, the chronological sequence, the philosophical meaning, the dramatic merits of the play, all these problems lie on another plane, with which the others frequently intersect. There is, however, a region of artistic criticism which is only indirectly dependent upon all this, a region of direct, nonscientific creativity, of subjective critique, to which the following text does not apply . . . But this text . . . does refer to some sort of criticism; we therefore consider it necessary to dwell on its peculiar conditions and features. This, it seems to us, is important because the tremendous mass of critical works about this great tragedy requires a rather strict delineation of competency in order to be able to achieve full and clear understanding. . . . Subjective criticism is the criticism of the reader, but this is a dilettante criticism. The three major features that distinguish it from other criticism are: its relation to the author of the play, to other critical interpretations of the same work and, finally, to the object of investigation itself . . . Such a criticism is not associated with the personality of the author . . . A work of art, once published, detaches itself from its creator. It cannot exist without a reader, since it represents a potential that only the reader can realize. In the inexhaustible variety and abundance of symbolic subjects which are the basis of a true work of art, we find the source of all its interpretations. The way the author himself understands and explains it is neither more nor less than one of many possible interpretations and does not commit anyone to anything . . . This is why a critic is not able to establish whether or not the author, on the basis of his historical and social position, and also as a specific personality (generally, if one may say so, *biographically*) can have those characteristics which he would attribute to him. He is unable to say whether the interpretation of the author's biography corresponds to the general spirit pervading his works . . . This is why the critic can create and produce his own interpretation without necessarily denying any others. By establishing that his interpretation is one among many possible ones, the critic tries to confirm it as such, to determine its validity without claiming it to be unique or exceptional and without engaging himself in a criticism of critics. This is the relationship between the reader's criticism . . . and other interpretations of a given work of art. Now we have to determine the most important point, namely, its relationship to the work of art itself. A literary work cannot exist without readers: the reader re-creates it and gives it life . . . From this basic fact concerning the relationship of the critical reader to the subject of investigation there issue two substantial objections to the two positions established above (the relationships with the author and with other commentators or critics of a given work of art). If, on the one hand, the critic is not bound by anything in the sphere of the work of art under investigation (either by the author's viewpoints or by the opinions of other critics), then, on the other hand, he is very strongly bound by the work of art itself. If his subjective opinion (impression) is not bound objectively by anything, then it will bind him. He must remain within the sphere of this work of art. It follows that, first, his interpretation must be the true interpretation of the work of art itself and not of something written about it; in this sense he is bound by the author, not biographically but rather by the content of the work of art. Second, he must maintain his opinion to the end, and must not piece it together from excerpts and fragments of the opinions of others. He must *objectively* recognize the freedom and equality of all interpretations, while *subjectively* he must stick to his own interpretation as the only true one . . . Two other consequences ensue from our view of the critical reader . . . First, such a criticism proceeds from the tacit assumption that the work investigated has an absolute artistic value. The criticism does not deal with nonartistic works: to expose their nonartistry amounts to an 'upside-down criticism,' the criticism of an advertiser or a publicist . . . From all this we see that the reader's criticism does not set as its task the *interpretation* of the work of art. To interpret means to exhaust, so that there is no need to read any further . . . More than anyone else, the critic in the course of his work feels the 'birth pangs of words.' Although no critic has ever complained about these pains, assuming that it is the duty of a critic to clearly state, interpret, complement, and explain what the author has not said or has mentioned only in part . . . The basic assumptions of the reader's criticism, its aprioristic postulates which we mentioned above, create totally different conditions for an investigation of *Hamlet.* The dilettantism of such a criticism makes it possible to leave aside the historistic problems in *Hamlet* (its first appearance, its sources, its author, the effects and influences of its setting, etc.), the biographic problem involving its author (the Shakespeare-Bacon question), and, finally, the entire, almost monstrous, purely critical literature about it. Only knowledge is required from such a critic, knowledge of the text of the tragedy itself. Thus, a totally different environment for the investigation is created. It is completely enclosed and becomes the exclusive property of the tragedy—even more: the exclusive domain of a specific interpretation of it. With regard to the technique of the work, this means that a given study has no questions or problems put from outside itself which need be solved. It must be noted, however, that in our case, Hamlet's problem is put on a different, almost inverse, level (opposed to that on which this problem was being solved until now). The reader will note that the question of Hamlet's weakness (or lack of will power) was approached by us from two sides. It must also be added that *Hamlet* is one of the few plays in which the plot, the sequence of scenes, requires an explanation, and since any new interpretation provides a new explanation of the plot, it comes in close contact with other critical interpretations. All critics have rationalized the characters of *Hamlet* in one way or another. They have tried to find an *understandable* sequence for the events. They have tried to explain the plot of the play and Hamlet's image in terms of known psychological, historical, literary, biographical, and aesthetic, events. In other words, they "explained and interpreted" Hamlet. For the first time, our criticism proceeds from the assumption of the impossibility of explaining the sequence of events and the image of Hamlet himself. Other critics acknowledged the "obscurity" of the tragedy, but they tried to overcome it. They adduced arguments like "irrespective of," "however," "in spite of," etc., whereas here everything is put straightforward. The mystery and the obscurity of the tragedy are not a blanket enveloping it; they are its core, its very soul. The tragedy has to be found behind the mystery and obscurity. The mystery is surrounded by characters, dialogues, actions, events, occurrences, which can hardly be understood but which nonetheless are required in that particular sequence by the mystery itself. The true critical essay tries to interpret and explain the tragedy as a myth. This is a "first" in Shakespearian criticism . . . the problems arise from the investigation itself and are determined by the interests of the critic. The text of the investigation looks at the tragedy through the reactions and emotions it causes in the heart of the investigator. There is no quotation, no reference to any text (except the text of the tragedy, of course), no matter how tempting it might seem to refer to the words or the ideas of another critic . . .

These excerpts from the introduction of Vygotsky's early work *Hamlet* are significant for an evaluation of his development in the ten years from the time he wrote his first essay on *Hamlet* to the completion of the present book, in which the *reader's* critique is replaced by analysis and the synthesis of the literary work as an objective value (independent of the psychology of the reader or the author).

40. Concerning artificial aspects of the structure of Shakespeare's plays, see B. L. Pasternak, "Comments on Translations of Shakespeare's Tragedies," *Literaturnaya Moskva* (*Moscow Literature*), Moscow, 1956, pp. 799–800.

41. For an analysis of the tragedy, the author uses the concept of stage time, which differs from everyday time, cf. what was said in note 34 concerning the analysis of time in the short story.

42. The analysis of the correlation between sense and nonsense in tragedy is of great significance for the contemporary theater theory. Where the problem of nonsense applied on stage arises in the plays by Ionesco, Becket, and Albee (the latter, more than any other author, sees Chekhov as the predecessor of this type of theatre, cf. *The Three Sisters*). More remote sources of certain aspects of this *antitheater* can be found in Aristophanes. Vygotsky correctly points out that Shakespeare regards nonsense as a "lightning rod" to protect the sense (unlike the situation in many contemporary plays where the balance between nonsense and sense is disrupted in favor of nonsense; this fact is quite frequently stated by the theoreticians of antitheater).

43. This idea is developed in greater detail in an early work by Vygotsky on Hamlet. "The symbolism of the scene is brought on stage here, that is, the laws of this mirror of life, the actor, who plays a role which is not determined by him but who nonetheless feels it. This is the order which is apparently opposite to life, but which by the hidden meaning of the tragedy is the same. We have stage on stage here, but then, Hamlet is nothing but stage on stage. This symbolism of the stage on stage (of Hamlet himself, taken as 'a mirror of life'), its sense, laws, and actions are brought to the fore here, are made abstract, are removed from the play, and set free . . ." Further, about the "Mousetrap" he says:

The pantomime begins; this is a very symbolic feature. It is only the plot, the skeleton of the play. It is the pantomime which dominates the entire play, precedes it, and determines it, showing in a symbolic way that the play is dominated and subjugated by the course of its action. Only then the oath of the Queen, the following events, and finally the play itself are developed. It is a significant place for explaining the laws of action in the tragedy *Hamlet*. Here we also have a pantomime, but it is not separate from the play, it is within the play itself, in Hamlet's soul, and in the action itself. The pantomime is the situation "as it was prior to the tragedy", without aprioristic motivation hanging over it.

Elsewhere in the same paper we find the following:

We have to mention the astonishing technique used by Shakespeare in this tragedy. We must say a few words about the technique with which its action is developed, a technique which imposes its style upon the whole play. *Hamlet* is saturated with accounts about events and actions, all the essential actions of the play take place off stage—all except the catastrophe (a particular emphasis is put on the sharp contrast of style between an actionless tragedy and a last scene so packed with action as to become hardly bearable, so that this last scene obviously acquires a special meaning). Thus, we learn from talks and reports about the murder of Hamlet's father and the marriage of his mother with the murderer, the duel between Hamlet and Fortinbras, the appearance of the ghost (twice), the political intrigues, Fortinbras' undertakings, Hamlet's love for Ophelia, his farewell from her, the struggle with the pirates, the murder of Guildenstern and Rosencrantz, the death of Ophelia, etc. The play is built on words, talks, and reports; this obviously contradicts the very nature of tragedy as a dramatic representation, where everything is expected to be reproduced before the spectator. This, however, makes for the particular actionless character of the play and determines its peculiar style. Everything seems to be clad in a mist of words. The tragedy occurs by reflex, reverberation, or reaction. It is as if it were shown to us behind a semitransparent screen ("words, words, words . . ."), as if it were taking place in a strange, dim light, not strong enough to be real; it appears to be a tragedy of reflections, a tragedy of shadows, where behind every shadow (the shadow of an event, of an "action"—in the dramatic sense) we sense a mysterious reflecting object; we sense behind every report or talk, a mysterious action or event (concealed by "words"). Everything is accomplished off-stage; onstage we have only reverberations, reflections, reactions of the real events; we have only a tale, a shadow. This is why the play contains a terrifying and fear-provoking beyondness of those events and actions that appear directly, when they can be witnessed and seen, when they are not reported by a talk or tale (catastrophe). After this, we have the monologues of the actors, the stage on stage, the songs of Ophelia and the gravediggers, the excerpts and poems of Hamlet and, above all, the review of the entire tragedy in Hamlet's last conversation with Horatio, as if it were a story, the review of Horatio's role . . . This speech is of great importance for the style of the tragedy, not for the course of its action (Horatio, is never involved in any action; he is the narrator, the *chorus* of the tragedy; so that we view it as Horatio's account, not as a tragedy in itself. It is as if Horatio were telling us a dream) and for the strict style, kept strict to the last limit, when, from the shadowy character of this tragedy, everything becomes clear.

Equally characteristic of Vygotsky's early work on *Hamlet* is the characterization of the role of the ghost:

The ghost, so to speak, is a double plot of the tragedy. This is the exact definition of the ghost's role: it is not understood how it is connected with what takes place here, but it is the real and true link that connects these "wars." The fateful duel of Hamlet and Fortinbras, of which Horatio speaks, is not finished—it is continued by the sons whom we never meet, and this actionless struggle represents the outward frame of the tragedy . . . At the height of Rome's glory, the graves stood empty, one felt the *beyond,* the dead appeared before destruction. This is how the appearance of the ghost is *reflected* in the soul of the *student* Horatio—it is a highly artistic trait. The ghost is also the premonition of the terrible events with which the scene is saturated; it is the omen of fate, *the premonition of coming evil.* Great events, when they reach the earth, cast shadows on it. A shadow, in our common acceptance of the word, is a reflected projection of something three-dimensional onto a two-dimensional space. Here instead, the shadow is the projection onto the three-dimensional space of the tragedy of something four-dimensional . . . the entire play (since it is single-centered and rotates around this one center), the whole course of events in the tragedy is under the spell of the shadow cast by the ghost (literally, as Hamlet says, "a shadow's shadow").

44. In his early work on *Hamlet,* Vygotsky expands the thought quoted above.

This same style, however, creates particular conditions for perceiving the tragedy. Everything is clad in a dramatic form, into the accounts of different characters. The reader-critic cannot identify himself with any of them (especially since nearly all of them report or tell us something), and this is why he has to talk not only about the events themselves but about the reverberations, the reflections of their accounts in the hearts of the characters. He must work only with this material. He must subject himself to the style of the tragedy and let himself be infected by it. In so doing (with reference not only to the events themselves but also to their reflections and the mirror-half of the characters) the critic must study thoroughly and carefully each and every mirror, since all of them are different; they give different reflections because some are concave, others are convex, still others are straight but of differing focal lengths. Thus they give distorted, magnified, or reduced reflections, and so on. To study the event itself in these reflections, one has to find the focus or the center of each individual mirror—of each character.

45. Again, in his early work on *Hamlet*, Vygotsky wrote:

The meaning of his inaction is that "this machine is not to him;" it is governed by another force, and is completely subdued by it; the meaning of his "will and lack of will," lack of action and activity, is in the *tragic automatism* of this "machine"; now his actions, his deeds, his lack of action, etc., do not depend on him. Everything is done by this "machine," which has only one motive, one reason: *the tragedy requires it.* . . . This is Hamlet's personal tragedy: he is a man, a person, not a machine; and at the same time "this machine" does not belong to him. This tragic automatism contains Hamlet's personal tragedy, and it also contains the meaning and significance of the entire play. [Elsewhere Vygotsky says]: If we compare Hamlet's role in the play with that of a magnetic needle which finds itself in a magnetic field in which forces are placed like invisible threads across the entire tragedy to direct it toward a certain spot, then the characters of the play must be compared with nonmagnetized iron needles thrown suddenly into the same field. The directing effect of the magnetic forces (hidden *offstage*) reveals itself on Hamlet, who transmits it to the "nonmagnetic" remaining characters; as a magnetic needle magnetizes other iron needles, Hamlet "magnetizes" or "contaminates" all the others with the tragic. In this respect, of course, his is the essential role in the play, the tragedies of the remaining characters are only shown in part. They are hinted at or shown only from one side, the side turned toward Hamlet. As such, however, they occur away from the main path of the play. In fact, they can interest us only from that aspect or that side (the side turned toward Hamlet), which receives the full impact of the magnetic forces of the tragedy, lit by the reflections of the tragic flame. . . . It is deeply significant that Hamlet controls himself, holds himself back from acting and the action which has matured in his heart and which he feels but does not understand. This is just as important as the fact that he drives himself to action, reproaches himself for being inactive; both aspects have the same origin. He feels that he moves freely, and therefore he condemns himself and looks for the threads that tie him and prevent him from acting until the very last moment, when he *must* do what he feels he has to do. . . . On the contrary, instead of pushing him into action, they divert him from the true path and help him to control himself. He will commit a murder, he senses that; he will drink hot blood, he knows that too, but all this will happen despite his will. Nonetheless he feels that he moves freely, that he stops himself from doing one thing and gravitates toward another. Like a magnetic needle in a magnetic field, he is bound by the movements of magnetic, invisible, but extremely powerful threads, which come from beyond and traverse the entire tragedy. The play is one great magnetic field in which this needle performs its predestined movement, predestined by the whirl of the magnetic forces.

This interpretation of Hamlet's personality, expounded in Vygotsky's early work (but not repeated in the substantially different present book which he finished ten years later) is quite close to Pasternak's. "From the moment of the ghost's appearance, Hamlet renounces his freedom in order to 'perform according to the will of the one who sent him.' " (B. L. Pasternak's remarks on the translations of Shakespeare's tragedies, *Literaturnaya Moskva* [*Moscow Literary Life*], p. 797.) Another similarity can be seen in the characterization of the role of music in the tragedy. See also the excerpts on the pantomime in the tragedy. Similar thoughts about *Hamlet* occur in Pasternak's verses as well as his prose.

This coincides with the general characterization of the tragedy given by Vygotsky in his early work:

This unusual tragedy, which bears no resemblance to any other, is lacking in what would seem to be the most important element, dramatic action. This is a tragedy without action. If we accept textbook definitions (and, alas, not textbook definitions alone) of the tragedy, which specify that it is the representation of the internal or external struggle of a hero, then we have to eliminate *Hamlet* from this category, because it is a tragedy without a struggle, a tragedy without action. But is struggle the tragedy's only substance? *Hamlet* touches the bottom of the deepest tragic abyss. The tragic, as such, issues from the very foundations of everyday human life. The very facts of human life, the birth of man, his individual life, his estrangement from the universe, his loneliness, his appearance from an unknown world into a known world which causes him to belong simultaneously to both worlds and to neither—all this is tragic. And if the tragedy be the highest form of artistic creation, then *Hamlet* is the pinnacle, because it is the *tragedy of tragedies*

. . . It defines all that is tragic in the tragedy. It is the tragic principle, its essence, its tone. It establishes that which converts an ordinary drama into a tragedy, that which is common to all tragedies; it opens the tragic abyss and the laws governing it. This tragic abyss, which we feel behind every word, gives meaning to this play. Could it be that *Hamlet* lacks all that is necessary for a common tragedy because it is the *tragedy of tragedies?* Every single episode contains enough material for a separate tragedy. The play can be divided into as many separate trage- dies as there are characters or, to go a step further, into as many as there are individual plots or intrigues, since some characters could be · the protagonists of several tragedies. But these separate, individual trag- edies are not worked out. They are only suggested. They are not singly developed but are put together and adhere to one another on a com- mon side. This abutting edge produces the tragedy of tragedies which contains all the common edges or sides of the subplots. Any tragedy is inexplicable in the final analysis. This is all the more true in the case of the tragedy of tragedies which is based on the tragic par excellence. Every single atom or link of this tragedy, if developed into a drama, would yield a separate tragedy in which the entire drama could be ex- plained in many ways. As a result, all the explanations that divide the drama into so many "subdramas" inevitably reach the indivisible core of the tragic. Our *Hamlet* contains several of these dramas evolved from tragic cores (the presence of which accounts for the play's apparent con- fusion, heteronomy, and lack of grace); all these dramas are turned so that one of their sides faces a common center, the inner focus of the play at which all their tragic sides converge. This focus is indivisible, and the tragic sides of the dramas are inexplicable and also indivisible. This is why everything that happens has its own rationale, and this is also why everything is enveloped in darkness and obscurity. Alongside the exter- nal, real drama, another deeper and more essential one develops. This latter drama takes place in silence (the former, on the other hand, is full of words). This external drama supplies the framework for this inner drama. Behind, or rather beyond, the audible dialogue, we sense the si- lent, inner dialogue . . . This is the external tragedy behind which the internal tragedy hides. It is the tragedy of masks behind which we sense the tragedy of the souls.

"I am dead." Hamlet is already dead; he is in the grave, and he knows everything; he could tell us everything. And thus he very clearly out- lines the two meanings of the tragedy, one of them being the external story of the tragedy, which Horatio must tell in some detail. He knows nothing, he is only a spectator. He will recount the plot of the tragedy and its development . . . and thus the tragedy neither stops nor ends.

At the end it closes a circle, because it goes back to the beginning of what has taken place on stage before the audience. The circle is closed: the incomprehensible tragedy, filled with the monstrosity of equally incomprehensible and unnatural events . . . will remain incomprehensible in Horatio's narration. Its second meaning, about which the dead Hamlet could talk (because in his soul and heart there took place everything that this second meaning does not reveal) is not given in the play; it is taken to the grave. What is this second meaning taken by Hamlet into his grave? What is the second meaning which he understood only when he was already standing in the grave? What would Hamlet have said if he had had time? What would he have told us, the poor, pale, trembling spectators of this overwhelming catastrophe? In his posthumous words the tragedy is clearly divided into two parts: one, the tragedy itself, its "words, words, words" (Horatio's narration), and the other, *the rest*. What is *the rest*, what is *silence?* This is the second part of the tragedy, "the rest," all that is not given in the play, but issues from it. Whatever its essence, it is obvious that it alone can explain the unnatural narration of Horatio, the first part of the tragedy, its "words, words, words . . ." We can understand Shakespeare's tragedy (Horatio's narration) only by substituting for its "words, words, words," the formula "the rest is silence." As I have already said, this second part is not given in the play; it is not explained. The tragedy completes its circle and goes over to Horatio's narration. Nonetheless, this second part is indispensable for solving the problem of the tragedy and for understanding what it tells us. If we look deeply enough, we shall find that this second sense is actually given in the play. It is the tragedy itself, and it is given like the root of an equation which is present even if it is irrational, that is, if it cannot be expressed or does not exist outside the equation. This "sense" does exist in *Hamlet,* in its course of action, its tone, and its words. This is why the tragedy is always moving in the silence which is its "underground" foundation, its tragic source . . . We are interested in this second sense only in a limited way, within the boundaries of the tragedy, within the close circle of its "words." We can sense it only in the words. This is why the synthetic impression of the entire tragedy to which this chapter is devoted must be transformed into an analytic examination of its components, its individual characters (their positions, speeches and destinies) etc. We think that the best way to proceed is through investigation of the characters and the plot of the play. These are the two parts into which the external tragedy is divided. The interrelation of these two parts determines the meaning of the tragedy (for instance, what are commonly known as tragedies of fate or tragedies of character are determined by this alone). The plot of the drama (that is, the course of events in it) and its characters (that is, the participants in these events) determine the tragedy or, more correctly, it is their interrelationship that determines it. Thus, if the course of events in the drama is governed by the character roles and depends upon them, then we have a tragedy of character. On the other hand, if the course of events dominates the fate of the characters, despite their roles, and thus has something fatalistic about it then we have a tragedy of fate . . . But in addition to these two parts, the *plot of the play* (the course of events, the intrigues, the catastrophe) and the characters, we have yet another part, an extremely important one, which envelops the interrelationship between the first two parts and gives it a very special quality. We are talking here about the invisible atmosphere of the tragic, its lyricism, its "music." As in a painting, the most important elements are not the colors, the representation of objects, or the canvas, but the atmosphere, the perspective, the spaces, the ambiance created by the combination of colors and objects that crowd the painting, that actually do not exist in the painting but arise from it. The same applies to the tragedy, where the author does not say a word, where he does not explain the course of events, where positions are reproduced, as are events, characters and conversations; so that what is most important is not the description of the characters or of their actions, fates, roles, etc., but that imperceptible air that fills the gaps between the characters, those infinite tragic spaces which arise from the combination of characters and their positions—in brief, the mood. In a tragedy, the most important element is not what happens on stage and can be seen. Rather, it is the one hanging over us, that is only obscurely perceived, felt, sensed, *understood* perhaps, behind all the events, talks, speeches, and monologues, that invisible tragic atmosphere which continuously presses upon the play and forces the images, characters, and events to issue from it. This atmosphere which envelops the second meaning of the play does not exist in the play itself. It is not given but issues from the material. Each character acquires a different meaning as soon as he comes up against another character who casts some light upon him. Each of the characters must be placed in the spot belonging to him. We must distinguish the genuinely tragic characters, who are the tragic heroes and carriers of the tragic principle, from the tragic victims, who perish under the weight of this tragic principle. Only thus distinguishing the characters will we be able to bring to life the space that exists between them and is filled with the invisible threads of the tragic.

46. In particular, this distinction applies to the so-called "actual articulation" of the sentence where the word (or phrase) that is particularly important to the speaker is placed first.

47. A combination of the tragic with the comic was already apparent in the earliest stages of art. We find it, for instance, in such phenomena as laughter about death. See in particular: V. I. Propp, "Ritual Laughter in Folklore," *Uchenyye zapiski Leningradskogo Gosudarstvennogo Universiteta* (*Proceedings of the Leningrad State University*), No. 46, Leningrad, 1939; P. Bogatyrev, "Les jeux dans les rites funèbres en Russie subcarpatique," *Le monde slave*, N. S., III, 1926. R. Jakobson, Medieval Mock Mystery (The Old Czech *Unguentarius*). "Studia philologica et litteraria in honorem L. Spitzer," Bern, 1958, p. 262; S. M. Eisenstein, Montazh, *Collected Works*, Vol. 2, Moscow 1964, pp. 364–366 (on the Mexican national festival "the day of death," taken in an unfinished film [*¡Que Viva México!*] by Eisenstein). The semiotic interpretation of laughter about death as applied to the finales of Shakespeare's tragedies, was given in the paper by Pasternak, quoted in note 45, p. 807.

48. Similar ideas can be found not only in ancient Greek poetry (Aristotle) but also in ancient Indian poetry, the teaching of *rasa*.

49. A stricter definition of the iamb requires one unstressed syllable followed by one stressed syllable, the foot rising toward the stress. See A. Prokhorov, "Mathematical analysis of verse," *Nauka i zhizn* (*Science and Life*) 6: 152–153, 1964.

50. A similar analysis of folkloristic texts, built upon the combination of opposites (for instance, spring and winter, etc.), was given in many of Potebnia's studies. See, for instance, the analysis of the Ukrainian spring songs (A. A. Potebnia, "The Saga of Igor's Army," *Ob'yasnenie malorusskoi pesni XVI veka* [*Explanation of the Ukrainian Song of the Sixteenth Century*], Kharkhov, 1914, p. 215).

51. These ideas are particularly effective for evaluating the deformation of proportions in artistic images. Limitation in disproportionate representation of objects was stressed by Eisenstein in his early papers: "Representation of an object in the proportions actually involved, is of course a tribute to orthodox and formal logic, dominated by the idea of an unshakable order of things. It appears periodically in painting and sculpture when absolutism is established, and changes the expressivity of archaic disproportion into a regular 'table of ranges' of an officially established harmony. Positivistic realism is not the correct form of perception. It is simply the function of a specific form of social order, the statist absolutism which requires uniformity of thought. An ideological uniforming, which grows from the long lines of uniforms of guard regiments . . ." S. M. Eisenstein, "Behind the Frame," in *Selected Works*, Vol. 2, Moscow, 1964, p. 288.

52. This analysis of *The Three Sisters* is particularly important when the

problems of stage significance, meaning and nonsense are considered (see note 42).

53. This interpretation of the psychology of an actor's emotions is very significant in overcoming the prejudices based upon the incorrect explanation of the profound ideas of Stanislavsky, which have apparently found a fairly wide audience.

54. L. S. Salyamon recently reproposed the hypothesis of a possible connection between the physiological assumptions of art and the *funnel principle*. He feels that the phenomenon known as the *funnel principle* or the *principle of the common path* can be applied to explaining certain assumptions of the emotional-aesthetic activity of man. See L. S. Salyamon, "The Possible Physiological Assumption of the Emotional-Esthetic Activity of Man," in *Symposium on the Complex Study of Artistic Creation, Abstracts and Notes,* Leningrad, 1963, p. 20ff; and also the ideas of Potebnia on language: A. A. Potebnia, *Iz zapisok po teorii slovesnosti* (*Notes on the Theory of Literature*), Kharkov, 1905, p. 644.

55. A note of Vygotsky's on the connection between art and morale probably applies to this. "From a social viewpoint art is a complex process of balancing the environment. As biological balancing, it is born from discomfort and directed toward eliminating this discomfort. Only in social psychology can we understand the practical value of art completely. Its educational role is not to serve certain moral purposes, and we are ready to admit, together with Yevlakhov, that 'creativity is antimoral.' " (See A. Yevlakhov, *Vvedenie v filosofiiu khudozhestvennovo tvorchestva* [*Introduction to the Philosophy of Artistic Creativity*], Vol. II, Warsaw, 1912, p. 122). More correctly, art has a complex relationship to morality, and we have reasons to believe that it contradicts it more frequently than it supports it. This is due to the essences of art and morality as such. Morality controls us and puts the brakes on us. Art, on the other hand, releases exactly opposite instincts. It is time, finally, to say that art contains nothing noble or high in a moral sense; on the contrary—it is a complete negation of morality (*Ibid.,* p. 190):

But he who says that art is an antisocial phenomenon is in error. He must proceed from the fact that the interests of art and society diverge; and this divergence becomes basic. He therefore considers the roots of art to lie in individual creativity. This is a very naive approach to the interrelationship between art and life, for it closes its eyes to the extremely complex social function performed by art. As Plekhanov has said, it can be directly opposite to life. It may give the city dweller the exclusive pleasure of observing a landscape. It can show us those aspects of our being which have not found any actual expression in life. This is why it will always remain deeply social.

The idea of the social function of art is well developed by Vygotsky. As concerns the banal approach to the association between art and morale, repeatedly criticized by Vygotsky, the reference to Yevlakhov is more or less casual. There would have been much more point in referring to Kierkegaard who studied the problem of the connection between the ethical and aesthetical and considered both paths to be quite distinct.

56. The problem of the relationship between the conscious and the subconsicous in art and in other forms of man's artistic creativity is being studied through cybernetic investigation of artistic creativity (see note 21). Vygotsky studied this problem in subsequent works by using materials from natural language and other higher forms of mental activity, which first become automatic (subconscious) and then can again be recognized (in other words, the possibility of controlling these subconscious behavioral programs appears). See L. S. Vygotsky, *Razvitie vysshikh psikhicheskikh funktsii* (*The Evolution of Higher Mental Processes*), Moscow, 1960.

INDEX

Actor, creativity of, 236
  emotions of, 294
  as physician, 79
Aesop, 93, 102, 119, 138
  fables of, 95, 97, 98, 103, 107, 108, 110, 115, 141
Aesthetic response, 199, 205, 206, 211, 213, 214, 215, 217, 240, 251
  contradiction in, 218
Aesthetics, from above, 10, 13
  from below, 10
  definition of, 247
  historical, 17–18
  task of, 236
  theoretical, 91
  traditional, 160
Alfonso, 185
Allegory, 93, 94, 97, 108
Ambiguity. *See* Dualism
  in fables, 125
Andromache, 33
Anna Karenina, 35, 180, 247
Architecture, catharsis in, 237, 238
  Gothic, 237
Aristophanes, 231, 285
Aristotle, ix, 91, 114, 203, 213, 230, 244, 293
Art, analysis of, 271

applied, 203, 253
biological basis of, 246
as catharsis, 227, 248, 249
changeability of, 40
content of, 39
definition of, 247
dualism of, 258
in education, 253, 255
emotion and, 37, 47, 240, 249
historical value of, 38
intellect and, 48
interpretation of, 72
Marxist theory of, 4, 11, 12
miracle of, 243
as mood, 206
morality and, 294, 295
nonfigurative, 83
as perception, 32
psyche and, 207
purpose of, 242
role of, 259
science and, 33
social significance of, 249
subconscious and, 76, 85
as technique, 56, 58
Artists, 79
Asafev, B., 270
Astrology, aesthetic, 18

Babel, I., 278
Babrius, 110
Bakhtin, M. M., 275, 278
Balli, C., 67
Balmont, K., 66
Batte, 103, 107
Baudouin, Charles, 277
Baumgardt, 168
Beck, 169
Bednyi, Demian, 273
Beethoven, Ludwig van, 65, 241, 243, 251, 252
Behavior, aesthetic, 205
  control of, 270
Bekhterev, V. M., 14, 15, 17
Belinskii, V., 132, 255
Bely, Andrei, 19, 66, 68, 218, 250
Bense, M., 272
Bergson, Henri, 233
Bergsonism, 19
Berlioz, Hector, 12
Bernays, Jakob, 213
Berné, L., 168, 170, 185, 191
Bernshtein, S. I., 277
Blok, Alexander, 66, 127, 159
Blonskii, 159
Bogatyrev, P., 274, 293
Boiardo, M. M., 59
Brandes, G. M. C., 168, 169, 171, 174
Braque, Georges, 275, 277
Brecht, Bertolt, 272
Breitinger, J. J., 98
Briullov, Konstantin, 36
Briusov, V. I., 38, 42
Brock, E., 276
Bruner, J. S., 269
Bücher, K., 245
Bühler, K., 43, 257
Bunin, Ivan, 145–165, 214
Bylina, 16
Byron, George G., 220

Cassirer, E., 272
Catastrophe, of fable, 142
  in Hamlet, 286
Catharsis, ix, 215, 217
  in architecture, 237, 238
  art as, 199–216, 227, 248, 249
  in comedy, 232
  concept of, x, 213, 214, 244
  in drama, 235

in fables, 215
in painting, 236
psychophysical, 244
in sculpture, 237
in theater, 236
in tragedy, 215
Chatskiis, 49
Chekhov, Anton, plays of, 234
Chelpanov, G. I., v, 14, 15
Christiansen, 46, 59, 157, 193, 194, 207, 208, 236
Cognition, art as, 272
  in defectology, 268
Comedy, 232
  purpose of, 233
Composition, in novella, 147
  in short story, 158
Contamination, theory of, 249
Content, 61
  form and, 156, 215, 228, 278
  of story, 150
Counterfeeling, 127
Creativity, 31, 75, 248
  artistic, 56, 81
  psyche and, 137
Criticism, aesthetic, 282, 283
  dualistic nature of, 254
  role of, 253, 254, 255
Croce, Benedetto, 18, 64, 140, 233
Cybernetics, 266, 267, 270

Dante, 42
Darwin, Charles, 12, 212
da Vinci, Leonardo, 48, 81, 82
Daydreaming, 74
Defectology, 267, 268
Deformation, 59, 61
  experimental, 86
  of proportions, 293
Delacroix, Eugène, 12, 20
de La Grasserie, 17
de La Motte, 91, 93, 107
Delbouille, P., 276
de Saussure, F., 278
Descartes, René, 268
Device, aesthetic meaning of, 174
Diderot, Denis, 212, 235, 236
Dilthey, Wilhelm, 19
Disposition, of story, 151, 158
Dmitriev, 137
Dos Passos, John, 278

Dostoevsky, Fedor, 76, 82, 204
Dowden, E., 168
Drama, 101
  analysis of, 290
  basis of, 231
  Elizabethan, 175
  fable and, 143
  heroes of, 227
  psyche and, 242
  Shakespearean, 173
  unreal motive in, 235
Dramatic composition, law of, 181
Dreams, 76, 84
Dualism, in comedy, 232
  in drama, 237
  in fables, 120, 121, 134, 141, 143, 192
  in music, 237
  in poetry, 237
  in short story, 195

Edson, W., 274
Eichenbaum, B. M., 55, 56, 175, 176,
    274, 275, 278, 279
Eichenwald, I., 91, 137, 255, 256
Einfühlung, 65, 207
Eisenstein, S. M., 272, 275, 276, 293
Emotion, 200. See also Feeling
  aesthetic, 206, 250
  antithesis in, 212
  art and, 37, 47, 240, 241, 249,
  economizing, 249
  explanation of, 212
  expression of, 209, 211
  fantasy and, 210
  fable and, 121
  individuality of, 243
  language of, 241
  lyrical, 41, 203, 221, 248
  purpose of, 202
  in short story, 159
  study of, 199
Engels, Friedrich, 22
Enjoyment, principle of, 252
Epic, 101
  fable and, 143
  Greek, 39
  heroes of, 227
Ethics, aesthetics and, 241
Eugene Onegin, 49, 54, 58, 59, 112, 148,
    149, 222–227

Fable, 89–115
  animals in, 99, 100, 104, 110
  catastrophe of, 142
  complexity of, 168
  definition of, 103
  form of, 141
  history of, 138
  Indian, 109
  love story in, 123
  lyrical, 93, 97, 104, 107, 108, 111, 118
  moral of, 91, 130
  motives of, 128
  parable as, 115
  parallel themes of, 139
  poetry and, 140
  prosaic, 93, 105, 107, 118
  purpose of, 100
  story of, 113
  structural elements of, 93
Fables, Aesop's, 92
  ancient, 108
  Greek, 96
  Krylov's, 93
  La Fontaine's, 93
  Lessing's, 93
  Tolstoy's, 93
Fabulists, 98, 99, 110, 111
Fantasy, 74
  feeling and, 209
  study of, 199
Fechner, Otto, 9, 18, 64
Feeling. See also Emotion
  aesthetic, 240
  art and, 211
  emotional, 201
  fantasy and, 209
  imagination and, 215
  psychology of, 200
Fischer, F. T., 207
Fischer, Kuno, 65, 168, 174, 184
Form, 61
  in art, 220
  content and, 215, 228, 278
  psychology of, 52
  of short story, 146
Formalism, 61, 64, 68
  in art, vii
  Russian, 68
Formalistic method, theory of, 56, 274
Formalistic principles, 58
Formalists, 54

Fossius, 93
Frank, H., 272
Frebes, J., 18
Freud, Sigmund, 14, 17, 73, 77, 79, 81,
    82, 84, 204, 248, 252
  art and, 247
  on daydreaming, 74, 76
  on emotions, 200, 201
  on wit, 233
Friche, V. M., 259
Frye, N., 276
"Funnel" theory, 266
Futurism, Russian, 62

Galakhov, 126
Gasparov, M. L., 271
Gauzenshtein, 21
Gegenständlichkeit, viii
"Gentle Breath," 154, 161–165, 279
Gershenzon, M., 20, 42, 255, 256
Gilbert, K., 277
Goethe, Johann W., 34, 166, 168, 191,
    220, 230
Gogol, Nikolay, 45, 76, 91, 112, 136
Goncharov, I. A., 68, 170, 194
Gorky, Maxim, 273
Grammont, M., 67
Grant-Allen, 247
Grib, V. R., 270
Grigoriev, K., 124
Grigor'ev, M. S., 19
Grinev, 95
Groos, Karl, 210
Gunzenhauser, R., 272
Guyau, M.-J., 42, 249, 250

Haman, R., 18, 91, 102, 233
Hamlet, 54
  character of, 169, 170, 171
  emotions of, 191
  enigma of, 181, 185
  monologues of, 182, 183, 189
  motivation of, 183
  original saga of, 180
  personality of, 177, 289
  personal tragedy of, 288
  procrastination of, 167, 181, 182, 185
  psychology of, 176, 177
  riddle of, 180
Hamlet, 166
  analysis of, 175
    contradictions in, 190
    device in, 173
    historical problems in, 284
    king's role in, 279–281
    murders in, 172
    paradox of, 191
    plots of, 188
    staging of, 172
    technique in, 286
    Tolstoy's view of, 178, 179, 180, 181
Hamsun, Knut, 55
Hebbel, Friedrich, 76, 170, 231, 232
Hedonism, 276
  aesthetic, 64, 65
Hegel, G. W. F., 233
Hegelian dialectic, 12
Heine, Heinrich, 57, 75, 102, 170
Hennequin, E., 5, 21, 211, 250
Hero, of *Eugene Onegin*, 227
  in fables, 99, 131
  Goethe's view of, 191
  mythological, 104
  tragic, 195, 231
Hessner, 168
History, fabular, 115, 133
Homer, 33, 34, 37, 102
Horace, 111, 138
Hornfeld, A. G., 32, 38, 41, 42
Hugo, Victor, 12
Humboldt, Wilhelm von, 30, 42
Huxley, Aldous, 272

Iliad, 101
Imagination, feeling and, 215
  study of, 199
Inhibition, 210
Intellect, definition of, 48
Isolation, in aesthetic experience, 211
  problem of, 277
Ivanov-Razumnik, 49
Izmailov, A. A., 106, 111, 234

Jakobson, R. O., 273, 274, 277, 293
James, H., 201
Johnson, 185
Jung, C. G., 277

Kant, Immanuel, 9, 63
Kayser, W., 276
Kenevich, V., 106
Khemnitser, I. I., 111

Kierkegaard, Sören A., 295
King Lear, 179, 180
Kirpichnikov, A. I., 122
Khlebnikov, V., 276
Klinger, Max, 236, 237
Köhler, Wolfgang, 60
Kolbanovskii, V. N., 269
Kolmogorov, A. N., 271, 277
Kondratov, A. N., 271
Kornilov, K. I., v, ix, 48, 210
Kovach, 75
Krasnova, N., 273
Kruchenykh, A., 273
Krylov, Ivan, 91–93, 97, 102, 103, 107,
    122, 124, 125, 129, 131, 135, 136,
    137, 139, 143
    fables of, 5, 97, 101, 105, 112, 113,
    118, 119, 120, 123, 125, 127, 128,
    132, 150, 256
    poetry of, 136
    style of, 132
    "subtle poison" of, 137
Kuhn, G., 277
Külpe, O., 9, 18, 22, 43
Kutuzov, Field Marshal M. I., 132

La Drière, G., 276
La Fontaine, J., 91, 92, 97, 99, 102, 103,
    104, 106, 110, 111, 115, 119, 120,
    124, 125, 129, 131, 137, 138
    fables of, 101, 105, 112
Lalo, C., 233
Lange, Carl Georg, 65
Langer, Suzanne, 272
Language, 266
    art and, 30
    of children, 268
    natural, 271
    poetic, 203, 272
    psychology of, 32
    Russian, 49
Lanson, Gustave, 56
Lazurskii, A. F., 81, 247
Learning theory, 268
Le Bon, Gustave, 14
Lee, Vernon, 234
Lehman, 47, 210
Lermontov, Michael, 44, 102, 140, 220,
    221
Lessing, G. E., 118, 119, 121, 138, 140,
    213

fables and, 90, 91–93, 95, 96, 98–108,
    110, 113–115
Lévi-Strauss, Claude, 274
Levy, J., 273
Likhachev, D. S., 279
Linguistics, structural, 279
Lipps, Theodor, 4, 10, 65, 155, 207, 208
"Literary mask," 112, 113
Literature, 48. *See also* Drama; Fable;
    Poetry; Story; Tragedy
    Latin, 93
    teaching of, 255
Lobanov, 125, 131
Lombroso, Cesare, 75
Longinus, D. C., 243, 254
Lotman, I. M., 275
Lunacharskii, A. V., 11, 244
Luria, A. R., 269
Lyric, 101, 242. *See also* Poetry
    fable and, 143
    psychology of, 41

Macbeth, 175, 176, 208
Maiakovskii, Vladimir, 62, 66
Mandelstamm, Osip Y., 44
Marty, A., 272
Marx, Karl, 20, 22, 80
    art and, 4, 11, 12, 39
McDougall, William, 14
Meiman, E., 208, 220
Meinong, Alexius, 47, 209
Melody, of short story, 152
Merezhkovskii, D. S., 169
Messer, August, 43
Meyer, H., 46, 47, 209, 210
Mezières, 185
Michelangelo, art of, 234
Moles, A. A., 272
Molière, J. B. P., 56, 230
Molozhavy, S., 257
Montague, 169
Moral, fabular, 107–108, 110, 112, 119,
    120
    in story, 111, 121
Morality, aesthetics and, 178
    art and, 294, 295
Morris, C., 272
Mukarovsky, I., 274
Müller, G., 279
Müller, V. K., 213, 230

Müller-Freienfels, R., 5–6, 23, 29, 76, 205, 208, 211, 212
Münsterberg, Hugo, 17, 211
Music, 53, 250, 252, 253
  art of, 36
  dance, 251
  dualism in, 237
  military, 242
  rhythm in, 218

Narrative, 149
  elements of, 157
  techniques in, 158
Neufeld, I., 82
Niepor, 67
Nonsense, problem of, 285
Novel, 54, 63, 90
  classic, 270
  tragedy and, 231

Objective-analytic method, 23
Ode, 58. See also Epic
Odoevskii, V. F., 111
Oedipus complex, 78, 80, 81, 82
Orshanskii, I. G., 201, 246
Othello, 31, 32, 179, 208, 229
Ovsianiko-Kulikovskii, D. N., 31, 32, 33, 34, 35, 37, 41, 44, 49, 201, 202, 203, 214, 242, 243, 248

Painting, 90
  art of, 36
  catharsis in, 236
  elements of, 157
  portrait, 193
Pansexualism, Freudian, 277
Pasternak, Boris L., 62, 194, 285, 293
Pechorins, 49
Perception, 56
  aesthetic, 279
  in art, 62
  child's, 258
  in defectology, 268
  experiments in, 60
  processes of, 31
  in psychiatry, 268
  study of, 199
  unconscious, 200
Peredonov, 84
Petrazhitskii, 189, 203, 242

Phaedrus, 103, 104, 110, 112, 119, 138
  fables of, 95, 96, 107, 108, 109
Piaget, J., 269
Picasso, Pablo, 275, 278
Pisemskii, 34, 35, 214
Plato, 72, 103
Pleasure, concept of, 77
Plekhanov, George V., 4, 11, 12, 13, 15, 20, 212, 244, 255, 294
Pletnev, 129, 137
Plot, 146
Poet, 68, 72, 73, 80, 112
  contradiction and, 192
  moral and, 112
  as paranoiac, 75
  technique and, 174
  tragic, 231
Poetry, 36, 45, 58, 79, 90, 103, 114, 143
  dualism in, 237
  elements of, 157
  erotic, 203, 242, 243
  fable and, 104, 110, 118, 140
  life and, 137
  lyric, 221, 248
  purpose of, 242
  rhythm in, 218, 219, 245, 279
  Russian, 62
  sound in, 276
  teaching of, 256
  tragic, 243
Polivanov, E. D., 277
Porebski, M., 272
Potebnia, A. A., 30, 31, 35, 36, 38, 40, 41, 43, 44, 47, 57, 68, 93, 96, 98, 100, 102, 104, 106, 108, 110, 113, 114, 115, 119, 122, 125, 139, 140, 203, 257
  fable and, 90, 92, 94, 95, 97, 99, 100
  poetry and, 42
Poulet, G., 279
Prels' law of temporal continuity, 174
Procrastination, psychology of, 176
Prokhorov, A. V., 271, 293
Prophet, The, 38
Propp, V. I., 275, 293
Prose, 114. See also Literature; Novel; Story
Proverb, 90
Psyche. See also Emotion
  emotional, 242
  function of, 202

Psychiatry, 268
Psychoanalysis, 73, 78, 79, 81, 82
Psychological Institute, of University of Moscow, v
Psychologism, vi
Psychology, of avarice, 54
  child, 257, 267
  collective, 17
  Freudian, ix (*see also* Freud)
  historical, x
  of perception, 199 (*see also* Perception)
  sensualistic trends in, 43
  social, x, 4, 14, 15, 79, 252
  Soviet, v
  theory of consciousness, ix
Pushkin, Alexander S., 16, 20, 34, 35, 38, 43, 47, 49, 55, 59, 67, 83, 84, 112. *See also Eugene Onegin*
  poetry of, 221
  stories of, 222
Pypin, 49

Quintilian, M. F., 93, 95, 106, 245

Rader, M., 277
Rank, O., 73, 74, 76, 77, 79
Reality, 252
  in short story, 154
Reflexology, 17
Representation, theory of, 52
Revzin, I. I., 273
Rhyme, 78
  nursery, 258
Rhythm, 218, 219
Ribot, T. A., 209
Richet, C. R., 103
Riddles, 44
Rilke, R. M., 277
Rohrschach tests, 41
Rossi, 17
Rosenkranz, Karl, 233
Rukavishnikov, 19
Rümelin, G., 169
Rutz, 253

Sachs, H., 73, 77
Salyamon, L. S., 294
Santayana, G., 279
Sapir, E., 276, 277
Saran, 218, 219
Satire, 140

Schizophrenia, 268
Schilder, P., 212
Schiller, Friedrich, 54, 136, 175, 176, 215, 248
Schlegel, August W. von, 168, 170
Schönberg, A., 275
Schopenhauer, Arthur, 43
Sculpture, catharsis in, 237
Sebeok, T. A., 274
Semiotics, 266, 268
Shakespeare, William, 32, 76. See also *Hamlet*
  aesthetics of, 179
  characters of, 179
  heroes of, 75
  language of, 179
  psychological method of, 189
  Pushkin's view of, 229, 230
  similes of, 45
  Tolstoy's view of, 169, 228, 229, 230
  tragedies of, 150
Shcheglov, I., 275
Shengeli, G. A., 271, 279
Sherrington, Charles C., 247
Sherrington's principle, 246
Shklovskii, V. B., 38, 44, 47, 52, 54, 58, 62, 67, 90, 146, 149, 272, 276, 277
Shostakovich, D., 275
Shpet, G. G., 272
Siegel, 17
Sievers, 253
Silverswan, 16, 174
Smirnov, A. A., 281
"Socialist realism," vi
Society, art in, 249
Socrates, 103, 104, 107, 212
Sokolovskii, A. L., 185
Solomon's Song, 44
Song, 54
  work, 245
Sounds, 258
  emotional shade of, 135
Spannung, 155
Spencer, Herbert, 202, 203, 204
Spinoza, Benedict, 6, 259, 268, 270
Staiger, E., 279
Stanislavsky, Konstantin, 294
Steckel, 75
Stepanov, N. L., 278
Sterne, Laurence, 147, 148, 278

Stoiunin, 126
Stoll, E. E., 179
Story, 54
    artificial leaps in, 155
    lyrical, 111, 115
    short, 145, 150
    words of, 154
Strada, V., 275
Subconscious, 72, 76, 295. *See also* Freud
    role of, 80
Sumarokov, A. P., 119, 120
Swift, Jonathan, 55
Symbolism, phonetic, 67
    Russian, 39
    on stage, 285
Syntax, 278

Taine, H. A., 244
Tale, 54. *See also* Epic; Story
Taranovskii, K., 271
Tarde, Gabriel, 17
ten Brink, B. A. K., 168
Theater, aesthetics of, 235
    catharsis in, 236
Tieck, Ludwig, 170
Time, literary, 279
    stage, 285
Titchener, E. B., 200, 212
Tolstoy, Leo N., 34, 35, 40, 46, 55, 63,
        68, 93, 179, 251, 252, 254
    aesthetics of, 236
    moralistic view of, 178, 241
    Shakespeare and, 169, 177, 178, 228,
        229, 230
Tomashevskii, B. V., 56, 91, 107, 146,
        189, 271, 279
Toporov, V. N., 276
Tragedy, 58, 77, 127, 136, 232
    affect of, 209
    analysis of, 180, 228
    art and, 190
    catastrophe in, 186, 187, 188
    catharsis of, 232
    of character, 180
    characters in, 192
    conflict in, 195
    contradictions in, 291
    dualism in, 195, 229, 291
    emotional effect of, 194
    of fate, 292
    feelings and, 189

Hamlet as, 167
    hero of, 193
    of jealousy, 229
    literary roots of, 170
    lyricism of, 292
    novel and, 231
    obscurity of, 284
    perception of, 287
    psyche and, 242
    psychological effect of, 192
    psychological planes in, 187
    psychological seed of, 140
    Shakespearean, 39, 106, 232. *See also*
        Hamlet
Tristram Shandy, 147
Trochee, 124
Turgenev, Ivan, 34, 42, 68, 112, 139,
        170, 171
Tynianov, Yu. N., 219, 220, 222, 273,
        275
Tyutchev, F. I., 42, 45

Uspenskii, Gleb, 221
Utitz, Emil, 4
Uzin, V. S., 222

Valter, V. G., 241
Verhalten, 9
Verhaltungsweisen, 13
Verli, M., 277
Verse, 53, 56, 149
    Alexandrine, 83
    poetical elements in, 219
    Russian, 271
    structure of, 220
    words of, 154
Vertov, Dziga, 278
Veselovskii, A., 10, 203, 204, 244
Veselyi, A., 273
Vodovozov, V., 119, 124, 128, 132, 135
Volkelt, J. I., 10, 63, 228
Volkenshteyn, V., 170, 171, 172, 228,
        231, 233
Voltaire, F. M. A., 169
von Lange, J. C. F. W., 247
Vygodsky, D., 67
Vygotsky, Lev Semenovich, v, 269
    death of, 268
    research of, 265
    works of, 266, 270

Wallenstein, 54
Weinreich, U., 269
Wellek, R., 274
Werder, 171, 191
Wit, 204
Words, 46. *See also* Language; Syntax
contradiction of, 230
Wundt, W., 14, 47, 65, 67, 210, 276
Würzburg school, 43

Yakubinskii, L., 66, 203

Yermakov, I. D., 20, 83, 84
Yevlakhov, A., 228, 241

Zeller, Eduard, 209, 213
Zenkovskii, 200, 209
Zhirmunskii, V., 45, 56, 58, 219
Zholkovskii, A. K., 273, 275
Zhukovskii, V. A., 124, 126, 129, 137, 138, 139, 140, 170
Zoshchenko, M., 278
Zvegintsev, V. A., 272